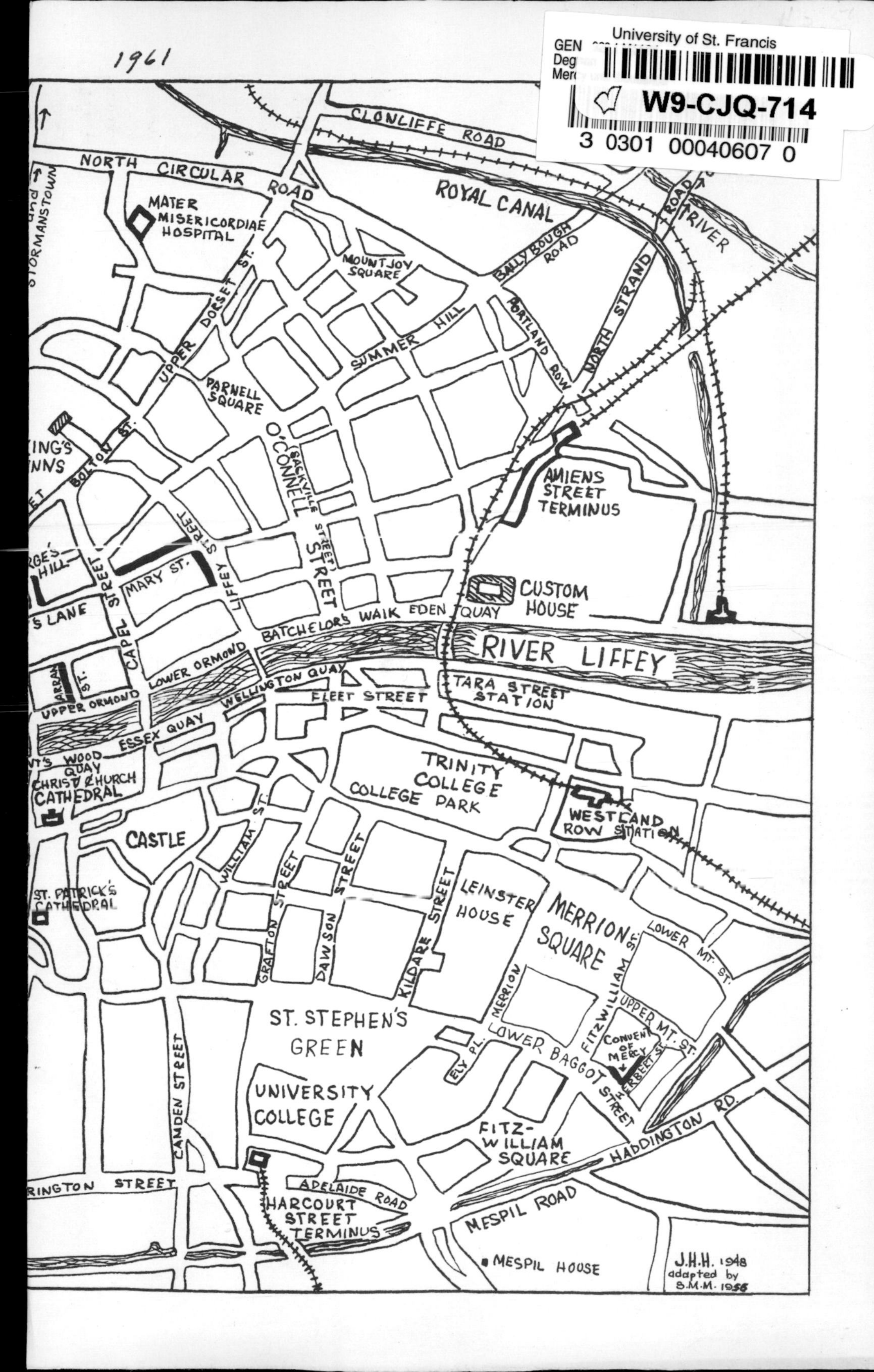
1961
CLONLIFFE ROAD
NORTH CIRCULAR ROAD
ROYAL CANAL
MATER MISERICORDIAE HOSPITAL
STORMANSTOWN
MOUNTJOY SQUARE
BALLYBOUGH ROAD
UPPER DORSET ST.
SUMMER HILL
PORTLAND ROW
NORTH STRAND ROAD
RIVER
PARNELL SQUARE
O'CONNELL (SACKVILLE STREET) STREET
KING'S INNS
BOLTON ST.
AMIENS STREET TERMINUS
LIFFEY STREET
MARY ST.
CAPEL STREET
CUSTOM HOUSE
BATCHELOR'S WALK
EDEN QUAY
RIVER LIFFEY
LOWER ORMOND
UPPER ORMOND
ARRAN ST.
WELLINGTON QUAY
FLEET STREET
TARA STREET STATION
ESSEX QUAY
WOOD QUAY
CHRIST CHURCH CATHEDRAL
TRINITY COLLEGE
COLLEGE PARK
WESTLAND ROW STATION
CASTLE
WILLIAM ST.
ST. PATRICK'S CATHEDRAL
GRAFTON STREET
DAWSON STREET
KILDARE STREET
LEINSTER HOUSE
MERRION SQUARE
LOWER MT. ST.
FITZWILLIAM ST.
UPPER MT. ST.
MERRION
ST. STEPHEN'S GREEN
ELY PL.
LOWER BAGGOT STREET
CONVENT OF MERCY
HERBERT ST.
UNIVERSITY COLLEGE
CAMDEN STREET
HADDINGTON RD.
FITZ-WILLIAM SQUARE
ADELAIDE ROAD
HARCOURT STREET TERMINUS
MESPIL ROAD
MESPIL HOUSE
J.H.H. 1948
adapted by S.M.M. 1956

922.1
M116d

31479

Degnan, Sister M. Bertrand
Mercy Unto Thousands

DATE DUE	BORROWER'S NAME	RECD

Mercy Unto Thousands

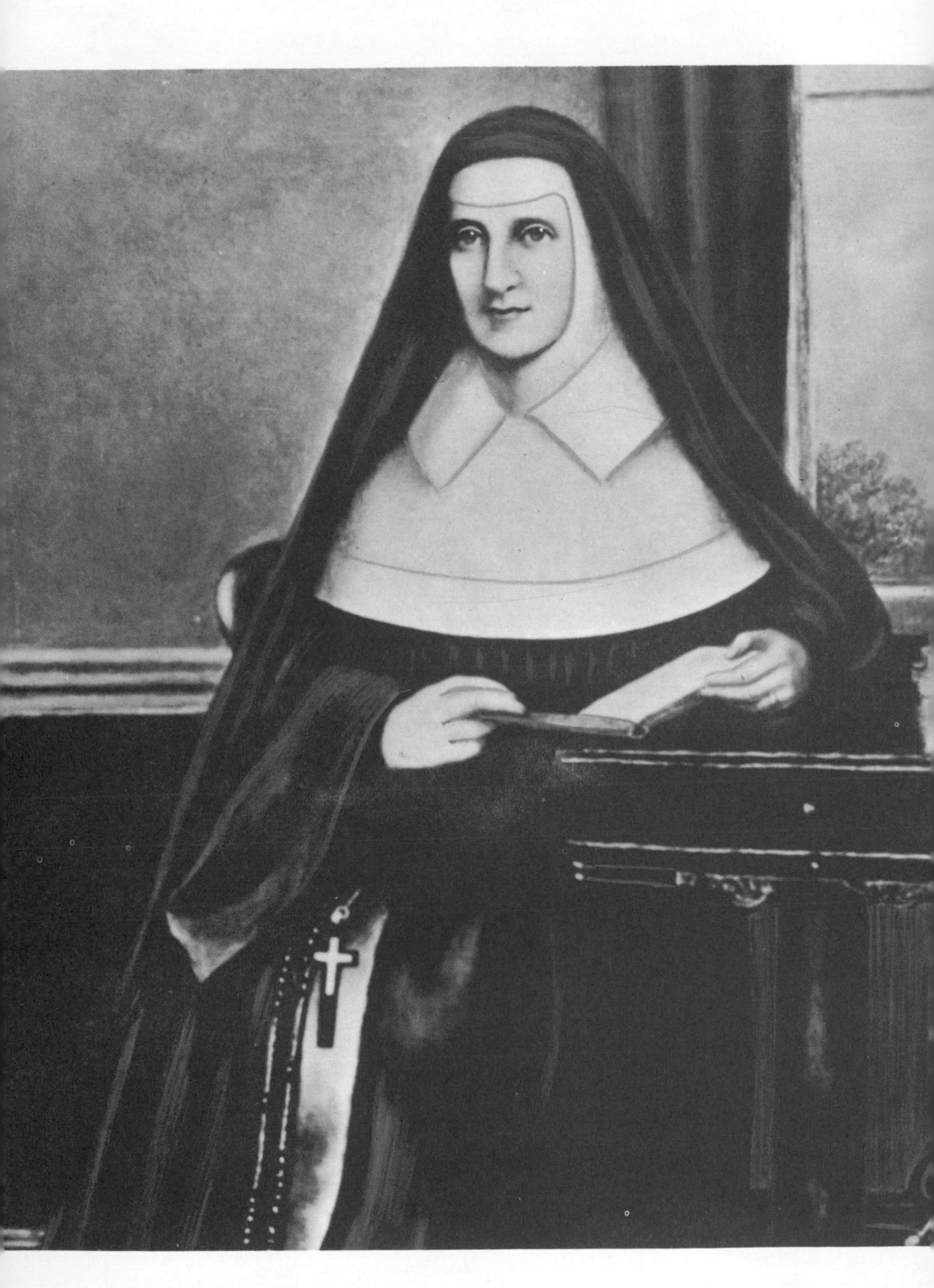

Mother Mary Catherine McAuley

Mercy Unto Thousands

Life of Mother Mary Catherine McAuley

Foundress of the Sisters of Mercy

BY SISTER M. BERTRAND DEGNAN, R.S.M.

with a Foreword by the MOST REVEREND EDMUND F. GIBBONS, D.D.
Titular Bishop of Verbe

"I am the Lord thy God showing mercy unto many thousands to them that love me and keep my commandments." (DEUT. 5:9–10)

THE NEWMAN PRESS • 1957 • WESTMINSTER, MARYLAND

First published October 1957
Second printing December 1957

Nihil obstat: FERDINAND MAYER, O.F.M.Conv.
Censor Deputatis

Imprimatur: WILLIAM A. SCULLY, D.D.
Bishop of Albany

Albany, New York, August 15, 1957

Library of Congress Catalog Card Number: 57-11809
Printed in the United States of America

MARIAMATAE

MATRI MISERICORDIAE

Foreword

MERCY, the Angelic Doctor teaches, is a virtue springing spontaneously from charity, by which the will is moved to compassion at the sight of another's misery and longs to alleviate it. All virtue is amiable, mercy particularly so. It recognizes in man the likeness of God, no matter how stained or scarred it may be. In fact the more wretched the condition, the more eager is mercy to relieve it.

The pages of holy writ are literally filled with encomiums of God's mercy. Our Blessed Savior even goes so far as to identify himself with the object of it: "I was hungry and you gave me to eat; I was thirsty and you gave me to drink; naked and you covered me . . . . As long as you did it for one of these, the least of my brethren, you did it for me" (Matt. 25:35-36, 40). The saints were all distinguished by it. When St. Martin, not yet a baptized Christian, divided his comfortable military cloak and gave half of it to the shivering beggar, he merited to see Christ clad in it and hear Him declare: "Martin while yet a catechumen clothed me with this garment." God the Father, Christ his divine Son, the saints his progeny, all exemplify the beauty and transcendent merit of mercy.

But what is more to the point in this brief Foreword, the holy Mother of God, who gave birth to the Savior of Mercy, is proposed by the Church for our veneration on September 24 under the title *Beatae Virginis Mariae de Mercede*, the Blessed Virgin Mary of Ransom, or, as it is commonly translated, of Mercy. It happened in this way. In the 13th century, Catholic Spain was in great part groaning under the yoke of the Moors, and many captive Christians were in imminent danger of losing the faith. A holy man of wealth, Peter Nolasco, now a canonized saint, had recourse to the Mother of Mercy, who then appeared to him and told him how pleasing it would be to her and to her Divine Son if he would institute a religious order to secure the liberation of the captives. The same night she appeared to Saint Raymond of Peñafort, St. Peter Nolasco's confessor, and to James, King of Aragon, delivering to them the same message. On August 10, 1218, Pope Gregory IX approved the plan. The Institute spread with amazing speed; many holy and charitable men joined its ranks and labored to obtain from the faithful the funds needed to secure the liberation of the captives. Some, bound by a fourth religious vow, went even further and delivered themselves bodily into slavery when no other means availed. Thousands were restored to freedom. Such was the power of faith in the ages of faith. Such was the response of the Church and the children of the Church to the appeal for mercy.

In the following pages a Sister of Mercy relates in detail a story of mercy, whose characters and whose action lie in a period six centuries later than that with which we have briefly dealt. I can testify to her piety, patience, and diligence over several years in collecting the material for this volume which she now presents in clear and becoming style to all who are privileged to read it. It is a narrative that should be deeply interesting and highly edifying to the thousands of Religious, especially Sisters of Mercy the world over, and many others called to the same holy state. While their titles may be different, they are all spiritual daughters of the same heavenly Queen, all cast in basically the same mold. All of them have chosen as their life work and their passport to a happy eternity to practice in one form or other the corporal and spiritual works of mercy: in the class room or hospital or asylum or home for the aged or refuge for the unfortunate; in city slums or in the cloister of prayer and mortification. What does it matter as long as they "do it" faithfully in His Holy Name, and under the patronage of Our Lady of Mercy or the glorious saints that form her court.

EDMUND F. GIBBONS
Titular Bishop of Verbe

Feast of the Holy Family
1954

Preface

ONE of the magazine notices anticipating the foundation centenary of the Sisters of Mercy (1931) began with a mild reproach: "Have the Sisters of Mercy made known to the world the hidden, inner life of their revered foundress?" Expressing regret that "no step has been taken toward enquiring into the saintly life of this noble woman with a view of having her raised to the altars of the Church," the author observed:

There can be no miracles without prayer, no prayer without confidence and trust, no trust without love and no love without knowledge. And where is this knowledge of Mother McAuley to be more surely obtained than from her spiritual children?[1]

Even as the above article was being written, Sisters of Mercy on both sides of the Atlantic were answering its challenge. Through their interest the Reverend John C. MacErlean, S. J., was designated to collect material essential to the introduction of a cause. After ten years' research he turned his findings over to the Reverend Roland Burke Savage, S. J., to assemble, for Father Burke Savage had already compiled a book on the history of George's Hill Presentation Convent, where Catherine McAuley prepared for her role as foundress of the Sisters of Mercy. Meanwhile, the general superior of the Sisters of Mercy in the Albany Diocese, Reverend Mother M. Borromeo Warren, had appointed a sister to write a biography of the foundress of the Congregation of Our Lady of Mercy. Mother M. Borromeo drew inspiration for the project from a remark made by the previous general superior, Reverend Mother M. Adrian Burke, under whose direction this book was completed.

Collecting data for *Mercy Unto Thousands* began in October

1945 at the General Motherhouse of the Sisters of Mercy of the Union, Washington, D. C. The following spring, superiors of the first foundations in Ireland and in England also opened their records to the author. Through these cooperative courtesies the present book became possible.

In Ireland the writer visited all the known residences of Catherine McAuley, as well as the various churches and convents connected with her life history. In England, also, the writer visited the convents established by Mother Catherine and examined archival material held by the respective communities The itinerary, pursued within a year of V-E Day, must have taxed our European Sisters; but the proverbial warmth of Irish hospitality and the flawlessness of English courtesy, expressed through the charity Mother Catherine had made a distinguishing mark of the congregation, concealed every hardship.

Nothing, of course, could hide the destruction caused by war. Bermondsey records had been moved to a less damaged convent at Eltham when the motherhouse became uninhabitable after the March 1945 bombing. The salvaged papers included not only Mother M. Clare Moore's memoir of Mother Catherine but unexpected items: retreat notes the foundress had copied during her noviceship at George's Hill and eight and a half finely written pages of instructions in her own handwriting, as well as a valuable letter fragment. The letter postscript, marked "private," contains the most intimate record extant on one of Mother Catherine's severest trials. The instructions explain the foundress' concept of religious life for her Institute: reciprocal support of action and contemplation. They also contain a warning against perverting the true spirit of the congregation.

In Birmingham the writer reviewed three letters and other material pertaining to the foundation of the Convent of Mercy there, which had recently come into the possession of the community from the Hardman family papers. At the Mt. Vernon convent in Liverpool hitherto unrevealed verses written by Mother Catherine were found. Principally narrative, these rhymes give a first-hand account of the Carlow foundation and other incidents. Such findings lead to the reasonable conclusion that other valuable bits may still be disclosed.

The biographer had difficulty in managing the foundress' family name because of variations in spelling. Catherine McAuley's parents' signatures preface a *G,* but Catherine herself always spelled her surname as given, evidently following the direction of her early tutors. Her sister's marriage into a Macauley family with a different orthography, her brother's adopting his brother-in-law's surname for himself, and the change her sister's children made back to their mother's family name could produce confusion. Except for certain references, I have used the spelling contemporary to the period under discussion.

With religious names I have taken the foundress' example. She frequently omits *Mary* in referring to a sister and rarely uses more than one of the given names. (Her nieces' religious names were Sister Mary Joseph Teresa and Sister Mary Anne Agnes.)

At the point in Catherine McAuley's history where her extant correspondence supplies first-hand information, I have quoted directly, at the risk of weighting the text.

Another problem arises from the rapid expansion of the foundress' work during her short life as a religious (hardly ten years). Her story remains incomplete unless it includes the extension of the Institute by her first associates. The biographer must either add chapters after the account of the foundress' death or write patently from retrospect. I have adopted the latter procedure.

In offering this new biography, the Albany community has aimed to reveal the personality and character of Catherine McAuley spiritualized through her vocation as a religious Sister of Mercy.

So many persons in several countries aided my research that it is clearly impossible to record their various services. My prayer is that all will find recompense from the Source of enduring benefaction. I am especially indebted to: His Excellency the Most Reverend Edmund F. Gibbons, Bishop of Albany, for his paternal interest in the work; His Lordship the Most Reverend Eugene O'Doherty, Bishop of Dromore, Newry, for time and personal effort spent copying the correspondence of Bishop Blake to Catherine McAuley and her associates; Right Reverend Monsignor Richard I. Glennon, Chancellor of the Dublin diocese, for the release of pertinent correspondence from the Archiepiscopal Archives and for obtaining permission to photograph the Liffey Street chapel altarpiece, now at the Archbishop's House, Drumcondra; Very Reverend Myles V. Ronan, Litt. D., P.P. of St. Michan's, Dublin, for personal letters supplying information on Dublin history; Very Reverend Michael Moylan, O.D.C., for making possible a visit to the crypt of St. Teresa's Church, Clarendon Street, and for supplying data from the Carmelite Archives and interment records; Reverend Robert Prendergast and other professors of Carlow College for receiving us at the College and permitting us to examine the Judgment Books and Bursar's Lists from 1829 to 1835 and for lending books on the history of the diocese and of the College; Reverend John Cadogan, S.M.A., President of Dromantine College, for the hospitality of the College during our stay in Newry and for securing the Reverend Jerome Sheehan, S.M.A., to do a reading of the first chapters of the book; Reverend Joseph F. Gallen, S.J., J.C.D., Professor of Canon Law at Woodstock College, Md., for supplying books on government and for checking the chapters covering the subject; Reverend F. X. Martin, O.S.A., Good Counsel House, Raheny; Reverend Conleth Kearns, O.P., St. Mary's, Tallaght; Father Canice Mooney, O.F.M., Dun Mhuire, Killiney; Brother J. D. Fitzpatrick of the Christian Brothers of Ireland, St. Patrick's, Marino; the Sisters of Charity of Mt. St. Anne's, Milltown, and the Loreto Sisters at Rathfarnham, for data from their community records; the Presentation Sisters of George's Hill, of Carlow and of Galway and the Poor Clares of Newry for receiving us with great cordiality and giving us access to their community records on the period of their hospitality to Mother Catherine; Dr. Richard J. Hays, director of the National Library of Ireland for valuable aid in follow-up work on my microfilm records; M. L. Hoyle, Assistant Keeper, Department of Manuscripts, British Museum; J. R. Lloyd, Superintendent of Records, Commonwealth Relations Office, Whitehall; Miss Mary Brewster, Reference Librarian at the New York State Library and Miss Maude Nesbit, Medical Librarian there; to Helena Concannon, Litt. D., Member of the Irish Senate, for critically reviewing the first chapters of the manuscript; Mrs. William R. Nolan, editor of the *Irish Library Bulletin,* for courtesies of heart and mind that opened avenues to living authorities on the period of research; Mr. Daniel Magee, publishing manager of Browne and Nolan, Dublin, for the opportunity to visit Stormanstown House and for courtesy copies of out-of-print books; Mr. John Harvey, Bookham, Surrey, author of *Dublin, A Study of Environment,* who magnanimously offered the use of any of his material, who permitted an adaptation of his map of Dublin, who supplied data from the London Society of Genealogists on Europeans in India, and who made pen sketches for this biography; Mr. William T. Kelly, Assistant Registrar, Registry of Deeds Office, Dublin, whose specialized knowledge and generous assistance were invaluable to me in locating documents; Miss Helen Fraser, Albany Medical College Librarian, for directing me to a wider vision of eighteenth and nineteenth century history and for indexing this book; Mrs. Vincent (Frances Gaynor) Hartigan for reading manuscript and proof; Miss Mary Francis, staff member of Westminster Youth Work, London, for giving her personal services generously, locating members of the Macauley family in England and securing from the *London Evening News* the war picture of Bermondsey convent; Miss Helen Landreth, author, curator of Irish Manuscripts at Boston College Library, for donating a copy of Malton's "Capel Street."

The heaviest debt of any biographer of Catherine McAuley is to the foresight and indefatigable efforts of Mother M. Teresa Austin Carroll who assembled data in the years preceding publication of her book in 1866 and continued research over a period of twenty years, expanding her account through four volumes of *Annals.* One of the sources for her biography of the foundress was Mother M. Vincent Hartnett's book[2] on Mother Catherine, published from Dublin in 1864. Now out of print, it nevertheless remains the first extensive biography of the foundress.

Sister Mary Catherine McAuley, Convent of Mercy, Kyneton, Victoria, Australia, Mother Catherine's grandniece, gave me through her letters over a period of several years not only personal contact with the foundress' family but contact with a living exemplar of the foundress herself. I here register my affectionate gratitude for her help and warm encouragement in this work.[3]

Without the cooperation and continued assistance of the superiors of the Convent of Mercy, Carysfort Park, Dublin, through their sister archivist, who is the best living authority on Mother Catherine, the present work would not have been possible. To them and to the superiors of the independent communities founded during Mother Catherine's life and to the Derry community, where Mother Mary Anne Doyle spent her last years, I owe the opportunity of reviewing original manuscripts and extant letters connected with the life of our Mother Foundress.

Also to the superiors of the Sisters of Mercy of the Union in the United States, Mother M. Carmelita Hartman, R.S.M., first Mother General, and Mother M. Bernardine Purcell, R.S.M., second Mother General, I owe a heavy debt for permitting me to begin my research at the General Motherhouse where Mother Carmelita had assembled letters and writings of Mother Catherine, and where Mother Bernardine had on file pertinent Roman documents through the courtesy and paternal interest of His Eminence P. Fumasoni-Biondi, Cardinal Prefect of Propaganda and Cardinal Protector of the Sisters of Mercy of the Union. To these superiors and to the sisters associated with them at the General Motherhouse in Washington I am indebted for many courtesies and services.

The title of the book was drawn from a collection of Biblical quotations on mercy, culled by a member of the Birr community. Their number, one for every day of the year, represents the devotion of a sister who inscribed and illuminated them on a single card, which hangs framed in one of the reception rooms of the convent.

Finally, for the privilege that has been mine in these years of close association with our Mother Foundress, I am deeply grateful to the general superiors of the Albany Sisters of Mercy, Reverend Mother M. Borromeo and Reverend Mother M. Adrian, whose inspiration made the present work possible. For the concurrence and support of the other superiors of my community and for the heartening interest and services of my sisters in religion everywhere, who as spiritual children of the Mother of Mercy and religious daughters of Mother Mary Catherine McAuley share in the dedication of this work, I make grateful acknowledgment.

SISTER M. BERTRAND DEGNAN, R.S.M.

Albany, New York
Feast of Our Lady Queen of All Saints
1954

Contents

Illustrations

Book One

Sifted as Wheat

"I have prayed for thee that thy faith fail not: and thou, being once converted, confirm thy brethren"
(LUKE 22:32).

I

Upon a Michaelmas

THE full misery of a people under tyranny and persecution eludes both historian and biographer. The historian can do little more than suggest wretchedness accumulating with event and legislation, and the biographer can expose only the measure of human woes at some focal point. Consequently, suffering visited on any nation year after year, century after century, remains largely unrevealed though registered in a library of biographies and histories.

Such is the case of Ireland. Records attest that the degradation of the Irish people reached its nadir under the Penal Laws which, though not the product of one mind, together form a markedly consistent policy. The persecution they set in motion attacked the most sensitive features of Irish nationality: right of land tenure, love of learning, tenacity of Faith. It was against the Faith that the Penal Laws leveled their particular genius, and it was through limitations on land tenure and prohibitions on education that they aimed to coerce or subjugate the faithful.

Political impotence of Catholics was easily effected; their social ostracism followed. Adherence to the Faith brought them to a state of pauperism that could scarcely be much alleviated by their only recourse, law evasion. One historian declares that the Penal Laws produced a "state of wretchedness hardly paralleled in Europe."[1]

Into penalty-ridden Catholicism Catherine McAuley's father and mother were born. "James Mc(G)auley, gentleman" was an architect—in other words, a contractor for new buildings, a builder himself, and a real-estate dealer. Existing records, though meager, indicate clearly that he had means. From this fact alone something of his story can be reconstructed because the prosperous Catholic was then a rarity. Evidence points to the second decade of the century as the likely period of his birth, and that decade closed the reign of Queen Anne under whom "the most crushing and vindictive of the penal laws against the Catholic religion had been enacted." [2] As a child he must have witnessed some of the most vicious effects of persecution.

His residence in Georgian Dublin, apparently from early childhood if not from birth, and his apprenticeship in and mastery of building as one of the trades open to Catholics were fortunate circumstances. Government concession of one "registered" priest to a parish assured in populous areas some accessibility to clergy and an opportunity for instruction in the Faith. Also a greater likelihood of toleration for "popish schools" existed where the weight of Catholic numbers and a few affluent Catholic townsmen contributed moral and financial support.[3] James McAuley was fortunate in his trade because expanding Dublin needed his services. Therefore he prospered, and his prosperity redounded to the poor of which Ireland, not surprisingly, had more than her share.

Catherine McAuley's recollections of her father, the only source of information on his personality, establish him as a person devoted to the poor. A lifetime of good works lay behind him " . . . when, rather advanced in years," he married "a young, very beautiful, very vain, but not very devout Catholic." According to evidencc, the phrase "advanced in years" must be taken quite literally, for James McAuley had been a builder's apprentice as early as 1730.[4]

The memoir-writer just quoted labels Elinor Conway "a philosopher above forms" and excuses the weakness of her Catholicism on the grounds that ". . . in those times and for some years afterward, Catholic education was a thing of impossible attainment."[5] It is useless to conjecture what Catholic education might have done for Elinor Conway. High-principled herself, she admired her husband's principles but she did not endorse the practical character of his charity when he obtruded the poor on her, his every free day. Of charity she certainly approved through proper channels and in proper places. In the ritual of social forms she did believe. But she condemned her husband's method, and her remonstrances were frequent. Was her home to be cluttered with derelicts?

Although he was otherwise devoted to Mrs. McAuley's wishes, Mr. McAuley cultivated indifference on this one subject. He knew Dublin well. Evidences of long oppression and accumulated privation confronted him in the streets and lanes of the Irish capital, and on Sundays, because he would have it so, the poor were no farther away than his own front door. He relieved their needs and taught them their religion.

The year of Catherine's birth at Stormanstown House to the north of Dublin,[6] Relief Bills began to grant as privileges what in reality were the rights of Irish Catholics. It was therefore in the cold but hopeful dawn of a better time that James McAuley took his baby daughter into his arms and blessed her with a name strong saints had borne through other troubled days.

Catherine was an autumn child, born on the feast of St. Michael.[7] Irish and English traditions honored the saint in homely and fanciful ways. In Ireland many sacrificed a sheep to feed the poor on Michaelmas. In England successful candidates for office garlanded their doorways and rejoiced. There the very bracken reputedly broke into flower at midnight to herald the feast of the Archangel. Small blue flowers in England's darkness, a victim sheep for Ireland's poor and the defensive sword of St. Michael—these were symbols to consider.[8]

Four other autumns came upon Dublin and its suburbs before there was any radical change at Stormanstown House. Five spring seasons passed over Ireland as Catherine grew from babyhood to childhood, awakening to the crisp beauty of her young mother, to the great, gentle compassion of her father, to the warm affection of her small sister, to the ever new familiar routine of each fresh day. Along the roads furze bushes grew candescent spring after spring; hawthorn trees fragrantly hedged in the farmlands; blackbirds and thrushes called across the morning; and on her own front lawn willie-wag-tails ran among the pink-tipped daisies and held Catherine fascinated with wonder. Then with the fifth spring a new wonder came to the House, for the little McAuley girls had a baby brother.

But soon the joy of this possession subsided in a strange quiet that fell over Stormanstown House. James McAuley died in the summer of 1783. A succession of strangenesses followed, culminating in Elinor McAuley's taking her three children away from the House to a new home farther along the road toward Dublin.

It was not her father's deathbed that little Catherine was to remember, but her mother's several years later. She hardly thought of her father in terms of death at all. Perhaps at four the only negative spiritual force in innocence is grief. A very young child can fill to the brim of its small being with grief. And a very young child's soul can expand in an ocean of compassion. Catherine was often to look back on this first decade of her life and see not the beautiful, square, ivy-covered house set in its gardens, nor the seasons' beauties folded one upon the other, nor the gay wheedling of her much-loved sister. Instead, she was to remember these only as a background for one persistent, vivid recollection: her father's at-home days; her father on the lawn in the sunshine surrounded by small hordes of the wretched; her father standing in the hallway on a rainy day with the tattered and vulgar huddled around him. She would carry for years within her, like a mystery of faith, the impression of something deeply vibrant. For years she would remember but would not understand.[9]

She would never be quite sure of her father's appearance. She would lose the certainty of the color of his eyes, the shape of his face. One certainty alone would stay with her: her father had needed these people about him; he was under some compulsion that flowed in his words and filled her soul, words she could never clearly recall though she would always remember their spell upon her and feel their force within her.

Before James McAuley died, he had made a will. Nobody knows its provisions because a registry entry in a recorder's office provides the only clue that it existed at all.[10] But the will is unimportant. James McAuley's greatest legacy, transmitted without benefit of script, fell to his daughter Catherine. He had established well a trust for her, inaccessible to thieves and secure from corruption. There had passed to her from him the wealth of God's love in a kernel of faith and the vast fortune of a compelling pity for the miserable.

II

Philosopher Above Form

ELINOR MCAULEY and the children lived for three years in the spacious new brick and stone house near Dublin.[1] In 1787, however, she sold it and leased No. 52 Queen Street,[2] where she could be close to a personal friend. Queen Street was a pleasant place in the 1780's, and Mrs. St. George was a companionable neighbor. The little McAuley girls looked upon living in Dublin as an unprecedented adventure.

Mrs. St. George was glad to have Elinor McAuley on Queen Street because she and Elinor had much in common. Even Mrs. McAuley's religion created no barrier since it lacked the "obnoxious" features of Catholicism as practiced by the ignorant. Elinor McAuley was broad-minded. She had been born into Catholicism; that she could scarcely help. Mrs. St. George was broad-minded, too; she overlooked Mrs. McAuley's religion as any well-bred person might overlook a congenital flaw.

But Mrs. St. George could not, of course, ignore Catholicism. No one in Ireland could. She talked a great deal about its errors and vulgarity. It was a popular subject, and she was an opinionated person. Elinor McAuley found her positive and sympathetic, a support in practical matters. The children found her attractive, and they took on impressions. If Catherine found these new influences disquieting, she did not know what to do about the matter. She sensed that her mother would be of no help at all, for the old impressions were rooted in her father's activities of which her mother had so strongly disapproved. Unconsciously she had long ago aligned herself with her father.

In after years, people observed an almost elusive sadness in the expression and bearing of Catherine McAuley. One of her associates put it thus: "There was in her exterior, voice included, a tender sweetness blended with a tinge of mournfulness. I cannot describe this, but there are strains in music that make one very thoughtful, though not the least gloomy."[3]

Though her natural disposition partly accounted for this feature of her personality, the habit of serious thought forced upon her at so early an age strengthened the characteristic. The long and trying conflict of soul that made her the woman she later became began here on Queen Street where life was pleasant enough but where something was lacking, something vital. Her thoughts were plagued with what she sensed to be a major inconsistency: religion warm, comforting, simple in practice as she had lived close to it through her father's example; religion cold, wordful, barbed, afflicting the mind as she found it on Queen Street. Still, a growing child surrounded by engaging distractions, by the tasks, recreations, and small excitements of a well-regulated household, had many diversions. The state of puzzlement came only on occasion with incident, overheard conversation, or invading memory. Only some forceful experience could make a problem of it.

Then Catherine's mother became sick. Extant accounts imply a long illness during which the patient neglected to make any provision for death until it was almost too late. That she made a swift readjustment of values in her last hour is evident from the effect the deathbed scene had on her sensitive daughter: it gave Catherine a dread of dying that was not relieved until her own final hours, and it made her forcefully aware of the inadequacy of religion as her mother had practiced it.

Elinor McAuley had tried to give her children a concept of right principle. She had also impressed upon them the existence of a personal God who cared about their conduct, and she had even arranged for their Confirmation and First Communion at St. Paul's, off Arran Quay. On this the London manuscript is specific:

Mrs. McAuley was a very amiable and accomplished person; her mind was highly cultivated, but her religious principles were defective; hence she considered liberty of conscience so essential that she thought constraint or the obligations of performing any duties of religion foreign to its spirit — yet she educated her children as Catholics and they were confirmed and made their First Communion in Arran Quay Chapel, and little Catherine faithfully adhered to the pious practices she became acquainted with.

Elinor McAuley had neglected the full practice of her Faith. Looking back, she saw her error; looking ahead, she fell into a confusion so painful to Catherine that she could never bring herself to refer in any detail to the experience.

Dr. Owen Conway, Elinor McAuley's brother, and a William Armstrong, probably a relative on the Conway side, are mentioned in contemporary records as being responsible from now on for the McAuley children. The latter is credited with making a home for them, securing and managing their finances, and directing their education. As a matter of fact, however, Catherine lived with her Uncle Owen at 28 East Arran Street[4] several years before going to the Armstrongs', and it is highly probable Mrs. McAuley spent her last months in her brother's home. She sold the Queen Street house in 1796. It is certain that Catherine remained with her to the end.

Mrs. McAuley had reasons for not entrusting the children's finances to her brother. Certainly the words "dissipation and recklessness" used by his granddaughter in referring to him imply carelessness with money, an implication borne out by his bankruptcy not long after his sister's death.

William Armstrong, on the other hand, was a reputable apothecary highly regarded for his business ability and personal endowments. Besides, as an official of the Company of Apothecaries,[5] he was in a position to invest money profitably in the newly organized corporation. In 1791 the Apothecaries Act had provided for an executive staff and a building in which the institute could operate and hold licentiate examinations. In 1792 it was established on Mary Street in the vicinity of the Armstrong business.[6] In fact, as far back as 1787 William Armstrong is listed at 34 Mary Street in the Dublin directories.[7]

Extant biographical data on this period of Catherine's life, though sparse, yield ample enough evidence that her association with Protestants during these years eventually produced in her a spiritual crisis. At the Armstrongs', Catholicism was a forbidden subject; her stay in the Conway household only increased her perplexity. That her uncle's Catholicism was not her father's Catholicism she had long known. Early biographies of Catherine actually call her uncle an apostate, but his daughter's eldest child, a Dominican nun at the time of their publication, wrote an emphatic denial of the charge.[8] Her letter of correction goes so far as to attribute Catherine's preservation in the Faith to the period of her residence with Dr. Conway. It reads in part:

> On the contrary, he was distinguished in childhood by the most fervent piety . . . accustomed to serve daily all the Masses in Liffey Street Chapel, which had just been built by his father and dear Mother Catherine's father, the former being contractor for the brick work, and the latter for the wood work. My grandfather in childhood was commonly called on account of his piety "Father Owen," but this early promise was not realized; association with the gay world in which he was eminently qualified to shine cooled his fervor, and his apprenticeship to Surgeon Read[9] was the occasion of plunging him into dissipation and recklessness. The Sacraments were neglected. Attending Mass on Sundays and observing the abstinence of Friday and Saturday were almost the only sacred duties which he attempted; but the seeds of piety sown in youth were never completely eradicated, and to quote a sentence which I have often heard from dear Mother Catherine's lips:
>
> "Amidst all his gaiety and revels, he retained to the last day of his life the highest reverence for religious things and religious persons."
>
> In her living with my grandfather, by whom she was much beloved, during the greater part of the time (4 or 5 years) which elapsed between her mother's death and her going to reside with Mr. and Mrs. Callaghan, dear Mother Catherine was, under God, indebted for the preservation of her Faith, which, by being thrown at an early age completely amongst Protestants, her brother and sister unhappily lost.

Clearly, Catherine's environment included both a strong Protestant atmosphere at the Armstrongs', and a worldly one with a Catholic label at the Conways'.

The Protestants close to her were, true enough, people of virtue and high moral principle. The only deterrent to her feeling quite at home among them was their polite contempt for everything Catholic. In her perplexity Catherine applied to William Armstrong for books that would explain the Protestant position. He gladly responded to this promising sign, but the books did not satisfy. Discerning in them a certain amount of sophistry, Catherine found herself in the further difficulty of not being able to refute their errors. Harassed by misrepresentations, she could at times scarcely distinguish between the specious and the true.

Yet her difficulties with religion served to increase her devotion, for she turned more and more to the Blessed Sacrament. An eighteenth-century description of the interior of St. Mary's, Liffey Street, mentions a detail that must have been dear to young Catherine McAuley: "fore-part of the altar covered with gilt leather and name of Jesus in glory in the midst."[10] Even when too young to write, Catherine had copied off, in imitative print, parts of the Psalter of Jesus,[11] had memorized them, and had developed the habit of reciting the aspirations hourly. She would stop on a doorstep, pray among the people on the street or wherever she found herself when the clock struck. The round of petitions, beginning with and repeating a plea for mercy, became the keynote of her spirituality: a tender, personal love of God with strong devotion to the Passion. It was to draw down upon her the Divine Compassion.

III

Georgian Teen-ager

DURING the last decade of the eighteenth century Catherine McAuley passed through her teens, at the same time manifesting a maturity beyond her years. The spiritual trials she was undergoing gave her an insight which her natural sympathy for people softened to discerning tolerance. She learned patience with herself and others, a humble waiting for God to work His way. This characteristic endeared her to older people.

Mary McAuley, Catherine's sister, enjoyed the popularity of those her own age, but Catherine was beloved by all. An early biographer contrasts the two McAuley girls in terms that require explanation: "Mary was fond of dress and amusements but Catherine felt only weariness and disgust for them."[1] To understand this statement one must know something of eighteenth century social life in Dublin. Descriptions come from varied sources, most of them written by travelers from the continent or by long or short term visitors from England. Referring to these, Constantia Maxwell, authority on Georgian Ireland, says:

> All were impressed by the air of gaiety in the houses of the well-to-do which went with a peculiarly splendid way of living— a multiplicity of servants, great profusion of dishes on the table, abundant wine.

Though manners tended to improve by the close of the century, drinking and gambling remained Irish vices. The same writer declares that Lord Chesterfield "was horrified at the amount the Irish gentry managed to consume." She adds:

> No one of any position in Dublin would have thought himself truly hospitable unless he provided large quantities of claret for his guests,

with the result that the men seldom rejoined the women after dinner in a state of complete sobriety.[2]

On the subject of dress this chronicler of manners begins, "A passion for show was certainly a weakness of the Irish gentry," and she borrows from a commentator the telling epithet, "gaudy frippery."

Catherine McAuley would certainly find such display repugnant. That she gave meticulous attention to proper grooming and had a definite regard for conservative styles is demonstrated in a description of her by one of her early associates, an artist alert to detail:

She was fair with brilliant colour on her cheeks, though not too red. Her face was a short oval but the contour was perfect; her lips were thin, her mouth rather wide. Her eyes were light blue and remarkably round. . . . In repose they had a melancholy beseeching look [but they] would light up expressive of real hearty fun. If she disapproved of anything, they could tell that too. Sometimes they had that strange expression of reading you through, which made you feel that even your mind was in her power and that you could not hide anything from her. She wore bands made from her own back hair, which were so well managed as to be quite free from the disagreeable look bands of the kind usually give; the colour was pale golden . . . very fine and silky. She was dressed in black British merino, which according to the fashion of the time fitted tight to her shape. She was remarkably well made, round but not in the least heavy.[3]

This description of Catherine's clothes and her coiffure in middle age is typical enough for an impression of her at any period. Surely a woman who dresses according to the fashion of the time and effectively manages fine, silky hair cares about her appearance. Even as a religious she counseled the sisters on clothes and manners, regretting the time that must be spent on appearance but insisting on its importance.[4] "A perfect religious is a perfect lady," she would conclude.

Conservative dress in the 1790's dictated that a young lady should wear her hair flat with side curls to accommodate a variety of hats. The princess dress with its high waistline and full-length skirt was standard not only for the well-dressed teen-ager but for the young matron, the elderly madame, and even for the little girl.

As for amusements, Catherine may not have devoted the greater part of the day to them as did many, but her references to the "Duval Trio" and the "Sir Roger de Coverly" show that she entered into the social life at the Conways' and Armstrongs'. Her position in the Conway household amounted to that of a favored daughter, and her friendship with the doctor's only child Anne guaranteed to young Catherine McAuley a full social program.

Of the Queen Street, Arran Street, and Mary Street area at the time Séan O'Faoláin has this to say: "With Arran Quay as center and the Circular Road as radius, Georgian Dublin was fashionable and residential." He adds significantly, "carpenters could design in those days."[5] Indeed, though this district has fallen from grandeur, the Georgian doorways retain vestiges of beauty.

In the matter of social life, Anne Conway, the McAuley girls, and the Armstrongs could not have been better favored by time. During the last decade of the eighteenth century, those years just before the political coup (Act of Union, 1800) that was to disrupt the whole social and economic pattern of Dublin, the social life of the capital expanded remarkably. Patronage of the arts, particularly music, had gradually refined coarse mid-century customs, and the social graces now flourished at gatherings of gentry and nobility. Moreover, lines of demarcation between these two classes had relaxed with the emergence of professions, particularly the medical profession. Benefit events for the hospitals became occasions of the first order on the social calendar.

Dublin Castle, the seat of English government in Ireland, was actually the vortex of social activity, which extended north and south to the town houses and beyond to the country houses and to the beaches. Georgian homes were resplendent with period furniture and old silver plate, foreign carpets and brocades, Irish silks, linens and laces. Imported foods and wines supplemented Irish fare. Such opulence, together with "bands of servants" managed under the easy discipline of the mistress at town or country house, testified to an amalgamation of Irish and English social life that, however hybrid, produced a conviviality running to heady brilliance.

Harps, organs, and harpsichords were the common musical instruments, and by the end of the eighteenth century the pianoforte appeared in the drawing rooms of the middle class. Catherine McAuley's taste for music grew out of this fortunate emphasis in the social life of her girlhood.[6]

Musicals, balls, card parties, and the theater supplied afternoon and evening diversion; horse-racing, hunting, bowls, and outdoor sports swirled with the seasons; and the whole gay dance included enough drinking and gambling to ruin scores of reputations and sink countless fortunes.

It is therefore not difficult to trace the cause of Owen Conway's bankruptcy, which occurred shortly before the turn of the century. Halted in his "gaiety and revels," as Catherine McAuley charitably described his way of life to his granddaughter, Dr. Conway finally saw his little family uncomfortably near starvation. The extremes of poverty they suffered were later recounted by Catherine herself: there were days when those of the household had almost nothing to eat, and there came at last nights when they had but the floor on which to sleep. Catherine McAuley thus learned by experience what it meant to be poor. In later years she evinced a particular sympathy for those suddenly impoverished.

One memoir gives this account of her experience:

> Surgeon Conway's affairs became embarrassed and at last he was reduced to ruin so that she suffered great poverty. Frequently after an entire day spent without food, they had nothing but a little bread at night . . . but her cheerfulness never failed and she has often said that she took her rest more contentedly on the boards than when surrounded by luxuries; from these circumstances she used to conclude that we are much better able to endure hardships in God's service than we usually imagine. [She would point out] that happiness does not depend on the enjoyment of temporal comforts, since many in great poverty are still most joyful . . . Christ our Blessed Lord and His holy Mother had not temporal comforts [she would say] yet were always full of peace and joy. She had a remarkable talent for thus drawing instructions from every occurrence and made useful reflections on all passing events, teaching us to be careful in like manner to derive spiritual profit from all things.[7]

It must be apparent that no ordinary young girl could take her rest "more contentedly on the boards than when surrounded by luxuries." Only an intimate knowledge and love of Christ reveal poverty as a spiritual privilege. Catherine therefore achieved more than preservation of her faith during the years at the Conways'; she also established a spiritual treasury. Love of God and pity for humankind, hitherto almost natural virtues, now assumed supernatural vigor.

IV

An East Wind

ABOUT the time Dr. Conway's furniture was being sold to meet creditors' demands, there came to 31 Mary Street a chemist of considerable reputation. William Callaghan had lived a number of years in India. He had been absent from Dublin since the time of his marriage in 1776 until 1786 and probably acted as army physician during those years, returning home when Warren Hastings resigned the governorship of India.[1]

Soon after reaching Dublin, he established an apothecary shop on Castle Street, at 18 Silver Court, and became eligible for membership in the Company of Apothecaries organized in the 1790's. He was elected to office in 1797 and maintained a connection with it till his death, serving as governor, deputy governor, secretary, or treasurer at one time and another for a period of twenty-five years. It was undoubtedly at the Armstrongs' that William Callaghan's wife, the gentle Quakeress Catherine Callaghan, first met Catherine McAuley. Through their frequent meetings, afterward, Mrs. Callaghan developed an affection for the young girl that became one of the great comforts of her life. This enduring friendship compensated Mrs. Callaghan to some degree for having no children of her own.

It has been said that the Armstrong, Callaghan, and Conway families were distantly interrelated, and an A. Conway Armstrong in the directory as well as the reappearance of Armstrong as a given name seems to lend support to assertions of a Conway-Armstrong kinship.[2] As for the Callaghans, Dr. James McAuley, Catherine's brother, and William Armstrong's daughter were both beneficiaries of the William Callaghan will. Certainly Catherine's first recruit in the Baggot Street social service work believed these Protestant connections were relatives. Of their influence she wrote:

Protestant relations, to whom she was much attached and whose conversion she ardently desired, induced her to think of forming a society of ladies, who would devote themselves to the practice of the works of mercy, without making vows, that they might be at liberty to visit their relations and remain with them in sickness and affliction.[3]

A point not made in early biographies is that when Catherine went to live with the Callaghans they as well as the Armstrongs had an apartment at the Apothecaries' Hall.[4] She was again on the premises with her sister and brother. It was, in general, a happy arrangement. Although her own brother and sister were by this time affiliated with the church of their guardians, Catherine still belonged to St. Mary's parish. Following her religious program as she had done at East Arran Street now had its own special difficulties.

Meanwhile, the political tempo of Irish life quickened. A new unrest had begun in 1791 with the Society of United Irishmen, established in the North by a Southern Protestant, Theobald Wolfe Tone. Through his career the kaleidoscopic character of Irish politics before the turn of the century can be graphically represented. Wolfe Tone, as he was familiarly called, first attracted attention by publishing a pamphlet urging Catholics and Presbyterians to unite in order to regain their political rights. With the nobler ideals of the French Revolution in mind, he aimed at "a brotherhood of affection, a communion of rights, and a union of power amongst Irishmen of every religious persuasion . . . a complete reform of the Legislature, founded on the principles of civil, political, and religious liberty."[5]

Had the Protestantism of the Irish Parliament been of his breadth, the Catholic cause need not have waited for an O'Connell; instead, the Protestants were so intent on bulwarking their minority position, shortsightedly and ignobly, so busy petitioning the British Ministry against concessions to Catholics and dissenters, that they constituted an effective block to any improvement in conditions. As for O'Connell, these years brought him back from France to London and finally to Dublin. Nobody could have foreseen at the time that he would be "the Liberator."

Concessions did result from Wolfe Tone's agitation, and the Ascendancy retaliated by outlawing his Society of United Irishmen and banishing their leader. Tone then went to France, where the new Republicans had proclaimed their readiness to aid any oppressed people against tyranny.

Meanwhile, England received and harbored hundreds of French refugees, among them scores of Catholic clergy, religious and ecclesiastics. Meanwhile, too, the United Irishmen quietly and illegally reorganized, though not without the knowledge of Crown spies. England became acutely aware of the danger of insurrection. She therefore sent to Ireland in January, 1795, Lord Fitzwilliam, a man known for his conciliatory attitude toward the Irish cause.

When His Lordship as Lieutenant Governor began to replace minor officials, however, he incurred the displeasure of Pitt and the Cabinet. His recall in March threw the Irish capital into a demonstration of mourning. Shops closed and business was suspended as crowds gathered to watch the passing of his carriage to the harbor. A discerning person would have sensed beneath the mourning a spirit of grim decision; for hope of peace sailed out of Ireland that March 25, 1795, and there were those who faced the sea and read the signs of trouble.

Henceforth the Society of United Irishmen recruited Catholics by the thousands and began underground operations. "By the end of 1795 the policy of the United Irishmen had become distinctly Republican," history records, "and they looked to an armed insurrection as a means of obtaining their end."[6]

Regrettably, the first skirmishes took place between Catholics and Protestants of the North,[7] for the Orange Society had flared into existence. Where now was Wolfe Tone's hope "to break connection with England . . . to unite the whole people of Ireland, to abolish memory of past dissensions, and to substitute the common name of Irishman in place of the denominations of Protestant, Catholic, and Dissenter"?[8]

By the time the Orange Society began to operate, Wolfe Tone, who had gone to America, had returned again to France to further his plan of invasion. He might have succeeded in spite of disrupting influences at home and the infidelity of some of his French allies, had not nature itself conspired against him. With an estimated 15,000 troops and competent French generalship, he set out from Brest with a fleet that would never disembark. Though some half of the ships arrived offshore of Bantry, the weather continued so unfavorable that after a fortnight's lying to, they returned to France.[9]

But the mere fact of their sailing had its effect at the Castle. After the French fleet left, government authorities multiplied security and defense measures. The secret Society of United Irishmen, whose membership too quickly and too openly swelled to a hundred thousand, included many spies. By 1798 martial law and free quartering were established throughout Ireland. Trouble did not begin in Ulster, however, as might have been expected, but in the southeast where free quartering became more than the people could bear.

It was from the borders of "bloody Wexford" that young Father Murray, later Archbishop, fled to Dublin when his pastor was killed; it was in Dublin that Lord Edward Fitzgerald and other prominent members of the United Irishmen were arrested; and it was to Dublin, the place of his birth, that the young lawyer Wolfe Tone was brought to be hanged when the trouble was over.[10]

While the insurgents of '98 were being put to death or were dying in prison, the fast-moving little metropolis of Dublin went on much as before, except for bursts of short-lived excitement in the form of arrests in Bridge Street, in Thomas Street, and at the various depots of arms of the United Irishmen. To escape the dangerous vicinity of Dublin Castle, William Callaghan at this time moved to the Apothecaries' Hall on Mary Street. Shortly thereafter, at Mrs. Callaghan's invitation, Catherine McAuley made her home with the chemist and his wife; it was a decision that was to influence thousands of people across the world for generations.

V

And Spiritual Storm

FROM her new home Catherine McAuley continued to frequent the Liffey Street chapel.[1] Probably some of the servants followed the same streets to the same church; certainly none of the family circle did. The loneliness of her position must have saddened her often; there is ample proof that her defenselessness did. She experienced a kind of spiritual exile that her charity might be perfected.

The matter of her spiritual direction brings several clergymen into the narrative at this point. In fact, their very number becomes baffling. Since Catherine's first biographers show uncertainty on her degree of communion with the Church, it is important to clear up the matter. Anne Conway's daughter is specific on this point: in one letter she refers to Father Andrew Lubé, curate of St. Mary's, Liffey Street, as "my mother's confessor and . . . confessor to her cousin, Miss Catherine McAuley." In another she deplores inadequate recognition of Dean Lubé in the first published biography of Catherine McAuley. She concludes her protest emphatically:

> Dean Lubé, then of Liffey Street . . . when Miss McAuley came to reside at the Apothecaries' Hall, Mary Street, with Mr. and Mrs. Callaghan, was until his removal to James Street her confessor, and by his charitable counsels contributed more than *any other* to the preservation of her faith, at times sorely besieged.[2]

Another early manuscript confirms this with the statement: "She was much indebted to the instruction and kindness of the Reverend Dean Lubé, who was her steady friend for eighteen years."[3]

Since Father Lubé served St. Mary's from 1785 to 1810, the period of his direction covered both the East Arran Street and Mary Street residence of Catherine McAuley and part of her subsequent stay at Coolock House. Besides Father Lubé, Father Daniel Murray, Father Betagh, S.J.,[4] and Father Michael Blake are mentioned as her spiritual directors.

All of this suggests that Catherine McAuley was at no time out of communion with her Church, however severe and complex the difficulties that exercised her faith. The autobiography of St. Thérèse amply attests that trial of faith is not reserved to the ill-instructed. Such difficulties exercise intellects in the process of growth as well as saints in the process of sanctification. The principal fault of nineteenth-century accounts of Catherine McAuley's life in her teens and early twenties lies in the interpretation of those who, having a few facts, tried to align her spiritual trial completely with her position among Protestants, as if spiritual patterns can be reduced to formulae or as if spiritual experience can be expressed in equations. Such interpretations do not take into consideration the sifting process designated by Christ Himself as a preparation for the religious leadership of others.

The siege was certainly a long one with something of a progressive character. Catherine herself always attributed perseverance in her religion to her fortunate reception of the Sacrament of Confirmation at an early age.[5] In the span from 1798 to 1810 Catherine continued under the able direction of her cousin's confessor, Father Andrew Lubé. By the very interdependence of virtues, the exercise of her faith matured her interior life.

A private letter of Anna Maria Doyle, Catherine's first associate at Baggot Street, states: "She told me that in some doubt she had recourse to the celebrated Dr. Betagh who quite convinced her. At another time she sought instruction from Most Reverend Dr. Murray, then a curate in the old chapel, Liffey Street."

The order of Miss Doyle's statements signifies nothing because the letter from which the excerpt is made contains reminiscent jottings without regard to chronology. It may have been Father Murray who advised her to apply to his former teacher, Dr. Betagh, pastor of St. Michael's, then in his old age teaching poor boys in the cold, damp cellar where they met for his instructions. This much is certain: Miss McAuley met Dr. Betagh in the last years of his life, and he influenced her profoundly. It is unlikely that a person of Catherine's disposition toward the underprivileged could meet Dr. Betagh without profiting from his ability as an experienced educator of the poor. Here a forward-looking circumstance must not go unnoticed. The future Dr. Blake was curate at St. Michael's for several years before he succeeded Dr. Betagh. Neither should the fact that Catherine McAuley's father had had connections with the parish in the last years of his life go without mention. He owned considerable property in the area, and the name of his only son appears on the St. Michael's baptismal registry for May, 1783.

A few facts about the aforementioned three great figures in the reassertion of the Catholic position in Ireland will help to clarify Catherine's connection with them.

Father Daniel Murray, curate at St. Paul's shortly after his ordination in 1790, was appointed to Liffey Street chapel from Wexford in 1798. In 1809 he became Coadjutor Archbishop of Dublin. Catherine's first contact with Father Murray was at St. Paul's when she received her First Holy Communion.

Father Betagh, S. J., on the other hand, had been ordained before Catherine McAuley was born. He spent his entire priestly career in St. Michael's parish where he took over the work of educating boys, begun by Father Austin, S. J., who had established a seminary and a boys' school. Father Betagh continued the educational work of his predecessor and extended it by opening a school for poor boys, where he taught till the year of his death, 1811. These schools still exist under his name. Father Betagh was curate at St. Michael's about the time the McAuleys moved into St. Paul's parish across the river, and he became pastor of St. Michael's just before the turn of the century.

Father Michael Blake, later Bishop of Dromore, was a native of St. Paul's parish where Catherine McAuley had been confirmed at an early age and later received her First Holy Communion. The fact that Catherine McAuley and Michael Blake grew up in the same parish at the same time, he being only three years her senior, does not necessarily imply that they knew each other. Though educated in Father Betagh's seminary and in Rome, he came to ordination in 1798 in Liffey Street chapel, which Archbishop Troy had then recently made his mensal parish. Catherine was certainly a St. Mary's parishioner at this time. Father Blake became curate first at St. Paul's, then at St. Michan's,[6] and finally went to assist Father Betagh at St. Michael's, succeeding to the pastorate when Father Betagh resigned in 1810. He also succeeded to Father Betagh's work in education and he fostered among the laity besides, through the confraternity movement, a form of Catholic Action. It might be observed in passing that whoever writes the history of Catholic Action, extended with much fanfare in our time, should give a substantial chapter to this period of Irish history. Among his activities Father Blake organized a society "for promoting the Spiritual and Corporal Works of Mercy," including lay-catechetical work with poor children. Here may be discerned the basis for a sympathy of interest with Catherine McAuley, who occupied herself in this type of service as soon as she was in a position to do so.

Catherine's interest in the poor of St. Mary's parish undoubtedly began while she was living on Mary Street. It is interesting to observe that during his ten years at St. Mary's, Father Murray met in their young womanhood the future foundresses of both the Irish Sisters of Charity and the Sisters of Mercy.[7] In fact, he there formed the idea of a religious order that would go out among the poor to relieve their misery—"the walking nuns," as people came to call them.[8]

The time was not far off when Daniel Murray, Coadjutor-Archbishop of Dublin, would be in a position to put his idea into execution, but the idea of a congregation spreading out of Ireland over four continents within a quarter of a century, was not in Father Murray's mind and most certainly not in Catherine McAuley's. She was vitally interested in some form of a lay apostolate of Catholic social service, but did not have any well-defined objectives.

Meanwhile, just as she did throughout her life, Catherine continued simply to rely upon the Providence of God. Convinced of her own insufficiency, of her complete spiritual dependence, she acquired that solid base upon which religious persons build complete confidence in God. With wisdom she was later to counsel her spiritual daughters: "While we place all our confidence in God, we must ever act as if all depended on our own exertions."

At 31 Mary Street Catherine was hampered by constrictions that lay partly within herself. If the Callaghans rarely adverted to her religion, she herself was sensitively conscious of it. She could scarcely help being so. The circumstances of her life had singled it out, impaled it, subjected it to scrutiny, passed judgment on it, cast it aside, granting it barely sufficient nurture for survival. Want of sympathy and meagerness of spiritual sustenance in her childhood had fostered an inner asceticism. To her, reserve meant more than a cultural asset, a mark of good breeding, more than a merging of good judgment and self-control. It was a quality of soul, the spiritual economy that produces the virtue of modesty.

Free to make her own way for religious observance, she did so inconspicuously from two motives. In the first place, it was the part of wisdom to protect her religion, insofar as she could, from the light comment of those in no position to understand it. Besides, consideration for her foster parents kept her from inconveniencing them on her account.

Knowing the negative value of religious controversy *per se*, she avoided it. With the family she was generally successful, for Mr. Callaghan's interests were scientific rather than polemic. Mrs. Callaghan, according to the kindly philosophy of her own sect, tolerated Catherine's religious beliefs without inquiring into them. But Callaghan hospitality was Irish hospitality. In a house open to many guests, some of them her own relatives, Catholicism became a frequent topic of discussion as the Catholic question rose in prominence. Catherine then had to listen to arguments and raillery that she felt she could not successfully parry if addressed directly. It was characteristic of her to do something about the situation. Her subsequent contacts with Father Betagh grounded her in apologetics and fortified her for the inevitable.

When Mr. Callaghan later had occasion to turn to her and ask what she could say to controvert certain statements, she acquitted herself so well that she won his commendation, and he never again called upon her to defend her position.

Meanwhile, she grew in affection for her foster parents, showing them every mark of the devotion of a reserved but warm-hearted nature. Meanwhile, too, Mary McAuley and Anne Conway accepted "opportunities of settling in life" and James McAuley entered what was becoming the family profession, medicine.

Toward the end of July, 1803,[9] William Callaghan leased the principal estate in surburban Coolock and shortly afterward moved from turbulent Dublin where the Emmet insurrection had just miscarried. Though she did not know it, Catherine McAuley now entered on a quarter of a century of preparation for a great work.

VI

Kaleidoscope

BY ONE stratagem or another the Act of Union had passed in 1800. The Irish had been deeply skeptical about the favoring arguments of better trade, better business, better human relationships; few were surprised, therefore, when the parliamentary welding did not achieve the better conditions. Emmet's abortive insurrection of 1803 and the clandestine activity of secret societies thereafter represented the real feeling of the people.

Dublin's social life lost much of its brilliance after the Act went into effect. With the dissolution of the Irish Parliament and the devitalizing of Castle authority, the pageantry of government and its attendant social trappings moved abroad to enrich the fringes of that more resplendent institution, the English court. Whole staffs of servants, hitherto an essential part of life in the big houses, were discharged, swelling the ranks of the many unemployed in Dublin. Members of Parliament returning from London sought their country estates, and the town houses remained closed until they were converted into offices, institutions, and finally tenements.

Those of the middle class who managed to survive adjustments in trade kept up the social life of the capital, which if less splendid, was not less gay. The Armstrongs, the Callaghans and the Macauleys were among the survivors. In 1804 Mary McAuley married William Macauley, a physician whose Protestantism was as firm as she supposed her own to be. He, however, was a Presbyterian, a "dissenter," whereas she followed the middle course and attended the Established Church. William Macauley was the son and namesake of a Dublin merchant who had married a Longford County Montgomery. The Montgomery estate, Cartrongarrow, had been in the family for nearly a century and a half and was to remain in it another quarter of a century.[1]

That Catholics were present at the wedding of Dr. William and Mary McAuley is relatively certain—among them, the bride's own sister. If Dr. Macauley could have foreseen when he married the pretty ward of the Armstrongs that his children would, through Catherine, adopt the religion he despised, he undoubtedly would have had a change of heart; and if the Orange Montgomerys could have foreseen that their estate would fall into "Papist" hands, they would probably have abandoned it to ruin.[2] As was to be expected, Mary and William Macauley conscientiously set about rearing their children as Protestants.

It was little Mary, born about 1811, who disturbed her mother's security one Sunday morning on the way home from St. Catherine's Protestant Church.

"Mama," she called out, "why do we say at our prayers 'I believe in the holy Catholic Church'? I don't believe in the Catholic Church. I believe in the holy Protestant Church!"[3]

Mary Macauley's early memories of St. Paul's stirred uncomfortably at her daughter's remark. By the time little Mary thrust this small wedge of doubt into her mother's mind, the child had two brothers of church-going age, James and Robert, and a baby sister Catherine. All of these children were born between 1810 and 1820. The first Macauley children had died in infancy. The only one born in the next decade survived to old age and died in Australia in 1904. William Armstrong Montgomery Macauley, on his own assertion, was the third child of the family to be named for his father.

The second family that was to be very close to Catherine also grew up between 1810 and 1820. This was the family of her cousin, Anne Conway. In the days of Dr. Owen Conway's opulence, he had planned that his only child would marry well, but, since he continued poor, he was unable to supply the dower that social custom then required.

Little concerned with her own prospects, Anne had set about making a match between a friend of hers, Kitty Sweetman, and a young printer, James Byrn, whose family had also fallen from affluence. Her efforts, however, resulted in James Byrn's declaring his interest in Anne, not Kitty. It so happened that Anne's spiritual director, Father Lubé, thought highly of James and tactfully recommended his virtues to Anne. Father Lubé always prided himself on having played a part in promoting James' cause.[4]

Instead of convincing either Kitty Sweetman or young Byrn, Anne finally persuaded herself. She then proceeded to try her persuasive powers on her father, but she was no more successful with him than she had been with Kitty. On his own daughter's assertion James was very homely.[5] Dr. Conway's objections fastened on his homeliness of features, his lack of money and of social position. Finally, however, Dr. Conway relented and gave his consent to the marriage.

The Byrns had four children: Catherine, born on March 19, 1812,[6] James, Ann, and little Teresa; the last was six months older than Willie Macauley. According to letters Catherine later wrote, protesting errors in the first published biographies of Catherine McAuley, her parents were exemplary Catholics. There is certainly ground for this insistence in the fact that Catherine was baptized three days after her birth.

It is impossible to write of Catherine McAuley's mature life without dealing at some length with people close to her for she devoted herself rather completely to others.

Life at Coolock House must have been pleasant. The lodge, the carriage house and stables, the gardens, the long driveway leading from the gatehouse to the mansion's sweep of white stone steps are still there. They and the woodbine on the garden wall, the walnut trees and copper beeches along the drive and on the grounds must have looked much the same for several generations. When one of the trees was cut down recently, someone detected Catherine McAuley's name carved so deeply into the trunk long ago that the spread-out letters could still be identified. Was this the work of one of the nine youngsters who used to romp the grounds? Many a family party was held at Coolock.

"Our dear foundress . . . doted on children and invariably spoiled them," one of her associates declares.[7] What holidays the children must have had there!

The lodgekeeper's wife points out the room at the gatehouse where Catherine McAuley, emulating her father, gathered in the children of the village poor, instructed them, and relieved their wants as well as she could.

What a lovely sight she must have been coming down the long drive to the gatehouse! Descriptions of her emphasize the dignity and grace of her movements, her pale gold hair, the earnest expression that could break so quickly into merriment or cloud over in sympathy for the suffering of others, her gentle voice with the Irish range of endearing terms so suited to it. How familiar and dear she must have become to the little children whom she loved with a special love! What the dour recorder of her talent for spoiling children overlooked was the amount of spoiling poor children can weather.

As has already been said, living with Protestants required some adjustment in Catherine's religious practices. Although Coolock village had a Catholic chapel and she busied herself with its parish poor, she also returned to St. Mary's, Liffey Street, from time to time for counsel, and she continued her interest in the sick poor of the city alleys. Experienced in spiritual and material poverty, she felt impelled to do something about the needs of others.

In a private letter, one of her associates tells how an amalgamation of natural and supernatural interests began to shape Catherine McAuley's vocation:

> Her charity and zeal, I need not say, were most remarkable. When she resided at Coolock House . . . she had much to exercise these virtues on account of the interference of a Protestant minister's wife with the poor. There she formed her first idea of a community or some society devoted to the instruction and protection of the poor.[8]

Catherine's vocation was being moulded by the needs of her day. Already in her twenties, she was showing that predisposition to service which emerged as a compelling force in her character. Her habit of conservative dress seemed particularly suited to her activities; she was as inconspicuous as an attractive young lady could manage to be.

Probably the best summary of the Coolock period comes from an early biography:

Miss McAuley devoted herself to her foster parents with all the affection of a child and gained their entire confidence so that they left the management of their household to her discretion. All this time she was most fervent and exemplary in the performance of religious duties. Though in the midst of Protestants, she observed rigorously the days of fasting and abstinence. . . . She never touched wine during Lent and practiced many other austerities. Prayer was her delight and refuge in all trials. She addressed herself to her good God with the utmost simplicity and confidence, even in the smallest difficulties. It was her chief recreation to copy prayers and pious books and to unite with one of the Catholic domestics in pious exercises. Being unable to have any holy pictures or other objects of devotion, they used often to kneel before a cross formed in the branches of the trees or even the cross-shaped panels of the doors. She was most careful to correct her faults and to practice a genuine humility and patient forbearance, but charity was her characteristic virtue. She loved all and sought to do good to all, but the poor and little children were her especial favourites. These she laboured to instruct, relieve and console in every possible way, so that she began even then to practice those works of mercy to which she afterwards so fully devoted herself.[9]

Catherine's life with the Callaghans became rich in service to others and marked by happiness and peace. If her foster parents had had a daughter of their own, they would have wanted her to be just such a daughter. Unusually strong bonds of friendship existed between Catherine and Mrs. Callaghan, but the petty troubles that sometimes arose around them never marred the relationship between the two. Through the interference of the minister's wife already alluded to, Catherine had differences over her interest in the village children. Mrs. Callaghan, on the other hand, suffered from the jealousy of relatives who resented her bringing Catherine into the family. Suppose the Callaghan money went to this stranger! Everybody knew how much influence Mrs. Callaghan had with her husband. Some unsuccessful efforts were made to cause dissension in the household. Failing in this, one of Mrs. Callaghan's own relatives began a series of insulting anonymous letters.

The letter-writer's handwriting was finally identified. When his mother later asked Mrs. Callaghan to intercede with her husband for money the young man urgently needed, Catherine's influence turned the matter in his favor. She pleaded so successfully with her foster mother to forgive the injury that Mrs. Callaghan burned the letters and secured the money from her husband.

Coolock House has the spaciousness of an old mansion.[10] A peculiar feature of its layout is a room off the main staircase with its own little flight of steps. The manner of access to it makes the room distinctively private. It could easily have been a hermitage or a shrine, and in the days of the Callaghan residence, it was something of both, for it is pointed out as Catherine McAuley's. The heavy cross-paneled door recalls the devotions she practiced here with her Catholic maid.

No one knows which of the large, pleasant rooms Mrs. Callaghan ocupied in her invalidism. The future foundress spent many hours there tending her foster mother day and night during a three years' illness. The only fretfulness the invalid ever showed was fear that those she loved might tire of her. There was no petulance in her distress but rather a delicacy of feeling for those whose devotion might conceivably be overtaxed. She had always been sensitive. If illness sharpened the characteristic, it also revealed Mrs. Callaghan's long fidelity to a philosophy that stressed human relationships as of prime importance. The word Friend has a particular meaning in the Society of Friends.

In devoting herself completely to her foster mother's needs, Catherine had to limit her service to others. This necessary neglect must have bothered her quite a bit. After readying Mrs. Callaghan for the night, she would sometimes fall asleep before her patient did. Alert to any sound, the nurse slept lightly, dreaming of all she had to leave undone. More than once Mrs. Callaghan asked her what she dreamed of that she showed so much distress asleep.

Of the poor, the unprotected, those in moral danger, the sick, the imprisoned she dreamed recurrently.[11] They were everywhere, the young, the old, little children—hundreds, thousands of them in need. She never finished caring for them, never finished reaching them, never finished. . . . Then she would hear Mrs. Callaghan's voice and be awake with only one person to tend.

Catherine was practical and wise. This was her work, God's will for her now. Parents had prior claim; relatives and friends had a claim; the poor had their claim. She saw the order clearly. Later it would be one of the marks of her institute, this well-ordered consideration of needs. Though the house was amply staffed with servants, Catherine had much to do. Before nursing became a profession, the kind of care later given by the trained fell to those personally devoted to the patient. It was an ideal in the old loyalties.

Perhaps without realizing it, Mrs. Callaghan began to recognize Catherine's religion as the vitalizing force in her character. She finally asked Catherine why she was a Catholic. In just what form she put the question and what specifically led to it are matter for conjecture, but the question opened the opportunity for which the devoted nurse had long prayed. Few appreciate faith like those who have reached it through trial. The desire to share it is both a natural and a supernatural consequent. Catherine McAuley's sensibilities and prudence deterred her from intruding her belief upon others or putting pressure on their consciences; yet she prayed continually for the conversion of those she loved.

She answered Mrs. Callaghan convincingly. Indeed among Catherine's outstanding gifts, according to her associates, were clarity of explanation and apologetic force. Mrs. Callaghan responded favorably to all Catherine's teaching, hesitating only when Catherine suggested bringing a priest to Coolock House. The patient's reluctance was entirely unselfish: she did not wish to displease her husband and at the same time jeopardize Catherine's position in the household. Catherine knew that ultimately no one is hurt by the right conscience of another. As for injuring her own prospects, she dismissed the subject.

The time would come when a bishop of the Church would confer upon the foundress of the Sisters of Mercy the title "Sister of Divine Providence" because of her reliance on God in material things. By then she had had years of devotion to Divine Providence. She succeeded in imbuing Mrs. Callaghan with her own spirit. Her last objection removed, the invalid consented to see a priest. He was the first to be admitted to Coolock House but not the last.

Catherine called in Father Michael Bernard Keogh, a Capuchin acting as pastor at Baldoyle not far from Coolock.[12] He was one of a brilliant group who met periodically at Archbishop Troy's hospitable table. Some Boswell among them should have recorded for history anecdotes connected with their gatherings.

At the time Father Keogh was the ablest pulpit orator in Dublin. He had a Protestant following that not only testified to his talent but to the changing times. He also had the reputation of being the most skillful impersonator of the period. "There was no public speaker from Grattan to O'Connell," Fitzpatrick says, "whom he could not personate to the life."[13]

Fitzpatrick, who collected enough fragments to give impressions of the principals at the clerical gatherings, further characterizes Father Keogh as "hospitable to a fault." Both his curates and creditors shared the effects of this paradoxical virtue. One creditor, Fitzpatrick relates, had the wisdom to request as a loan the amount owed him, and he was given in charity what he would hardly have elicited so promptly by collection. Catherine McAuley's early biographers add another telling bit of evidence, for this versatile divine forgot one of his appointments at Coolock House.

Contradictory statements have been made about Mrs. Callaghan's conversion. Dr. Conway's granddaughter (Sister M. Raymund Byrn) certainly detaches its incompleteness from any connection with Father Keogh's lapse of memory. Mentioning clergymen who had aided Catherine McAuley at various times, she listed "the celebrated Father Keogh who took such pains though fruitlessly with poor Mrs. Callaghan."[14] Another of Catherine's associates wrote: "She prayed unceasingly for the conversion of her friends and succeeded so far that Mrs. Callaghan shortly before her death consented to see the Reverend Mr. Keogh but died before she could receive baptism."[15]

VII

Lending to the Lord

MRS. CALLAGHAN'S legacy to her husband was their adopted daughter. If William Callaghan believed he knew Catherine's worth when he consented to Mrs. Callaghan's inviting her to share their home, he had had years of observation to confirm him in the wisdom of his wife's choice. Yet his affection for Catherine had been largely vicarious; he appreciated all she meant to Mrs. Callaghan. The years of Catherine Callaghan's illness proved how necessary the second Catherine was to both of them, to him because of the comfort he had in the unnumbered little things she knew about the care of the sick. What personal affection attended every service he was well aware. Now that no one could perform any office for his wife, he found consolation in Catherine's presence. As they had had their affection for Mrs. Callaghan in common, they now shared bereavement. Besides, during his wife's long illness, Catherine had learned so many ways of making him comfortable that adjustment to his loss was less painful than it otherwise would have been. His appreciation of Catherine continued to grow, and he observed with satisfaction how she turned again to her work among the poor when there was no longer the sick at home to tend.

Meanwhile, Catherine faced the realization that life at Coolock could not go on forever as it was. What then? Besides her devotion to the sick poor and to little children, she felt a keen sympathy for one class of persons particularly, young servant girls exposed to moral danger. Their situation came to her attention more than once, but the incident that affected her most concerned a pretty young girl she had unsuccessfully tried to extricate from a common dilemma. The story has all the elements of a nineteenth-century melodrama.

Those bound to service were almost completely dependent on the household they served. It is true that servants were provided with food and sometimes clothing, but little actual money was paid out. Servant girls, therefore, often found themselves exposed to moral danger. They frequently had nowhere else to go and no money to take them elsewhere. Not only did the master and mistress fail to assume responsibility for the morals of their servants but an attractive young girl could be victimized by members of the household.

Just such a young girl appealed to Miss McAuley for help. Catherine asked a Dublin organization to harbor the servant till work could be found for her away from the neighborhood. She learned that admission would have to come through a committee of well-intentioned ladies who met at stated times. Rules were inflexible. Miss McAuley's interest could not be represented till the next regular board meeting. Meanwhile the girl disappeared. This experience caused Catherine so much grief that she determined to do something for such persons. She even considered engaging rooms to lodge them temporarily.

That Catherine McAuley was actually mistress of Coolock House after the death of Mrs. Callaghan showed in her charities to her own relatives as well as to countless others. Catherine adopted Anne Conway Byrn's frail infant daughter in the early summer of 1821 and brought the few days' old Teresa to Coolock House. As Mr. Callaghan's health had begun to fail, children might be expected to disturb him; yet he seems to have endorsed wholeheartedly any project Catherine undertook. He himself was charitable. Though not a church-goer, he practiced virtue on principle.[1] His features may have been sharp,[2] but he had a gentle nature. His material holdings attested to superior business ability; his plan for distributing his wealth attested to genuine kindness of heart.

One day he asked Catherine what she would do after he died. She told him quite frankly that she would devote herself first to the protection of young servant girls through teaching them to support themselves and by guiding them in Christian living. He asked her what amount of money would carry on such a project. He was not surprised at her conservative estimate.[3]

She had always impressed him with unusual judgment and consideration in her disbursements. Her economy was the more marked because Mary Anne, a young cousin of Mrs. Callaghan, who lived at Coolock House on equal terms with Catherine, had little sense of money value. Nor was Mary Anne's judgment in other matters more sound. She had married Robert Moore Powell who liked her open-handedness and her connection with the Callaghans. This disposition of Mr. Powell became increasingly evident after their marriage. Continued liberality toward the Powells speaks much for Callaghan charity; yet Mary Anne's husband was to learn that William Callaghan could be as prudent as he was kind. On January 27, 1822, he made his will.

Catherine observed with distress that he considered his preparation for death complete when he closed his material accounts. Seeing him set his face toward eternity with the calm fortitude of a man whose life had been full of good works, she thought with longing of how much closer he could be to Christ if only she could share with him as he had shared with her. He was not unaware of her concern. Among his friends was a minister to whom he finally turned for advice. This much he would do to satisfy Catherine. He asked his clerical friend how a man could best prepare for death. Undoubtedly with good intentions, the reverend gentleman brushed the question aside, advising the sick man to think of living not of dying, to order up some of his best wines and tone up his system and his mental outlook. The interrogator had been in earnest and had, moreover, a scientist's dislike for evasion. Whatever conversation had passed between Catherine and him and whatever followed, he consented to see a clergyman of her faith.

Not bound to any secrecy as in Mrs. Callaghan's case, Catherine brought the village priest openly to Coolock House, much to the annoyance of Mr. Powell. Father Joseph Nugent became a regular visitor and so satisfied Mr. Callaghan that a series of instructions followed. He was received into the Church November 9, 1822.[4] The next day was Martinmas Eve, and Martinmas was traditionally a time to settle accounts and to make new beginnings. It was William Callaghan's last day on earth. In the liturgical year the feast of St. Martin commemorates the death of the Celtic Bishop of Tours who as a catechumen had divided his cloak with a beggar shivering at the gate. From one act of mercy Martin the catechumen advanced to baptism and went forth to the spiritual conquest of Gaul. Martinmastide was therefore symbolic. By harboring the harborless in consenting to his wife's adopting Catherine McAuley, William Callaghan had opened the way to Catholicism for himself, and, by leaving the bulk of his fortune to Catherine's charities, he provided the means for an apostolate of Mercy that has circled the globe.

Only after his death did Catherine learn of the import of the previous January 27. The first provisions of Mr. Callaghan's will, besides sundry bequests including his half-sister living in London, the poor of Coolock village, William Armstrong's daughter of Mary Street, James McAuley, "Surgeon to the Military Hospital in the Park," and other named beneficiaries, left a large income "to my kind and affectionate friend Miss Catherine McAuley, who resides with me, for her many kindnesses and attentions." The will named as residuary legatees Catherine McAuley and Mary Anne Powell. A codicil of the same date, however, dissolved this partnership and nominated Catherine McAuley "sole residuary legatee of all my estate and effects real or personal subject to the specific legacies mentioned in my will."

Stimulated by the presence of the lawyers, Mr. Powell unfortunately made statements that provoked the change. According to the will, Mr. Powell and Catherine McAuley would have been joint executors. The former, however, unaware that the patient had been temporarily moved to a chair near an upper window, expressed himself forcefully at a window below about changes his wife would make when she had control at Coolock House. For one thing, Miss McAuley would no longer be free to bring priests there. Realizing through Mr. Powell's bigoted remark that Catherine's charities might suffer from the arrangement already planned, William Callaghan added the codicil that gave Catherine McAuley, excepting only the particular bequests, the entire Callaghan fortune. To Father Nugent he said, "She will do good with it."

It is difficult to evaluate in American equivalent today the worth of the estate Catherine inherited. Besides the regular income, it amounted to approximately $100,000. A twentieth century exponent would probably give it another digit.

Only one clause of Mr. Callaghan's will went unhonored: "... it is my request that said Catherine McAuley do take and assume the surname of Callaghan." William Callaghan could not have paid his principal beneficiary a higher tribute, for she would thereby become his wife's namesake. Although Catherine did not adopt the surname Callaghan, her work has memorialized it equally with her own father's. Rightly so, for the two persons most directly responsible for the apostolate of Mercy initiated by her are James McAuley and William Callaghan. Of the others who influenced her toward it, one now comes into prominence in her life story.

Catherine's father had been twenty years dead when she sought out Dr. Betagh at St. Michael's; he was forty years dead when she applied to Dr. Betagh's successor for advice on the project taking shape in her mind. In the first decade of the century, St. Michael's was much as her father had known it,[5] but by the end of the second decade Dr. Betagh himself, had he been alive, would not have recognized it, and the reason was Father Michael Blake. A new site, a new church, and a merging of parochial boundaries had given a new name to Sts. Michael and John's and had made Father Blake one of the most experienced priest-financiers in the capital. He was the logical adviser for Catherine McAuley, now about to enter on a building project in Dublin.

Almost as soon as she began to consult Father Blake on extending her Dublin charities, circumstances arose to hamper her activity in them.

Anne Conway Byrn, whom Catherine loved as a sister, died on August 9, 1822, leaving three children, Catherine, James, and Ann, besides the year-old baby Teresa. These children now came in for a share of Catherine's attention. Records at the Dominican Convent in Drogheda, where Catherine Byrn (Sister Mary Raymund) died, assert that Catherine McAuley adopted Catherine Byrn at this time:

> When little more than ten years of age . . . she was adopted by Miss Catherine McAuley, her mother's first cousin, afterwards foundress of the Sisters of Mercy. Under the care of this relation she was confirmed in Clontarf Chapel, October 1822, by Most Reverend Dr. Murray, and

she made her First Communion in Sts. Michael and John's on the Feast of Corpus Christi, 1823.

The Dominican chapel at Clontarf in October 1822, a few weeks before Mr. Callaghan's death, and Sts. Michael and John's the following spring furnished a setting for memorable days in young Catherine Byrn's life. There was some reason for Catherine McAuley's arranging her young ward's First Communion at Dr. Blake's church. Apparently she was already under the pastor's advice. Though litigation over Mr. Callaghan's will could not yet have been settled, Catherine was assured of a moderate income even if the terms of the codicil were rejected. On her own assertion she began her plans for the Dublin house two years before they actually materialized.[6]

According to the Dominican records Catherine McAuley certainly had contact with Sts. Michael and John's early in 1823. No one knew better than the pastor, Father Blake, how little a single generous worker and one fortune could do to lift to respectable poverty even a small part of the wretched of one Dublin parish. Yet none knew better how much could be accomplished by the persistent efforts of an earnest person, for Father Blake had spent most of the twenty-five years of his priesthood in social uplift in his native city. When Catherine told him that she planned to erect a social service center in Dublin, he became convinced that she was destined for a special work in the Church. He not only encouraged her but he also aided her in every way he could, and he lived to see his opinion confirmed. Dozens, then hundreds, then thousands were to be inspired by the dedication of the one compassionate lady who now humbly applied to him for direction. Counterparts unto thousands rose up in Ireland, in England, in Australia, in North and South America, in Africa and in India to carry on her project. Hovels, mansions, schools, orphanages, hospitals and battlefields became other centers for the work she now initiated. The pastor of Sts. Michael and John's did not die until all this and the beginning of much more had come to pass.

Father Blake selected a site on the corner of Baggot and Herbert Streets in a neighboring parish. The parish happened to be Archbishop Murray's. With the death of Archbishop Troy that very year, Archbishop Murray had secured permission from Rome to make St. Andrew's a second mensal parish.[7] In July he appointed the Reverend Edward Armstrong administrator. It was therefore Father Armstrong that Father Blake consulted about opening the center in St. Andrew's parish. Father Armstrong agreed that the residential district chosen would be ideal for it. The poor were never far away, and their daily excursions under the eyes of the well-to-do might profit both.

The property selected belonged to the Earl of Pembroke who leased it on June 20, 1824, at the annual rental of £60 for 150 years beginning March 25, 1824. Though the Earl's son, the Honorable Sidney Herbert, succeeded his father in ownership, he was not party to the lease. Therefore, the ancedote of the Honorable Sidney Herbert's demur, incompatible with his nature as Bishop Donnelly characterized it,[8] must be discarded.

Before going to Rome that summer to continue a drive for reestablishing the Irish College, Dr. Blake laid the first stone of the new building. The following month, August 1824, he left Dublin, turning over the direction of Miss McAuley's project to Father Armstrong. The administrator of St. Andrew's had a particular advantage in being a close personal friend of the Archbishop. This connection assured his new parishioner an accurate representation of her aims in the quarter where approval was essential. His Grace's regard for Miss McAuley's adviser went back to their curacy together at St. Mary's, and Father Armstrong's regard for his new parishioner may also have gone back as far. At any rate, he was as convinced as Dr. Blake that Catherine McAuley was destined for a special work in the Church.

No one can study the religious history of the Irish capital in the transitional period from Relief Acts to Catholic Emancipation without being struck by the spirituality of the Dublin clergy. The character of the times, moreover, highlighted administrative talent, and administration brought into play the whole range of a man's character, exposing any and every peccadillo—hence the impression of eccentricity associated with some names. The priest who without caricaturing himself gained prominence in such a society would be a man of singular selflessness and extraordinary natural and supernatural benevolence. To such a man Dr. Blake had consigned Catherine McAuley's affairs.

In the letter appointing Father Armstrong to St. Andrew's, Archbishop Murray had written to the chapel house: "I have no doubt he will meet in Townsend Street with the same brotherly affection he deservedly experienced in Liffey Street for so many years."[9]

Father Armstrong had arrived at St. Andrew's providentially for Catherine McAuley. Of his connection with her work Bishop Donnelly says:

After Dr. Murray, to Dr. Armstrong may be attributed the foundation of the Sisters of Mercy. He was a spiritual guide, philosopher and friend of Mother Catherine McAuley whilst groping her way through many charitable labors before they crystallized into a new religious foundation.

During the three years the building was under construction Catherine busied herself as usual and extended her interest to teaching methods as developed in the most reputable schools. In the teaching of religion she excelled. Hitherto, however, her religious teaching had been done on a small scale at Coolock lodge or in the homes of the poor. She now became one of the regular instructors at St. Mary's Poor School and gained an insight into work of the kind on a large scale.

Her most constant companion in these years was a young Galway woman who spent a great deal of time with her aunt in the Dublin vicinity, probably at Clontarf. Some proximity to Coolock certainly existed, for Catherine Byrn refers to Miss Frances Tighe as the principal influence in the former's Dominican interest "at the age of eleven years." Since Catherine Byrn was eleven years old when she went to Coolock House to live, her friendship with Miss Fanny, to whom she refers as "one of my oldest and dearest friends," must have begun at that time.

Miss Tighe was twenty-four years old in 1822 and was dividing her time between Galway and Dublin charities. Back in her Galway parish she did catechetical work so successfully that her name was held in veneration for more than a hundred years.[10] About this time a relative of Miss Fanny entered the recently founded Presentation Convent in Galway city, and this incident was to influence Frances Tighe's life. For the present, she continued her activities to the great consolation of Catherine McAuley, who began to look forward to Miss Tighe's assistance in the Baggot Street project. Not satisfied with the Lancasterian system, Catherine decided to visit France to observe methods used for the instruction of large classes in that country. Regrettably, there is no record of the visit beyond mention of it. Since she had already acquainted herself with the work of the Irish Sisters of Charity,[11] the most likely place for her to go would be to the Sisters of Charity of St. Vincent de Paul. Their work in Paris slums and elsewhere in France presented an ideal that scarcely allowed of improvement in method. Catherine's itinerary must be left to conjecture, since the trip to France is obscured by other incidents that lead to the opening of her poor schools and house of refuge on Baggot Street. The journey to the continent, however, shows with what thoroughness Catherine prepared to extend her work.

About mid-May, 1825, she heard that Father Nugent was sick. The account of his illness and death shows the great need professional nursing eventually filled. One of Catherine's associates describes his case briefly:

> He was always delicate, but he took ill suddenly and for a few days Miss McAuley heard nothing of it. When she did, she went to him immediately and found him in a sad state of dirt and neglect. She hardly left him till his death.[12]

Father Nugent died May 30, 1825. Catherine thereby lost a great support. Not only had he befriended her and Mr. Callaghan at Coolock, but he had been her adviser through the legal proceedings that contested Mr. Callaghan's will. The account says in conclusion: "He was a true disciple of Dr. Blake, always giving." This reference to Father Nugent's connection with Father Blake may imply that the pastor at Coolock had directed Catherine to Father Blake for advice on her building plan.

A spiritual kinship existed among these religious persons who had in common a great love for the poor and wretched. When Catherine McAuley as Mother Catherine said that the tomb was never closed to her, she spoke not only of the loss of her family and of her spiritual daughters but also of those others who, having ideals like her own, had served her in helping her serve God's poor.

Father Nugent, connected with Liffey Street chapel at the time of his death, was one of these.

Again and again Catherine had the spiritual discipline of losing by death or otherwise the very person who seemed most necessary to her.

Detachment from the comfort of family, friends, and worldly possessions is the ordinary way to acquisition of virtue and eternal beatitude, but deprivation of spiritual support is, by Divine provision, the way to hardiness of soul and close union with God. In her case the need was certainly great, embracing as it did pressing needs of countless others. The loss, therefore, was proportionately great, each divestment making her more acutely aware of the soul's only unfailing Resource. As circumstances pressed her to lean more heavily on Divine Providence, her trust in God deepened, though not without the pain to nature that attends spiritual expansion. Blind faith had led her to the work she was to do; blind trust was to support her in it.

Of Catherine's social life meanwhile, the Derry manuscript gives this survey:

While the building was carried on, Miss McAuley resided chiefly at Coolock House, still keeping her intentions with regard to the proposed institution a secret, as she had reason to know that her family would resent it extremely. They rather wished, or affected to wish, that she should marry, and she had some advantageous proposals; for, though no longer young, she lived in what is usually called good style, that is, she kept a carriage, dressed well, went into society and sometimes gave parties at her house but employed the greater part of her time in works of piety and charity especially in the instruction of poor children in the female schools of St. Mary's, Abbey Street. She was also very regular in the performance of every duty of religion, fasted rigorously and during Lent never tasted wine; she arose very early, prayed much and was most assiduous in her attendance at sermons and at the public offices of the Church.[13]

During Mary Macauley's final illness, Catherine lived almost entirely at the doctor's residence near the Royal Hospital at Kilmainham. Dr. Macauley knew that his wife had a tendency to tuberculosis, and he used every precaution to prevent its development in both her and the children. He did not live to see his children die young of consumption. Only their last child, his namesake, escaped.[14] Willie's letters, written years later from Australia to his former playmate Teresa Byrn, name the disease that marked his mother's family for generations. Both he and Teresa supply child's-eye recollections of life at Coolock in the 1820's. Teresa remembered relief of the poor as part of daily routine as far back as she could recall.

Regrettably, the autobiography Willie wrote toward the end of his life did not survive.[15] After white ants mutilated the manuscript, his daughter Emily destroyed the remnants, not realizing that even excerpts would be valuable to the Mercy congregation records.

Among recollections revived for Teresa Byrn through his letters, Willie gave graphic details of the children's interest at their aunt's home. Who was Paul Tanner that Willie conjured in reminiscence fifty years later for Teresa?[16] If only they could go back to Coolock House as they had known it, they would see Paul, Mrs. Harper, and the dog! Using the vivid present, Willie reminds his cousin: "Old Drake is done barking . . . Robert has thrown a stick for him to fetch."

Mrs. Harper fascinated the children. From one of Catherine's excursions to Liffey Street she brought home this neglected creature, somewhat deranged, who had been in good circumstances till misfortune impoverished her. The London manuscript makes a point of Mrs. Harper's religion and mental state as if to demonstrate that Catherine's charity was free of sectarian zeal. She could have had no hope of converting Mrs. Harper.

As Mother McAuley, Catherine later counseled her associates to have "compassion for those who have seen better days or are ashamed to make known their indigence . . . . Assist them privately," she advised. Because this poor old woman had been accustomed to refinement, she elicited Catherine's particular sympathy. Even though Mrs. Harper caused the household servants a great deal of annoyance by the untidy habits she had fallen into and by making off with and hiding things, she freely ranged about the place till she sickened and died several years later. With the perversity of mental disorder she took a strong dislike to her benefactor, subjecting Catherine to rudeness and abusive language, but the charity of Catherine McAuley already knew how to "endure all things." It is said that nothing Mrs. Harper did could ruffle the lady of the household.

"No sight of misery ever repelled her," the writer of the London manuscript asserts. Only unusual virtue can control the revulsion of feeling a sensitive nature suffers when confronted with ugliness. Yet supernatural charity, which overcomes repugnance, perfects itself in compassion or union of suffering. If Catherine McAuley went her way unrepelled, her secret was identification with the afflicted. Every misery was her personal burden. Her external practices during the Coolock period and intimations garnered from advice she later gave her associates permit some evaluation of her spirituality at this time. Her known devotion to the Divine Humanity in its most appealing aspects, the Infancy and Passion of Jesus Christ, interprets her charity. She had long been in the habit of living unselfishly. Gradually her services assumed a new character: self-effacement had prepared her for conformity with the Divine Will, and active charity united her to Jesus Christ.

VIII

Why This Waste?

CATHERINE MCAULEY lived in a day of apprenticeships. Observation and practice formed a large part of training even for professions, though teaching was scarcely considered one of them. A letter by her first permanent associate[1] attests that Miss McAuley gave as much time as she could to the study of school management and classroom procedure through visiting educational institutions of repute. Since the Kildare Place Society sponsored the most modern of these, she called often at their schools while her own was being built. She thereby learned that there were many Catholics registered. She secured their addresses and subsequently paid a visit to their wretched homes with the information that the Baggot Street Poor School would include religious instruction as well as the advantages offered by the Kildare Place Society. She urged parents to remove the little ones from the proselytizing influences for which the Kildare Street schools had a well-deserved reputation.

This last statement requires explanation, since efforts to win Catholic children to Protestantism continued beyond Penal times, despite legislation. Motivated partly by fear, proselytizing received fresh impetus from the political situation in the 1820's. The O'Connellites were making headway toward Catholic Emancipation, and Protestants feared the Catholic preponderance.

George IV had succeeded to the throne in 1820. As king he had no more enthusiasm for Catholic M. P.'s than his father had had, though as Prince of Wales he had married a Catholic.[2] His fidelity to this marriage over a period of years had given him the opportunity to modify his prejudices, but it was not his way to improve opportunities for generosity. George IV certainly represented no threat to the *status quo;* the threat lay in the already ascendant power of one man, a man of the Irish people.

The Catholic Association, founded in Ireland in 1823, excited alarm in Parliament by its unprecedented success and was suppressed under general terms in 1825. Reorganized almost immediately by O'Connell's evasive skill, it effected such startling results in the Waterford and Clare elections that it threw adherents of the old Ascendancy into something like a state of panic. Their concern fastened on the active membership of hundreds of Catholic clergy in the Catholic Association.

Repeal of the Test Act against Protestant Dissenters, supported by the Association, struck members of the Established Church as a prelude to an Act removing Catholic disabilities also. At every fresh success of the Catholic Association, old-line Protestants stirred themselves desperately to counter-activity. Nevertheless, the current against them grew stronger. Their political power, weakened at the beginning of the century by the Act of Union, was nearing a crisis.

In the light of the rising threat to their position, efforts to swell their numbers in the years immediately preceding 1829 are understandable. Comparative estimates of population on a religious basis show Protestants outnumbered as high as ninety per cent in some Dublin parishes.[3] Conditions in the populous capital therefore show cause for Protestant activity. Deceived by bigotry and fired by tenacity for their advantageous minority position, the party in power operated through individuals and organizations to prevent Catholic ascendancy. Proselytizing was a traditional obligation, the *sine qua non* for the continued existence of the ruling minority.

Inasmuch as the Kildare Place Society was government subsidized "for the education of the poor without religious distinction" and was "by one of their fundamental rules pledged to impart the benefits of instruction to all Christians without interfering with the religious tenets of any," their activities offended the sense of justice of a number of Protestants, some of whom withdrew from the Society. Among these was the Duke of Leinster who resigned the presidency.[4]

From her connections Catherine McAuley was often assumed to be Protestant. On that assumption authorities at the Kildare Street schools exposed to her their methods of undermining the Catholic Faith.[5] This information strengthened her determination to do all she could to remove Catholic children from such influences. During the months immediately preceding September 1827, Catherine McAuley had a constant reminder of perverted faith, for lack of common ground with her sister on the matter of religion became increasingly painful as the year progressed. Two circumstances made it so. In the first place, Mary Macauley had reached the final stages of tuberculosis, and she needed the consolations of religion. The other circumstance was the building on Baggot Street. In Mary's happiness over the prospect of the work that would be done there for the poor, Catherine felt again the union of interest that had been theirs in childhood, and she knew that basically Mary had not changed.[6] The Macauley residence on Military Road offered almost no opportunity for a confidential talk, especially since Dr. Macauley did not entirely trust his sister-in-law's influence in the matter of religion. Her latest venture on Baggot Street proved that she was an extremist. It made both Dr. William and Dr. James uncomfortable, for it involved the family name. They were probably more often interrogated than Catherine on the great box-like house. In her presence they engaged in ironic witticisms. She, on her part, would put an emphatically defensive word to her brother and brother-in-law. Their misrepresentations of her religion hurt and at times angered her; yet her sympathy was close to the surface. She well knew how hard it could be to work a way clear to truth. Catherine and her brother-in-law not only did not see eye to eye on faith; James and William were never to discern what had become so clear to herself.

The house particularly nettled Dr. James, who referred to it as "Kitty's folly." On the word of his cousin Catherine Byrn, Dr. James "was from youth a shrewd, calculating man of the world," who had "made his way amidst almost unconquerable difficulties." Facts support this terse characterization, to which she adds redeemingly: "but he was not devoid of generosity as I could advance good proof."

Dr. James' long life bore out Catherine Byrn's estimate of him.

He lived to his ninetieth year, spending his last days in residential Blackrock, and left an estate worth close to £14,000.[7] His sons and grandchildren have carried on the army and medical traditions. One of his grandsons, Brigadier General Sir George Bohun Macauley, K. C. M. G., K. B. E., C. B., died in 1940. The old doctor would have been pleased with Sir George's record.[8]

His reaction to his sister's use of her inheritance recalls his mother's remonstrances with her husband over earlier unreasonable charities. Dr. James did heartily wish that Catherine would conform to worldly standards for her own good, as he saw it. In his estimation, her adherence to the old Faith, which she let carry her to ridiculous lengths, seriously marred her personality. With her beauty, charm of manner, and wealth she could easily be a social figure and he would have been proud of her as such.

It is true that Catherine McAuley retained a rather youthful beauty till she was close to fifty, but little Willie with a child's observation of detail discerned that a trick of coiffure camouflaged her graying hair. To the younger children she was a story-book lady of wonderful reality. Coolock's acres and the people of the House were a story-book land. Its mistress they loved with the undisguised selfishness of childhood. To Mary, however, her aunt represented an ideal. This eldest of the Macauley children, about sixteen when her mother lay dying, is described in the Dublin manuscript as "a lovely, highly-gifted child . . . her aunt's favorite . . . of whose Protestantism the parents were particularly jealous." Mary's love for her Aunt Catherine was a response to something not yet clear to herself. It was Mary's mother who put the distinguishing finger on it.

Dr. Macauley had consented that they take a house in the mountains to give his wife whatever temporary relief she could have. Necessarily, since his work was at the Royal Hospital, he could not maintain at Stillorgan the close vigilance possible at the residence on Military Road. In his absences Catherine found the opportunity she had so earnestly desired, a chance to talk to her sister Mary on the separation they foresaw. The conversations that followed opened the way for Mary's return to the Church. A Father McCormick[9], brought from Booterstown nearby, was able to make several visits during which he effected the reconciliation and administered the consoling Sacraments.

Mary then took her daughter into her confidence and earnestly recommended that the young girl follow her aunt's guidance. Mrs. Macauley could not have made an easier request of her eldest child. From early childhood little Mary had loved her mother's sister with a particular affection and had been stirred by her aunt's references to God and by her way of praying. So this was the secret of Catherine McAuley's attractiveness! It was her aunt's religion that made her different from anyone else Mary knew; it was Catherine's intimacy with God that drew her niece.

Mary Macauley was reconciled to the Church during July, 1827, and died early in August. Catherine then had three houses to manage. Staying principally at Dr. Macauley's residence, she made regular excursions to Coolock and to Baggot Street. Her friend Frances Tighe had not returned to Dublin that year. Just when Catherine needed her most, Miss Tighe entered the Presentation Convent in Galway city. As if to balance the scales, however, a candidate for the Presentation Convent in Dublin, unknown to herself or to anyone else, was on her way to fill Miss Tighe's place at Miss McAuley's side.

The building going up on the corner of Baggot and Herbert Streets had assumed proportions. Of all the people who passed by and wondered, one had a more than ordinary interest in it. It certainly looked institutional, and Anna Maria Doyle was interested in institutions. She had decided to devote herself to the education of poor children by entering a Presentation convent. The example of her only brother, curate in Sts. Michael and John's, may have been her inspiration, for he had established a seminary in Castle Street shortly after his appointment to the parish. It seemed inevitable that a priest sent to St. Michael's should become interested in education, or perhaps it was inevitable that Father Doyle be assigned there. He had been a school principal before he decided to study for the priesthood, and St. Michael's seemed traditionally the parish for priest-schoolmasters.

His sister had certain misgivings about entering a cloistered order, since her elderly parents would then be alone. One day she induced the foreman to let her go through the huge building under construction on Baggot Street. She learned that it was the project of a charitably disposed Catholic lady who planned to make it a center for work among the poor of Dublin. Her parents brightened at the interest their daughter took in the information and eagerly seconded her decision to look up Miss McAuley. If only Anna Maria could content herself to do good where she would be free to come to them and care for them when they themselves fell into need!

The channels through which Miss Doyle secured an introduction to Miss McAuley are unknown, but secure it she did with the directive information that Miss McAuley could be found at Dr. Macauley's residence near the Royal Hospital at Kilmainham. There the two met, each instantly recognizing in the other similar ideals. Both longed to work among the poor. The difference lay in the fact that Catherine McAuley would never think of entering a convent to do so. She must go out among the poor or gather them in according to their needs; nor would she exclude her own from her charity. How these two points of view merged is the story of the founding of the Institute of Mercy. A coincidence worthy of mention is this first meeting of the new institute at Kilmainham[10] on the site of the ancient Priory of the Knights Hospitallers who long ago were vowed to "service of the poor and defence of the Faith." Three other members of the new order of hospitallers, the Institute of Mercy, were recruited from the house on Military Road, Mary Teresa and Catherine Macauley and their friend and frequent visitor, Frances Warde.

Miss Doyle's father and mother rejoiced over Anna Maria's account of her visit. They admired Miss McAuley's comprehensive ideal. Some sacrifice, however, attended Anna Maria's decision in favor of Miss McAuley's work, for the Presentation Order had appealed to her not only because of its dedication to the interests of the poor but also because of its dedication to our Lady, to the Child Mary's oblation of herself to the Will of God.

By Anna Maria's sacrifice, however, she came nearer than she then knew to the original ideal of the foundress of the Presentation Order. It may be that the merits of her patroness, good St. Anne, on the occasion of the Presentation had something to do with Anna Maria's recompense, for in joining herself to the new project, out of deference to the wishes of her aged parents, she compassed all her aspirations.

After Mary Macauley's death, it became clear to Anna Maria that Catherine would stay on at the doctor's for the children's sake. She grew a little anxious about the projected plan for Baggot Street and finally wrote asking Miss McAuley when the work would begin. Early in September she received a satisfactory reply. Enough of the building would be ready by the twenty-third or twenty-fourth of the current month for the Poor School to open. Miss McAuley would assign her young ward, Catherine Byrn, to live at the house with Miss Doyle and assist her. Miss McAuley herself would come daily and bring her niece to help with the classwork. Anna Maria, unaware of coincidence, sent word that she would arrive September 24. Only after the letter was on its way did she learn that September 24 was the feast of Our Lady of Mercy.[11] She then followed up her first note with a confirmation of the date, remarking its significance and suggesting that the Baggot Street building be named House of Mercy.

The hour of the Psalter had struck. Mercy had built herself a house.

> Jesus, God of Compassion, have mercy on us . . . Help us to spend our time in the practise of all the virtues, and in such works and labors as obedience will render most acceptable to Thee . . . Help us in our endeavors to imitate Thee, that we may promote Thy glory, attain our own sanctification, and cooperate in the salvation of others.

Book Two

Cloak of Mercy

"Put ye on as the elect of God, holy and beloved, the cloak of mercy, benignity, humility, modesty, patience . . ." (COL. 3:12)

IX

Beneath the Brown Scapular

ON SEPTEMBER 24, 1827, two departments opened at the new social service center on Baggot Street. The Poor School had a heavy registration, but the residence for working women had only two applicants that first day. Catherine McAuley, Anna Maria Doyle and Catherine Byrn managed the business of admissions, the last with more competence than might be expected from a fifteen-year-old.

Besides youthful venturesomeness, Miss McAuley's young cousin had certain native qualities that fitted her for the work she now undertook. Precocity of a kind overrode any disadvantage of age, and the advice of her spiritual director, which she kept to herself, made her sure that, for the time being, this was her proper place. In the beginning, most of Miss McAuley's associates were part-time workers. It was not that they lacked the generosity of complete sacrifice; they were simply not asked for it. Her idea offered opportunities for gratuitous service to those willing to devote some of their leisure to a good cause. The world has many people whose resources for good are incompletely or wastefully expended because they lack example or leadership or even so small an incitement to service as merely to be shown how to proceed. Catherine Byrn's circumstances gave her the leisure, the example, and the method. If she had ideas of her own for the future, that future was still several years away.

Miss McAuley's invitation to a temporary service in which a recruit retained full exercise of her individuality depended for smoothness of operation on Christian rules of good breeding, on reasonable docility to a nominal authority, on fidelity to engagements made, and on consideration for others. Presumably Christian motives were already present in such as offered themselves. So was individuality. A noteworthy feature of these years which, unknown to all concerned, initiated a new religious foundation lies in the fact that diverse, strong personalities did actually launch a major work without friction.

Miss Doyle was in immediate charge, Miss McAuley in remote control—though not too remote, for she came almost every day with her young niece and entered into the business going on. The business soon included not only day school and night refuge but a kind of employment agency as well for young women temporarily harbored and trained in the House of Mercy.

As is the way with projects for good if they are to accomplish anything, the work attracted both favorable and unfavorable attention. In this case the attraction was so immediate that friends and opponents rose side by side in the same ranks.

From the mansions in Merrion Square and vicinity came young ladies to offer their services. First among them appeared the Misses Costello and O'Connell. Theirs was not a service limited to the classroom; it also extended to the workroom and other departments as these were added. In fact, of all who took advantage of Miss McAuley's invitation, these two families were pre-eminent and should never be omitted from any account of the success of the venture.

The O'Connells need no identification, nor did the Dublin Costellos a century ago. At the time of her service to the day school, Miss Louisa Costello had not yet attained the recognition she later shared jointly with her brother for reviving the ancient art of illumination. In her late twenties when the Mercy Poor School opened, she had already published two books, and she brought to the classroom the gifts that later distinguished her.

To the O'Connells and Costellos must be added the names of James and John O'Farrell, and the first community lawyer, Charles Cavanagh.[1] These last were of the cordon functioning effectively in the background.

Some time during this year Mary Macauley introduced to her aunt a vivacious young lady in middle teens whom Mary had met socially. Whether Frances Warde herself had asked for the introduction or whether Mary had proposed it; whether the meeting was inevitable from the friendship between the two young women and from Miss McAuley's position in the doctor's household, or whether Frances Warde's Carmelite confessor had already interested himself in the activities centering in the big house on Baggot Street, the introduction brought together the future foundress of a religious community and the missionary who within two decades carried the new work to the United States.

At the time, however, a religious vocation was in the mind of neither. Frances Warde, seventeen years old, was enjoying life in the Irish capital, and Catherine McAuley, nearly three times her age, was busy with the maintenance of a country estate, the supervision of her brother-in-law's family in their residence, and the care of a larger family—as many of the poor and needy as she could reach.

There was a serious side to Frances Warde. In her childhood she, too, had known a pious father and had had the environment of a happy family in comfortable circumstances. The Wardes then lived at Belbrook House in Queen's County. Death and injustice intervened, and she with an older brother and sister passed what was left of their childhood under the care of a maternal aunt, the only mother Frances remembered. Frances' seriousness showed itself in fidelity to her religious obligations and in a certain uneasiness about her somewhat frivolous use of time.

Though she had a buoyant manner, she also possessed dignity, a combination of qualities that, all other things being equal, never failed to attract Catherine McAuley. Frances Warde was in fact already marked for a place in Catherine McAuley's affection. She wanted only the specific direction of her confessor, almost immediately forthcoming, to point the casual way to her vocation. Soon after the House opened, Frances Warde entered into the work of the "ladies," as they were then called.

They with their charges went regularly to St. Teresa's Church on Clarendon Street and thus came to the attention of the Carmelite Fathers who, under Father L'Estrange as Prior, administered the parish.[2] The services the Carmelites rendered to Miss McAuley, the ladies associated with her, and the young women residing in the

House of Mercy were so valuable to the pioneer effort that their worth cannot be overstated. To enumerate them all would be impossible, and although some will be mentioned in the historical account of the Institute, the debt of the Sisters of Mercy to this venerable Order can never be computed. It was appropriate that the oldest Order in the Church dedicated to the Mother of God should sponsor the new Institute, named for her under the appealing title of Mercy. The friendship shown Miss McAuley and her co-workers by the Provincial, Father Raymund O'Hanlon, and his successor, Father Francis L'Estrange, established a precedent followed to the present day.

How well organized the work must have been from the beginning can be judged from Miss McAuley's taking time out the first week of November to be present at Miss Tighe's formal reception into the Presentation Order. Catherine took with her Teresa Byrn, then six years old. What an adventure for the little girl, and what lovely, homely details the trip would yield if there were any record of it! Whether it was made entirely by sea or by stagecoach and canal, it must have been more than a day's journey. Even a child would notice a difference between the friendly Dubliners and the reticent strangers in that other ancient city. It was but a part of the wonderful strangeness of almost everything little Teresa saw, even to Miss Fanny in the dignity of her quaint black and white attire.

Poor little Teresa Byrn! At six or at sixty she was to be called "little," and the next time she set her face westward in journey she would cross not only the expanse of Ireland but the great ocean beyond it. It would be she who then wore quaint black and white attire. Not the hand but the spirit of her godmother would guide her in that later time, for the capable hands of Catherine McAuley would have finished their work.

Other future American missioners were present, too—Sister M. Magdalen O'Shaughnessy and three who would be the first nuns of their order to found a Presentation convent in the New World, pioneer religious in Newfoundland six years later. Before Teresa Byrn found her way to New York, these four had welcomed the first Mercy missioners Catherine McAuley prepared for the foreign field.

How incredible this would seem to any of them, could they have known! The middle-aged social worker and the new Sister Mary Louis had much to say to each other with the Baggot Street House only six weeks opened and thriving in both its departments!

The brief holiday came to an end, and the next big event at the new House in Dublin was Christmas dinner for the poor, the first of many but by no means the first Miss McAuley had given and superintended. One of the "ladies" wrote reminiscently a number of years later:

> We had also the Christmas dinner, which even before Baggot Street Reverend Mother was accustomed to give to the poor children. For some years in Baggot Street many respectable persons used not only send large presents of beef and other supplies, as I suppose they still do, but they used be present and serve the poor women and children. O'Connell used to carve for them.[3]

In that last casual sentence the writer of the London manuscript introduces the most central figure in early nineteenth century Ireland.

X

St. Andrew's New Parishioner

THE RELIEF ACT OF 1793, reopening higher education to Catholics, had admitted to law a young Irishman eminently suited to the profession. Daniel O'Connell, forced home from college in France by the excesses of the French Revolution, arrived in Ireland in time to profit by concessions on education. The Relief Bill of 1813 brought his latent power before the people and took Coadjutor Archbishop Murray and Father Blake off to Rome to represent Irish opposition to the proposed veto privilege.[1] Morale at home improved when the committee's efforts defeated the proposal to give English monarchs veto power on appointments of Catholic bishops in their dominions, and O'Connell's popularity rose. At last auspicious forces were conspiring for a renascence of Irish liberty.

Two antithetical occurrences exposed a trend in the new spirit: an epidemic of fever multiplied the sufferings of the Dublin poor, and the "walking nuns" appeared among the people. The Irish Sisters of Charity, sponsored by His Grace, the Coadjutor Archbishop, and guided by Mary Aikenhead, one of the socialites of the time, began to relieve the wretched state of thousands on the north side of the Liffey.

Conditions in Paris slums during the eighteenth century have been widely recounted, but in the filth and vice-breeding squalor of poverty-pocked Dublin, a Paris counterpart survived well into the nineteenth century. A similar incongruity of spacious town-house lavishness with huddled, fetid humanity *en masse* a stone's throw away, marked both cities, except that Dublin from its tributary arrangement of alleys and its around-the-corner juxtaposition of contrasts was probably the more offensive.

But such exposures come better from an Irishman. In his sermon for Archbishop Daniel Murray, the Rev. William Meagher, pastor at the Pro-Cathedral, refers graphically to conditions at the beginning of His Grace's administration.

Dublin was very wealthy and very wicked—very gay and very dissolute. . . . Catholicity had just begun to breathe a little freely after a struggle maintained for mere existence, through two full centuries and upwards . . .
There was weakness from within—there was wide-spread treason amongst the soldiers of the faith; and alas! there was division in their ranks. There was the fatal treason which consists in a general depravation of Christian manner—the prolific cause of more ruin to religion than all the power combined of earth and hell—and Catholics were contending amongst themselves, whether or not they should sell the purity, and the independence, and efficiency of their chiefs, for the sorry baubles that cunning politicians offered in exchange. The morals of the people of Dublin, Catholics among the rest, were hideously corrupted . . . every hour through a series of years [with] indulgence of vilest libertinism and wildest extravagance.[2]

Specifying as sources of disorder the vices of drunkenness and gambling, Father Meagher describes conditions of poverty in such terms as *squalid, shivering nakedness, famine-stricken emaciation, ruined families, houseless orphans.* "Vice did more to fill the town with the agonies of human suffering," he declared, "than famine and plague and abject poverty have wrought in these latter days of woe."

Referring to the "handful of clergy and a dozen small, mean and incommodious chapels . . . the frenzy of recent revolution, the false liberality of the day, and the desolating philosophism of France," he admits "that in Dublin at the period alluded to, amid many Catholics there were but few practical Christians." With such statements for background he traces the changes wrought during Dr. Murray's episcopate.

Archbishop Troy had used all the force of his position to keep Irish Catholics from French Revolutionary example and to promote peaceful resistance to injustice. With the exception of one or two disturbances, he had succeeded remarkably well. Parish priests, through the parochial activity they had been promoting for the relief of the poor, contributed effective support to Archbishop Troy's policy. Lay Catholic action was already an extensive movement. Catholic merchants and tradesmen who had managed to prosper in Dublin, where the very weight of their numbers protected their interests, gave of their money and time to the confraternities. Priests had been their teachers and continued to influence them by directing their charities. Under such direction earnest laymen took up teaching catechetical and poor school classes, preparing themselves for a new role in the political history of the country.

During the 1820's those who had been working to improve the condition of the masses became agents in rallying them to the support of the organization that would re-establish their liberties. The Catholic Association was a success chiefly because of their efforts. All other organized effort ranging from secret societies to Catholic Committee had failed.

The Association was not like any political organization that had yet operated for reform, and the chief difference lay in the genius of its leader, Daniel O'Connell. His firm belief in peaceful resistance to injustice was political ground on which his Prelate and he could meet. During his stay in France O'Connell had seen with his own eyes the violent way of the French Revolution and he would have none of it for Ireland. Endowed by nature to be a leader in the people's cause, he possessed the orator's gift of estimating and commanding an audience and the statesman's ability of perceiving and of using every advantage. Active in the parish apostolate of Sts. Michael and John's, he knew the influence of the priests with the people and the value of a layman's experience in confraternity work on a parochial and inter-parochial scale. Without any directed collaboration, the groundwork for the Catholic Association had been effected. Approximately two-thirds of the Irish people were Catholics, and their leaders were in sympathy with O'Connell's principles.

When Archbishop Murray succeeded Archbishop Troy the very year the Association came into existence, there was no change of policy on the matter of peaceful measures of forwarding the

Catholic cause. In fact, Archbishop Troy had designated Dr. Murray coadjutor because the two were in accord on policy, and he had almost immediately delegated administrative powers to his new appointee. In other words, Archbishop Murray had had more than a nominal position since his elevation in 1809. This was fortunate because by the time Dr. Troy died, Dublin was astir. In fact, all of Ireland was astir, and Daniel O'Connell was the spokesman of the people. His aim, based on a sincere belief that conditions had never been more propitious for good feeling between Catholics and Protestants, was to unite both against injustice.

In 1827 a recurrence of fever created new orphans and widows. Providentially, the Baggot Street social service center opened that year. To the poor school and refuge for unemployed servants an orphanage was added through the circumstance of Miss McAuley's gathering up from an alley a little girl[3] whose parents had been living in a cellar. Father and mother had died and the child had literally no place to go. Her predicament gives an insight into conditions in Dublin, for it constituted no unique situation.

It was inevitable that an orphanage should become part of the work at the House of Mary of Mercy. Miss McAuley's experience with and love of children foreordained it. Christmas dinner for the poor had been one of her practices for years. Who were the recipients of this Christmas charity before 1827? The children of Coolock village certainly. Yet from Catherine's long connection with St. Michael's, Dr. Blake's little charges may also have been among her pre-Baggot Street interests. He had established an Orphan Society in 1816 with O'Connell as president.

Whether or not Catherine McAuley met the Liberator before she opened her social service center, his daughters early enlisted in the Baggot Street charities. By 1828 their father became a benefactor, probably through the direction of his confessor, the Carmelite prior Father L'Estrange. O'Connell was then at the height of his career, exerting all his powers toward Catholic Emancipation.

Daniel O'Connell and, in her obscure way, Catherine McAuley were among those born for the time. The dates of relief measures and the movements of counter pressure are like so many guide cards in his biography and, with less obvious connection, in hers. The year 1828 moved along toward events of great historical import. However regrettable the Act of Union, it guaranteed to Catholics in England, as was ultimately demonstrated, the benefit of any concession that could be wrung from the government by Irish agitation. The activities of O'Connell and the Irish majority during 1828 culminated in the political coup of 1829.

At the big house things moved along quietly toward another kind of climax. Though Father Armstrong had been promoted to pastoral charge of St. Michan's from his administrative position in St. Andrew's, he had kept a careful eye on the erection of the building till its completion. As Chancellor of the diocese and close personal friend of the Archbishop, he continued his efficient support to Miss McAuley's interests.

In the spring of 1828 Catherine was beset the second time by a temptation to discouragement. Father Armstrong had seen her through an ordeal of this kind once before when the financial weight of her undertaking began to bear heavily. Would she be able to finish what she had begun? Or, finishing it, who would help to support it?

Who? One alone, Father Armstrong had told her.

Now that the building was actually occupied and the charities flourishing, how was she to maintain the numbers that came to her for help? Her charges often needed more than housing for the night.[4] They had to be supported during unemployment and, so inadequate was the compensation for their services, that they had to be assisted at times even when employed.

How could she meet the need? Again Father Armstrong told her: "Place your confidence in no human aid but God alone."

All her life, as the work expanded beyond the city, beyond the diocese, beyond the country, she would suffer the same misgivings. Again and again she would hear in memory the words: "Put your trust in no human help but in God alone," and she would be strengthened by trust in the one unfailing Resource.

While he lived, Father Armstrong gave a practical turn to his advice, for he furnished the first dormitory in 1827, and now in 1828 he counseled Catherine to solicit patronage by letter.[5]

The first letter, written in her own name, began "C. McAuley takes the liberty of soliciting." It drew a show of resentment from a number of persons, the first intimation she had of opposition. The resentment, variously incited, had principally one source. As far as the neighborhood itself was concerned, she had offended by bringing a charitable work into the residential section.[6] Nor did the patronage of the Merrion Square aristocrats and the great O'Connell help the situation, for the motives of her early opponents had no veneer of virtue. Some of the responses were aimed at putting her in her place. The most offensive reply ran:

————knows nothing of such a person as C. McAuley and considers that C. McAuley has taken a very great liberty in addressing her. She requests that C. McAuley will not trouble her further.

Considering the sequel, one might ask in the words of an American humorist: Why are women like that? The writer of the formal indignity followed it with lavish benefactions and an undeviating loyalty. It is a truism that staunch supporters of a good work come often from the ranks of early critics. Human nature is so constituted that if people give their attention to a cause at all, there is some hope of attracting their interest.

A later letter of solicitation, signed by Archbishop Murray, reads:

Poor schools and House of Mary of Mercy, Baggot Street, [are sanctioned] by His Grace the Most Reverend Doctor Murray, superintended by the Reverend Matthew Kelly and kindly assisted by the Reverend Doctor Armstrong under whose pastoral charge of this parish the intention was formed and building erected.
In these schools five hundred poor girls may daily experience the blessing of religious instruction, and being practiced in various branches of industry come forward shielded from all the evils incident to ignorance and idleness, prepared as Christians to discharge the duties of the humble state in life to which it has pleased God to call them.
Young tradeswomen of good character who have employment yet not sufficient means to provide safe lodging are invited to this house at night as their home—practiced in prayer and meditation, prepared for Sacraments and guarded against the dangers that surround them.
You are most earnestly entreated to contribute to the support of this institution.[7]

In the midst of the rising opposition of Catholics, a bazaar for the support of Miss McAuley's charities was successfully held in the spring of 1828 at Morrison's Hotel. It netted nearly three hundred pounds, contributed largely by Protestants. Protestant patronage had a two-fold source, the loyalty of Catherine's family connections and charity to the poor as a Christian ideal. Promoters drew part of their advantage from a tradition among the aristocracy favoring this comfortable type of almsgiving.

The most enduring persecution of Miss McAuley's work arose, as is often the case, from misdirected zeal. It will be remembered that Father Murray of St. Mary's had an idea for alleviating the misery of the parish poor when they were his charge, that he then selected the young lady he hoped to interest in establishing a new religious community and that, finally obtaining her cooperation, he succeeded with his plan. The Irish Sisters of Charity had been at work several years when Catherine McAuley established her social service center in St. Andrew's parish.

Catherine was quite unprepared for any wide misinterpretation of her work. The ignorance of her brother and her brother-in-law she could condone, but she could not anticipate anyone's thinking she would go into competition with a religious community. The London manuscript explains her intention:

> She was convinced Almighty God required her to make some lasting efforts for the relief of the suffering and instruction of the ignorant, and she thought of establishing a society of pious secular ladies who would devote themselves to this service, with liberty to return to their worldly life when they no longer felt inclined to discharge such duties—for although [she] was gifted with much piety and was always a most zealous Catholic, she had imbibed certain Protestant prejudices which she retained for a very long period. She did not like the idea of religious vows and disapproved of conventual observances, having constantly heard them ridiculed and misrepresented by Protestants. Her own house not being well situated for the purpose, she resolved to employ part of the large fortune she enjoyed in building one suitable to the designs she had in view.

The new building with her great family of poor children and the young women for whose needs she undertook to appeal, aroused the fears and animosity of the clients of Mother M. Augustine Aikenhead, foundress of the Irish Sisters of Charity. It was natural that in the thirteen years of its existence this young congregation should have made loyal friends among both clergy and people.

As the intense loyalty of the Irish people to any espoused cause tends to make them partisan, both Mother M. Augustine and Catherine McAuley were embarrassed by party spirit beyond their control. That it included the clergy made their position the more difficult. It is to the glory of the older community that their foundress evinced the perfection of Christian charity in this contingency as well as in the more usual channels of its exercise.[8]

By the spring of 1828 the trouble was just beginning to show itself. Since there was as yet no religious community at Baggot Street, the burden of reproach was entirely Miss McAuley's. She was supported in her trial by the wise and holy pastor of St. Michan's, Father Edward Armstrong, mentioned with unconscious irony on the appeal sheet in the same phrase with her greatest adversary among the clergy of the immediate vicinity, though she was as yet unaware of his opposition.

Just as her need for Father Armstrong's counsel became acute, he developed a fatal illness. His Christlike character is strongly intimated in the community records. There is, moreover, the testimony of scapegrace little Willie McAuley that Father Armstrong's face registered beauty of soul.[9] "Let me now tell you," he wrote in 1884 to Teresa Byrn, "I never saw a face like it in all my travels—so beautiful," and it was not a few faces Willie had seen in those fifty and more years.

Father Armstrong's illness gave Catherine an opportunity for many an informal conference. The Mercy tradition of nursing care to the clergy began with Miss McAuley's service first to Father Nugent, then to Father Armstrong.[10] From her years of experience in caring for her own and from attending the sick poor, Catherine had become an excellent practical nurse. She devoted herself to Father Armstrong with all the skill of her experience, only to realize with the passing days that his strength would not rally. With the seriousness given to the words of a dying parent she listened to his counsel, realizing with dismay that he ardently hoped her charitable undertaking would eventually develop into a religious congregation.[11]

One of his earnest recommendations was that she secure a chaplain to care for the spiritual needs of her dependents, adding that it would be a mistake to draw on the clergy at St. Andrew's.

Though he knew his successor was interested in the work of the Sisters of Charity, the dying priest gave his advice with more than personalities in mind, as Catherine learned. Far-sighted wisdom prompted his words, for almost ten years later she wrote emphatically to her Mother Assistant on the subject of a chaplain: "Mr. Armstrong has engraved on my mind an objection not to be overruled."

Inasmuch as he had great influence with Dr. Murray and had managed all the business of the new undertaking on Baggot Street with the Archbishop's benign approval, it could be expected that Dr. Murray would continue his support to Miss McAuley's work. In fact, His Grace called at the House a number of times during his friend's illness, encouraging the workers and promising, as Catherine Byrn avers, "every assistance in his power."[12] Archbishop Murray loved and revered the pastor of St. Michan's, accepting his opinions with something of the confidence reposed in saintliness.[13]

Father Armstrong's advice to Catherine McAuley shows that this holy priest's security was God alone. His repeated exhortation, to place her trust implicitly and solely in Divine Providence, presently took on meaning, for the complete detachment he counseled came to include relinquishing such spiritual guidance as seemed necessary to her work.

One day after the visit of a clergyman from St. Andrew's, Catherine, reviewing in her mind the visitor's qualifications, asked Father Armstrong whether this priest might not be relied upon to direct her till Dr. Blake returned from Rome.

"I do not think so," was the weighed reply, followed by the now familiar words: "Do not put your trust in any human being but place all your confidence in God alone."

The wisdom of spiritual clear-sightedness dictated this counsel. Father Armstrong had been years at St. Mary's. Seeing Miss McAuley's work rise almost of itself, he discerned in it the finger of God and knew that it would not falter.

With the death of Father Armstrong on Ascension Thursday, 1828, Catherine McAuley found herself without the spiritual support of "any living person." Around her, opposition gathered, its principal clerical exponent being the very priest whom she would have elected as adviser.

XI

Because Thou Hast Enlarged My Heart

LATE IN MAY 1828, shortly after Father Armstrong's death, Catherine moved permanently to Baggot Street and began to negotiate the sale of her Coolock estate. She opened a second dormitory[1] to accommodate those she brought there to live with her: two from Coolock, her godchild, Teresa Byrn, and Ellen Corrigan, an orphan; from the house on Military Road her two nieces Mary Macauley and little Catherine. To these she added the child Ann Rice, who had been gathered homeless from the street.

The sale of Coolock House in September included everything on the estate except Miss McAuley's Swiss carriage and some pieces of furniture suitable for the Baggot Street house. Catherine retained the carriage till she could complete arrangements for extending her work according to a plan she had in mind. Meanwhile, it transported the little group to Mass at St. Teresa's on Clarendon Street.

Almost immediately, life at the House began to take on regularity and a certain religious character. That very month an unusual young lady about Mary Macauley's age came to Baggot Street in answer to a call for a governess for Catherine Macauley and Teresa Byrn. By October the new governess was devoting all her spare time to the charities centering in the House of Mercy. "I became acquainted with dear Reverend Mother in September, 1828," she wrote to her sister years later; "I went to reside in Baggot Street on the thirteenth of October."

Georgina Moore had been born into Protestantism. About five years before she met Catherine McAuley, her widowed mother had become a Catholic and had had all her children instructed in the Faith. Mrs. Moore thereby unwittingly prepared to enroll her two daughters among the first Sisters of Mercy.

In admitting the tall, dark, self-possessed young governess to her charities Catherine McAuley had no intimation that she recruited a future religious who would establish the Congregation of Mercy in England and would become the ally and personal friend of Miss Nightingale in the Crimea.

Mrs. Moore's daughters had been educated according to their mother's strong-minded ideas, on a plan not only including the best in the way of general education at the time but allowing supplementarily for their individual differences. Since Mary Clare liked to sketch and paint, she specialized in art. The younger, with an aptitude for languages, selected Latin as her forte. It was therefore an accomplished young lady with a grave intensity of manner who called at Baggot Street in September 1828 to enlist her services in Miss McAuley's work. Georgina had much of the good sense and clear judgment that characterized her mother. Otherwise, her energy of purpose might have run to a kind of impetuosity. As a Protestant she had been conscientious in goodness and sensitive to the repellent aspect of anything less than good. Catholicism opened a way of service complementary to her endowments, which she concealed under a maturity of manner that belied her seventeen years.

In the same month Miss McAuley addressed a letter to the Very Reverend Francis J. L'Estrange, O.C.D., leaving no doubt as to the status of the ladies on Baggot Street. Whatever recommendations Father Armstrong had made to Archbishop Murray concerning Catherine and her work had been resolved during the summer, apparently with due consideration for the presiding lady's wishes.[2]

Baggot Street
September 10, 1828

Very Reverend Sir,
With full approbation of His Grace the Archbishop, the Institution in Baggot Sreet is to go on according to the original intention. Ladies who prefer a conventual life and are prevented embracing it from the nature of property or connection may retire to this House. It is expected a

gratuity will be given [i.e., to create a fund for the school] and an annual pension paid sufficient to meet the expense a lady must incur. The objects which the charity at present embrace are daily education of hundreds of poor female children and instruction of young women who sleep in the House.

Objects in view—superintendence of young women employed in the House, instructing and assisting the sick poor as may hereafter be approved.

I have the honor to remain,

Very Reverend Sir,
With great respect,
C. McAuley.[3]

There was, in other words, to be no religious congregation at the House of Mercy. The scope of the work already under way and the plan to train young women on the premises and to attend the sick poor in their homes or elsewhere, are clearly presented. It is clear, too, that young ladies identifying themselves with the work not only gave their services but contributed financially to its support and covered their own maintenance. Volunteers must have lofty motives and, according to the terms, must necessarily be recruited from upper social levels.

Catherine's "original intention" aimed at a corps of Catholic social service workers. When it began to materialize, she asked the Archbishop to allow the work a title, "Institute of Our Lady of Mercy." His Grace granted the permission September 24, 1828. The concept of a group of workers loosely bound together by common ideals has had many counterparts. Simultaneously with hers one developed in the Irish midlands and in the next decade another in London. Both eventually became identified with her congregation.

Meanwhile, the ladies rose at six A.M. Two, and sometimes three of them, in the new dormitory, however, rose quietly at four or half-past to say the entire Psalter by moonlight or candlelight, "read some of *The Sinner's Guide* and transcribe" excerpts from the few spiritual books available. Miss McAuley with her more constant companion copied out passages for sick-room reading. She had accumulated a quantity of manuscript when it accidentally caught fire one morning as she opened her desk. In her preoccupation it ran against the candle flame and burned beyond salvaging. Young Georgina Moore registered with admiration Miss McAuley's composure on this occasion.[4] From Miss Moore's intimate knowledge of this and other early morning sessions in the improvised oratory and scriptorium, it could be deduced, if she had not admitted it in a private letter to her sister, that it was she who had volunteered to be first up. Frequently mistaking the hour in winter, she aroused Miss McAuley at "three o'clock instead of four or half-past four as they had purposed." The other young person who rose "sometimes" was Frances Warde.[5] The three o'clock error was never corrected by a return to bed. It furnished extra time for transcribing.

"As to the form of life," wrote Mother M. Clare Moore in retrospect, "it was primitive Christianity." Miss Doyle and Miss Byrn had had private rooms from the beginning, "cells" in convent parlance. A third cell, when appropriately furnished, served as their oratory. Miss Doyle and Miss Byrn joined the others after six; Miss McAuley said prayers from Gahan's *Catholic Piety* and then read meditation from the same book. At an appointed time during the day the ladies walked together and recited the rosary. In the evening they made another meditation from Father Gahan's book and Miss McAuley read aloud a section of *The Elevation of the Soul.*[6] Certain days had particular devotions: Monday, the short chaplet for the dead; Wednesday, St. Joseph's chaplet; Friday, that of the Sacred Heart. Young Miss Moore thought the prayers in common about all that could be managed with an horarium carefully laid out so that none of their time might be lost by mismanagement. "Each hour of the day had its allotted duties," she recorded. She therefore observed Miss McAuley's extra meditations now and again with deeper admiration.

Women of the refuge joined in the morning prayers before leaving for work and in the evening prayers said between eight and nine. In fact, others came in for night prayers by the Herbert Street door, left open for their convenience. Pleased with this arrangement, Miss McAuley enthusiastically commented on the honesty of the poor who crowded there. "Not a pin's worth has ever been taken," she observed to her associates. Almost immediately the only portable piece of furniture in the room disappeared, the chair on which she sat when she gave out the points for meditation! Since furniture was scarce, the loss of the chair was a serious matter. Prayers were said in the ladies' sitting room downstairs, an improvised oratory converted daily into a workroom to supply unemployed young women with a means of support.

Sewing was the first work undertaken. This was no new procedure for Catherine McAuley. During the years of her services to the Poor School of St. Mary's Parish she had trained her charges to self-support. In Mother M. Clare Moore's words, she then "established a kind of shop or repository for the sale of articles of female clothing."[7] If her linen coif retained at Baggot Street is a sample of her own handiwork, she was an expert needle woman.

From having this untrained group of young women under her roof Miss McAuley learned how great a task she had set herself. Whatever delusions she had about the uplifting effect of pleasant, clean surroundings, underwent the adjustment all optimistic enthusiasts for social betterment have to make. Undesirable habits developed in early years can be eliminated only by training of a tactful and rigorous character. Slovenliness, faulty manners, and crude speech had to be corrected as well as skills taught so that Catherine could recommend her charges to prospective employers. Nor were these young women always amenable to correction. As for gratitude, Miss McAuley came to know what a pleasant surprise it could be.

Once when there was a serious illness among her associates, she went out to the women, then recreating in the yard, and asked them to lower their voices.

"Humph!" she overheard one remark, "What a fuss she makes! I thought the House was built for us, not for them."

Catherine not only learned the rarity of gratitude but also the perseverance needed to effect any lasting good among those of untractable spirit.

Mary Macauley and "Kate," as Willie called the younger of his sisters, went home at times to their father and brothers. Their Aunt Catherine accompanied them when she could. Mary would sometimes have difficulty getting permission to return to Baggot Street. Since she wished to go to Sunday Mass with the others, Frances Warde would be sent out to coax the doctor to let his daughter return. Dr. Macauley invariably gave in, though he had considerable uneasiness over Mary's being so much in an entirely Catholic atmosphere. In all but the matter of religion he was inclined to let her do as she wished because what she wished had always seemed to him reasonable. It was apparent, moreover, that her aunt's care compensated in a measure for the loss of her mother's. It had certainly been a factor in his daughter's rallying from symptoms of decline after her mother's death; so the poor man was in a difficult position.

Before the end of the year 1828, Mary did something which her father certainly would not have approved, had he known it, however it might square with her own conscience: on St. Cecilia's day she received conditional baptism in the now nearly completed chapel, called St. Mary's.

Her interest in Catholicism became more evident, and it disturbed her father. On one of the occasions when his sister-in-law was home with the girls he ventured to make himself clear on the matter of his daughter's religion, expressing himself with unaccustomed emphasis.

This emphasis took on so much color in retelling that by the time it reached publication in the first biographies it drew emphatic protest. Whatever demonstration William Macauley made over his daughter's interest in Catholicism, it was directed primarily against young Mary, not against his sister-in-law. The latter acted as arbiter. Both Catherine Byrn and William Macauley, the one in Drogheda in the North of Ireland when the incident became public, the other half way across the world in Australia, independently of each other protested the details given to the public in the 1860's. In the published version the Macauley children were represented as witnesses of their father's frenzied anger when he learned from his sister-in-law one evening that his wife had been reconciled to the Faith before her death. Since Willie Macauley was supposed to have been present, his indignant denial must be accepted.

Catherine Byrn softens the affair to a statement of the doctor's becoming one evening "rather excited on the subject of his wife's having died a Catholic and his eldest daughter's predilection for the Catholic religion." She added, "but there was no disturbance of the usual harmony." Recalling the impressions of her teens, she considered the doctor incapable of violence.

The Dublin manuscript, however, makes it clear that the doctor was more than a little excited when he learned not only that his favorite child had adopted the religion against which he had an unconquerable prejudice but also that his wife had set her a final example in it. Mary Teresa "escaped," the memoir-writer asserts, to the protection of servants and did not venture to meet her father again that evening. His sister-in-law, wise enough not to try to reason with him in his "excited" condition, withdrew for the night, prevailing on the doctor next morning to interview his daughter with some degree of self-possession.

"That interview was a most painful one," the Dublin manuscript avers. "She had been his favourite child, but he told her that her conversion made a marked difference between his affection for her and his other children." The writer concludes with the comment: "It certainly did in his manner."

These incidents in what proved to be the last year and a half of Dr. Macauley's life imply great personal sorrow. His wife had been dead little more than a year when the worry about his eldest child's religious interests came to him. Mary Macauley's long illness had been a grief that he knew must end in bereavement, but just when her loss should have been compensated somewhat in the companionship of their daughter, to learn that his wife had wounded him doubly by example turned his grief to anguished hurt. In human relationships free of moral blight there is no greater loss than that effected by misunderstanding.

It would be soul-revealing to know the trend of the doctor's thoughts through the few weeks from December 1828 to his death, January 25, 1829. One day, late in January, he went across the city to his sister-in-law to tell her that he was not feeling well. His going to her for advice and sympathy reveals much. She urged him not to depend on his own remedies but to return home and call in another physician. She herself followed him there with Mary Teresa. Whatever the character of his illness, he lived but a few days.

It was not Catherine McAuley's nature to see him die without making an effort to win him to her point of view in religion, though only a person of her optimism could have had any hope of success. In their conversation he admitted what had escaped the youthful perception of Catherine Byrn, his religious bias.

"You know the prejudice in which I was reared," he said to his sister-in-law a few hours before his death. "I desire to belong to the Church of Jesus Christ, whatever that is."

His arrangements for his children further confirm his sincerity. They were to share equally in his estate and he left them free to select either their maternal aunt or uncle for guardian. Dr. James McAuley was as strong in his Protestantism as his sister Catherine was in Catholicism. Dr. William certainly understood that a choice of guardian implied in the ultimate a choice of religion. What a long way he had come in a few months!

At the end of his life he certainly merited Catherine Byrn's characterization of him as "one of the kindest and most consistent of Protestants, for he allowed to others the same liberty of private judgment which he claimed for himself."

The boys, James about twelve, Robert, ten, and Willie, seven, had been a great deal with their father and uncle. The only opinion on record is Willie's. He liked his Aunt Fanny, Dr. James' wife, but he did not like his uncle. In the formalities of settling matters after their father's death, each declared Catherine McAuley his choice. That Mary Teresa and little Catherine would favor their aunt was no surprise, but that the boys should do so discomfited their Uncle James and displeased their father's family.

The girls settled permanently at Baggot Street, and their brothers registered at the lay school connected with Carlow College. They stayed a few days at Baggot Street while arrangements were made, but before the end of February they arrived at Carlow under the kindly vigilance of Dr. Fitzgerald, O. P., and his efficient staff.

From thc casy discipline of an indulgent father and the exciting atmosphere of the Royal Hospital grounds to the junior division of a Catholic college in a quiet town was a great transition for three little Protestant lads to make in one short month. Carlow College still has among its records the "judgment books" carrying their weekly status, and the bursar's lists showing their rather free expenditures. Something must be said for the thoroughness of those records.[8] A perusal of them gives almost a psychograph of each pupil.

"McAuley (primus)," "McAuley (secundus)," "McAuley (tertius)" are listed March 2, 1829, with no given names and no marks across a chart beginning with "Greek" and ending with such telling supplementary details as "dress," "walk," "conduct," and "times absent from Mass, prayers, study." The signatures of the teaching staff appear on every charted sheet.

The curriculum for the lay school included Greek, Latin, French, history, geography, arithmetic, tables, spelling, reading, writing, bookkeeping and geometry. The second week, ratings were given to James and Robert in history, geography, reading and writing. Their penmanship was poor. By the third week the two older boys achieved marks in two more subjects, Latin and spelling, and seven-year old Willie did better than his older brothers in writing, his only subject.

The following week Robert was sick; James added Greek to his studies and Willie showed a weakness—spelling, *pessime!* Before the end of March James and Robert were both receiving ratings in Greek.

As for the interesting supplementaries, Robert just did not bother about prayers: "4 times absent from prayers," "always absent from morning prayers," "5 times absent from prayers" the conscientious prefect entered on the books, though eventually the record improved to twice absent, then a long triumphant period of no times absent!

Dr. Fitzgerald, president of the college, read reports in the lay school every week. What an influence that simple public castigation had! Willie would rise to *bene* in "dress" for several pages after one *male,* though sooner or later he would fall again into temporary disgrace—as low as *pessime* even.

Poor little spoiled Willie, whose individualism now suffered its first curb! Long years of unspoiling lay ahead of him. His mother had been sick as far back as he could remember. She was dead before he was six years old. Both at home and at Coolock he had given the servants a time of it, but everybody loved him. If life had not been so interesting, he might have been baffled by the radical changes in his surroundings.

"Bad dog!" Dr. Fitzgerald would say in disapproval of Willie's record, whisking the leaves of the record book over the lad's already rumpled hair, and "bad dog! bad dog!" emphatically when at Confirmation Willie added the name of the old doctor's patron to his own collection: William Armstrong Montgomery *Dominic* McAuley.[9] Dominic indeed! But it was the schoolmaster in the college president who spoke. Dr. Fitzgerald must do what he could to mend the ways of his undisciplined young charge.

Willie's record certainly showed wild fluctuation. Excellent in spots, it indicated capabilities unevenly exerted. In one subject, however, he was consistently *male*—French, as in one he was almost consistently not just *bene* but *optime* even. The subject was Latin! Since ratings for French and Latin begin to appear on his record the following year, Willie was all of eight years old.

As to the bursar's list of purchases for the McAuley boys—there were combs enough to keep Willie's every hair in place and clothes enough for all to be well dressed, if quantity would do the grooming. Silk handkerchiefs must have been the badge of wealth. Splendid indeed must their accessories have been at four shillings apiece when modest pocket handkerchiefs sold at five shillings a half dozen.

"Primus," "Secundus" and "Tertius" could hang on to gloves no better than the rest of mankind, and they bought as much headgear as the vainest of women. Parties at five and six shillings studded the account. The barber's services at a shilling with the frequency of comb purchases at 7d could have kept any boy *optime* in appearance, had he been so minded.

"Vacation—four pounds, four shillings, eleven pence"—three small boys can go a considerable distance in Ireland even today on that! This was apparently the old doctor's gift, for the appended note reads: "allowance made by Dr. F.—not to be charged."

"Broken delft" had to be paid for, and one terse item is eloquent: "1 pane of glass by James in the trunk room, ditto by William—4/6." What a tussle that must have been!

Dublin was still home to the boys. On one of their visits to

Baggot Street that year they received conditional baptism in the convent chapel.[10]

Willie had a venturesome strain that made life worth while under many vicissitudes. Over fifty years later he wrote from Australia to Teresa Byrn, then Sister Mary Camillus of Baltimore:

Let us in imagination enter Baggot Steet, fly downstairs, turn to the right, leave the kitchen door to my back, enter a room—it is the refectory. I sit down at the head of the table (no Sisters there) to a good feed. Enter my dear Aunt and little round-featured healthy looking girl . . . called Teresa . . . Teresa's eye follows my hand from the plate to my mouth and back to plate . . . Presently I hear a little slap on poor Teresa's hand with a "How dare you!" (I feel that slap.)
Let us run up the back stairs. I come to the first door and I look straight out and see the wall of the House of Refuge, look to my left and see into the Chapel; on still. Next [up stairs] over the Chapel. There my darling sister Kate died. On still. I come to a long room. There are four little girls; their names are C. McAuley, T. Byrn, E. Corrigan, M. Quin—and an impudent brat of a boy *past redemption*. What are the girls singing? I think it went—*Ellen, Elena, Mary, John* . . . .
Now what more do I see? My Aunt's front of ringlets—her own hair cut off when it began to turn grey (that was pride for you!). Well, I do not want them although what few hairs remain are snow white. We are told it is good to keep the feet warm and the head cool. My head is naked enough . . . after all the curling it got in Baggot Street . . . .

Scapegrace Willie, eight years old, on holidays in Dublin, his bad French and excellent Latin temporarily forgotten!

XII

Ladies of Mercy

WHEN ARCHBISHOP MURRAY called at the House that November day in 1828 to administer conditional baptism to Mary Teresa Macauley, he granted the ladies ecclesiastical permission to visit the sick poor.[1] On the feast of St. Andrew, Catherine took Miss Doyle, Miss Byrn, and Miss Warde with her to the Sir Patrick Dunn Hospital, which was within walking distance of Baggot Street. On this occasion, however, Catherine used the equipage she had had at Coolock House. She was known at Sir Patrick Dunn's because of her relationship with Dr. James and Dr. William. She explained to the head physician the nature of the service she and her associates were prepared to give patients, and they received gracious permission to come there as often as they liked. It took Catherine just two weeks to organize her visitation schedule, which included two other hospitals within walking distance and many by-streets and lanes that housed the poor.[2] She then sold her carriage and began to dress in the plainest manner permitted by fashion. She also gave up her social program.

Of December 7, 1828, and the daily work thereafter, the writer of the London manuscript says:

The going out dress was a grey cloak with hood and black silk bonnet with muslin veil; in summer a black shawl . . .
They visited and relieved many poor sick persons in the neighboring courts and lanes, and went daily to Sir Patrick Dunn's Hospital at a short distance from Baggot Street where the effects of Miss McAuley's zeal and tender charity were soon very apparent. She spent much of her time in the poor schools, having an admirable method of conveying

religious instruction and considering the early culture of poor children's minds a work of paramount importance. Out of her affection for them and her devotion to the Divine Infancy of Our Lord, she used to prepare a Christmas dinner for them every year and wait upon them herself. In this act of humility she was for many years assisted by that great and good man Daniel O'Connell, who used to go to the Convent School on Christmas Day to carve for the little children.[3]

In 1828 Christmas dinner at the Institute was unforgettable. It is deserving of eyewitness detail, particularly for the ancedote value of the part taken by O'Connell:

Every Christmas day she gave a dinner of roast beef and plum pudding to the children of the school and all the friends of the Institute were invited to be present. That given at Christmas 1828 excited great interest. The Liberator carved, the ladies and gentlemen served. O'Connell was exceedingly fond of children. Now among these children was the orphan of one of the nurses at Sir Patrick Dunn's Hospital, who had died about a week before,—the ugliest, most ill-formed, uncouth little being you could fancy. She was almost an idiot with a most startling voice. Beside her sat three or four pretty little girls, orphans, who were some time longer in the house and had learned to behave prettily before company. These were the pets with the ladies. Not so with the illustrious orator! He helped their ill-favored companion to dainty pieces, said droll things to make her merry, and when she had done eating took her in his arms, kissed her (she was about four years) and told her she was his favourite of all the little girls there.[4]

Again the Christmas holidays merged with a new year, the year of liberation. Optimism, so suited to the Irish character, reached at last the buoyancy a well-founded hope warranted. There was a new face on things. The natural light-heartedness of the people escaped old restraints and permeated the busy capital with a fresh vigor. Even the wretched hovels of the poor shared the rejuvenating influence because Mother Augustine and her Sisters of Charity and Miss McAuley and her Ladies of Mercy had been organized long enough to put a new spirit, if not a new face, on the lanes and alleys of the Irish capital.

In the first month of that eventful year the priest who had attended Mary Macauley in her last illness a year and a half before, the chaplain of the Carmelite nuns at Blackrock near the sea, brought his young niece, Ann O'Grady, to assist in Miss McAuley's work. Young as she was, about eighteen, she had spent a year in the Presentation Convent at Wexford and had left only when her health failed. In view of her later history the failure in health is explicable. She was a person of indefatigable application and imprudent zeal. Love of the poor and a dauntless spirit of making a way for Christian charity in their behalf marked her gentle character with strength. She required a wise spiritual director to curb her natural inclination to overdo both spiritually and physically. A thorough-going person, she was over-conscientious and inclined to scrupulosity. This was reflected in her dread of making religious vows, for which she had a deservedly exalted regard. Miss McAuley's Institute of Mercy gave Miss O'Grady's piety and charity scope without troubling her conscience, for there were no vows.

At the time, however, the Institution lacked restraints necessary for the physical well-being of the over-zealous. By the very nature of their spirit of sacrifice, people who devote themselves to service under religious influence require the moderating guidance of the Church's centuries of experience. Ascetical ideals have been made practical by Rules now hundreds of years proved. All groups working in common under Church approval have adopted a modified form of one of these.

Providentially, the presence of Miss O'Grady became one of the circumstances that brought to an issue the status of the Institute, for her arrival introduced the custom of using the term "Sister" in personal address among the Ladies. Probably because of her experience in religious life Miss O'Grady wished to be called "Sister Mary Aloysius," and the habit of acceding to her request began merrily enough. In fact, the custom developed in lighthearted good fun and was perpetuated by what someone has called divine humor.

A few days after Ann O'Grady joined the Institute, Georgina Moore's brother and elder sister called at Baggot Street. They had not come to visit Georgina. "My brother took me to introduce me," Mary Clare Moore explained. With an artist's appreciation of detail, she appraised the lady "sitting in the little parlor to the right of the hall" as they entered. Dressed in black merino modishly fitted . . . white skin . . . high color . . . pale gold hair . . . expressive blue eyes peculiarly discerning . . . graceful bearing—nothing escaped the trained eye of the elder Miss Moore. Judging Miss McAuley's age to be "upwards of forty," Mary Clare observed that the lady in charge of Mercy Institute "looked at least ten years younger." Actually, Miss McAuley was past fifty.

"She broke down very soon after," the description concludes, "for when I saw her again in six months I scarcely knew her."

The context shows that Mary Clare Moore does not refer to a constitutional breakdown but to evidences of age, though several descriptions of Catherine McAuley as a religious recognize her claim to beauty and to a more youthful appearance than her years warranted. No one else has described her so tellingly as Georgina Moore's sister because none of the others had so objective an attitude. The only aesthetic flaw the artist observed was the heavy white hands which should have been graceful and shapely to perfect the picture. They were "remarkably white," she records, "but clumsy, very large with broad square tips to the fingers and short square nails."

By the time Catherine McAuley reached her fifty-first birthday she began to lose her youthful appearance. Though the accumulating years changed her appearance, she had had enough anxiety in the preceding six months to age her.

XIII

Of Shoals and Beacons

DR. BLAKE's stay in Rome stretched out to a fifth year, much to his disappointment, for among his priestly interests, parish activities were second to none. He had been the obvious choice for the work that had to be done in Rome, and when he succeeded in leveling opposition to the reopening of the Irish College in the Eternal City, he was the obvious person to be made rector. So it was that Archbishop Murray sanctioned his stay. When the College was firmly established, he was recalled to Sts. Michael and John's. The cornerstone he had laid in 1824 now supported a thriving center of charitable activity. The first Mass had been said in the chapel at Christmas in 1827.[1] That more Masses had not been offered there was not the fault of Archbishop Murray, but of Dr. Armstrong's successor, the administrator of St. Andrew's.[2] On his return from Rome Dr. Blake found Miss McAuley, whose wish was to be hidden in her work, anything but obscure. She whose reverence for the priesthood he well knew had become a focus of clerical displeasure.

From Dr. Armstrong's death until Dr. Blake's return home, the Carmelites on Clarendon Street seem to be almost the only clerical friends Miss McAuley and her associates had. In this friendship she and her spiritual daughters have never been disappointed. St. Teresa's received them daily for Mass and ministered to the needs of the school children and the young women of the refuge. All went to St. Teresa's for confession and Sunday Mass, and the ladies chose the Reverend Raymund O'Hanlon for their regular confessor.

Since clerical opposition constituted one of Miss McAuley's severest trials, some analysis of it must be made. It resulted from misunderstanding, narrow-visioned zeal, and accidental affront. A Catholic layman who plans to do good among those of his Faith frequently meets with unexpected opposition. The higher his aim and the broader his objective, the more numerous the difficulties. Not that Church authorities always wish to make difficulty, but they see or anticipate obstacles for which the layman with his eyes only on his aim has neither the experience nor the perspective. Besides, on account of the administrative organization of the Church, the greater the scope of the layman's activity the more complicated his problem, since his contacts with Church authorities necessarily grow more diverse. Authorities may differ widely on the matter and manner of lay activity. Yet all elements must be harmoniously resolved if the layman is to be successful in his endeavor. Among hierarchy and clergy there is often a *laissez-faire* attitude on trivia in lay activity. What may seem of great incidental importance to the projection of a charitable work may actually be trivia in the eyes of those looking to the greatest good of all concerned. Conversely, what may seem unimportant to the layman may from contingencies known only to those in authority prove a real obstacle to some projected plan.

The element of human nature, confounding enough in the case of men dealing with men, can be further complicated by the intrusion of a woman. The position of women in the eighteenth and nineteenth centuries makes this observation pertinent, and the attitude of the Reverend Matthias Kelly underscores it.[3]

For years he had been curate at St. Mary's, Liffey Street, and knew Miss McAuley's rise from Conway poverty to Callaghan opulence. The Dublin manuscript comments:

> This gentleman had no great idea that the unlearned sex could do anything but mischief by trying to assist the clergy. Furthermore he was prejudiced against the Foundress, whom he considered as *parvenue*. His opinions perhaps influenced the curates, by whom he was greatly beloved, for certainly they did not affect to be glad of the establishment either as a secular or religious institute.

Still it must not be inferred that the Reverend Mr. Kelly[4] fixed his annoyance entirely on the monetary aspect of the situation. He resented the authority people sometimes assume when they have money to support them, and he erroneously estimated Miss McAuley as one who had taken advantage of his predecessor's patronage. The resemblance her work bore to the activities of Mother M. Augustine Aikenhead and her group added affront, for Mother Augustine was an acknowledged handmaid of the Church. Father Kelly considered a woman out of her sphere in presuming to initiate a charitable work in the Church. In the Church?—Why, in what was now his parish. It was fortunate for Miss McAuley that he was only parish administrator. It was fortunate, too, that at this juncture Dr. Blake returned from Rome.

Dr. Blake lost no time in taking up the matter of daily Mass at St. Mary's, Baggot Street, and he began to forward a plan for a change of status in the Institute. Both he and the Carmelites were in accord on this, with Dr. Blake as Chancellor in the better position to press the matter with the Archbishop.

Now the Archbishop, in common with Archbishops generally, had many things on his mind. One of them was his administrator Father Kelly, for a reason of far more concern to him than the Institute on Baggot Street. Dr. Armstrong had found it necessary to enlarge St. Andrew's and had been wholeheartedly supported by the parishioners. With Father Kelly's administration the plans had outgrown the original intention and had become a drive for an entirely new building. Whatever the difficulties that arose with parishioners, Archbishop Murray remained aloof, trusting probably that the trouble would dissolve. He had an ear for Dr. Blake's interests, however, so that in June St. Mary's Chapel in the House of Mercy was dedicated.

Dr. Blake had brought several paintings from Rome with the new chapel in mind. It would be interesting to know the artist's title for the Madonna Catherine selected as an altarpiece.[5] The Virgin has a communing seriousness of expression. Supporting with her right hand the Infant standing on her knee, she holds in the other hand her heart issuing a full flame and disseminating soft rays of light. The Divine Child clasps against His breast His Heart burning and aglow. He looks sadly out across the universe while His Mother with a nearer vision seems to look out over mankind. The painting was symbolic. Devotion to the Sacred Heart and to the Immaculate

Heart, given Papal approval at the beginning of the century, had enkindled new fervor. The picture of the Compassionate Hearts, therefore, represented fresh religious ardor as well as *Misericordia.* Incidentally, it represented a favorite devotion of Catherine McAuley and Anna Maria Doyle. Catherine was particularly devoted to the Sacred Heart of Jesus and Anna Maria had special devotion to the Immaculate Heart of Mary.

Everything was in order in St. Mary's Chapel of the House of Mary of Mercy, June 4, 1829, when Archbishop Murray, Dr. Blake, and the officers for the Pontifical Mass arrived—everything but the sentiments of the celebrant.[6] Undoubtedly he had been accorded the honor as a courtesy. Deference to his ecclesiastical superior obliged him to accept, but he had no enthusiasm for his position.

Nor did Dr. Blake's sermon change his humor, for Dr. Blake had not changed his attitude toward Miss McAuley and her work. According to his fixed belief, she was a chosen instrument in a divine plan. He went so far as to include in the sermon his conviction that anyone opposing her would summon divine disfavor.[7] And the reverend celebrant had been opposing her as effectively as he could! It was a difference of clerical opinion, to say the least. If Dr. Blake seemed to take unfair advantage of Miss McAuley's principal opponents by issuing a pointed condemnation from the pulpit, one of the reverend gentlemen was to have his moment. The guests were served after the ceremonies, and during the pleasantries of table talk the reverend celebrant used the opportunity to express *his* opinions, already well-known to some there. It was not a little advantage his position gave him, for he was generally liked among the clergy. In St. Andrew's parish at the time Miss McAuley had one solitary clerical supporter, the Reverend Mr. McDonogh, a Trinitarian.

The protagonist for the opposition pointed out the conventual appearance of the institution, the uniformity of dress adopted by the ladies in charge,[8] and the usurpation of conventual custom in the form of address among themselves—that is, use of the title "Sister." If these matters had escaped the Archbishop, it would be no fault of the present administrator of the parish if they did not soon come to His Grace's attention.

One of the incidents connected with June 4 amused Miss Warde, who had much to do with the business end of matters. Miss McAuley, wishing to assure privacy to the institution and to give less offense to the neighborhood, had made an early effort to secure the permission of her Protestant neighbors to add more height to the garden wall between their property. Since Miss McAuley had made it clear that the extension of the wall would be her expense, it is hard to understand an objection. The neighbors, however, held stubbornly against the improvement. The outdoor ceremonies on dedication day had an unexpected result. The ladies were surprised and amused to discover the wall hastily raised to more than satisfactory height the following day.

The wall Miss McAuley's clerical opponents were building against her activities was, by a subtler paradox, to be even more serviceable to her, and the builders were that morning at work on her premises.

The Archbishop kept as aloof from it all as he did from the building difficulties centering in the chapel house over on Townsend Street. What chagrin the Reverend Matthias Kelly would have suffered could he foresee that the new Institute would reach out and take over for a school the very chapel house in which he presided! To Miss McAuley Archbishop Murray was most gracious on this happy occasion. Perhaps memories of his beloved priest-brother Dr. Armstrong stirred him, for it was the octave of Ascension, the feast that a year before had separated them with whatever finality death can manage.

His Grace, the pastor of St. Andrew's, appointed a chaplain[9] and advised Miss McAuley to erect tribunes in the chapel of Our Lady of Mercy[10] so that Catholics of the vicinity might attend Mass there. He also told her to accept any contributions to support the needy young women of the House. Considering the size of the parish, the convenience to parishioners in the district, and the limited capacity of St. Andrew's Chapel, one might have expected the Reverend Mr. Kelly to be relieved; but considering the revenue he believed would be diverted from the pressing necessities at St. Andrew's, he could not be expected to be pleased. It is hard, nevertheless, to account for what he subsequently did to make Miss McAuley uncomfortable in her position.

Presumably he had little opportunity on June 4, 1829, to make known his attitude to her personally. In the first place, she was not present at the ceremonies to hear herself panegyrized by her unfailing ally, Dr. Blake. Something like consternation attends the reading of this passage from recollections of the day: "She was much affected and would not be present but remained in prayer in the [House]; at this time and long after she had much to feel from disapprobation especially of many priests and others. Much jealousy existed regarding the Sisters of Charity."[11]

So the principal lady was not present at the dedication of her own chapel because the experience was more than she could bear!

XIV

Contradicted Sign

ON THE Vigil of Pentecost, 1829, Mass was celebrated for the third time in the Chapel of Our Lady of Mercy on Baggot Street. Georgina Moore wrote of the occasion:

On the following Saturday [after dedication] the Reverend Mr. L'Estrange said Mass and O'Connell served his Mass and went to Holy Communion. He then took collation with his daughter Kate and Mr. L'Estrange in the community room.[1]

Fitzpatrick supplies the information that the Carmelite Prior was then O'Connell's confessor.[2] Father L'Estrange was more than a spiritual influence, however, for the same writer tells of his popularity, his worthiness, his prominence in the Catholic Association, and refers to him as a "political lion." The Emancipation was an actuality at last, and these were glorious days for the "political lions." But Miss Moore writes casually without regard to personalities or glory. She merely records community history, registering the Carmelite services, which were now brought to Baggot Street, and the fidelity of the O'Connells to the House.

"After the chapel was dedicated," she continues, "more regularity was observed. The Reverend Mr. Burke was appointed chaplain and Reverend Mr. O'Hanlon now came to hear confessions so that the Sisters went out no more to Clarendon Street or any place except to visit the sick . . .

"They [the Carmelites] supplied us with vestments and almost everything for the altar and continued for nearly three years to give altar breads, incense, charcoal and other things."

When Father L'Estrange became Carmelite Provincial the following month, these kindnesses continued to come to the little community through him, and covered the transitional period of the Institute.

Meanwhile, the Chancellor urged Miss McAuley to look toward a better organization of her group. He asked her to examine the Rules of all the religious orders of women in the Dublin area. Catherine was persuaded to examine the Carmelite Rule by Father O'Hanlon, who pointed out the practical advantages of certain customs observed by that Order. She did not need to be convinced of the need for regularity and prudent management, and she did see the wisdom of some procedures. But she had a pronounced aversion for conventual life. Catherine particularly disliked the distinction between superior and subject as well as other aspects of conventual practice. After all, she was Elinor McAuley's daughter. Catherine was to struggle with this repugnance even when she herself headed a religious community. The Dublin manuscript goes on:

> But Dr. Blake was urging her, and dear Father O'Hanlon managing it—in fact, I may say he did manage to bring her to the point he all along had in view, and by drawing her attention to particular bits of propriety now and then, prepared her mind to appreciate the advantages of uniform observance.

The Feast of the Sacred Heart, 1829, was observed at the House of Our Lady of Mercy with special ceremonies. High Mass was celebrated before the beautiful Madonna of Divine Compassion, and the Confraternity of the Sacred Heart was established.[3] The occasion marks the beginning of certain convent-like observances at the Institute. The dormitory hitherto used by the ladies was turned over to young women of the refuge, and the "Sisters" went into separate cells. At first the bed curtains and spreads in the Sisters' quarters were white, as they were elsewhere in the House, but when the Institute became a convent these accessories were made of blue and white checked gingham of a type still used in many European Mercy convents. Besides the bed, the cell furniture consisted of a chair and a wash stand.

The Sisters, as they were generally called among themselves, now had their devotions apart from the young women. The former convened in chapel at six in the morning where Sister Catherine read an Act of Oblation to the Sacred Heart. Then they meditated till seven. They made up their cells, assisted at Mass about 7:30, and had breakfast in the refectory at eight or eight-fifteen. Immediately following breakfast Sister Catherine read a short biography of the saint commemorated for that day. The ladies of the Institute dispersed after the reading in the refectory to work among the poor either in the classroom or the refuge on the premises; in the homes of the sick and distressed in the alleys and back streets beyond the residential section; or in one of the three hospitals they now regularly visited.

"I do not think we had any more prayers till near four o'clock when we assembled for examen," wrote Georgina Moore years later. "After dinner we had the 'Visit of the Blessed Sacrament' read out of Liguori; in the evening the rosary, private reading and prayer."[4]

Such a change of program was scarcely calculated to allay criticism. However misunderstood in Dublin, the Institute seems to have been rightly interpreted elsewhere as a social service to which a person might freely devote herself without relinquishing independence financially or otherwise. Yet Miss McAuley's ideas were gradually being modified. Daily Mass within the House and reservation of the Blessed Sacrament caused adjustments shaping toward stability and permanence.

During the summer of 1829 Dr. Blake introduced Miss Marcella Flynn to the work, and in September he presented Miss Margaret Dunne who had been hesitating on the very ground of the impermanence of the Institute.[5] When she consulted Dr. Blake, however, Miss Dunne was reassured and she cast in her lot with the other six at Baggot Street. In November Mary Teresa Macauley joined the group and in December the latter was followed by a friend of Miss Warde, Elizabeth Harley.

During these months after the opening of the chapel Miss McAuley provided further occasion for lay criticism and clerical indignation by accepting two lay sisters quite as would be done in a convent. The patrons of the Sisters of Charity found fresh cause for considering the venture a competitive project, and there was a great deal of conjecture about its ultimate destiny.

Early that year an incident occurred which underlined the real need for a refuge operating with the wide experience and great understanding provided by Catherine McAuley. After some unpleasantness with a tyrannical stepmother, a young woman had abruptly left a respectable home and set out for Dublin, expecting to be admitted to the Stanhope Street Refuge.[6] "She was denied admission," the Derry MS relates, "but as some consolation was told that in Baggot Street a Miss McAuley had a great house where every sort of people were let in; for thus did the pious and charitable speak of our poor institution." She reached the south side of the city late at night, terrified as well as hungry, cold, and "stupefied by fatigue." She gave her name and told her story incoherently. Her unkempt appearance after miles of travel on foot and her exhausted state caused Miss McAuley to hesitate before admitting her to the dormitory until her history could be investigated. Catherine secured safe lodging for her "in little James Street" the following day and secured a position for her until a reconciliation could be effected with her family.

Gossip about and opposition to the Baggot Street project continued. Gossip among the laity had it that Miss McAuley would become a Sister of Charity. The opposition of the parish clergy fastened on the unorthodox character of the Institute. Unorthodox it certainly was, for who had ever heard of a group of Catholic women living in community without canonical vows, without obligations beyond what their charity dictated, free to come, free to go! One of the group[7] had already withdrawn for a time to return when she pleased.

Father Kelly, the Reverend Administrator, had done everything in his power to prevent the opening of the House Chapel, but the Chancellor had parried his opposition. Perhaps Father Kelly now heard of Catherine McAuley's interest in religious rules for women. At any rate, he had a proposition of his own; so one day not too many weeks after the dedication ceremony he paid a visit to Miss McAuley at the House of Our Lady of Mercy and asked to be shown around. Though Miss McAuley must have wondered at his interest, she received him as graciously as if he were one of the greatest benefactors of the Institute, as indeed he quite unconsciously was. While she conducted him through the House, he explained the purpose of his visit, unaccountably giving her the impression that he represented the Archbishop's decision. The Sisters of Charity were to have the institution. Under their supervision Miss McAuley and her helpers would be allowed a few rooms to continue work among the poor of the parish.

In this plan Father Kelly was certainly expressing his own desire. He spoke authoritatively, referring to the Archbishop in a way that led her to believe the matter settled. The composure so often ascribed to her served her well. Informing her visitor that she had already put the House completely under His Grace's direction so that he was free to do whatever he wished about it, she saw Father Kelly out, sat down and wrote to Archbishop Murray. She told him that the plan proposed through his administrator was quite agreeable to her, since it represented His Grace's wish.

It developed that the Reverend Matthias Kelly had not been so clear with his ecclesiastical superior as he had been with his parishioner, for the real pastor of the parish, the Archbishop himself, came over to learn what the letter meant. The ensuing interview provided the turning point for the Institute.

In spite of the difference in their respective positions, the two principals had much in common. In addition to dignity of bearing, affability, and great personal charm, Archbishop Murray and Miss McAuley possessed a similar spiritual temper. Their particular discipline of soul marked both with longanimity. Consequently they managed difficulties with great forbearance. Several passages in the Meagher eulogy of Dr. Murray could be applied with equal force to Catherine McAuley. Generalizing on the character of the Archbishop, Father Meagher observed:

There were few salient points of character about him. Every passion was so subdued, every inclination so regulated, every act and movement so circumspect, every sentence he uttered so cautious and deliberate, all about him so void of ostentation or vehemence or sudden impulse that little remained visible to excite, surprise or create admiration except the beautiful repose and symmetry and completeness of the character at large.[8]

His Grace told Miss McAuley that he had in mind no change of plan for her House. He did say, referring to the title "Sisters of Mercy," "The idea of a convent starting up of itself in this manner never entered my mind."

She might have replied that it had never entered hers either but, remaining silent, she left herself open to misunderstanding.

"Really, Miss McAuley," he ended, "I did not think the founding of a religious order was part of your plan."

The seriousness of his manner and his words, particularly the word *convent,* struck her with far more force than anything Father Kelly had said and stayed with her disturbingly after His Grace had left. Slow to judge, slow to censure, lenient and kindly, Archbishop Murray[9] commanded more than respect when he made a critical pronouncement. Spiritually sensitive, diffident of self, submissive to authority, Catherine McAuley drew from His Grace's few words what no amount of clerical criticism, no amount of friendly counsel had succeeded in registering: she had unwittingly founded a convent, an irregular one at that! She who had taken no step without expert spiritual direction and the Archbishop's express sanction had erected more than an institution for the poor.

When architects had turned out a conventual building, she was amused. When in her absence during Dr. Macauley's illness the carpenters had introduced a grating in the chapel, she was annoyed. Under Dr. Armstrong's and Dr. Blake's guidance with the approbation of His Grace, Archbishop Murray, she nevertheless became involved in the ground plan of a new religious congregation. The situation left her in perplexity. She now turned again to Dr. Blake whose resourcefulness in spiritual emergencies seemed inexhaustible.

"A convent?"—he was neither surprised nor chagrined. Though he had not expressly planned it, he had for some time foreseen the ultimate destiny of the Institute. After his return from Rome he tried to prepare Miss McAuley for the inevitable, but he had had to wait for the intervention of Providence to convince her. The circumstance he felt sure all along would eventually arise had finally arisen. He offered her words of comfort: the Institute had the mark of the Divine Master, "a sign to be contradicted." It was time, he added, to rescue her and her associates "from the anomaly of their position." He therefore began a series of conferences with the Archbishop.

The close co-operation between His Grace and Miss McAuley was outlined by Sister M. Raymund Byrn, O.P., when she replied to an inquiry made by Father Meagher after Archbishop Murray's death:

From the time the idea was first entertained of founding an establishment for the objects now pursued by the Sisters of Mercy, His Grace gave the project his most zealous cooperation. Our lamented revered friend, Mr. Armstrong, to whose advice dear Mother M. C. McAuley paid the most implicit deference, being then Administrator of the parish, His Grace and he fixed upon the site of the present convent in Baggot Street.

The building being completed and being opened for the instruction and protection of the poor, His Grace gave it the title of House of Our Lady of Mercy. He often honored it with his visits, particularly during Mr. Armstrong's last illness, and promised that every assistance in his power should be given to the completion of the good work, which was then only sketched; for though the community performed with regard to the poor the same duties as at present, they were under no rule, the original intention of the foundress being that the members should form a sodality rather than a religious congregation.

In three years, however, from the opening of the establishment, the good Pastor who had all along fulfilled his promise by giving and procuring donations, expressing his fullest approbation to such ladies as wished to co-operate and animating in each of his visits the zeal of those who had joined the community, finding that misconstruction and even disedification arose from the difference of opinion which prevailed as to the religious position of those ladies, desired that some of their number should serve their novitiate in an approved religious house and fixed upon the Order of the Presentation, whose original objects had been almost the same as those embraced by the community at Baggot-street.[10]

The remainder of the letter pertaining to the foundation of the new congregation and the withdrawal of Miss Byrn to the Dominicans will be quoted in another place.

During the weeks following the July visit of His Grace to Miss McAuley, Dr. Blake came to Catherine with a proposition: she might complete the work by conforming to canonical regulations on women living in a religious community, or she should proceed along secular lines. With an appointed chaplain, flourishing charities, and an increasing staff of workers, the decision should have been easy. Of the rules that had been read, the sisters unanimously favored that of the Presentation Order. It was Catherine's choice, too, if not her inclination. Perhaps she still entertained hope that there might yet be a middle course. If so, Dr. Blake's spiritual counsels effectively dispersed it.

XV

The Staff of the Little Poor Man

WHATEVER the circumstances which led to the appointment of a Franciscan to the chaplaincy at the House of Our Lady of Mercy, the event was to prove an enduring blessing. The disciple of the Little Poor Man brought the joyfulness and simplicity of his holy patron to the young Institute, characteristics that ultimately marked the spirit of the entire congregation. The House had no other chaplain in the foundress' lifetime.

In 1829 the Reverend Daniel Burke, O.F.M., had but recently come to the Merchant's Quay monastery from Limerick.[1] There he had been guardian of the friary from 1822 to 1828. Except for approximately two years spent in the South African missions, where he died toward the end of the next decade, his principal services for the rest of his life were devoted to the Sisters of Mercy and their charges.

When he assigned Father Burke to the Institute, His Grace gave the latter permission to say two Sunday Masses as well as daily Mass in the chapel. Meanwhile Miss McAuley had carried out the Archbishop's suggestion that a place in the chapel be reserved for the laity. The arrangement proved a great convenience to Catholics in the vicinity, for the parish church on the east side was not only a considerable distance away but was then under reconstruction. Dr. Murray had told Miss McAuley to accept offerings and use them for the needs of the refuge. The generous response of those who took advantage of the hospitality of St. Mary's on Baggot Street obviated the need for letters of solicitation.

Although it silenced some of the lay criticism, the new arrangement increased the annoyance of Miss McAuley's clerical antagonists. New letters of censure rebuked her for usurping masculine prerogatives, and criticized her efficiency in the establishment of a flourishing center of charity. Her habit of signing herself simply "C. McAuley" gave one clergyman his cue. According to Miss Warde, who was present when Catherine received the letter, he addressed her *C. McAuley, Esq.* and proceeded to lecture her on the masculine character of works of philanthropy, business, and finance.

Now femininity was a thing very dear to a nineteenth-century woman, but far more dear to Catherine McAuley was the name *Catholic* which she had suffered so much to retain. Inured to disapproval of her religion, she was particularly sensitive to clerical criticism, which she associated with ecclesiastical censure. She had never expected to draw either and was never quite prepared for it.

She who had withstood unflinchingly the oral and written criticism of some of Dublin's most prominent Catholics, she who without tears could suffer bereavement that cost her dear belied the address of the letter and re-acted most femininely. She cried at having unintentionally offended a priest of the Church. Nor did she offer apology, because her misdemeanor consisted in harboring the harborless and setting others an example to do the same.

There would have been scarcely time for an apology, had she one to give, because the writer of the letter dropped dead in the street not many days afterward.[2] Intermingled with the prayers that rose from St. Mary's chapel for his eternal peace was the awesomeness of eighteen-year old Frances Warde who in that very place had heard "the truly sanctified"[3] Dr. Blake warn the opposition of Divine displeasure. Her youthful imagination interpreted the occurrence in terms of retributive justice. Catherine reproved Miss Warde for this judgment, pointing out that the good priest's opposition had been well-intentioned. Not only was it well-intentioned but also well-directed, for his untoward sentiments proved a good discipline. C. McAuley, Lady of Mercy, however virile of mind and strong in virtue, needed an exercised spirit, a yet more pliant will for her new role as a Religious Sister of Mercy.

Before another year was far along, Catherine McAuley came to a decision. She would put herself as well as all her possessions completely in the hands of her spiritual directors. That meant one thing: she must submit to a canonically approved novitiate and become a religious.

Ironically, the only rule not accessible was that of the Irish Sisters of Charity, the community with which so many interested persons, cleric and lay, wished to affiliate the ladies at the Baggot Street House. Besides the Carmelites, the Poor Clares offered to share with the Mercy Institute their rule which had already been adapted to the needs of Ireland. Because of the long period of penal restrictions through which they had managed to survive, this Order had added the active charity of teaching to their usual contemplative service of mankind.

Archbishop Murray proffered his full co-operation, and proposed a plan which he thought might ease the transition. His plan is explained in the Derry manuscript.

> The Archbishop, knowing that it would be a source of much inconvenience if she must leave the infant establishment, with great kindness and consideration proposed to spare her the restraints of a novitiate among strangers by sending hither two professed religious of any order to whose rule she might choose to assimilate ours, so that she and the sisters thought fit might serve a novitiate under them. The remainder with the management of our temporal affairs should be directed by her. In this, however, she perceived many causes of objection, so that eventually it was decided that, if permission could be obtained from the superiors of the Presentation Convent, George's Hill, she and two of our little community should serve a novitiate there.

Therefore instead of introducing another phase of Franciscanism or forming the first active community of Carmelites in modern times, the Institute on Baggot Street was to continue its original dedication to Our Lady of Mercy and under that title become a new religious family in the Church.

Too much cannot be said of the kindness of the Carmelites, both priests and nuns. They were eager to have the Sisters of Mercy adopt and adapt their rule, and they were disappointed when the Sisters decided against it. If Miss McAuley had been less practical or less humble she would have accepted the honor of the ancient rule. Adaptation of it would have given scope to the foundress of a new religious congregation, but Catherine McAuley was too single-minded to perceive the opportunity. The Presentation Rule would require little revision to accommodate her needs. Besides, she saw the inconvenience of putting the Institute completely under the direction of an Order whose Provincials could be frequently changed. It so happened that Father O'Hanlon was consecutively Prior of St. Teresa's from the expiration of Father L'Estrange's provincialship till the end of Catherine McAuley's life. Yet she could not anticipate this favorable circumstance, and probably would not have been influenced by it, since the objection would surely apply at some future time.

Adoption of the Presentation Rule proved no impediment to Carmelite influence. The Sisters of Mercy remained the spiritual wards of the Discalced Carmelite Order during the entire period of their formation, and the contemplative strength of the congregation must be attributed largely to this early spiritual relationship.

In the spring of 1830[4] while Archbishop Murray was negotiating with Rome for permission to have some of the Sisters of Mercy admitted to the novitiate of an enclosed order, there came from Rome a Rescript of Indulgences for "Mme. McAuley of Dublin with companions and associates of the same charitable disposition." The mover in obtaining this favorable recognition from His Holiness Pope Pius VIII was not far to find, for the new Provincial of the Carmelites had gone to the Holy City in March with the ex-Provincial, Father Raymund O'Hanlon. Sometime in June probably, for the rescript is dated May 23, the new prior Father Whelan, who was substituting at Baggot Street for Father O'Hanlon, brought "*omnibus mulieribus in supradicta Domo*" the grant sent from Rome by Father L'Estrange. Coming as it did when opposition pressed and when currents of change disturbed the little group, this comforting mark of approval from the Vicar of Christ himself stimulated and consoled the sisters.

The petition, submitted by the Reverend Secretary of Propaganda, set forth so clearly the status of "Signora McAuley di Dublino," outlined her objectives and summarized the pursuits of her companions so comprehensively that there could have been no doubt in the mind of His Holiness Pope Pius VIII on the character of the Institute to whose members he made the monthly grant of plenary and partial indulgences.

By then, however, it had been decided that three of *"alle medesime"* would go to George's Hill novitiate, and "Signora McAuley" was in the midst of preparations.

On June 10 Georgina Moore returned to Baggot Street, followed on June 18 by Caroline Murphy. Neither Caroline nor anyone else at the time knew that her short life would burn itself out on the threshold of the venture like a holocaust of the Old Law.

She had a literally remarkable beauty and a precocious spirituality. Georgina Moore says of her life before she presented herself to Catherine McAuley: "She was born in the South of Ireland and from her childhood manifested dispositions of extraordinary piety. At the age of twelve or thirteen she made a private vow of perpetual chastity, and her devout and penitential exercises proved how sincerely she desired to give herself to God without any reserve."

Other details on those eighteen years before June 1830 are few.[5] Her father, a Killarney doctor, showed a particular interest in his daughter's talent for music. He had died suddenly the previous year. Caroline's mother must have been a deeply religious woman to permit this beautiful, gifted child to enroll in the Mercy Institute so soon after their bereavement.

July 12 Mary Anne Delany of Castle Durrow,[6] "whose prudent manners seemed to fit her to have charge of others," came opportunely. This eleventh-hour arrival actually had charge of household arrangements when the three left for George's Hill.

Sometime in July Dr. Blake asked Sister Catherine to assume a care that shows with what difficulty a person reputedly rich dispels the impression of inexhaustible wealth. Mary Ann Redmond, orphaned in one of the cities of the southern coast, had come to Dublin where she lived in some comfort on her inheritance. A swelling that doctors seemed unable to relieve developed on her knee and kept her confined to her apartment where a young cousin and an old nurse also lived. Dr. Blake first asked that the Sisters attend Miss Redmond in her home, but when the doctors decided on amputation he requested that the operation be performed at the House of Our Lady of Mercy so that surgeons could have the assistance of those skilled in tending the sick.

Miss Redmond was removed to Baggot Street and was given

the large front room upstairs. Anna Maria Doyle and Margaret Dunne, older and more experienced than the others, attended the doctors. Since surgery had been lifted from its barber-guild association not too many years before and since modern anaesthesia was not yet widely accepted in medical science, the operation proved a gruesome experience for the entire household. For several weeks Miss Redmond was attended night and day until she withdrew to a country place to complete recuperation.

She died there toward the end of the year, distributing her money with no mention of the charities at Baggot Street.[7] This was not the only instance of unrequited services to persons well able to pay professional nurses, had there been such. In the words of Georgina Moore, there were "a great many others, I assure you."

Though the Sisters devoted themselves freely to any recommended to their care, their dedication was to the poor and they necessarily depended on those in good circumstances for offerings to support their principal work. Miss McAuley's wealth had been considerably depleted by the building and the initial cost of establishing the charities.

One day in all this busy summer stands out in lovely relief: "wild" Willie's First Communion day. He and his sister Catherine, then about eleven, received in the convent chapel. Vacation in Dublin that year apparently included an intensive period of preparatory instruction and catechizing, which must have been a colt-breaking process for the gentle Franciscan chaplain, for Sister Mary Catherine and Sister Mary Teresa. When the First Communion day finally arrived, feminine beauty must have paled into secondary importance before the washed and combed lamb, Willie McAuley, who went forward with folded hands for his first personal contact with the Lamb of God, a contact that was to be maintained with fair regularity for nearly seventy-five years. He was the only one present who would see the twentieth century.

Always impressed by attractive persons with pleasing manners, Miss McAuley increased the number of lay sisters to five, only to learn that piety and personableness left something to be desired. Out of experiences like these she came to favor the quotation "Common sense is the most uncommon of qualities." She dismissed three of the lay sisters as part of her insurance of good order in the House during the proposed fifteen months' absence.

However long-suffering, she looked upon the stretch to 1832 as an emergency and provided for it with decision and prudence. She tactfully arranged the withdrawal of the socialites giving part-time service to the House. Merrion Square volunteers who had followed the O'Connell and Costello lead had not followed their good example on the premises but had interspersed their work with conversation degenerating into gossip. Since sisters completely devoted to the charities now numbered twelve, Sister Catherine used the pending change of status as an opportunity to eliminate the social chatter. "The House was no more thrown open to seculars except particular persons," Miss Moore declares, "and for fear we should look out of the windows white muffing was put on all windows facing the street."

With that final cloistral touch Miss McAuley appointed Mary Anne Delany to household affairs and Frances Warde to household finances, and took with her Anna Maria Doyle and one of the more recent arrivals, Elizabeth Harley. They crossed the city to George's Hill on the feast of the Nativity of Our Lady, September 8, 1830.

XVI

Whither Thou Wouldst Not

A CARRIAGE drew into the dingy street in ancient St. Michan's parish on the north side of Dublin and discharged three somberly dressed ladies at the Presentation Convent. From the agility with which they alighted one could hardly discern difference in their ages, but Reverend Mother M. Angela Doyle who awaited them within had no difficulty in distinguishing among them. The senior was definitely past middle age; the other two were very young indeed, being little beyond twenty.

There had been difference of opinion among the Presentation Sisters on accepting and training subjects for another congregation. With superiors concurring and the majority assenting, a favorable decision had been returned to Dr. Murray, and the Reverend Mother now met her Mercy novices not only with the hospitality of the Irish but with the kindliness of a far-sighted religious of no ordinary spirituality. If anyone could make Catherine McAuley feel at home in a convent, Mother M. Angela would seem to be the person.

To expect Catherine McAuley to feel at home in a convent, however, was to expect a prodigy that was not forthcoming. If there were to be miracles, they were to be in the order of grace, not of nature.

Referring to Catherine and September 8, 1830, Georgina Moore, as Mother M. Clare wrote: "She often said it was so hard a struggle for her to remain on account of meeting there many things repugnant to her feelings, that had she not the establishment of the Institute most deeply at heart she would that very evening have sent for a coach to take her back to Baggot Street."[1]

There in a sentence is Catherine McAuley's personal history not only for September 8, 1830, but also for the 460 days following. Convent life held no more attraction for her at close range than it did speculatively.

Though someone has said that souls are drawn to religious life either through attraction or conviction, it seems reasonable to conjecture that most religious vocations are attended by some degree of both. Few persons arrive by the stark way of conviction alone. Of these one might venture to say that the toughness and flexibility of spirit developed in such constant struggle against nature augur special purpose in the designs of Providence.

As for Anna Maria Doyle, she was exactly where she had aimed at arriving, had she not been diverted by a walk down Baggot Street some half dozen years previous; but Miss Warde's friend, Miss Harley, had arrived where a year ago she had no notion she would ever be. Her Presentation superiors came to support Anna Maria Doyle's opinion of her. "She was a saintly creature," the latter wrote.

No sixteen-year old novice in a foreign community far from her native land felt more interiorly bleak than the gracious, smiling postulant, already past the half-century mark, who that September eighth sat among the Presentation novices toward the end of the table. Practiced in dissembling her feelings, Sister Catherine, as she was entitled to be called by Presentation custom, joined cheerfully in the recreation until it was time for community prayers. She then retired to the chapel and knelt with the others, not *before* the altar since at that time the altar faced the small chapel. God Himself seemed to be looking away from her.

As she climbed the long flight of stairs to her cell, she would have taken comfort could she have known that the Jervis Street Hospital outlined against the sky on the near horizon was waiting for her spiritual daughters or could she have seen beyond to the north the great *Mater Misericordiae* rise out of the future. To her that evening the window on the landing framed only as much of Dublin as it could claim, her native city, so familiar yet now so strange.

In the next corridor she turned and mounted a second flight of stairs. Every step was an effort of will. How gladly would she send for a coach to take her back across the river to her small religious family!

At the top of the second stairs she turned into an inner hall running parallel to the main third. This small corridor was dedicated to St. Teresa. Making her way to her cell in the *magnum silentium,* that great aid to meditation and union with God, she should have found consolation in the thought of that other foundress, the patronal guide of her present way. But the role that St. Teresa had shaped through spiritual inspiration and initiative was being shaped for Catherine McAuley; therefore she made no connection. Whereas St. Teresa carved her way "with the sword of the spirit," Catherine McAuley operated as part of a "machine that went on of itself." After her congregation came into being, she gave this explanation whenever anyone imputed credit to her. A fresh figure of speech in the early days of the Industrial Age, it more aptly applies from the period of the assembly line. Piece by piece circumstances fitted her to providential usefulness. All her religious life, now beginning, Catherine McAuley knew the sense of uselessness except as a piece in a plan. Perhaps at no time did she feel more bereft of any direction of herself than this first night as a postulant.

Sister Catherine's cell, the last in the corridor, also looked out on the Jervis Street Hospital, but its one window was effectively shuttered to remind the religious of her cloistered position. No occupant ever needed the reminder less. Though the future was as effectively shuttered as the world outside, Catherine McAuley must have thought of the past that night with Queen Street and St. Paul's so near, with Arran Street and St. Mary's to the east. True, St. Mary's was dismantled now. That could have been a comforting thought. As those other times had passed, this too would pass, the months till December eighth, then the year of her novitiate. December 8, 1831, would come at last. Perhaps because of Carmelite guidance and their semi-cloistered life since June 1829, the postulancy might be waived. She would ask Dr. Blake.

Whether this idea was an inspiration of her first or later hours at George's Hill, she did ask Dr. Blake about a concession. One of the Moore letters recalls:

She used to relate the conversation in which she represented the right she thought she had to get the habit at once. She complained to Dr. Blake, who was not pleased at her seeking any exemption. His answer was: "The devil is there."[2]

In other words, God works from eternity in patience. Catherine McAuley's natural repugnance, her natural impatience, assuming the guise of practicality, revealed a ruse familiar to every spiritual director, the plea for exemption or change under pretext of a greater good.

Sister Catherine, humbled under the rebuke, set herself to follow common life under the Presentation Rule. Often during the succeeding months she must have been struck by the similarity in the original intention of her two predecessors, Nano Nagle and Teresa Mulally. All three as seculars had set out to establish schools for poor girls. Miss Nagle's ideal, more nearly like her own, included visitation of the sick poor also. The failure of Miss Nagle's every attempt to introduce a religious community to the work of visitation shows how difficult it was to break down traditions. Nuns wanted to be nuns and that meant enclosure. Moreover, the religious Rule adapted to service among the people was far to find. Having brought one group from the continent to learn belatedly that they would not work beyond their convent, Nano Nagle established with Papal approval just such a religious congregation as would carry on her work, only to have it succumb to tradition after her death. Her congregation, originally dedicated to the Sacred Heart, became the Presentation Order.

Teresa Mulally began her work independently in Dublin, identifying it with Miss Nagle's on perceiving the similarity of their aim. The very month of Catherine McAuley's birth Teresa had journeyed to Cork to negotiate affiliation with Miss Nagle. The results Sister Catherine now saw all about her. They served ultimately to strengthen the character of her congregation in its active service beyond the cloister. On an occasion in her later life she made direct reference to the thwarting of Miss Nagle's efforts.[3] Pointing out the pernicious effect of adding to prescribed prayers, she set an emphatic example against the practice. By then she had learned that innovation is another form of the delusion of greater good.

Archbishop Murray had proved the practicability of the uncloistered ideal by founding the Irish Sisters of Charity. Its desirability needed no demonstration.

All modern religious statutes derive their substance from one of the ancient monastic Rules, minor changes requiring specific Papal endorsement. The Presentation Rule is basically Augustinian. More telling than the Rules and Constitutions are the variously titled supplementary manuals that explain and amplify the text. An outline of Catherine McAuley's manner of life at George's Hill can be found in the *Presentation Ceremonial.* Anyone familiar with the daily schedule of a Sister of Mercy is struck with a similarity and a dissimilarity: the order of prayers and even the principal prayers are the same; the emphasis differs. From her experience of cloistered life Catherine McAuley determined on two fundamentals for the congregation of Mercy: in prayer simplicity rather than multiplicity; in penance the self-discipline of an unfaltering charity as rudimentary. The Presentation Rule she adopted almost in its entirety; the Ceremonial she reduced to essence. A charity-imbued simplicity should pervade the atmosphere of every Convent of Mercy and a single-minded kindliness should characterize every member of the congregation. What Archbishop Murray's direction on the Presentation Rule did to synthesize these features will be explained in its place.

In Mother M. Angela, Catherine McAuley again found the right person for her need. Reverend Mother took the senior Mercy postulant under her own direction, exempting Catherine from the jurisdiction of the novice mistress, Mother M. Teresa Higgins, a convert of old-line asceticism. This arrangement prevailed through Catherine McAuley's postulancy and halfway through the noviceship.

Meanwhile, the three candidates were admitted to Reception. The ceremony, due December 8, was deferred till the following day because the Archbishop officiated at St. Mary's on its patronal feast. Below the very altarpiece before which Catherine McAuley in old St. Mary's had fought her way clear to faith Archbishop

Murray that day offered Mass in honor of Mary Immaculate. "I will greatly rejoice in the Lord," sang the Introit, "and my soul shall be joyful in my God: for he hath clothed me with the garments of salvation, and with the robe of justice he hath covered me, as a bride adorned with her jewels."

The novices-elect spent the feast in retreat looking forward to their clothing on the ninth. The two juniors undoubtedly had the enthusiasm of the young for the bridal attire worn symbolically by the candidate on this occasion. In recognition of the color proper to the ceremony, Catherine McAuley wore a long white shoulder scarf over a lavender brocade gown. Perhaps as a mark of special consideration Mother M. Angela gave some attention to the coiffure of Sister Catherine, but neither Mother Angela nor a sister who volunteered her services could have qualified as hairdressers. When the procession formed, the nuns were so much amused by Catherine's appearance that their reaction became one of the ancedotes of the day. Catherine was sent to rearrange her hair before being presented to the Archbishop. Her unconcern at the spectacle she made might indicate subjugation of whatever vanity little Willie had perceived. Her indifference, however, was probably more philosophical than virtuous.

Regrettably, there is no record of guests, no mention of Miss Doyle's priest brother and elderly parents, no reference to Miss Harley's military father[4] nor to any witnesses from Baggot Street, no allusion to Dr. Blake. Besides the Sisters, only the Archbishop is mentioned in the account.

It is quite certain that no members of the Institute attended. Georgina Moore's assertion that after the chapel was dedicated the Sisters "went out no more . . . except to visit the sick" finds support in the entire period of Catherine McAuley's direction of her congregation. The business of foundations, the necessity of going out to Mass in the absence of a chaplain, and purposeful visits to other Convents of Mercy later took the Sisters from Baggot Street, but for the present they left the House only to visit the sick. In those days, of course, ordinary business could be transacted either by letter or by summoning merchants, lawyers, and other business men to the convent parlor. Eventually the Sisters staffed schools not on convent premises, and changing times broadened their field of service beyond their own grounds. The only persons from Baggot Street who visited George's Hill during the fifteen months of Catherine's stay were her younger niece and her godchild, neither yet members of the Institute.

The relationship between Reverend Mother and the Mercy foundress was more consultative than superior-subject in character. Undoubtedly from her experience with Mother M. Angela, Catherine drew some of her own wisdom in dealing with subjects. The writer of the Dublin manuscript says: "[Mother Catherine] was with us precisely as my own mother was with her family, or rather we used less ceremony than was used at home."

When the names *Teresa, Clare* and *Angela* were proposed to her for herself and companions, Catherine felt quite free to insist that they retain their baptismal names, prefixing *Mary*. The Blessed Virgin thereby became their personal as well as their community patroness. Co-foundresses though they were, Catherine never lost sight of how incidental her position was. How hard she had tried to avoid the role!

Modification of the Presentation habit for the new congregation was long under consideration. Vetoing Catherine's preference for a black guimp of habit material seems more in keeping with Mother M. de Sales' suggestion than Mother Angela's. At any rate, a white guimp won favor with the Mercy foundress only on the Presentation superior's insistence that linens were traditional in the Church. For the novitiate period the three novices wore Presentation dress, and evolution of the Mercy habit was left temporarily to the future.[5]

On other matters Mother M. Angela gave Sister Catherine the benefit of her experience and wisdom. She would not permit the Mercy foundress to follow her practice of complete abstinence from food on Good Friday but required her to submit to the Presentation custom of a slight collation taken in a penitential attitude. Knowing to what lengths imprudent zeal can go, she inquired into practices at Baggot Street and recommended changes. She realized that strenuous work and daily out-of-door walking in Dublin alleys in Irish weather were new to the young ladies supporting the charity center on the south side, and Mother M. Angela feared the effects of such unaccustomed hardships on delicate constitutions. Two of her recommendations were to have ale served at dinner and to replace with hair mattresses the Carmelite palliasses in use at the House.

Georgina Moore's account of Reverend Mother's influence runs:

We used to sleep on straw palliasses. Those who desired to be comfortable cut the stitches, but most of us were quite happy on the hard stitched ones . . . To get so many [hair mattresses] at once was expensive. Someone offering to do it cheap, instead of horse hair put in cows' or dogs' or something so dreadful that the smell for several months was most sickening—I assure you, a penance.[6]

That penance they would never have conceived, though their penances were as diverse as individual attraction to particular saints and unguided fervor could devise. Georgina's sister describes these in a paragraph:

Sister M. Delany had been left in charge of the household affairs and of the duties of the Institute, but as to the spirituals, the others were not much inclined to be guided by the junior of all, so everyone mismanaged her own spiritualities in her own way. One took to fasting, another took the discipline, another slept in haircloth, while a fourth and fifth thought proper to remain up half the night at their prayers. To this last piece of perfection, however, Father O'Hanlon put a stop. I am not sure whether it was he or Father Burke who, having to be out late at night to upper Baggot Street, saw lights in the cells, but it was he who came the next day to forbid it and went to George's Hill to tell the Foundress, who also forbade it. Moreover, he and Father Burke made it a point to walk round the House odd nights just after ten o'clock to see that all the lights were out. These freaks [of penance] told on the health. All grew more or less sickly . . .[7]

The year 1831 was full of trial for Catherine McAuley. Of all the reports from Baggot Street none concerned her more than the state of health of the sisters. Catherine Byrn was a bed patient during the early months of the year. The Presentation Sisters sent over a relic which seemed to effect an instant cure. The foundress, however, questioned the imputation of a miracle. Apparently she knew her young cousin's temperament, for the doctor's comment tells much. "There was nothing surprising in the suddenness of her recovery since the nerves were involved." As it sometimes happens, the real invalid among them was that day one of the most active members of the household, concealing her debility and serving anywhere her alertness to need directed.

This first illness gave Sister Mary Catherine an opportunity to send to Baggot Street a visiting priest trained in asceticism. The Reverend M. de Luynes said Mass on the feast of St. Joseph and applied the relic afterward. The patient rose for Benediction that day and thenceforth gave every evidence of complete recovery.

The foundress hoped that the Reverend Father Luynes[8] might use the occasion of his visit to leaven with prudence spiritual practices at Baggot Street, for she wrote recommending that the sisters consult him and listen to his advice. How much profit resulted from his visit cannot be judged, since Georgina Moore's comment is the only one extant: "Although I tried and thought to get some difficulty to propound with him, I was unfortunately too stupid." She dismisses him and the subject with this information: "He afterwards went to America as missioner." By the time Georgina Moore was writing her reminiscences, one of the twelve that day present was herself a missioner in the United States where she established the congregation in the Middle Atlantic States, in the Middle West, and in New England.

But Frances Warde, twenty-year old manager of House finance, had immediate problems concerning neither missions nor finance.[9] As housekeeper, the treasurer had nominal charge of the lay sisters. Of the two left at Baggot Street when Catherine McAuley went to George's Hill, one remained.[10] Hannah Fulham was an attractive and active little person of some piety and considerable peculiar inventiveness. Frances Warde, who was fond of her, persevered in the hope that she could be trained; but either the chaplain or the spiritual director on one of his visits to the foundress advised dismissal, for word came from George's Hill that Hannah was to go. Her final performance serves as well as any of her behavior to substantiate the report made to Sister Mary Catherine.

Notified that she must leave, Hannah appeared next morning with her head completely shorn. The story she told was probably her masterpiece. She did not know how or when nor where her hair had gone but its disappearance proved, she pointed out, that her head was meant for the veil.

Ladies who had never before had ambition for sleuthery set to work and with great difficulty uncovered the evidence that broke the case. Faced with it, Hannah admitted the tonsorial feat and withdrew with her peculiar talents, leaving Frances Warde at last convinced that her lieutenant's wayward imagination eluded reform.

By the time Catherine Byrn laid vestments for the High Mass to be celebrated on the Feast of the Sacred Heart this year, lovely Caroline Murphy was dying. In the last weeks of her life the sisters became acutely aware of her virtues. Then they remembered how much they had taken for granted. Then they realized her serviceableness. It now occurred to them that, having no superior, she had considered every one of the eleven hers. They recalled, too, that when a particularly disagreeable task had to be done, she arrived first and stayed latest or contrived to direct them elsewhere while she did the most menial work.[11] As they looked back on the times she had appeared with work-blackened hands, someone remembered a habit she had of brushing a hand up across her face when she saw that she could not avoid a visitor in the hall. Her smudged face provoked a smile. This was her ruse to spare herself the embarrassment of an appraising look.

Mother Austin Carroll wrote of her: "A perfect blond, her beauty was more striking than Mary Teresa's—the latter grew on you, the former dazzled you at once."

Perhaps she was beautiful as she lay dying. The eyewitness, Georgina Moore, does not advert to superficialities:

Although she lived but a short time, she gave examples of virtue rarely to be met with. She practiced an entire obedience to all and on all occasions, though there was then no religious obligation to it. With profound humility she employed herself in the most abject offices in such manner that it was not till after her death that many of her humiliations were discovered. As her appearance was highly calculated to attract admiration, when she knew that strangers were to pass through, she used to blacken her face, as it were accidentally, that she might be despised. She had very delicate health but concealed her illness until it was too manifest and too late for remedies. When forced to yield to the violence of the malady (rapid consumption) she continued to evince her joyful resignation to the Divine Will with sincere humility. She prepared for her last hour by a general confession of her whole life and, having received the Last Sacraments on the Feast of St. John Baptist, she expired on the Eve of Sts. Peter and Paul in sentiments of piety which edified and surprised not only her companions but the Confessor and Chaplain who knelt beside her in her dying moments recommending her soul to God.[12]

Attended therefore by Father O'Hanlon "of the Virgin of Carmel" and by one of the spiritual sons of the Little Poor Man, Sister Caroline, age nineteen, died on June 29, 1831. The record just quoted closes:

As we had then no habit, she was buried in the brown Carmelite habit of the Third Order . . . . The good priests of Clarendon Street also allowed us a place in their principal vault under the altar where only priests were allowed to be interred before.

Twelve other Sisters of Mercy were interred in the same holy place in the next nine years, among them the foundress' two nieces.

XVII

A Piece in a Machine

When news of Sister Caroline's death reached George's Hill, Sister Mary Catherine was already in the most trying period of her noviceship. Pentecost elections that year had brought to the office of Mother Superior Sister M. de Sales Knowd, a person to be admired rather than loved. Retaining Mother M. Teresa Higgins in charge of the novitiate, Reverend Mother made no distinction among its constituents. Neither did Mother Teresa. To use a conventual figure, Sister Mary Catherine became a number on the bell card, assigned to routine duties in routine manner and corrected impartially with the youngsters who, for the most part, comprise a novitiate.

She was appointed to assist Sister Mary Anne Doyle in the sacristy, to serve the sisters at table and to perform tasks she had given to her servants three years earlier. One notable difference distinguishes the comparison: she was directed to her work with none of the affability she had shown servants. It was not that Mother M. Teresa lacked affability but that she had definite ideas on where and how it should be displayed. Being very young, only a dozen years professed, she had definite ideas on a great many subjects.

To understand Mother Teresa one must remember that she was a convert accustomed to interpret by the letter as is common in the early years of conversion. A Presentation Sister trained by her has left a brief memoir from which the following excerpts are drawn:

> Though she attended to the secular education of her novices to fit them for school duties, her greatest concern was to implant in their minds and hearts true and solid virtues . . . She was vigilant in the extreme so

that scarcely a step was taken by the novices which came not under the eye of this watchful Mother . . . . Her anxious turn of mind caused at times over-solicitude for the progress of those under her care. She would lead them to a profound sense of their own nothingness, real crucifixion of the senses and passions, true obedience, great poverty of spirit, perfect disengagement from creatures, death to self and devoted love for the duty of instruction. If in her desire to maintain regular discipline she seemed rigid in her ideas, she was still more austere toward herself . . . . I cannot fail to remark her sweet spirit of general charity. This precept she ever labored to instill in the novices, warning them in the strongest terms against particular friendships, the bane of religious communities. This was not mere precept, for she did not teach until she first practiced, being convinced that the force of words avails little if not preceded and accompanied by example.[1]

Young, exacting, confirmed in an ascetical ideal borrowed from the continent, Mother Teresa represented the essence of conventual life as it had repelled Catherine McAuley. Mother Teresa and the new Reverend Mother, moreover, had been among the unyielding in their conviction that the Presentation novitiate could not train candidates for another congregation.

So while the death of Sister Caroline grieved the heart of Sister Mary Catherine, the trials of her daily life invaded her very soul. The middle-aged novice underwent discipline established to curb the impetuosity of teen-agers and to groom unformed characters. It included activity suited to supple muscles and ready joints. With equanimity she went through paces aimed at grounding a novice in *a profound sense of her own nothingness, real crucifixion of the senses and passions, true obedience, great poverty of spirit, perfect disengagement from creatures, death to self and devoted love for the duty of instruction.*

Whatever Sister Mary Catherine lacked in these ways was to be supplied. Since she had been teaching almost as many years as Mother M. Teresa had lived, one might suppose that Catherine McAuley could train Mother Teresa, particularly since she had only recently been doing intensive study and observation to prepare herself for the Poor School on Baggot Street. She had visited the most estimable schools in Dublin, had evaluated the English systems and, not entirely satisfied, had journeyed to France to examine the best in general education there. But all this she had done as a secular, however religiously minded, and a Catholic school classroom operates on an integrated philosophy. Catherine's associates considered her not only a born teacher but an inspired one, particularly in her teaching of religion. Yet the excellent teacher is always the unfinished learner, and there can be no doubt that Sister Mary Catherine learned much from her experience in the classroom at George's Hill.

On the matter of "disengagement from creatures" Sister Mary Catherine also had something to learn, and the vigilant Mother of Novices used her own teaching methods.

When the guardian of Dr. Macauley's children showed pleasure at Dr. Fitzgerald's being announced, she was told to send him a polite message of excuse. She probably had not seen her nephews for months and the prohibited visit left her in a state of concern. What had Dr. Fitzgerald come to tell her?

Once she was penalized for being a little slow in dismissing her godchild, ten years old, and her niece, twelve. The next time Teresa Byrn and Catherine Macauley came from Baggot Street to see her, she had to read the *Imitation* to them for the entire half hour. During another of their visits, Mother M. Teresa entered the parlor and scolded Sister Mary Catherine in their presence. Upset by the incident, little Teresa exclaimed: "Do, dear godmother, come home from that cross lady."

Thereupon the two future Sisters of Mercy received their first instruction on the nature and purpose of religious discipline. They seem to have gone away impressed by Sister Mary Catherine's sweetness and lovableness rather than by the homily which, however, bore its fruit.

These and other examples of Catherine McAuley's virtue under trial Sister M. Camillus (Teresa) Byrn later set down in a memoir unfortunately lost.[2] What the children were in no position to observe, Sister Mary Anne Doyle summarized for the writer of the Dublin manuscript:

Reverend Mother went through her noviceship in a most edifying manner. Her cheerfulness was the admiration of all, though she had much care on her mind, still directing Baggot Street and suffering from a disease of the gums. For some time she was treated with indulgence and respect but, a change of superiors taking place, she was put under a young and very strict Mistress of Novices. She then went through every humble office. Our noviceship was severe, being only one year. Our holy Mistress left nothing undone for our spiritual improvement. My dear companion, Sister Mary Elizabeth, was not sufficiently strong (besides being very scrupulous) so that her health was broken down. Her death about four months after her Profession was a great trial to us, particularly to me. There was some difficulty regarding our Profession as our vows could not be the same as those made by the community. They submitted the difficulty to most Reverend Dr. Murray, who removed it by the form of vow which he proposed. He came himself some time before our Profession and examined us, particularly on our Profession in the new order we were about to erect, called "of the Sisters of Mercy."[3]

A less sympathetic account than this appears in the Dublin manuscript:

Sister Mary Anne was the favourite. Sister M. Elizabeth Harley they pronounced a living saint, but keeping her employed cleaning shoes and cooking utensils in a damp underground kitchen without fire fostered her constitutional tendency to consumption. The Foundress ventured to remonstrate but it was then too late. She was incurable before Profession. As for the Foundress herself, a few of the nuns understood her and valued her highly but the Reverend Mother and Mistress of Novices kept her in perpetual agitation by giving her to understand that they would receive her companions to Profession at the end of the year and postpone hers, or even reject her altogether. This, had it been done, would have ruined the Institute altogether, for much less than charge of motherhouse proved too much for Sister Mary Anne and, as I have said, Sister M. Elizabeth was dying.

The best that can be said for this second account is that the writer was a realist. Against her implied criticism stands the foundress' appreciation, reported by Mother M. Clare in the London manuscript:

She often said that, during no time of her life was she so happy as when a novice, living under obedience and, were she to have a choice, it would be to continue always in that state . . . .

She used often tell of the edification she had received in the Convent of George's Hill from one of the nuns who never spoke of herself or her employments so that it was not until a change of offices that our Reverend Mother discovered she had previously exercised an important and busy charge in the community. But it was not only this nun whose piety was remembered by her; the Superioress, Mother Mary Francis Knowd, had been a subject of her admiration for her humble patience and extraordinary regularity. Though suffering greatly from rheumatism, this holy religious never failed to rise at five and was one of the first in the [chapel.] With regard to humility she had so entirely overcome a naturally violent temper that she did not seem to know that anything unkind or disrespectful could be said of her. As it happened one day, that our Reverend Mother had, in ignorance of facts, said something which might seem a censure on [Mother Francis de Sales'] arrangements, she went as soon as possible to beg pardon. The good Superioress told her it did not signify and added impressively the following maxim which our Reverend Mother used to repeat: "Never let anything cause you trouble or anxiety which is not an offense against God."

Hard as Sister Mary Catherine's novitiate was, her attitude toward it implies that she had brought to it a great deal of solid virtue which increased under drastic exercise.

If she was helpless to relieve Sister Mary Elizabeth, she was no better off with regard to her associates at Baggot Street. When donations for the poor began to dwindle, Anne O'Grady had sought and had reluctantly been granted permission to solicit in person. The summer of 1831 was particularly warm for Dublin, and all-day walking in the heat and other self-imposed rigors told on Sister Mary Aloysius' health. By fall she was in a state of hopeless decline. Meanwhile, Mary Teresa Macauley had suffered hemorrhage, the forerunner of fatal illness.

These reports came from Baggot Street when Sister Mary Catherine was most harassed by the likelihood of having her profession postponed or denied, for a religious community sits in council two months previous to the expiration of a canonical period and decides whether candidates may be admitted to profession. The term of Sister Mary Catherine's novitiate would expire December 9, and early in October the Presentation Sisters would have to determine by vote whether or not the Mercy novices could be admitted to vows under customary form. Anyone familiar with the form will readily perceive the problem. Vows are made "according to the rule and constitutions" of a particular order or congregation.

Whatever of self lurked in Catherine McAuley's devotion to her work was now on the rack. Her naturally compassionate heart must, like the Hearts of those other Two pictured over the altar at Mary of Mercy chapel, be proffered in her own hand to Divine purpose. The exclamation that later came so spontaneously to her lips, "Whatever God pleases," was wrung from her now when her human heart yearned toward one dedication: the poor as she had seen them suffer, as she had ministered to their needs for nearly thirty years.

Was God going to refuse her the only way that opened or that, till now, had seemed open? The Presentation superiors thought it likely. Mother Teresa recommended the Litany of the Saints to Catherine and her companions as support in the few remaining weeks till a decision would be reached. Winged by Obedience, the daily plea, so soon to rise from hundreds of Mercy Convents, now petitioned aid of the Church Triumphant: *God the Father, the Son, the Holy Ghost; Holy Mary, Mother, Virgin; Angels and Archangels; Patriarchs, Prophets, Apostles; Disciples, Innocents, Martyrs and Confessors; Holy Founders and Foundresses; Men and Women, Saints of God; from all evil, through All-Good, deliver us; vouchsafe to confirm and preserve us in Thy holy service; spare us, hear us, have mercy on us, have mercy on us . . .*

XVIII

Religious Called Sisters of Mercy

THE Presentation Sisters decided to lay their difficulty before Archbishop Murray. How could they in conscience give vows according to *their* approved rule and constitutions to religious who would not observe enclosure? This was no mere nicety, for even yet solemn vows are not permitted to uncloistered religious women.

Archbishop Murray resolved the difficulty by proposing a form of simple perpetual vows to effect the transition:

In the name of Our Lord Jesus Christ and under the protection of His Blessed Mother, I, Catherine Elizabeth McAuley, called in Religion Sister Mary Catherine, do vow perpetual poverty, chastity and obedience, and to persevere until the end of my life in the Congregation called of the Sisters of Mercy, established for the Visitation of the Sick Poor, and charitable instruction of poor females, according to the Rules and Constitutions of the Presentation Order, subject to such alterations as shall be approved by the Archbishop, you, my Lord and most Reverend Father in God, Daniel Murray, Archbishop of this Diocese, and Reverend Mother Elizabeth Knowd, called in Religion Mary Francis de Sales, Superioress of this Convent of the Presentation in the year of Our Lord one thousand eight hundred and thirty-one on this twelfth day of December.

Since simple vows have remained the norm of the Holy See for religious congregations of women, the status of the new Institute as herein established had only to be confirmed by Papal endorsement. The Presentation Order retained a signed copy of the vow form for each of the three and gave the new religious their individual professions.

Except for a circumstance already mentioned, Foundation Day would have been the feast of the Immaculate Conception. On December 8, the patronal feast of the Archbishop's parish, His Grace officiated at the Pro-Cathedral. He therefore appointed December 12 for the profession of the first Sisters of Mercy.

What meditations the liturgy of the feast offered those preparing for religious profession!

The Lord possessed me in the beginning of His ways . . . . He that shall find me shall find life and shall have salvation from the Lord . . . . They that work by me shall not sin . . . . They that explain me shall have life everlasting . . . . Draw us, O Immaculate Virgin: we will run after thee . . . . Come and hear, all ye that fear God: and I will tell you what great things the Lord hath done for my soul . . . . Wisdom hath built herself a house.

By coincidence, the dates assigned for both reception and profession still made specific connection with Our Lady of the Immaculate Conception, since December 12, 1831 was the tercentenary of the apparitions of Mary Immaculate in the New World. These apparitions from their detail have been identified with the Immaculate Conception. December 9 to 12, moreover, covered the time span of the Guadalupe message.

Those who like to draw parallels will find one in Catherine McAuley's effort to evade the responsibility of founding a religious congregation and the Indian neophyte's taking another road to avoid the Lady's importunity about the business of a shrine in her honor. The compassionate Mother ("*piadosa Madre*") would not be circumvented or denied in either case.

"What road is this thou takest?" she had asked Juan Diego,[1] as she intercepted him and reconfirmed him in her service.

Foreshadowing attended this connection with Our Lady of the Americas,[2] for the greater part of the Western Hemisphere was still missionary territory and, unlikely as it might seem that December twelfth, a half dozen years later the foundress of the new congregation dedicated to the "merciful Mother" would volunteer her personal service to the cause.

But the Dublin poor and the needs of her spiritual children formed the boundaries of Sister Mary Catherine's missionary vision on December 12, 1831. They were so present to her that she declined further hospitality from the foster community and accepted Dr. Blake's offer of transportation to Baggot Street.

"So impatient was she to return," Georgina Moore declares, "that she offended the nuns by leaving the very day of her profession." In fact, Sister Mary Anne's recollections seem to imply that they left before breakfast.

That breach of Irish courtesy a person of Mother M. Francis de Sales' disposition might condone, but Mother Teresa must have had a momentary impulse to correct. Yet the needs of Sister Catherine's religious family had grown acute, and need superseded the code of hospitality. Besides, Father Blake represented authority. He who had counseled severely against shortening the time of probation now sanctioned immediate departure.

Of the leave-taking Sister Mary Anne reports: "Before we left the convent, Reverend Dr. Blake in the presence of the superiors congratulated us on the manner in which we spent our novitiate, the edification we had given and hoped we would infuse the same spirit into those to whom we were returning."

On the way across the city Dr. Blake reminded them that this was the real beginning, the foundation day of a new congregation in the Church. It was, in fact, part of a great movement[3] that swept upon Rome a flood of petitions to recognize religious institutes of women for active charity among the people. Nearly six hundred such congregations came into existence in the nineteenth century to care for expanding missions and to combat the evils of the Industrial Age. The Holy See, as if under pressure of canonizing a saint through popular acclaim, reversing an attitude of centuries, gave approval to the uncloistered religious state. Ever alert, however, to the dangers of uncontrolled fervor, she set up a new tribunal and codified norms, incidentally establishing another school of spiritual experts, the Doctors of Canon Law for Religious.

But this was the dawning future. Dr. Blake discharged the three Sisters of Mercy at their House where, crossing the threshold, they entered what now became the first Convent of Mercy. Fifteen months before, they had left nine ladies in charge, and nine postulants awaited them in the chapel, two recruits replacing two absentees.

Several weeks before the death of Sister Caroline (June 28,

1831), a Miss Mary Jones of Wales had come to Dublin to join the Sisters of Mercy, and the foundress herself arranged the admission of Miss Anna Carroll (July 24, 1831), niece to one of the Presentation Sisters at George's Hill.

Miss Jones' history bore a certain resemblance to the foundress', for a childhood impression had also been her guiding star. During an illness early in Mary Jones' life, the family nurse had taken her to a Catholic Church to petition a cure. The recollection of a priest with a chalice in his hand stayed with her. Yet so completely Protestant were her surroundings that she could never learn the meaning of the scene. Then in young womanhood, while visiting relatives in London, she came upon a Catholic chapel and saw again a priest with a chalice in his hand. The end of her search was the beginning of a spiritual transition. In London she met the founder of the Irish Christian Brothers who recommended the Sisters of Mercy to her.[4] He, like many others, had the impression that Catherine McAuley was a convert.

Ceremony days in a religious community are marked by spiritual jubilation and a particular joyousness. The atmosphere has something of First Communion Day about it, though it actually resembles nothing the religious has known. In its joyful character this ceremony day has never had an equal in the congregation. Even Anne O'Grady took on hope. Hope of recovery?—no, a larger view opened as her eyes examined the habit of the Sisters of Mercy, so like the Presentation habit she herself had worn for many months. So like, yet so unlike! The soft puckered coif front and short deep-hemmed coif resembled the headpiece of the Irish Sisters of Charity.[5] Catherine McAuley's choice of headdress for her congregation certainly testified to her admiration for Mother Mary Augustine's wisdom in designing a habit for "walking nuns." Had the Presentation superior not insisted on a linen guimp, there would have been a black cape. The white coif, fitted to the face by a draw string run up through the coif hem, across in the small dimity hem, and down to be tied and concealed under the chin, was strikingly like Mother M. Augustine's.

Anne O'Grady would never wear the Mercy habit nor make religious profession. Her desire had been to devote her life to the poor in an organized group, but the prospect of taking vows had always upset her. She had spent herself for the poor, and others would enter into her labors. She, too, was a piece in a plan, a test piece. Work and suffering and, yes, dying were her contribution. Sister Mary Catherine, who had taught so many to die well, had come home in time to teach her, too, and Anne O'Grady was happier than the rest.

One of the household that day has left her recollections of Catherine McAuley as a religious superior:

She was in stature rather above middle height, well proportioned and erect, with a fair complexion and high colour; her eyes were large and penetrating, of a very bright blue with a most kind expression; her manner dignified and reserved, tender and compassionate to the poor, maternally affectionate to the Sisters; her movements quiet, her words few; her whole demeanour showing constant recollection of the presence of God.[6]

The tempering influence of such a person must have brought glad recognition to her associates. Her presence at the evening recreation was what it had always been, a cheerful leaven. Sister M. Vincent Hartnett says:

Whatever trials or difficulties Reverend Mother had to contend with, she never appeared sad or dejected and except those Sisters whose position in the community made them aware of her crosses, none knew she had any, and even to those there was not the least trace of care discernible at recreation. The seniors used, in fact, to be surprised at her liberty of spirit and at her unembarrassed playfulness and cheerfulness while the young sisters would crowd round her, charmed with the joyfulness and sweetness of her conversation as well as with the pleasure it evidently gave her to contribute to their happiness. She never failed to introduce some passage or reflection that would raise their thoughts and hearts above this passing scene, yet so judiciously and pleasingly that, while her words produced the desired effect, no one ever thought them approaching to a sermon or in any way unsuited to the unbending of the mind for which recreation is established.[7]

The topic of this evening's recreation was the Archbishop's visit next day. Many matters had to be discussed before His Grace arrived. The horarium must be made completely conventual. How could the Presentation Rule be adjusted to meet their needs till the Mercy Rule was ready? Those longest in the work must be interviewed preliminary to receiving the habit—Catherine Byrn, Frances Warde, Georgina Moore, Mary Teresa Macauley, Margaret Dunne and Mary Anne Delany. For some reason, Anna Carroll was added to these six.

As for nineteen-year-old Catherine Byrn, how could she tell Sister Mary Catherine what she must tell the Archbishop tomorrow? Her mother's cousin may have had no intention of becoming a religious, but for several years Catherine Byrn had thought of doing so. Miss McAuley's ward would have affiliated with the Dominicans in 1827 if she had had any encouragement from her director. Father Harold, Dominican himself, had thought her too young then and had advised her to accompany Miss McAuley to Baggot Street and take part in that project for two years. In the meantime, Father Harold developed a lung condition and removed to Cork, where he died in the spring of 1830.

On December 13, Archbishop Murray settled Catherine Byrn's problem temporarily by counseling her to continue at Baggot Street under the new regime to see whether she could adjust there.

He appointed Sister Mary Catherine mother superior. To her demur over the title he responded by saying that there should be one mother in every house. She interpreted this as excusing her from the usual prefix *Reverend* and required the sisters in those first years to call her simply "Mother Catherine." It was not until foundations were made outside her own diocese that the more formal title came into use, and it is interesting to note that the superiors of filial houses under her were addressed "sister."

His Grace approved the horarium with two minor alterations: he required the Office to be said in English and he introduced a short recreation after dinner. Sister Mary Catherine had provided only one recreation at the end of the day, intending the Sisters to have no alleviation till then, as was the lot of the poor. There was wisdom in placing a short period of relaxation at four-thirty. The advice was psychologically sound. Since spiritual reading frequently occupied the dinner time, from four o'clock till nearly seven would have required uninterrupted concentration on spiritual exercises. Any prolonged serious application at the end of a busy day profits by some recuperation from earlier fatigue.

Dr. Murray saw that adapting the horarium of a cloistered

order to a program of active charity among people required more adjustment than inserting a half dozen hours of strenuous work into an already full day. Fortunately Archbishop Murray had had a little experience with uncloistered religious communities. Besides the one he himself founded, he had brought the Loreto Sisters to his diocese nine years before.[8]

Sister Mary Catherine's modification of the Presentation horarium consisted principally in reducing lengthy prayers and eliminating others. Yet the result, emphasizing the liturgy and the common litanies, seems the effect of inspiration. During her life Mother Catherine put forth special effort to maintain the character of this spiritual framework by insisting that no prayers be added. She realized that alterations in the time schedule might sometimes be needed, but she remained confirmed in her attitude toward the number of prayers. Disciplinary practices she gradually added, but not prayers.

Those said while putting on the religious habit she reduced almost to aspirations in order to leave the mind free for the subject of meditation. The only haste Mother Catherine ever counseled was hurry in dressing; yet she increased by ten minutes the fifteen-minute period allowed at George's Hill.

At six o'clock the *Angelus,* the Little Hours, and meditation preceded Mass. Breakfast was followed by a half hour of spiritual reading in common, the superior presiding.[9]

Except for three *Paters* and *Aves* after the Little Hours there were no other prayers till noon and these were not obligatory upon sisters out all day. A note in her own handwriting states:

> Sisters engaged in the visitation of the sick are exempt from any choir duty from 10 till 4—but all in choir at Office and all attend lectures. The rosary is said by obligation but no time marked; it is often said going on the visitation.[10]

The "choir duty" referred to was a visit to the Blessed Sacrament (examen) shortly before noon, the *Angelus* and Acts of Faith, Hope and Charity with the Litany of the Holy Name offered for vocations. The Act of Contrition was part of the particular examen. Vespers, Compline and the Litany of Our Lady followed the dinner hour. From the *Presentation Ceremonial* Mother Catherine retained six *Paters* and *Aves* for the Pope, the clergy, the propagation of the faith, benefactors, friends and other specified intentions. Probably because of the general scarcity of appropriate books at the time, the superior presided also at the second half-hour of spiritual reading listed at five-thirty.[11] At six the *Angelus* preceded Matins and Lauds. The litany for a happy death that followed was replaced on Mondays by a litany for the dead.

At quarter to seven a light collation was allowed, followed by the long recreation. Night prayers afterward included the Litany of the Saints, which had so heartened the three Mercy novices toward the close of their stay at George's Hill. General examen and preparation of the next morning's meditation closed the nine o'clock prayers. The final bell rang at ten.

With the exception of certain psalms said daily before and after meals and two short prayers at the beginning of night prayers, all others were occasional, one every Friday at three for those in mortal sin and for the dying, one on the feast of Our Lady of Mercy, the Thirty Days' Prayer in September, the Psalter during Lent, and novenas preceding special feasts.[12] For sick and dying members of the congregation and for sisters in retreat particular prayers were also reserved.

When Mother Catherine asked His Grace to direct her on the matter of the rule until their own would be ready, Archbishop Murray opened the Presentation Rule to the chapter on "union and charity" saying that its observance would suffice. It was a master stroke, for though Dr. Murray almost immediately appointed a priest to assist Mother Catherine in writing the new chapters, a half dozen years were to pass before the revised rule would be completed and approved. Meanwhile, the uncompromising charity imposed by the Presentation Rule gave single direction to spiritual energy hitherto diffused in a dozen individual ways.

Beginning with Christ's words "Love one another as I have loved you," the first section reminds the religious that charity fulfills the law. It further enjoins charity so perfect "as to resemble, in some manner, the love and union which subsists between Christ and His Heavenly Father." With no redundancy the second section recasts the injunction: "This love for one another should be such as to emulate the love and union of the blessed in heaven."

The third, fourth and fifth sections exhort and warn:

They shall therefore in conversation, manners, and conduct most cautiously avoid whatever may in the least disturb their union or lessen in the smallest degree their mutual charity and love; and shall be solicitous to repair the smallest offense by quickly asking pardon, which should be immediately granted without contention or reserve . . . They shall on all occasions assist and help one another, bearing with patience and charity each other's defects, weaknesses, and imperfections. They shall never dispute, but should they happen to differ in opinion on any subject, they shall propose their reasons with moderation and charity. . . . They shall always bear in mind . . . the noble description of charity given by the Apostle: "Charity is patient, is kind, envieth not; dealeth not perversely, is not puffed up, is not ambitious, seeketh not her own, is not provoked to anger, thinketh no evil, beareth all things, hopeth all things, endureth all things."

The Sisters of this Institute shall not admit any particular friendships, attachments, or affections among them, and shall studiously avoid all private parties and unions, as the source of discord and division, and as hostile to purity of heart, to charity, and the spirit of Religion.

At the first lecture Mother Catherine read the tenth chapter of Rodriguez on obedience, the vow that consecrates and liberates. Four principles coordinated in their one rule: mercy to the afflicted, union and charity among the sisters, child-like obedience, and the discipline of common life as marked down in a "daily distribution of time"—this was the spiritual norm for Sisters of Mercy. The foundress' own life modeled it, and her dying words were to confirm it.

On the subject of lectures Sister M. Vincent Hartnett, who often heard her, says:

Her language was simple and unstudied but sweet and forcible: her instructions were the fruit of prayer to which she had recourse in every difficulty; and they were given with such authority and dignity as left the sisters no doubt that what she inculcated was the holy Will of God. Our venerated foundress established spiritual lecture as a community exercise to be made in common, and she always read the lectures herself. The morning one she usually selected from Rodriguez on *Christian Perfection* and that of the evening from the *Lives of the Saints*. Her method of reading was so delightful that everyone considered it rendered the subject quite new to them, though they might have been familiar with it and might often have heard her on it before; for she considered it most useful to adhere to a few solid, religious books and read them over and over rather than to go hastily through many. Whatever she read she rendered most impressive; all who had the happiness of hearing her admitted that they never heard reading comparable to hers.

If spiritual desolation foreruns consolation, respite should have come to Mother Catherine at this point, and it does seem that such an interlude now began, for that very month Dr. Blake was appointed not administrator but pastor of St. Andrew's. Father Kelly's subsequent procedure throws further light on the character of the man with whom Catherine McAuley had had difficulties. He accepted his transfer to St. James, and one might have expected that he would be glad to relinquish his building worries at St. Andrew's. If hardship attended his appointment, it would seem to be on the side of St. James' parishioners who had lost by death their venerated and beloved parish priest, Dean Lubé. Father Kelly persevered in his new charge just two months, then resigned. Bishop Donnelly in his history of Dublin parishes tells of Father Kelly's "free lance" activities afterwards in St. Andrew's, where he appeared in the gallery as spokesman for the opposition at a business meeting. If he hoped to embarrass his successor in plans for a new church on a new site, he was disappointed, for O'Connell arose in defense of Dr. Blake and the Reverend Mr. Kelly's arguments suffered total eclipse.

XIX

Compassion on the Multitude

On the feast of the Espousals, January 23, 1832, Archbishop Murray conferred the habit of the Sisters of Mercy on the seven candidates he had previously examined. Death was close to Anne O'Grady by then and almost as close to thousands of unsuspecting Dubliners, for Asiatic cholera was on the march.

Because expenses at the Presentation novitiate had made inroads on an already depleted treasury and because Anne O'Grady was critically ill, Mother Catherine decided on a private ceremony. The black uniforms of the postulants were remodeled for habits and others freshened up as a substitute for bridal array, though Mother Catherine reverted to the Presentation custom of bridal white at all subsequent ceremonies of reception.[1]

To save expense, guimps worn by the three professed during their novitiate were fresh-laundered for the seven and but one new white veil was made up for each. After all, those brought home from George's Hill had to be worn out. At this time Mother Catherine allowed only a brass crucifix on the beads. She considered the ebony used at George's Hill too expensive. Later, however, she adopted the plain ebony cross with white inset that is a common part of the Mercy insignia.

The decision to exclude outside guests was a mistake the foundress never made again. Not only relatives and friends of the postulants were disappointed but a number of wealthy patrons of the charities had expected invitations. Some of the relatives came anyway to assure themselves that others had not been admitted, and the clamor outside the chapel was distracting, to say the least.

The junior postulant's mother made a scene, declaring that she would withdraw her daughter to the Presentation Convent, a threat she carried out before the end of the month.

Sister Catherine now redeemed herself for declining the names proposed by Mother M. Angela for December 9, 1830, and conferred them upon three of the received. To her niece she gave the name Sister Mary (Joseph) Teresa; to Georgina Moore, Sister Mary Clare; and to Margaret Dunne, Sister Mary Angela. Catherine Byrn became Sister Mary Josephine; Frances Warde, Sister Mary Francis Xavier; and Mary Anne Delany received the family name of the great mystic and lover of the poor, that other Catherine to whom Catherine McAuley had particular devotion, Caterina de Pazzi, listed among Carmelite saints as St. Mary Magdalen de Pazzi.

The penitential character of life at the Convent of Our Lady of Mercy now achieved balance under the direction of a trained religious. Hours of silence were set and strictly observed. Sister Mary Clare has left it on record that Mother Catherine "would reprove for even one unnecessary word, being convinced that future regularity depended in great measure on beginning well and fervently." Sister immediately adds that Mother Catherine herself was "a model of regular observance." How the superior managed to keep herself in the practice of submission the same writer explains, inviting an inference that she may have been the junior sister appointed.

In order that she might have the advantage of practising submission, she enjoined one of the junior sisters to tell her of any fault or omission of duty she might perceive; and when reminded that she had not performed some exercise, though hindered by urgent business, she would humbly acknowledge it and supply for it without delay.

Sister M. Vincent Hartnett also describes the change that occurred when a secular institute became a religious congregation:

Our dear Reverend Mother was most solicitous that silence should be observed religiously and with the utmost exactness, and she established it in every department of the convent. The young, ardent sisters were at first quite at a loss to know how silence could be practiced in the schools, but she instructed them and soon quite a new face was put on all the works of the institute.

The same zeal actuated the sisters. Their whole deportment was changed, their movements moderated, their step noiseless and self-possessed; for she taught them that silence is the guardian of interior recollection . . . . She had been much edified by the virtue of silence during her noviceship, and she sought to have her spiritual children not only equal what she had witnessed but, if possible, surpass it.[2]

The program of poverty Mother Catherine initiated was rigorous. Only necessities were provided and sometimes not those. She later modified her procedure but for several months she imposed a strict economy. Plain and even frugal fare was the rule. Milk should no more than color tea, for example, and all other recommendations on food were in keeping with this.

"We were even spoken to at table to remember we were not come to a house of plenty," recorded Sister Mary Clare. [We were told] "We should be more sparing, [though] we had been most sparing during her absence."[3] In the London manuscript the same writer comments: "She yielded neither to human respect nor to human feelings; her exactitude with regard to poverty was extreme."

What hardship this worked on young people reared in homes of middle class Irish lavishness soon became evident.

That poverty and cheerfulness were compatible Mother Catherine strove to show in the refectory as well as elsewhere. Though she dispensed with some conventual practices that she later adopted, she never permitted formal penances in the refectory as was customary in cloistered orders. Her efforts to avoid anything that would create an austere atmosphere were successful even after she gradually evolved the code of discipline she considered suitable to a Convent of Mercy.

Freed of prejudice against religious life by the experience of novitiate training, she had come away from George's Hill impressed more by example than by discipline, convinced that practical religion was above all else Christ among people. She knew that human nature must reach toward this Ideal by discipline, but she had concealed her own penitential practices for over thirty years and was not likely to favor anything demonstrative.

The instruction she gave on mortification is summarized by one of the six forming the first Mercy novitiate:

She was particularly desirous that [we] should adopt the practice of small acts of mortification, for example, in the refectory, saying that [we] ought never let any meal pass without denying [ourselves] something (being careful not to injure health), and that these mortifications were often of far greater value before God and caused Him to bestow more abundant graces than rigid austerities which might spring from or occasion vanity.[4]

The same sister in a private letter describes Mother Catherine's efforts to give a homelike atmosphere to the refectory without dispensing with conventual silence and customary spiritual reading.

When Reverend Mother first came home, she would have no server but a carver and a reader for each week. The table was like an ordinary table, not divided, and the carver occupied her own place as it came her turn. I was appointed to carve the first week, Sister Angela to read. I never shall forget [my first experience], a leg of mutton and how I laboured to cut it up, for I scarcely knew how to cut bread and butter. The next week I was reader and Sister Angela carver, which finished that plan. Reverend Mother took the carving entirely herself, and one was to serve, another read a day at a time. Supper was at 8 o'clock, no silence.
When Elizabeth Harley died or soon after, we had no server at all, but the little girls waited at table. Five or six of them used to stand against the wall and hand the plates, etc. Little Mary Quinn used to sit between Reverend Mother and Sister Francis Warde but no absolute want of silence. We went on this way till Sister Mary Teresa's death. Then Reverend Mother reproached herself for not attending to these matters. She thought, she said to me, that perhaps the Sisters' health might be injured by the constraint of convent discipline, but Almighty God had made her see that without it their health was lost.
After that the refectory took the form it now has pretty much, with a few minor changes such as helping the juniors first; then the seniors were helped first; then it went back to the juniors—I suppose they were considered to be most hungry.
Mother M. Anne got [Reverend Mother] to try dinner at 3 o'clock or thereabouts, no lunch—[a procedure] which lasted only a few days or weeks.[5]

While these experiments were being tried in the best interests of the sisters' spiritual and physical well-being, as the foundress believed, Anne O'Grady and Elizabeth Harley died.

The sister, unwearied in efforts for the poor, showed exhaustion at last. Anne O'Grady's debility toward the end was extreme. "She was greatly beloved by the sisters, for no one could be more meek, humble and charitable," the Derry MS states. "She suffered a great deal during the whole course of her long illness, yet when she was laid in the chapel preparatory to her interment, her features looked even more lovely than when she was in the prime of health and beauty." Sister Mary Aloysius O'Grady died February 8 and was laid with Sister Caroline among the Carmelites under the main altar of St. Teresa's Church.

If grief could fill hands as well as heart, Mother Catherine and the sisters would have had no time for it, because to all their work Dr. Blake now added a charge. The contents of the poor boxes at St. Andrew's had been regularly distributed by the curates. The new pastor, believing that a greater number of the parish poor could be benefited by a dinner plan, asked Mother Catherine to open a room in the House of Mercy to give free dinners to those he would send. This was not an entirely new procedure, for besides the annual Christmas dinner, meals were provided for unemployed women of the refuge. The new charge, however, required separate bookkeeping, more cleaning, and a great deal more work, since the number who came averaged close to a hundred daily. It would have been a joy to "Sister Mary Aloysius" to see so many hungry fed and a joy to the sisters to have her unruffled, tireless help in the new work, for the old work grew heavier too.

Indeed the new work would have been a keener joy if the curates at St. Andrew's had been better pleased with the arrangement, but Father Kelly's assistants remained loyal to his ideas, and now that the status of the ladies on Baggot Street was satisfactorily established, the curates found other excuses for their prejudice.

On March 22 the first cholera victim died in Dublin. Thereafter pastors and curates were too busy with the dying to advert to petty grievances, and all Mother Augustine's and Mother Catherine's spiritual daughters were not enough "walking nuns" to care for the stricken. The penances of that Lent were of a most practical nature. Without these religious women, the poor would have been a thousand times more wretched and many others would have died unattended.

A terror that did not stalk the open streets nor assail the Georgian fronts ranged the by-ways. Schooled to distrust of authority, the alley-hutched had had too few years of "Emancipation" to recuperate, and panic among the ignorant made a graver threat of the plague. Rumor spread that the hospitals were death traps where the poor were dispatched with poison or buried alive among corpses hurried into the earth to halt contagion. A shocking arraignment of their oppressors stands in the ease with which the alley wretches believed this atrocious report. Concealment of cholera meant widespread disaster.

Then a softer rumor moved down familiar footways and into hovels recently brightened by repeated visitations of hope. "The walking nuns," this rumor said, were in the hospitals. Such a one had seen them going, such a one had seen them there, such another one had spoken with Mother Catherine herself who had assured him that "the walking nuns" would be there every day, all day, as long as the cholera itself.

Though the disease marched on and the death list, numbering thousands, mounted still, the poor no longer feared to make known their sick. Die they might but not unattended nor unprepared for eternity. A docility fell upon them that made it easier for the authorities, for the afflicted, and for the "walking nuns" themselves. Kneeling nuns they became; too busy to rise, they moved from cot to cot for long intervals on their knees.

Authorization for work in the cholera hospitals had come from Archbishop Murray himself. After receiving a letter from the Board of Health asking the sisters to help at the Townsend Street station, Mother Catherine wrote to His Grace, enclosed the request and asked permission for the sisters to attend the plague victims in this improvised hospital. The Archbishop came in person that evening to grant permission. After a long conference with the foundress, he went to the community room and spoke to the sisters. The Derry MS gives the best account of this visit:

He gave his sanction to the good work which he said could not fail to be pleasing and meritorious in the sight of God. At the same time he required that the sisters should take all due precautions for the preservation of their own health, make use of the prescribed remedies against infection, take port wine, boiled meats, etc. He then spoke of the visitation in general and laid great stress on the unobtrusive manner in which they should appear and act, appealing to Mother Catherine's experience of the unpleasant feelings always excited in Protestants when certain points of difference were drawn prominently forth. On this account he wished our outdoor costume might exhibit no remarkable difference from that of secular persons of respectability who did not enter into the vanities of the world, and above all things [he exhorted] that the cross and beads be concealed. [He said] we should not wear in the street any dress that would make us remarkable.[6]

The recommendation on diet "was literally obeyed for a week or two," Sister Mary Clare discloses, "but it was found too troublesome. We used also at first change our habits and use vinegar."[7]

There is no point in detailing the treatment of cholera at which the sisters became so proficient that the death rate at the Townsend Street Hospital was one of the lowest on record.[8] One of the efficient Mercy nurses on duty that spring was to use her skill again as an ally of Miss Nightingale in the Crimea.[9] It is this sister's record of the work in the Townsend Street Hospital that explains Mother Catherine's procedure. Short staffing the convent for visitations, the school, and the House of Mercy, the foundress assigned sisters in relays of four to be relieved every three or four hours. She herself remained all day. They set out shortly after 8 A.M. in "Kirwan's car" and returned before 9 P.M.

One evening when the car drew up, the waiting sisters were startled by the weak, persistent cry of a new-born infant. Mother Catherine had wrapped it in a shawl and brought it with her from the hospital where its mother had died a victim of the disease. The foundress directed a little bed to be put in her cell, apparently with the impractical purpose of taking care of the baby herself, but it cried all night. By morning the self-appointed nurse realized that she would have to turn it over to someone for permanent care, particularly since she herself must be on daily duty at the cholera hospital.

Meanwhile, however, the first Lent of the Sisters of Mercy had closed with Holy Week practices that have since become traditional in the congregation. Mother Catherine again took no food from Holy Thursday till Holy Saturday, but she required the sisters to follow the Presentation custom of a small collation at usual mealtime. Silence, of course, was observed. She made a slight change in the penitential practice at George's Hill: the sisters were to stand while taking the little provided. Out of regard for the common life Mother Catherine herself ultimately conformed to the community custom of taking collation.

Sister Mary Elizabeth's example in this ideal of the common life crowned the First Lenten observances, for Easter Sunday she attended Mass and received Communion with the others, though she died the following Wednesday. While attending twenty-year old Anne O'Grady in her last illness, Sister Elizabeth, seeing the patient's extreme debility toward the end, observed to a novice that till then she had always looked upon lingering consumption as a blessing, a long time in which to prepare for death. "But now that I see how much the mind is weakened," she remarked, "I hope Almighty God will permit that my last illness be short."

Her prayer was answered. She served in the refectory Ash Wednesday and appeared in the community room daily during Lent. Though she suffered much in Passion Week and Holy Week, she walked till the last week of her life and "enjoyed the perfect use of her faculties to the last moment."

During Easter week, plans for the annual benefit for the poor were nearing completion and Mother Catherine was called upon for consultation at times. The benefit bazaar was an item on the social calendar, and polite differences among distinguished ladies had to be adjusted as well as the business in general forwarded. Criticism, too, was poured upon Mother Catherine.

She was called from Sister M. Elizabeth's deathbed to a lady who came to speak her mind. Supposing the interview would last but a few minutes, Mother Catherine said to the dying religious: "Now, my dearest child, say nothing but 'Jesus, Mary, Joseph, assist me in my last agony.' "

The Derry MS describes the visitor as "an old lady, very rich, very charitable, rather odd, having a great dislike to bazaars, and she came to lecture on the impropriety, the utter sinfulness of this way of raising money for the poor." The "charitable" lady's diatribe lasted nearly an hour. Finally, moved by the patience of her listener or by a grace descending from the merits of the dying, she changed her mood and, rising to go, gave Mother Catherine fifteen pounds for the poor. Nothing in the meekness of the foundress had betrayed anxiety or had given an impression that there could be urgency in a convent.

On the departure of her advisor, Mother Catherine returned to Sister Mary Elizabeth and found her still repeating the aspiration. Such was the patient's obedience that she would not change the prayer till her superior returned.

Of Sister Elizabeth's spirituality the Derry MS gives the following account:

In this holy sister two virtues were especially remarkable, humility and obedience, and these she had acquired in so high a degree that no trial of either could disturb her equanimity . . . . After her profession she was for some time ranked below the postulants who entered before her; yet she never complained—in fact, never seemed to perceive that she was not in her place. No reproof, however unmerited, ever tempted her to justify herself; no contradiction, no want of attention ever seemed to give her pain and never by act, word or look did she give pain to others. On the subject of obedience she was particularly edifying; she never seemed to feel the slightest repugnance to any sacrifice it required.

So grieved were the sisters at Sister Mary Elizabeth's death that Mother Catherine, to relieve their personal sorrow and to remind them that this bereavement was God's appointment, recited the verse of the Easter *Benedicite*: "This is the day the Lord hath made; let us rejoice and be glad therein."

Sister had managed her illness so well that they had not realized her death was near. She had actually lived over half her religious life at George's Hill Presentation Convent. Yet the eight months previous to her novitiate and the four months after her profession had set an example the sisters could not forget. Before Low Sunday, the Carmelite Fathers recorded in their interment register the first professed member of the congregation: "Sister Mary Elizabeth Harley, O.M., died April 25, 1832, age 24 years."[10]

XX

The New Rule

WHETHER or not Father Myles Gaffney was assigned to St. Andrew's parish by the arrangement of the Vicar General, Dr. Blake, he arrived shortly after Father Blake himself and was directed by the Archbishop to assist Mother Catherine with the new chapters of the rule. Father Gaffney's services to her and his subsequent history show that His Grace had reasons for the choice.

Of the Mercy Rule one of the sisters who lived several years at Baggot Street has stated:

Reverend Mother often said that every word of the rule was the result of prayer as were also those retrenchments she made in some parts of the Presentation Rule, on which the new rule was grounded.[1]

By summer the cholera epidemic was under control, though cases of it continued to appear till 1833. As was to be expected, many reversions and conversions to the Faith resulted from the sisters' ministrations to the sick and dying. Toward the middle of June Mother Catherine brought with her to the Townsend Street Hospital a young lady in her middle twenties. Her garb differed somewhat from that of the other sisters, for she was a postulant. Miss Anne Moore had entered on Pentecost Sunday, which that year coincided with her birthday, June 10. This was Father Blake's protégée who had been disappointed in not being admitted to the ceremony of reception five months before.[2] Active as she had been in parish work among the poor, her work in the cholera hospital revealed new miseries to her.

On August 6 the Sisters were relieved of hospital duty to attend the first annual retreat, preached by the Reverend Myles

Gaffney. An account of it appears in the London manuscript in context with Mother Catherine's instructions to the novices:

Her lessons on humility, supported by her own unvarying example, necessarily made a deep impression on the minds of her spiritual children. The least shadow of pride was odious to her. She told them that their very tone of voice and manner of walking should be humble and subdued; that they should carefully shun speaking of themselves or of their works and try as far as possible to banish even the words *me* or *myself* from their conversation, that they should never attribute to themselves anything but faults and imperfections, sincerely acknowledging that they were not merely incapable of promoting the good in which the Almighty deigned to employ them but that their unworthiness would very likely obstruct its accomplishment. She taught them to love the hidden life, labouring on silently for God alone, for she had a great dislike of noise and show in the performance of duties. "See how quietly," she would say, "the great God does all His mighty works. Darkness is spread over us and light breaks in again [without] the noise of drawing curtains or closing shutters" . . . .

When instructing the sisters, [she] loved to dwell on those words of our Divine Lord "Learn of Me because I am meek and humble of heart," saying, "If His blessed words ought to be reverenced by all, with what loving devotion ought the religious impress them on her memory and try to reduce them to practice."

Her own feelings of self-abasement she carried, it might be said, too far. She could not be prevailed on to hold the prescribed Chapter of Faults for a very long time after being made superior and was pained when the sisters manifested their faults to her in private. She allowed any of them to guide and direct her (being occasionally abstracted or forgetful of the ceremonies) and would good-humouredly call those who perhaps had been rather importunate her "Mistresses" . . . .

Not content with her own instructions, our Reverend Mother procured for her novices the advantage of making their first annual retreat under the direction of a most pious and enlightened priest, the Rev. Mr. Gaffney, since made Dean of Maynooth College. His simple but inflamed discourses were well calculated to excite in their hearts ardent desires of perfection, which were prudently regulated by his private instructions in the confessional. His views accorded entirely with those of our holy Foundress. Humility was the virtue he recommended to all, desiring them to make that the subject of their particular examens and to let the first practice of it be never to speak of themselves either in praise or dispraise. It was to this priest Dr. Murray confided the charge of assisting our Reverend Mother to adapt the Presentation Rule to our institute.[3]

But the influences affecting the novices were not confined to Mother Catherine's instructions and Father Gaffney's exhortations. Four of the six had been at Baggot Street through the entire transitional period; besides, the year of Mother Catherine's absence had also left its mark. Subtle results of the variously inspired asceticism of those months began to appear. One sister conceived the idea that the hardships of intensive charitable service in several fields were a lesser offering than the formal penances to which they had been accustomed. She decided to be a Carmelite. Paradoxically, another who had practised Carmelite austerities the previous year but had been physically unequal to the challenge of exhausting activity decided also to be a Carmelite. What the Carmelites might conclude about admitting them does not seem to have entered their consideration. Catherine Byrn, too, had remained unsettled.

In accord with canonical regulations, the Archbishop or his representative must interview candidates for profession two months before the expiration of their novitiate term. By autumn several personal crises were in process. The novices had the advantage of Father O'Hanlon's guidance, however, and the Carmelite Provincial had no difficulty in distinguishing between spiritual mirage and contemplative vocation.

His direction of one of the three wavering candidates is on record because she made a point of leaving it on record in the Order where she spent the greater part of her religious life. Because her version differs in certain respects from the accounts in the Dublin manuscript, it becomes necessary to reconcile the two.

According to Dominican records at Drogheda, the Reverend William D. Harold in directing Catherine Byrn to accompany Miss McAuley to Baggot Street had pointed out that there would be no commitment in doing so because no profession of vows was involved. "These were his words" is the parenthetical explanation. Father Harold further declared that the Baggot Street project would supply an excellent testing ground for the Dominican vocation of the fifteen-year old aspirant.

By the time the institute changed character Father William D. Harold was dead and his protégée was under Carmelite direction. She explained her position to Father O'Hanlon who advised her to tell Mother Catherine. The words of the record are:

Four and a half years having elapsed, Father O'Hanlon authorized Miss Byrn to announce formally to Mother Catherine McAuley (then just professed at the Presentation Convent, George's Hill, and appointed by Most Rev. Dr. Murray superioress of the new Convent of Mercy) her desire to become a child of St. Dominic. He, however, advised her to comply with the request of Mother Catherine and take the habit of the Sisters of Mercy and try, at least during ten months, if she could persuade herself to remain at Baggot Street. The Archbishop gave the same advice, and Sister Catherine Joseph was accordingly clothed January 23, 1832. Father O'Hanlon laid down strict regulations for her observance, forbidding her to speak to him of her Dominican longings except at stated times. However, near the expiration of the time appointed for decision, finding, as he said, her vocation strong, he exerted himself to obtain her entrance into the Dominican Convent of J. M. J., Cabra, on December 1st, 1832, and there she received the habit, February 9, 1833.

Whatever Catherine Byrn said to her guardian that January day apparently did not make a strong impression. Presumably Mother Catherine knew of the Dominican interest, for in Coolock days she had brought her young charge to the Dominican chapel at Clontarf to be confirmed, and she could scarcely have been unaware of whatever enthusiasm Frances Tighe communicated to Catherine Byrn. Certainly Catherine McAuley's generosity of spirit and of purse when Frances Tighe entered the Presentation Order and her gracious release of Anna Carroll a few months before, as well as her liberality on such occasions, relieve her of blame for Catherine Byrn's procedure.

Catherine McAuley, moreover, must have had some reason for not selecting Catherine Byrn for George's Hill. It may or may not have had anything to do with her young cousin's dispositions. She also had some reason for questioning the reputedly miraculous cure of Catherine Byrn on March 19, 1830, that had so convinced Dr. Blake. Not even Catherine Byrn leaves the impression that she made a confidante of her guardian, though she seems to have had a lasting affection for her. This is testified in letters to Ann Byrn and to others after the publication of Mother M. Teresa Austin Carroll's biography—emphatic, even indignant letters in which her references to Mother Catherine are always reverent and affectionate.

To understand this novice's character, one should consider that she was past ten years old when, at her mother's death, she became Catherine McAuley's ward. Though from early childhood she had had an affectionate regard for her mother's cousin, it was too late for a child of her disposition and temperament to find in Catherine McAuley what she had lost through the death of her mother. Little Teresa's situation was different; she had never known any mother but her godmother.

Having no money, Catherine Byrn could not face the embarrassment of expecting Mother Catherine to finance her departure. She therefore made a successful effort to reach the Reverend William V. Harold, O. P., uncle of her deceased Dominican director.

She effected the contact through her office of sacristan, placing at the extern door the orphan assigned to help her. This child received from one of Catherine Byrn's pupils replies to messages sent out from the classroom. It was the Reverend William V. Harold who came that first day of December, 1832, to transfer her to the Dominicans at Cabra and who fourteen years later transferred her to the Second Order Dominicans at Drogheda, where she spent the rest of her religious life.

This Order was so convinced of her sincerity, which certainly cannot be questioned in its Dominican allegiance, that they gave her the responsible office of Novice Mistress several years later.

Commenting on Miss Byrn's method of reaching Father Harold, the Dublin manuscript declares:

> Reverend Mother had not the least idea of what was going on till the Reverend friend came to remove [his protégée]. Though she felt it painfully, she never uttered a word of remonstrance nor made any effort to shake [Sister] from her purpose, a circumstance which puzzled the good friar and perhaps disappointed his protégée. It was himself told me a great deal of this. The rest I learned from Reverend Mother herself and from the child employed to watch, who was a lay sister when I entered.

Mother Catherine certainly felt pain as she parted with Anne Conway Byrn's eldest daughter who had been a cherished member of her household for over ten years. Anne's two other daughters, however, were to compensate her in some measure. Both became Sisters of Mercy.

Some time between Catherine Byrn's departure and the day set for profession, Mother Catherine's especially loved niece, though already consumptive, revealed her desire to be a Carmelite.

Catherine Byrn as Sister Mary Raymund, O. P., refers to this in her letter to the Very Reverend William Meagher:

His Grace professed the first three members in 1831 and, immediately on their return from George's Hill, appointed Mother McAuley superioress, examined the vocations of those in the house and induced two of them, members of Mother McAuley's family, who were there only from circumstances, having all along felt themselves called to a different order, to remain at least for some time. He accordingly gave the habit to several postulants during the ensuing year, 1832. This is the last act of His Grace in favour of the Sisters of Mercy to which I was witness, for the time allotted for the trial of my vocation having expired, I joined another order, the object of my early and continued aspirations.[4]

Mother Catherine's response to her niece's confidence was: "If God wants you to be a Carmelite, my darling, you shall be one. I myself will help you . . . . I only ask that you do nothing rashly."

But God wanted neither an active branch of Carmelites at St. Mary's nor Carmelite subjects from among the first Sisters of Mercy. Sister Mary Teresa's health continued to fail. In fact, of all Mother Catherine's trials, ill health among the sisters became her gravest concern. Some time during this first year all the sisters but one became bed patients at the same time. Always particularly compassionate toward the sick, Mother Catherine called in an eminent physician, so advanced in his ideas that he might seem to have drawn them from the twentieth century. Sir Philip Crampton inquired into their way of living and prescribed conversation at meals, change of diet, and discontinuance of social work in the slums!

Mother Catherine's reaction was characteristic: what was compatible with their religious state she would do, change the food and allow more recreation at dinner. The realistic writer of the Dublin manuscript comments:

More recreation days were appointed than she afterwards found convenient . . . . He tried to convince Reverend Mother of the real unwholesomeness of the visitation, but she never could understand and always maintained that fresh air must be good, forgetting that it must be taken by us mostly in Townsend Street and Bull Alley.

The memoir writer's prejudice in the matter of food is revealed by her reminiscences: "Even when I entered, the diet was most unfit for persons doing our duties: leg of beef with onion sauce, beef steaks that seemed as if they had lain in a tanpit and, for dainty, fried liver and bacon, though boiled and roast mutton came in sometimes."[5]

Her preference for mutton would hardly be shared by people living in a cattle country. Only the truly mortified, however, could dispute her on the morning collation: "The breakfast table was a trial to one's nerves: sugar of the blackest and coarsest kind, weak tea, very little milk, plates of thick stale bread with a thin scraping of butter."

Most of the patients were in their late teens or early twenties, and which of them that day of Sir Philip's visit was the ambulatory case helping Mother Catherine with the sick, ringing the bells, and answering the prayers? The fact that the community exercises were not slighted is mentioned but not the name of the hardy one who carried on for all.

In the usual order, it would scarcely take the diagnosis of a Surgeon General to prescribe relaxation, fresh air, and nourishing food, but these young ladies had not been living according to any usual order. Ascetics who had fasted by choice the previous year now fasted of necessity, and those who had then adopted Carmelite penances now drew mortification from the exhaustion and contacts of the classroom, the hospitals and the alley hovels at a time when plague harried every department. Mother Catherine was to tell future novices that she saw some of these first fall asleep mounting the stairs to their cells at the end of a day in the cholera hospital.

On January 24, 1833, Archbishop Murray received the Vows of Sister Mary Francis Xavier Warde, Sister Mary Clare Moore,

Sister Mary Angela Dunne and Sister Mary de Pazzi Delany. This was the first ceremony conducted according to the Mercy ceremonial, on which Mother Catherine had spent a great deal of time and prayer. A contemporary wrote the following comment on the 1833 profession:

Immediately after the ceremony in October, Reverend Mother devoted every spare moment to drawing up the ceremonial for reception and profession . . . and the [first] ceremony was gone through in conformity with its direction. The Archbishop presided, as at each of the other ceremonies . . . . The sisters seemed almost inspired while devoting themselves. The procession and the music choir were equally effective.[6]

Which of the four had been the second prospective Carmelite has never been disclosed. Sister Mary Joseph Teresa still clung to the idea that she might yet be one of her holy patron's spiritual daughters. "The six black and five white veils gave now to the institute the features of an established religious community. A few postulants, both lay and choir, were added. For the government and guidance of the latter Reverend Mother had given a special chapter in the rule, there being no provision for such aspirants in the rule of the Presentation Order."[7]

The day after the Mercy profession Mother Mary Augustine wrote her admonitory letter against "false zeal or false love of our own Institute," exhorting Sisters of Charity to rejoice that others are "also made the chosen instruments of God's mercy to the poor and afflicted."[8] Her noble sentiments were soon to be put to the test. Exhort as she did, the saintly foundress of the Irish Sisters of Charity could not stem the tide against Mother Catherine and her community of five professed nuns. On March 17 the administrator at the Pro-Cathedral, who was devoted to the interests of the Irish Sisters of Charity, succeeded Dr. Blake at St. Andrew's. Very Reverend Walter Meyler had been associated with St. Mary's, old and new, for twenty-six years. He knew Catherine McAuley and, unfortunately now for her, had been annoyed with her in some issue at St. Mary's. Dr. Blake proceeded to Newry as Bishop of Dromore.

Anticipating the new pastor's wishes, Mother Catherine asked to be relieved of the responsibility of distributing parish alms and was promptly accommodated. Since Father Meyler's appointment to St. Mary's had come after Catherine McAuley's removal to Coolock, earlier "unpleasantness" between them undoubtedly arose from her charitable work in his former parish. The prominence of money in the issues now arising seems to indicate that financial policy may have caused the earlier disagreement.

The very attitude that had influenced Mr. Callaghan to make Catherine his principal beneficiary had irked members of her own family and doubtless others: she held her wealth in trust for the poor. She reserved the right to make disbursements according to her own judgment, supported by the guidance of self-selected advisers. By 1833, Catherine McAuley was no longer wealthy. She was relief agent rather than philanthropist. Mother M. Clare says of this period: "Just after the cholera Reverend Mother got printed tickets sent to each house, begging old clothing, carpeting, bed clothing, etc., and the result was that for a long time carriages used to stop and great bundles [be] handed in so that the store room was filled and the supply lasted a long time."

In her management of charities Mother Catherine seldom dispensed money. Her direction on this point reads:

> In the visitation of the sick the Sisters are obliged by their regulations to employ every practicable means to promote cleanliness and to be exceedingly cautious in the distribution of relief, making every inquiry that may lead to a true knowledge of each case. The Sisters carry nourishment and clothing to the sick and very seldom give money except for fire and light.

Long experience with relief dictated this policy.

An epidemic of influenza in the late spring of 1833 and the aftermath of cholera brought great pressure on all departments of the Baggot Street charities, but an influx of subjects implemented the business of supplying needs. Among the postulants were Father Gaffney's sister, Sister Francis Warde's sister, the first of two daughters of a Dublin magistrate, a Mr. White, and two widows, one in her early thirties, the other considerably older.

Again casually, a controlling circumstance enters the formative influences on the new congregation. Mrs. McCann was a wealthy young widow, suddenly bereaved. Her husband had been physician to the sick at the House of Mercy from the beginning. When stricken, he in turn was served by the young community, Mother

Catherine herself attending at his deathbed. She was soon to know the impression her ministrations had made on the doctor's wife, for in that sorrowful hour Mrs. McCann resolved to follow Mother Catherine's example by devoting herself to the service of the sick and needy.

Placing her ten-year old daughter in the boarding school of the Loreto Sisters, the young widow became a postulant a few months after her husband's death. At the same time another circumstance was shaping a decision of the foundress.

In late summer Sister Mary Joseph Teresa, still a novice by choice, broke a blood vessel trying to rescue an orphan who had climbed to a dangerous position on a low roof. Illness brought on by this mishap aggravated her anxiety about her vocation. Mother Catherine called in two types of physicians, the medical specialist and the spiritual expert. The former ordered change of air. Mother Catherine, concerned and grieved as she was, responded that he must confine his recommendations to what was suitable to poor people "who might indeed procure some little nourishment or delicacy for their invalids but could not have the means of removing them to a country place."

Yet the reporter of the interview, one of the sisters then living at Baggot Street, testifies that Mother Catherine was "most tender and careful for the sick and infirm among her spiritual children. No expense seemed to her too great when there was question of procuring them any comfort." The account continues: "She sought to alleviate their pains by every affectionate contrivance which the heart of a fond mother could dictate and spared no labour and fatigue in their service, but even in her extraordinary care of the sick she evinced her love for religious poverty."[9]

To her niece's spiritual need she brought the discernment and wisdom of Archbishop Murray who had baptized her in 1828 and had conferred upon her the religious habit in 1832. The patient recounted to Sister Francis Warde the reasoning His Grace used and Sister Francis years later gave an outline of the interview to Mother M. Teresa Austin Carroll.

His Grace first asked Sister whether she would be satisfied with his decision. She had no difficulty in resting an unqualified confidence in his spiritual direction for, in common with thousands in the city, she revered the saintly Archbishop. She told him that she would follow his advice. Encouraged then to lay her problem before him, she proceeded with the optimism of the consumptive, and he tactfully dealt with it as if she could recover. He listened with paternal kindness to the arguments that had deterred her from profession. Influenced by a conviction that the contemplative life was superior to the active and by her recent inability to participate in the works of the Institute, she had concluded that her vocation lay with the Carmelites.

His Grace pointed out that Christ Himself had set the example of active contemplation or contemplative action by performing the works of mercy. "Your vocation," he said, "is to imitate Him as far as your superiors direct." As for impediment, the decision rested with superiors. The substance of his comment, as Mother Austin reports it, was: "It is not always those who *wish* to perform the works of mercy that are required to do so in religion but those *appointed*."

The Archbishop reminded the novice of the years of service she had given to the Institute before her health failed and emphasized the importance of her desire to help in the active work. He told her that all her doubts would presently evaporate, as they did.

By early November it was clear that she could not live much longer. Archbishop Murray, then sick, delegated Father Gaffney to receive her vows, and she made her profession on November 3. She lived a novena's length as a professed religious, dying shortly after midnight November 11, 1833. Her death is therefore registered for the next day.

The estimate of one who lived with her during her years at Baggot Street is worth quoting. Referring to her as "deservedly beloved by all who knew her," Mother M. Clare Moore summarizes:

From childhood her amiable disposition had endeared her to all and, as she advanced in years, she gave proofs of great virtue and piety. Having attained the happiness of becoming a member of the true Church, she from that moment devoted herself ardently to every religious duty. Listening only to her fervour while her aunt was at George's Hill Convent, she practised austerities which seriously injured her health. From the time she put on the religious habit she applied herself to acquire the virtues of that holy state with so much ardour that she was in some measure carried too far by her zeal and, anxious for greater perfection, sought to join an Order too rigourous for her delicate frame, but on her deathbed she begged to be admitted to Holy Profession and most fervently made her Vows a week before her death, which took place on the 12th of November, 1833.[10]

In her last illness she had been attended daily by her uncle, Dr. James McAuley, who had a great affection for her. He summoned other physicians, one of whom had been able to bring her to recovery in an earlier attack of the disease, but it was evident to all that there could be no recuperation from this. Those who had known her thought she had never been so lovely as on the last day of her life. Her joy at the prospect of death astonished the doctor who had known her from infancy. She thanked him for his many kindnesses to her and asked God's special blessing on him. She reminded Dr. James that he had never refused her anything and made the only request he seemed unable to fulfill, that he return to the Faith of his baptism.

Before that Martinmas ended, the Faith within her was to be obscured. After nightfall she struggled in a deeper darkness for two hours. Suffering to see her suffer, Mother Catherine interrupted the prayers with an exclamation: "I know Our Lord would comfort her if the Mother of Mercy would only say one prayer for her!"

At the mention of the Mother of Mercy, Sister's agonized face relaxed into a faint smile and she gradually regained her calm. Her last prayer was for the wayward, her last aspirations the holy Names of Jesus and Mary. Shortly after midnight Mother Catherine eased her up that she might breathe more freely. Her face grew radiant and she relaxed in the arms of her aunt.

Without a tear Mother Catherine said the prayers for the departed. To the sisters she said, "I loved my Mary Teresa too much and God took her from me. We must love Him as well when He takes as when He gives. May I never be free from His cross!"

She who had been willing to release the young novice to the Carmelites now applied to Father O'Hanlon for a place among the other Sisters of Mercy in the vault at St. Teresa's. On the day of Sister M. Joseph Teresa's funeral the new Vicar General, Father Coleman, presided at the Office chanted by priests. It was followed by a High Mass sung by the Carmelite Prior.

XXI

Growing Time

EARLY IN 1833 the chapters on visitation of the sick and protection of young women were submitted to Archbishop Murray. That very fall the rule of the Irish Sisters of Charity was confirmed and the rejoicing of their patrons revived old comparisons. Mother M. Augustine and her spiritual daughters had reason to rejoice, for eighteen years was a short span to compass approbation and confirmation of a religious rule.[1] But the ill-considered comparison brought embarrassment to the foundress of the younger Institute that could claim only eighteen months of existence. Therefore, when toward the end of 1833 an Augustinian friar, Father John Rice, called at Baggot Street on his way to the Holy City and asked Mother Catherine whether he could serve her when in Rome, she told him of her desire to have the new chapters of her rule confirmed. To understand Father Rice's interest in Mercy Institute, one must know something of the life story of Edmund Rice, his brother.[2] By 1833 Edmund Rice was a prominent figure in Catholic education in Ireland.

He had been born near Kilkenny over seventy years before and had procured a good education in spite of discrimination against Catholics. He spent his young manhood in Waterford in his uncle's import and export business, which he later inherited. Though active in relief work among the poor, he felt called to religious life. At that time a noviceship had to be made on the continent, since penal restrictions still had force in Ireland. The plan to go abroad for this purpose was well formed in his mind when his Augustinian brother stopped in Waterford on a return trip from Rome about the middle of the 1790's. Edmund confided his intention to Father Rice who, realizing the loss to the Irish poor, dissuaded him. Several years passed before the subject came up again. He then consulted Dr. Lanigan, Bishop of his native diocese, who told him that his vocation lay in the field of education among poor boys of his own country. Repeating this advice to others whose opinion he valued, he learned that all agreed with Dr. Lanigan. He therefore went to the Bishop of Waterford and arranged to build a school. His business had never been so lucrative as in 1800, the year he disposed of it and engaged two salaried assistants to begin his work. A little experience proved that no amount of salary would induce paid teachers to stay. What that implies can be imagined. Others came, however, to do for love of the Boy Christ what money could not procure.

As helpers increased in number, Mr. Rice found himself in a situation similar to Catherine McAuley's twenty years later, and he did what by coincidence she was to do. He adopted and adapted the Presentation Rule. Invitations to other dioceses followed upon the success of his Waterford schools and he organized units in Cork, in Dublin, and in Limerick. Since the Presentation Rule designated the diocesan ordinary as principal superior after the Holy See, Brother Rice up to 1820 had no jurisdiction over houses in other dioceses.

From the time Dr. Murray invited him to establish in Dublin, His Lordship, then Coadjutor Archbishop, maintained an active interest in the new institute. He advised the founder to apply to Rome for confirmation of his rule. With the aid of Father Peter Kenny, S. J., Brother Rice in 1817 submitted to the Holy See a set of rules and constitutions for the Irish Christian Brothers. Three years later by Apostolic Brief Pope Pius VII established the "Fratres Monachi" as the first congregation of religious men in Ireland. In accord with the provision of the Brief for a superior general, the Irish Christian Brothers elected Brother Rice.

A circumstance that was to have unexpected results now interposed. Bishop Murphy of Cork refused to relinquish his authority over the Christian Brothers in his diocese, but by going one by one to Waterford to place their vows in the hands of the Brother General, the Cork members were enabled to conform to the wishes of the Holy See. By 1826 Brother Rice finally succeeded in including all of his houses under the government of the superior general. One of the Cork members, Brother Austin Reardon, remained with Bishop Murphy and became founder of the Presentation Brothers.

Subsequent to the promulgation of the Apostolic Brief in favor of the Irish Christian Brothers, the Superior General received so many applications for admission and so many invitations to open schools that before his death in 1844 his congregation had twenty-three houses in Ireland, England, and Australia with requests to establish in Newfoundland, Canada, and the United States.

Edmund Rice was already past seventy when in 1833 his Augustinian brother called on him before leaving for the Holy City. The opportunity that came to Mother Catherine at this time must be attributed to the sympathetic interest of the Founder of the Irish Christian Brothers. From Rome the venerable Augustinian sent to her for the necessary documents of appeal. On December 8, 1833, she forwarded a copy of her vows and a transcript of the new chapters. To these were added a statement from "Mr. E. Rice" and the formal petition. It is apparent from the petition that she and her advisers supposed confirmation could follow approval of the intercalary chapters.

Most Holy Father

Catherine McAuley, prostrate at the feet of Your Holiness humbly begs that you deign to confirm a congregation that she with certain other pious women has founded. The principal purpose of this congregation is to educate poor little girls, to lodge and maintain poor young ladies who are in danger, that they may be provided for in a proper manner, and to visit the sick poor. With the attention they find in this institute these poor escape dangers menacing their faith and morals on all sides. Already in a short time 772 poor women have been provided for, more hundreds of children have been taught and admitted to the Sacraments, and the poor come here with their disputes and quarrels; and it is unbelievable the good that is done on all these occasions. The petitioner has made vows into the hands of Archbishop Murray of Dublin, and another twenty-three sisters have followed her example. They make profession according to the rules and constitutions of the Presentation Order with such changes as will be approved by the Archbishop so that all that remains to confirm are two chapters necessarily added because of their different purpose. They humbly supplicate Your Holiness to grant that they be placed on the same footing [*medesimo piede*] with the religious of that Order.[3]

The following spring Archbishop Murray received a letter from the Holy See asking him to express an opinion on the representations made for Catherine McAuley. In reply he affirmed the content of the petition and gave in brief the history of the Institute, concluding:

There remain up to the present in the above-mentioned house, twenty-three really devoted women. Of these, only eight up to this time have pronounced their vows; ten having been clothed in the holy habit, are occupied in fulfilling the period of training and five (of whom two are lay sisters) are in the first period of probation asking the holy habit. And with much benefit to souls they assiduously devote themselves to the pious works mentioned in the petition. I myself judge them completely worthy of receiving every mark of kindness from His Holiness that will render permanent this most propitious beginning for furthering the Divine Glory.

This favorable testimony was directed to "the Most Eminent and Most Reverend D. D. Cardinal Pedicini" under date of June 21, 1834.

While correspondence was going on preliminary to the approbation of the rule, the twenty-three Sisters of Mercy were trying to meet charity demands that would have taxed the abilities of three times twenty-three. Conditions among the poor after the cholera were appalling. Experienced now in the most successful procedure for the annual benefit bazaar and encouraged by the patronage of the titled and the influential, Mother Catherine directed an appeal to the Duchess of Kent for samples of her handiwork and that of her fifteen-year old daughter, the Princess Victoria, so soon to be Queen of England. Mother M. Clare Moore comments:

The spirit of mercy and compassion for the poor which animated and, as it were, consumed her made her sometimes adopt plans for their relief which to some appeared beyond the limits of prudence, but the success with which her undertakings were usually attended showed that she was guided by a heavenly wisdom. She sent by post a letter to Her Royal Highness the Duchess of Kent, entreating that she and the

Princess Victoria would give some of their work for a bazaar about to be held for the relief of the poor. A gracious answer was returned, and the Duchess of Kent sent some of her own beautiful work with drawings and transferred boxes done by her royal daughter. This extraordinary contribution was of considerable benefit to the Institute and realized, as may well be supposed, a very large sum of money.[4]

If previous bazaars had found a place on the social calendar, the flurry over the royal donations made this affair one of the most brilliant occasions the Rotunda[5] had known, accustomed though it was to social splendor.

Whether it was the success of the spring benefit or another determining influence, Dr. Meyler decided to cut off the only source of regular revenue to the charities, the weekly donations made by those attending Sunday Mass in Our Lady of Mercy chapel. Since the new St. Andrew's had been completed early in the year, parishioners in the Baggot Street area could all be accommodated in the parish church. Dr. Meyler's prohibition, issued in the fall of 1834, is so in accord with general practice today that it is difficult to see how Mother Catherine had a claim. The Archbishop himself, however, had been responsible for the arrangement made in 1829; therefore, Mother Catherine consulted her friend Bishop Blake. It was not the first time since he had been elevated to the See of Dromore that she had turned to him for direction. Shortly after he left Dublin, she had received an application for admission from a Miss McGuinness of Newry. Since this lady did enter into the Baggot Street charities in the role of benefactress and since her interest became a source of trial at a time when Mother Catherine was much tried, both of these early letters of Bishop Blake are given here.

Under date of June 5, 1833:

You should not have been so long without receiving an answer to your kind letter of the 27 April had I not been ever since immersed in the duties belonging to the Jubilee time and were I not anxious, before I would reply, to have my mind properly informed on the subject of your inquiry. As I have no personal acquaintance with the lady herself and have not seen her but once for a moment, my information has been necessarily borrowed from others. But I have consulted several dispassionate persons and all have agreed in acknowledging the strict morality and religious habits of that lady, all are persuaded that she has means for doing extensive good, all finally regret that one little drawback from the excellence of her other qualities is found in a certain peculiarity, a singular mode of thinking and judging by which she is distinguished. I hope that you and your community all continue to enjoy good health now that everything there is going so well.

Under date of October 23, 1834:

Your kind letter of the 13th must have arrived in Newry, I should suppose, on the following [day], but as I was then just commencing a second week's retreat with some of my clergy, it was not brought to me until the salutary business was entirely over. Otherwise you should have received a few lines from me before now.

I most cordially sympathize with you and your edifying Community in the trial which the closing of your chapel [to the public] must have caused, although I am sure from my knowledge of the natural kindness of your revered Archbishop and of his frequently declared sentiments respecting the merits of your Institution, that nothing short of an imperative sense of duty could have induced him to insist on such a sacrifice. If he has not explained his reasons to you, be persuaded that they are strong and cogent. I have not forgotten you in my poor prayers. Trusting in the efficacy of Divine grace, I hope that you and all the members of your Community will be superior to the workings of human weakness and will not utter a murmur of complaint. It would be right, however, that you should know clearly the will of His Grace, Dr. Murray, and beg as a favour that he would express it directly himself to you. You seek nothing from selfish motives; he will require nothing but what is right, and if his decision causes some pain, he will alleviate, he will reconcile you to it by his consoling and healing advice. I beg you to present my most affectionate and respectful compliments to His Grace, and to remain assured that I shall have always the kindest sentiments toward you and your community.

Sometime during 1833 the foundress parted temporarily with her niece Catherine, then about fifteen years old. Dr. James had invited her to live with him and his family, and she consented to go. A weighty consideration and undoubtedly Father O'Hanlon's advice must have induced Mother Catherine to agree. That she feared her brother's influence with her nephews is clear from a letter she wrote on an occasion to Dr. Fitzgerald. Yet she seems to have had confidence that Catherine's faith could not be affected by the Protestant atmosphere of her brother's household. Mother

Austin, who had both Teresa Byrn and Frances Warde for reference, states that the arrangement was a deliberately planned test of young Catherine's vocation.

At any rate, Mother Catherine and Dr. James for different reasons saw the wisdom of removing their niece from Baggot Street for a time. If it is true that after the death of her sister, Catherine expressed the desire to become a Sister of Mercy, it was certainly wise to give her a change of atmosphere in order to learn whether she had a true vocation or whether she had been unduly impressed by the example and loss of her sister. Willie's love for their Aunt Frances, as well as the friendly relations between her and Mother Catherine, speaks much for the personality and character of Dr. James' wife. Young Catherine's stay in their home must have been a profitable and happy experience. Meanwhile, the services of the governess who had been teaching Catherine Macauley and Teresa Byrn at Baggot Street were discontinued and Teresa was placed in a boarding school.

During this year Mother Catherine seems to have been turning over in her mind the possibility of purchasing a house away from the city where sick sisters might recuperate their health, and circumstances now concurred to enable her to carry out the advice given by Sir Philip and the recommendation made by the specialist who had attended Sister Mary Teresa McAuley. Little Kate McCann died from a childhood illness while her mother was still in the novitiate of the Sisters of Mercy.[6] Sister Mary de Chantal (McCann) therefore planned to put her money at Mother Catherine's disposal for the express purpose of buying a house in a locality where sisters could do the work of visitation as well as care for sick members of the community. The young widow's mother cautioned prudence. After all, Mrs. McCann was just out of her twenties when the doctor died. She should have some security, her mother told her. She might not persevere or the new venture itself might fail. What would she do then?

"Won't I have my sweet Lord?" Sister asked, reminding her mother of other days when she used to reprove the young matron for giving to every beggar she met.

"Better to help a hundred imposters," the doctor's wife said then, "than turn away one deserving person."

And now she would devote all her resources to opening the second convent of the Institute. With Father O'Hanlon's approval, the foundress enlisted the aid of the convent chaplain to locate a house. He in turn must have consulted one of his religious brothers, chaplain to the Poor Clares in Kingstown, for a suitable house there came to his attention. Its situation, close to the newly built parish church, obviated the necessity of a separate chaplain for the convent. With the permission of the Archbishop, Mother Catherine now opened at Sussex Place, Kingstown, the first branch house of the congregation.

Bishop Donnelly lists the completion of a new church, dedicated to St. Michael, the beginning of the Dublin-Kingstown rail service, and the opening of St. Patrick's Convent of Mercy as significant incidents of the year 1835, all contributing to the period of progress on which Kingstown then entered. His Lordship eulogizes with some undertones the Reverend Bartholomew Sheridan, P. P., into whose debt-encumbered parish the Sisters of Mercy moved in 1835. Looking back on Father Sheridan's thirty-three years of service to the city, Bishop Donnelly comments:

None can dispute or question the energy of his character or his zeal or personal piety, but he got the repute of a shrewd and close financier; yet few can show such lasting and prolific results. Kingstown Church completed and four new churches with a fifth commenced are standing monuments to his economic administration, especially when we remember that he accomplished all this without almost any appeal to his people.[7]

Endowed though she was with business acumen, Mother Catherine was not prepared for the particular shrewdness of the Reverend Mr. Sheridan. Therefore, by reacting with characteristic zeal to conditions that fell under her observation, she involved herself in a situation both amusing and exasperating. While making visitations to the sick, she was struck by the number of young girls idle on the streets. How much opportunity she had for observing them Mother Clare implies in telling of the work in Kingstown:

They visited the sick going often a very great distance, and our good foundress, notwithstanding the difficulty she experienced in walking, never spared herself in those labours of charity and mercy.[8]

Mother Catherine's natural impulse to gather in these neglected girls and train them found a momentary check in the practical questions: Where? How?

Where? The unused stables and coach house could be put into condition if the parish would support the project. "Nobody expected the parish priest would," the writer of the Dublin manuscript comments tersely. The same writer elsewhere mentions Mother Catherine's fund of optimism and, unfortunately now for the foundress, the curate at St. Michael's, the Reverend William Walsh,[9] seems to have been likewise endowed. He sounded out affluent parishioners who supported him with enthusiasm if not with money. Father Sheridan countenanced anything that would improve his parish but was too shrewd to particularize on finance. A local builder offered long credit. With the good will of all and the promises of no one but the foundress, hers limited specifically and stated definitely, the remodeling was done and the school opened. It met with instant success to the gratification of everybody, and the long-term credit stood the test. Meanwhile, progress marked the parish and redounded to the credit of its pastor.

Having established her first branch house, Mother Catherine returned to the parent house. While she had been attending to the business of St. Patrick's Convent, Kingstown, Archbishop Murray had received from the Holy See a letter of the highest praise for the society called "of Mercy" with the approval of His Holiness on its establishment. The letter was specific on the matter of vows, showing that the copy of Catherine McAuley's profession had been carefully examined. The Holy Father adhered to the tradition of the Church, reserving solemn vows to religious orders of women having papal cloister. The perpetual vows of the Sisters of Mercy were to be simple. The letter authorized His Grace to complete the adjustment of the Presentation rule and constitutions to the needs of the Institute of Mercy. The Archbishop therefore asked Mother Catherine to put the two new chapters in context and to make any other alterations she thought necessary so that he might deliberate on the rule of the Sisters of Mercy in its entirety. He would then comply with the direction of the Holy See and give it a finished form.

Father Gaffney, appointed by His Grace in 1832 to aid Mother Catherine in drafting the new chapters, had meanwhile been made

Dean of Maynooth. Neither the responsibilities of his new position, however, nor the death of his sister caused him to lessen his interest in the congregation. Sister M. Mechtildis Gaffney died June 14, 1835.

Mother Catherine continued to direct the novitiate to the great profit of the novices.[10] On the tenor of her instructions the London manuscript gives the following:

Our Foundress's time being constantly occupied with necessary business, she could not devote herself so fully as she wished to the instruction of the novices; nevertheless she provided excellently for the preservation of due order and regularity by establishing the strict observance of silence. Her exhortations were most animated and impressive, especially on the duties of charity and humility. These were her cherished virtues which she inculcated more by her example than by words. She taught the sisters to avoid all that might be in the least contrary to charity, even the slightest remark on manner or natural defects, so that they should make it a rule never to say anything unfavorable of one another. She was not content with their avoiding the smallest faults against this favored virtue of Our Blessed Lord; they were to evince it in their whole conduct. She instructed them to observe in speaking mildness and great sweetness, to be ready always to yield and condescend to others and careful to edify by word and example . . . .
While she passed over without seeming to notice them many inadvertent offenses, she was most watchful to correct in their conversation or manners the least failure against politeness, and anything which could discover the want of a good education, being convinced by experience that the inattention of some religious to these minor points often lessens charity in a community, as it tends to diminish the respect which seculars should have for the religious state.

Mother Catherine had many little devices for enlivening the recreation hours or for correcting without seeming to correct. One of these was composing simple rhymes and requiring the reply to be made in kind. A number of examples have fortunately been preserved by those who took a particular enjoyment in them. One from the period of her direction of the novices concerns her own feast day:

Dear Reverend Mother, our cook and your namesake
Wants to compose a most beautiful tea cake

For materials of which 'twill be needful to pay
And therefore for cash your petitioners pray.

The Sisters of the Noviceship

The reply in her own handwriting is:

Dear Sisters,
Early this morning on leaving the choir
I did anticipate this your desire
And sent out an order in time to bespeak
What I hope you will find—a very nice cake.

Another example in the same vein began with Mother Catherine herself. The sister to whom it was addressed had received a half crown from a visitor and wanted it for the sick poor, who were her charge.

To my great surprise you demanded last night,
The enclosed as your own—your particular right:
I am sorry to find such a matter distract you,
I did not suppose such a crown could attract you;
But since with reluctance from it you would part,
Take it—there is no such tie on my heart.

The Sister answered:

Dear Mother, in spite of your jesting I own
That I ever ambitiously sigh for a crown
Which the one you surrender may aid me to gain
And therefore the right of my poor I maintain.
This very day twelvemonth it was that you bound
With a black leather cincture my waist and will round
And to tell of my happiness humbly I pray
That the Sisters may have recreation today.

To this Mother Catherine replied:

I rejoice in your motive for liking this day
But not in your wishing to spend it in play

I must freely confess it were more to my mind
If to reflection your heart were inclined:
But since you're not weaned nor alone cannot walk
I suppose you must do what you can do—then talk.

On the foundress' manner of correcting, Sister M. Vincent Hartnett says:

Reverend Mother truly acted on that lesson of an ancient spiritualist never to command anything that she had not first practiced herself. She lost no time in useless discourse. When she had to find fault, she did so as briefly as possible, impressively but mildly. It evidently was a duty that gave her great pain. Even with those ladies who aided her with the bazaar, she spoke little. She wished everyone to work for God and say little about it . . . . It was only in matters which dear Reverend Mother considered of great moment that she gave reprehension and then in few words.[11]

Further ancedotes on Mother Catherine's method of correction appear in Mother Austin's biography. From the latter's practice of using a true initial of a person whose name she withheld, it is now possible to identify many of her references.

Among the postulants admitted during 1834 was young Catherine McAuley whose taste of social life in her uncle's family had made her only more determined to work among the poor. Like her mother's sister she possessed a natural compassion for them, supported by a supernatural urge to spend her energies in relieving their distress.

Perhaps the presence of her niece influenced Mother Catherine to withdraw from immediate charge of the novitiate. Whatever her reason, she appointed Sister Mary de Pazzi mistress of novices toward the close of 1835. Fortunately for the novices, several months passed before Mother Catherine began foundations. She therefore remained in a supervisory position. To use an expression of those first sisters, Mother de Pazzi was "a little on the severe side."

Stormanstown House, Dublin. Birthplace of Catherine McAuley

James Malton's sketch of Capel Street, Dublin, in the 1790's

toria and Albert Museum

Coolock House, Dublin

Convent of Our Lady of Mercy, Baggot Street, Dublin

resentation Convent, George's Hill, Dublin. Garden and St. Michan's Church

hapel of Our Lady of Mercy, Baggot Street, Dublin, dedicated on June 4, 1829

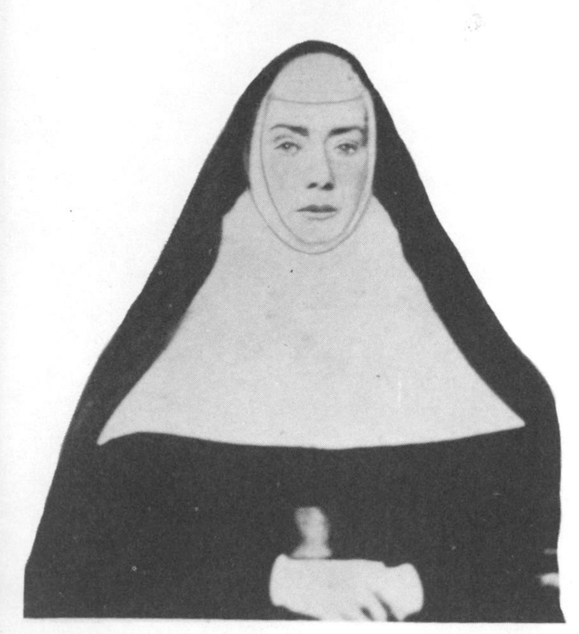

Sister Mary Francis Xavier Warde, first Sister of Mercy received and professed at Baggot Street

First Convent of Mercy outside the Dublin diocese, St. Joseph's, Tullamore

St. Anne's, Booterstown

St. John's Convent of Mercy, Birr

St. Mary's Convent of Mercy, Limerick, showing entrance to garden through the ruins of St. Saviour's, thirteenth century Dominican Church

First building erected as a Convent of Mercy, St. Leo's, Carlow

onvent of Our Lady of Mercy, Carysfort Park, Dublin, present motherhouse of e parent community

Mt. Vernon Convent, Liverpool

The London Evening

Bermondsey Convent, England, after March, 1945, bombing

Convent refectory, Birmingham

onvent chapel, Birmingham

Parish Church, Birr, where Mother Catherine McAuley renewed her vows the last year of her life, January 1, 1841

Convent infirmary where Mother Catherine McAuley spent the last days of her life

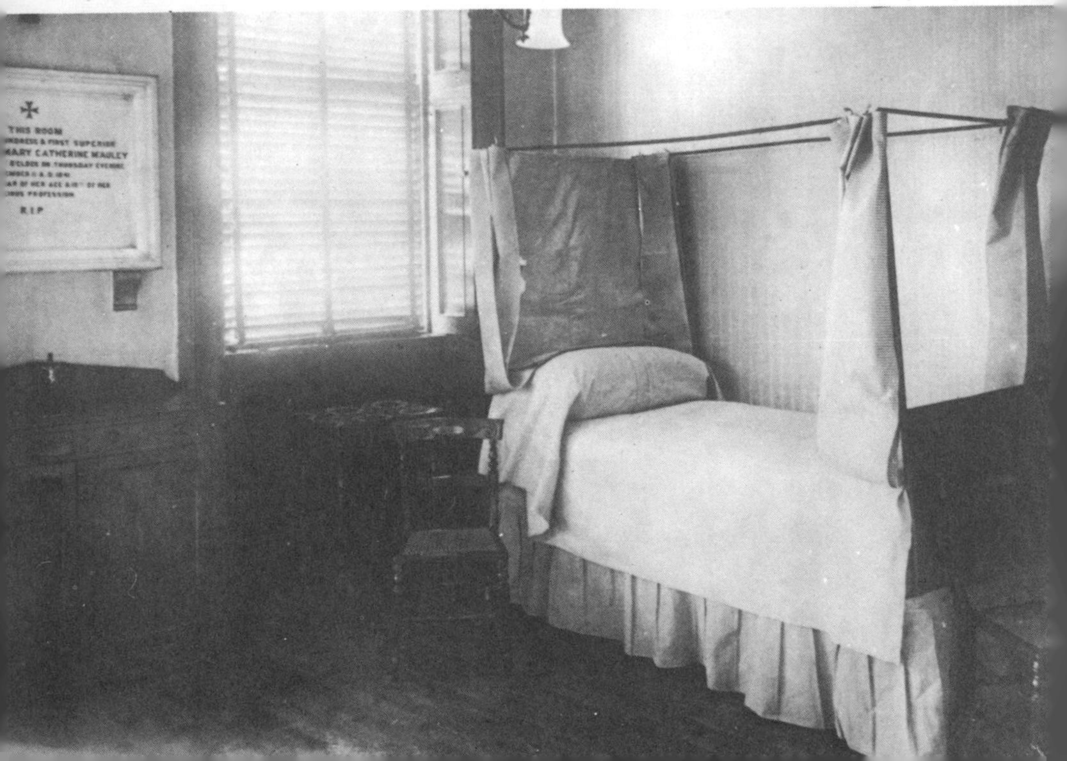

Mother Mary Agnes O'Connor, present at MotherCatherine's deathbed

Keogh Bros. Ltd.

Hall of relics of Mother Catherine McAuley
Baggot Street, Dublin, left side view

Hall of relics, right side view

Keogh Bros. Ltd.

XXII

Multiplied Mercy

IN THE fall of 1835 an old lady died in Tullamore, a town on the rim of the Irish midlands. At the age of seventy-five she had come from Dublin to live in retirement and use the income of a substantial legacy[1] for the poor of her native town. A rather usual circumstance arose. The will on which she depended was successfully contested, leaving her little more than an annuity. Had she been willing to defend her claim, she could probably have supported it, but she preferred to remain in retirement doing good with whatever God provided.

When Miss Pentony returned to Tullamore in 1824, she hoped to open a way for a foundation of Irish Sisters of Charity. Loss of income, however, obliged her to proceed with only the assistance of a personal friend, Catherine Barnewall. Another young lady, Elizabeth Locke, came to their aid and applied herself zealously to the program: to teach religion to the young, "to visit and comfort the dying poor and to relieve distress."[2] For a dozen years the three carried on these charities simultaneously with Catherine McAuley's lay activity in Dublin. At the age of 86 Miss Pentony died leaving her small house and garden in the hands of her pastor with the specification that it should become a convent. Little was secured to it for maintenance because she had little. Nevertheless, Reverend Dr. O'Rafferty, Vicar General of the diocese of Meath and parish priest at Tullamore, set out for Dublin to try to carry out the terms of Miss Pentony's bequest. If he had some misgivings on its adequacy, he drew courage from the enthusiasm of his curate, Father Murtagh.

In Dublin Father O'Rafferty learned that he could not then secure a foundation from Mother Augustine. At a loss to know how to proceed further, he called on the Carmelite Prior, Miss Pentony's friend and advisor before her return to Tullamore. Father O'Hanlon suggested that Dr. O'Rafferty lay his problem before Mother McAuley over on Baggot Street. Whether he had ever heard of her till that moment, he was never to forget the interview. Her grace of manner, the spiritual force of her calm, the compassionate tenor of her words made an impression that he rehearsed to his old age for Sisters of Mercy of another generation.

Sister M. Vincent Hartnett confirms this impression of the foundress:

> Her own manners were most pleasing and a perfect exemplification of what she required of others both as regarded her intercourse with the sisters and seculars. She was gifted with great observation and she seemed to be intimately acquainted with the workings of the human heart; so that with ease she adapted her conversation either for edification or instruction to the circumstances of the moment and always agreeably and with dignity. Though so cautious, her manners were neither formal nor stiff. There was nothing of self about her. She never cared for nor studied self but made everything in her conduct subservient to God's honour and her neighbour's good. For these she conversed and worked and lived.[3]

The needs of the Irish poor she understood. Father O'Rafferty therefore stressed the poverty awaiting those who would undertake the work. As if he had mentioned a valuable asset, Mother Catherine seized upon the very condition he had been reluctant to disclose. She would make the foundation, she said, in honor of the beginning of Christ's earthly life in Bethlehem.

It has been said that she thereby set aside a request from her friend Bishop Kinsella who had been importuning her for a foundation in behalf of unemployed servants. Certain objections, however, entered into her refusal of an opening in Kilkenny. Whatever the inducements otherwise, Mother Catherine considered the house offered too public for either the sisters or the young women to be sheltered.[4] She told His Lordship that she could not undertake work in his diocese until the sisters and their charges would have privacy. Tullamore, therefore, secured the first Convent of Mercy outside the archdiocese.

Before the foundation materialized, Mother Catherine's niece had received the religious habit with the name Sister M. Anne Agnes.[5] By 1836 the two elder McAuley boys had returned to the capital to study law and Willie was thinking of going to sea—that is, if he could induce his brother James to outfit him. These three dearly loved nephews became a source of anxiety and grief to Mother Catherine in the next few years. From now on, too, trials connected with her work increased. On this subject the writer of the Dublin manuscript observes:

> The greatest trial of all to her was the frequent deaths of the sisters .... She had a great awe or even fear of death, and she never saw the approach of a sister's death without great emotion. She had really a tender affection for us.

Before she went to Tullamore—in fact, before or during almost every foundation—this trial of bereavement came to her. On February 10, 1836, Sister M. Agnes Marmion died of erysipelas. She had made her novitiate under Mother Catherine herself. One of her sisters was a novice when Sister Agnes died and another entered later. Nor was the liberality of the good parents of these gifted children limited to the sacrifice of their three daughters. The community treasurer could have testified that their benefactions far surpassed those of wealthier patrons.

In early Paschaltide Mother Catherine set out on her first foundation. Accompanied by Father O'Rafferty, who had come into the city to escort the sisters, and by their spiritual director Father O'Hanlon, sisters for the new mission left Dublin, April 21, before 7 A.M. on the "Fly-boat" that plied the Grand Canal between the capital and the Shannon. With Mother Catherine were Sister Mary Anne Doyle for superior; a novice, Sister M. Teresa Purcell, who was to remain, and Sisters Mary Clare Moore and Anne Agnes to help establish the works of the congregation in the Diocese of Meath. At three o'clock they arrived in Tullamore where a rejoicing congregation awaited them. To the embarrassment of the sisters, all were helped to "an outside car" except the foundress who had a place of honor in a carriage with the pastor and the Carmelite Prior. Driven slowly through the crowds but never out of them, the sisters reached the parish church accompanied by the parishioners. There God's blessing was invoked on the work about to begin. Dr. O'Rafferty then introduced Elizabeth Locke as one of two postulants who had been waiting for the sisters to arrive, and he invited her to have dinner with them. Afterwards she and Father Murtagh brought them to their new home which had somehow been fitted up as a convent, though the tiny chapel would not be ready for another month. Meanwhile, a private choir had been arranged in the church. No account of the Tullamore convent would be complete without Mother McAuley's remark in a letter written to Dublin:

> Mother M. Anne has at last met her "beau ideal" of a conventual building, for our rooms are so small that two cats could scarcely dance in them! The rest of us, however, would have no objection to larger ones.

Visitors today must use their imagination on the original rooms, for the old building was merged with the house next door in 1840 and, by taking down partitions, was converted into a school in 1841.

The original house was blessed as a convent the Sunday after the sisters arrived and dedicated to St. Joseph in honor of the feast of his patronage. The works of mercy were immediately begun by visitation of the sick. Since it was impossible to establish a school in their confined quarters, the sisters helped out in the Thomas Street garret school of Miss Alwell, a fully qualified National School teacher. Proficiency in the system, then new, was no mean accomplishment. Yet when this excellent teacher applied for admission to the community two years later, when parish schools opened, Dr. Cantwell advised that she be accepted as a lay sister. Her entry speaks much for her character, and it is unnecessary to add that she was a definite asset to the Institute. Elizabeth Locke came to stay on the feast of St. Catherine of Siena, and Mary Delamere, a personal friend of hers, entered on Ascension Thursday, May 10. A third postulant arrived ten days after Mary Delamere. Since there were neither rooms nor beds for all, Mother Catherine arranged a dormitory with "shakedowns" for the sisters and assigned the postulants to the rooms, or cells as they could now be called. "She always showed extreme consideration for the young," one of the three as community annalist recorded.

Of Mother Catherine's usual procedure with regard to foundations Sister Mary Clare Moore, who accompanied her on several, says:

When she went to found convents, she invariably chose the poorest and cheapest mode of traveling, often to her own great inconvenience. Her bed was usually on the floor, as she never waited for a new convent to be comfortably arranged, satisfied to have any kind of opening to extend the good effected by the institute. She relied on the loving Providence of her Heavenly Father that all necessaries would be supplied, and she was never disappointed.[6]

Tullamore was certainly a case in point. There she began the practice of remaining at least a month, saying for the new mission the two Thirty Days' Prayers in honor of the Passion. She once confided to Sister Mary Clare Moore that "she was careful what she petitioned by means of [this devotion], as the request was sure to be granted."[7]

In Sister Mary Clare's opinion Mother Catherine's marked benignity drew from her devotion to the person of Jesus Christ. In the London manuscript she wrote of the foundress:

Her sweet compliance was not so much the effect of innate benevolence as of her desire to resemble our Blessed Lord. She constantly repeated: "Be always striving to make yourselves like Him. You should try to resemble Him in some one thing at least, so that any person who sees you or speaks with you may be reminded of His blessed life on earth."

Sister M. Vincent Hartnett says further:

Reverend Mother compared humility to the root of a tree which strikes deeper in proportion to the loftiness of the branches and which lie concealed while it imparts life and stability. Though it is the source whence the beautiful head and spreading branches derive all that makes them worthy of admiration, yet does it hide itself away in the soil.

She was very earnest in teaching poverty and carefully excluded superfluities. She often drew comparisons between the poverty of which our Divine Lord from His birth to His death set the example and that practiced by religious; and she used to say that, though His was incomparably greater than ours, yet it possessed one trait of resemblance, that of being voluntary. She said that labour should always accompany poverty as a constant attendant and even a consequence, as labour was the lot of the poor. On this she used sometimes quote: "He that will not work, let him not eat." She showed how these virtues harmonized and promoted not only spiritual good but also health and cheerfulness.[8]

During the month the foundress remained in Tullamore she prepared Sister M. Teresa Purcell for profession. The annalist states that the fortunate novice kept a record of the instructions, which the community has preserved.[9] In note form they lose something of their original force but retain the spiritual character of Mother Catherine's teaching.

The little convent received the Blessed Sacrament on Pentecost Sunday. On Thursday of the week following, the Most Reverend Dr. Cantwell, Bishop of the diocese, called and confirmed Sister Mary Anne's appointment to the office of Mother Superior. The following morning Sister M. Teresa made profession of vows at ten o'clock Mass in the parish church, the Bishop officiating. The value of a public ceremony to introduce the aims of the community in new territory impressed itself on Mother Catherine that day, and she thereafter made it a practice to bring with her on a foundation a sister about to be received or professed so that people and clergy might become acquainted with the purpose of the congregation through the ceremonial and the sermon.

The custom of wearing the crucifix visibly is attributed to a remark of the foundress on this occasion. The Mercy cross, a white inset in ebony, completed the rosary. To the religious it conveyed a message, conformity to the Cross of Christ. The crucifix was displayed in the sick room and in classrooms, in the chapel and in the convent corridors and cells where it could always receive the respect and veneration it deserved.[10] It was carried concealed on the person of the religious as an intimate memento of her dedication. On the profession morning, the young aspirant placed her crucifix momentarily on her breast, resting it in the cincture. The foundress, looking up, observed it and made a remark construed as favorable to wearing it so. The Tullamore community consequently adopted the custom of conferring the crucifix at profession to be worn in the cincture, a practice that became almost universal in the congregation.

Dr. Cantwell said Mass in the convent chapel the next morning and set August first for the reception ceremony. Before confirmation of the rule the Bishop had the power to shorten probationary terms and often exerted his privilege for the first ceremonies of a new foundation.

Promising to return for the reception, Mother Catherine left for Dublin on Monday, May 30, taking with her Sisters Clare and Anne Agnes. Dr. Cantwell called at St. Joseph's again that day to console the community in the loss of the sustaining presence of their Mother Foundress—"to them their living Rule," Mary Delamere wrote. As Tullamore convent annalist from 1836 to 1844 this religious deserves mention. From her faithful account the story of the foundation can be easily reconstructed. A letter the foundress wrote this postulant in the intervening two months exists as her first extant letter to any of the sisters.

By the time Mother Catherine returned to Tullamore in July the people had responded generously to the sisters' needs, and wealthy parishioners had come to the support of the pastor in plans for a new convent and schools. Father Murtagh meanwhile presented what he considered a practical gift, a cow. The annalist observes, however, that lacking so much as a blade of grass for its maintenance, the community sent it out to the country to graze. Reports on "Madame La Vache," as Mother Catherine referred to the animal, supplied considerable amusement to the Dublin sisters. Before Mother Catherine returned to Tullamore she received a visit from the pastor at Charleville, a town on the northern border of County Cork. Father Croke had come to complete arrangements for a foundation in his parish. Tentative plans had already been made by one of his outstanding parishioners. On Mary Clanchy's visits to the Dublin convent she had met Sister Mary Angela Dunne whose vocation inspired her and she determined to establish the Sisters of Mercy among the poor of her own town.

Both the Bishop of the diocese and her pastor knew and approved her plan. Whatever her charitable interests before 1830, they intensified with the death of her father. She was the only daughter of John Clanchy whose solid mansion stood like an old manor house just out of Charleville along a hawthorne-lined road to the east. Besides the mansion and its grounds "John Clanchy, gentleman," owned the last row of houses on the town side and stables lodging some of the finest horses in Ireland.

The Clanchy mansion had bright spacious rooms made brighter with trophies and curios according to the tastes and interests of its owner. Though the small family had grown smaller with the death of Mrs. Clanchy and the marriage of Mary's elder brother, there were servants and visitors enough to keep the place lively at any season. But the life and brightness died for Mary with the death of her father. When her younger brother John married in 1832, Mary decided to become a Sister of Mercy with the hope of bringing a foundation to Charleville. She sent her musical instruments to the motherhouse, offered one of her father's houses for a convent, and pledged £500 for a beginning.

Meanwhile, however, she found in Arthur French, eldest son of Jeffrey French of Tomona House, Elphin, the sympathy and affection that she needed and married him. Since she did not withdraw the proffer of the house, her pastor felt sure that she intended to contribute the money pledged. With the permission of his Bishop he therefore called at Baggot Street in July and completed arrangements for the Charleville foundation.

Consequently, when Mother Catherine returned to Tullamore at the end of the month, she expected to pass that way again in the fall. By post she had promised Sister Mary (Delamere) a real holiday spirit at the time of the reception. The letter, written in a light vein, has some well managed points, ending on a note characteristic of Mother Catherine's genuine warm-heartedness:

> Of one thing, however, I am sure—and seriously so—that I seldom look forward to any change in this world with such happiness as I do to our meeting.

Accompanied by the convent chaplain, Mother Catherine, Sister Mary Clare Moore, Sister M. Elizabeth Moore, and Sister Mary de Chantal McCann arrived in Tullamore on Friday, July 29, for the first Mercy reception outside the Dublin Archdiocese. Almost immediately Father Burke set out for Dublin again to bring two more sisters to assist at the ceremony. No reason is given for the decision, but the annalist's reference to music favors a conjecture that in rehearsal Mother Catherine realized that the special music of the ceremonial needed more support. Though she herself had a poor singing voice, with which she sometimes amused the sisters at recreation, she had a good ear and excellent taste in music. What she lacked personally God had supplied through her religious subjects. If she had a keen appreciation of and love for music, she had keener relish in seeing talents applied to the service of religion. She therefore managed such assets with the judgment she exerted in the use of other resources and expected of the sisters the disinterestedness she herself manifested. This communal attitude, so perfectly represented in her charity, had a characterizing influence. The family spirit that continued to mark the congregation in spite of the dispersion now begun has been variously attributed, but a study of Mother Catherine's concept of charity yields the true source.

Elizabeth Locke (Sister Mary Catherine Teresa) and Mary Delamere (Sister Mary Clare Teresa) received the habit on Monday, August 1, in the parish church. Father Gaffney, Dean of Maynooth, preached the sermon. The next day the foundress and the four sisters from the motherhouse returned to Dublin. Whether Mother Catherine had set up the nonsensical club over which she had promised to preside, she did "effectually remove all painful remembrance of former parting" and fortified them for the second separation.

With the new foundations the title "Reverend Mother" came into use. The Dublin MS effectively depicts Mother Catherine's attitude toward it and toward any mark of special deference shown herself:

For a long time she would not be called *Reverend Mother* but only "Mother Catherine." Even to the last she would not allow the least ceremony to be used towards her . . . . At recreation she moved about the room, but the sisters were not to stand up or she moved off. I had a trick for keeping her. She liked to look at me drawing or working and I always contrived [to have] an empty chair I could reach without standing up, and by drawing it to her I have often got her to sit half an hour at the end of the table.

XXIII

West and South

BEFORE Mother Catherine left Baggot Street again, she received a letter from the Reverend Gerald Doyle, parish priest of Naas, a military town about twenty Irish miles southwest of Dublin. The letter recommended a young lady and inquired about qualifications for admission. Father Doyle had a foundation for Naas in his mind but, under prohibition of his Bishop, he could not mention it. Not that his namesake Dr. Doyle lacked zeal—he was one of the great churchmen of Ireland a century ago, "J. K. L.," James of Kildare and Leighlin, known throughout the land for his controversial skill. Dr. Doyle was practical enough to see that Father Doyle could not do everything at once. He had built a church, still in debt and unfurnished. To turn the old church into a school would require money, and Father Doyle's parishioners were poor. Yet with his eyes on the needs of the children, the zealous pastor had proposed opening a school as early as 1829. His Bishop offered the counsel of patience and prudence. Biding time, Father Doyle learned that it would be well to send subjects to the novitiate in Dublin so that trained teachers would be ready when his debt decreased or his Bishop relented.

Mother Catherine's reply, full of sense and clear in its implications, confirmed him in his choice of a community. On the feast of the Nativity of Our Lady, the foundress wrote:

In compliance with your desire, Reverend Sir, I shall submit what seems "generally" requisite for a Sister of Mercy.
Besides an ardent desire to be united to God and to serve the poor, she must feel a particular interest for the sick and dying; otherwise, the

duty of visiting them would soon become exceedingly toilsome. She should be healthy, have a feeling, distinct, impressive manner of speaking and reading, a mild countenance expressive of sympathy and patience; and there is so much to be required as to reserve and recollection passing through the public ways, caution and prudence in the visits that it is desirable she begin rather young before habits and manners are so long formed as not to be likely to alter.

I beg again to remark that this is what seems generally necessary. I am aware exceptions may be met and that when there is a decided preference for the Order and other essential dispositions, conformity in practice might be accomplished at any period of life.

Mother Catherine never wrote a more characteristic letter, ample without being diffuse, cordial though concise. Inherent in it is one of the tenets of her spiritual code, development of the supernatural on basic prerequisites or natural virtues—not that Mother Catherine's faith was deficient but that prudence leavened all her spirituality. She knew that ordinarily God does not work by miracle nor is the usual way of man heroic. Though a high degree of virtue can make a hard, unyielding character habitually pliant and can so control natural aversion as to produce effects of devotedness, such change seldom occurs instantaneously. Mother Catherine's own soul had experienced gradual development; her compassionate nature expanded through contemplation on the life of Christ. As foundress of an institute dedicated to works of mercy, Mother Catherine expected a candidate to bring some natural inclination or aptitude to the classroom and to the service of the sick and dying.

While she made plans for the Charleville foundation, Bishop Murphy of Cork began to press his interests. Since he had befriended the congregation from its infancy, his insistence became something just short of mandatory. There are several possible explanations for the ensuing delay, one of them in the character of the good Bishop himself, as Mother Catherine was to learn. His Lordship was better supplied with religious communities than most ecclesiastics of that time. Nano Nagle had established the Ursulines in Cork and had founded the Presentation Order there. Dr. Murphy's predecessor had introduced Brother Rice's congregation for poor boys, and Dr. Murphy himself brought the Irish Sisters of

Charity to his episcopal city in 1826. Besides, as has already been explained, he was responsible for the development of the Presentation Brothers as a distinct institute. By 1836, however, he seems to have diverted his attention from the rule and constitutions of the Irish Christian Brothers to that of the Sisters of Charity. In February Mother Augustine wrote to the rectress of the Cork convent in some concern. Bishop Murphy had called at two of their Dublin convents and had said Mass. He then called on Mother herself and baffled her by bringing up a plan for a second house of their congregation in Cork, a plan that she had approved four years earlier. Finally he came to the real purpose of his visit.

"He questioned me," she wrote, "as if we . . . had not made perpetual vows. I assured him that we never had made any other, but he really appeared as if he did not credit what I said." [1]

Two weeks later Mother Augustine wrote again, warning the sisters against jealousy of "this rising congregation" and exhorting them not to commit themselves before seculars or clergy on the partisanship that had evidently followed them to Cork. The news was therefore out: Bishop Murphy was bringing the Sisters of Mercy to his diocese. Mother Augustine had to wait yet eight years for Dr. Murphy's "delays" to end, but the opposition and trials that her congregation suffered in Cork brought out her own expansiveness of soul—her patience, her charity, and her power to summon the right spiritual dispositions for this contingency as for others.

When Mother Catherine set out for Charleville in October, she was aware that she would make a foundation elsewhere in the county not too many months hence. Father Burke accompanied the missioners to Tullamore where the pastor of Charleville came to meet them. Again Sister Mary Clare was Mother Catherine's companion. In a private letter to her sister she wrote reminiscently: "This journey was amusing. I find that I shall not have sufficient time to give particulars of it today,"[2] and she seems not to have resumed the subject at any other time.

The superior of the Charleville foundation was to be Sister Mary Angela Dunne, one of the 1831 ascetics whose fasting had elicited remonstrance from the foundress. Penance enough waited her on the new mission, though she had been selected for her maturity rather than for her ascetical leanings. Sister Angela was older than any of the others professed in 1833 and the Charleville foundation, remote from Dublin, needed a mature person in charge. Besides, she would undoubtedly be the personal choice of the charitable lady who had proposed the foundation, and Mother Catherine deferred to the wishes of patrons when she could. As it developed, no other mission had the intensity of trial that the Charleville convent endured from the beginning.

The sisters arrived in Tullamore on October 29, the day Miss Pentony's friend and confidante, Catherine Barnewall, entered. The poor already knew and loved her, and as Sister Mary Gertrude she was long and reverently remembered. Mother Catherine rejoiced in the good fortune of the growing community. The Jesuits of Tullabeg had come to their assistance with the loan of spiritual books, then rare, and retreat notes. Handwritten copies accumulated at St. Joseph's, giving the community a library of manuscripts for spiritual reading. Mother Mary Anne had had the pleasure of presenting a Communion class in white on the feast of Our Lady of Mercy, the first formal reception of the Sacrament the parishioners had ever witnessed, for penal times had accustomed the people to a minimum in preparation and no formalities. Sister M. Angela and the two novices for the Charleville foundation surely took heart at the evidence of what had been accomplished in six months.

The first hardship of these home missioners lay at the door. Canal travel, always slow and inconvenient, was cold and in late October particularly uncomfortable from the length of time the rest of the journey took. The cross-country boat did not stop at Tullamore till the middle of the night, and it was one thing to arrive in a town where their sisters awaited them and another to leave at midnight for a strange city with no convent to receive them.[3] They reached Limerick at nine in the evening, October 30, and went to Charleville by stage coach the following day. Nor did the foundress' cheerfulness fail when late in the afternoon of a chill day they were conducted to a narrow, tomb-like house in a row of flat-faced brick dwellings that looked across the Clanchy meadows.

Not till next morning did Mother Catherine's reflections begin to take on the bleakness of her surroundings. Whatever inconvenience the house on Clanchy Terrace might present at another season, it appeared at its worst with winter coming on. Though a pilgrim today will look in vain for the rivulet that made it uncontrollably damp, Sister Mary Clare wrote of it a hundred years ago:

> She [Mother Catherine] found the house very far from being as convenient as it had been represented to her and, on account of a little stream running close by, extremely damp, so that [our] clothes were quite wet each morning.[4]

In fact, their garments could not have been wetter if the freshet ran through or under the house. Perhaps some of its tributaries did, since the area had been at one time noted for springs. The little group needed the intercession of All Saints that first day of November, 1836. If work had been the only requisite, there was enough to be done, for the amount of poverty seemed appalling.

Three days later His Lordship Bishop Crotty came to look over the situation and bless their undertaking. Though only three years consecrated, he already had a reputation for a sharp eye, for insistence on meticulous care of the altar, and for love of good order generally. Nearly seventy years old at the time, he nevertheless lived to rule his diocese with vigor for another decade. Though he left the management of affairs at St. Joseph's Convent in Charleville principally to the parish priest, his keenness did not falter here either. On this occasion His Lordship must have observed with satisfaction the neat little convent chapel. Indeed daily Mass was the sisters' only comfort.

They had begun the Thirty Days' Prayers on which the foundress leaned heavily for guidance, but day after day she and her companion returned from errands of mercy with her perplexity unrelieved. How could she in conscience leave Mother Angela and the two novices to face winter in a place where the threat to health was so menacing? The work was taxing and a middle class practically non-existent. Without a middle class there was no prospect of subjects nor of resources for the sisters and the poor, if Mrs. French's support should fail. What decision to make remained a problem. Of all the negative prospects, the one that gave her greatest anxiety was, as usual, the health of the sisters.

In the spring skeins of furze would light the hills and hawthorne blossoms would brighten the roadside, but in November the landscape was as bleak as their prospects. Did Martinmas summer come to Charleville that year? The sisters do not mention it, but one day toward the end of the month as Mother Catherine and her companion made their way along a dreary lane from one miserable hut to another, light and warmth rose in the cry of a poor woman that blessed their presence: "Ah, it was the Lord Himself that drove you in amongst us!"

So God had driven them to Charleville, the foundress reflected, as God had driven her into this spreading work of His. Then she would never withdraw the sisters. No amount of importuning thereafter, and she suffered a great deal of it from the disheartened superior, altered her resolution.

The last Clanchy holder of the estate sold it while this book was being written. Dealers came from as far as London to buy up old plate, furniture, and curios representing several generations of Irish culture. Before the dealers closed in, however, the Sisters of Mercy of Charleville secured from heirs the miniatures that John Clanchy's only daughter had mounted together, with the inscription:

> Portraits of John Clanchy, Esq., and his only daughter Mary French, who exerted herself to establish a convent of the Sisters of Mercy in Charleville as a tribute to the memory of the best of fathers and most benevolent of men—may he rest in peace.

This memorial had had a place of honor in the reception room of the old mansion. It is treasured by the Sisters of Mercy as a memento of the benefactress whose niece became Sister Mary Angela Clanchy of the Charleville Sisters of Mercy, and whose descendants contributed to works of mercy in Charleville to the present generation.

At three o'clock in the morning, November 29, Mother Catherine and Sister Mary Clare Moore left Charleville expecting to arrive in Limerick seven hours later. They arose at two to be ready for the stage and went fasting in the hope of receiving Communion in Limerick. Of Mother Catherine's "tender devotion towards the Adorable Sacrament" her companion later wrote:

[The Foundress'] instructions on the subject, whether to seculars or to her religious, were calculated to awaken sentiments of lively faith and most confiding love. It was a cause of much sorrow to her when any sister through scrupulosity or other motive absented herself from Holy Communion, "for," she said, "it is by means of the grace therein bestowed on us that we are enabled to persevere in our holy state" . . . . She directed the sisters to make [devotion to the Blessed Sacrament] a frequent subject of their instructions to the poor whose happiness and eternal welfare depend entirely on their approaching the Sacraments with due dispositions. She herself had observed that converts do not seem to understand fully the instructions given them until they receive the Sacraments but afterwards find many difficulties cleared up. However, she did not at all like the sisters to spend a long time making their confessions lest they occupy the priest's time unnecessarily.[5]

Love of the Holy Eucharist brought Mother Catherine and Sister Mary Clare fasting to Limerick that late November day and a snow storm tested their devotion. The stage was late. Not being familiar with the city, they had to find their way to a chapel in a heavy fall of snow. It was nearly noon before they heard Mass and it was one o'clock before they breakfasted. They set out again by stage coach and arrived in Dublin the following day in time for a late Mass said in the convent chapel by His Lordship, Dr. Murphy of Cork. He had come again to talk about a foundation for his diocese. Bishop Murphy's admiration and affection for Dr. Crotty had begun long before on the continent when one was a professor, the other his student; the friendship had lasted through years that brought Dr. Crotty back to Ireland as President of Maynooth and now into the neighboring diocese as its bishop. That his venerable friend had so quickly secured Sisters of Mercy for one of the least promising of parishes off on the remote border of the county stimulated the younger Bishop to action. He left Dublin assured that when he would be ready he might have sisters.

It pleased Mother Catherine to learn that during her absence Archbishop Murray had paid a visit to the Convent of Mercy in Tullamore, had "expressed his pleasure" over progress there and had left his blessing. But the next news of Tullamore was not so happy. An epidemic of fever swept the town in December keeping sisters and clergy busy to the point of exhaustion. As the early snow had augured, it was a severe winter. Finally Father Murtagh himself became a victim, and there followed an anxious time. The sisters in Dublin added their prayers for his recovery, and he did fortunately recover. Toward the middle of the month, Mother Catherine wrote to Sister M. Teresa Purcell:

I have just had the pleasure of seeing Reverend Mr. O'Rafferty and receiving your letter. Indeed I am heartily sorry to hear of Mr. Murtagh's illness and earnestly hope God will soon restore him. We have been seriously alarmed about dear Sister Lubé and thought we were going to pay our annual tribute to the tomb but this day, thanks be to God, there is a more favorable opinion, though strong symptoms of rapid consumption appeared. Her brother appointed Dr. Graves to visit her and his treatment has been quite different from what we have seen on similar melancholy occasions. So far it has been wonderfully successful and we have great hope. I am sure you will pray for her recovery in choir as we do. She is now so much affected by mercury that a decided opinion cannot be given for some days.

Father Lubé's patient direction of Catherine McAuley brought many spiritual dividends, one of them the Mercy vocation of his own sister.

The Christmas season came on cold and busy. There were Mercy Christmas dinners for the poor in three dioceses this year. No word survives for St. Joseph's, Charleville, but the Tullamore annalist wrote wistfully:

Naturally the sisters missed the many merry faces that graced the frugal board at Baggot Street but the community was a brave little band. The usual Triduum was kept by the two professed sisters who renewed their vows on the feast of the Circumcision, 1837.

As for the motherhouse, during the holidays His Grace called. Mother Catherine brought him to the community room where, despite foundations, he saw no vacancies. Looking along the table and recognizing novices and postulants whose families he knew, he exclaimed pleasantly:

"I declare, Mother McAuley, I believe you are the greatest enemy the fashionable world has."

XXIV

Need Is Our Cloister

THE YEAR 1837 began propitiously with the arrival of the rule carefully collated and revised by Archbishop Murray. It now had to undergo a period of trial before it could be submitted to the Holy See for confirmation, and the spread of the congregation offered testing ground for its practicability. Just here lies the difference in the history of the rule of the Irish Christian Brothers and that of the Sisters of Mercy. Brother Rice lived long enough to see that the modified Presentation Rule left much to be desired in the government of his congregation, whereas no circumstances in the rapid spread of Mercy Institute during Mother Catherine's half dozen years of experience with foundations showed inadequacy in a form of government intended for cloistered religious. In fact, she evidently cherished the hope that some elasticity of interpretation on enclosure would permit solemn vows and include her Institute among religious orders.

No major change appeared in her manuscript copy of the rule, though one short chapter had been significantly canceled:

> The religious of this Institute of the Sisters of Mercy, always keeping in mind that in consecrating themselves in this holy state they have totally renounced the world, shall hold themselves obliged to a strict, exact and faithful observance of enclosure so that, after having made their vows, it shall be no longer in their power to pass the limits of the enclosure, which shall be marked out, except *first,* to comply with the duties of their institute, *second,* for the reasons assigned in the Sacred Canons and Apostolical Constitutions.

Archbishop Murray struck out this chapter, entitled "Enclosure." His Grace also drew a line through all the warm little expressions Mother Catherine had introduced elsewhere in the rule.

"The sisters shall bear to each other great and cordial respect and affection, not in outward behavior, looks and words only, but also really in deed, in heart and in mind," she had written, copying the Presentation Rule but inserting *affection*. The word was crossed out.

"The young shall reverence the more advanced in years and all shall with true humility endeavor to bear with each other *in tender concern and respect*." His Grace ran a line through the four words at the end of the sentence and wrote: "exhibiting toward their sisters a respectful demeanor 'in honor,' as St. Paul expresses it, 'preventing one another.' "

Besides the chapter on enclosure only one other passage was marked for omission, an exhortation that the Archbishop may have judged to belong properly to a directory or manual:

The sisters shall at all times appear with those cheerful yet reserved manners which characterize religious modesty and form the dignified deportment that becomes persons consecrated to God. This deportment will be the index of a mind equally free from restraint and levity. It will give the eyes that humble expression which bespeaks a feeling recollection of mind almost natural because wholly unaffected. The countenance should be ever serene and cheerful and exhibit that sweet religious gravity which is never lost by loud laughter, hasty and noisy words. Every action and gesture, even the walk of a religious should show the recollected mind, free from all that agitates and disturbs. Haste may be necessary but hurried steps or precipitation shall be carefully avoided.

That Mother Catherine herself exemplified this inheres in descriptions of her belonging to these final years of her life.

Mother McAuley looked about forty-five though she must have been more. Her figure was rather tall but not slight. Her countenance though not small was well-shaped; her complexion fair, of a peachy tint; her eyes such a lovely blue as is rarely seen. She had a particularly sweet expression about her eyes and mouth. No photograph could give the expression of sweetness and holiness that marked her entire bearing. Her voice, particularly in reading, possessed a charm not to be forgotten. Her conversation fascinated those with whom she came in contact, and such was her humility that self seemed utterly ignored.

In the early months of 1837 Mother Catherine met the uncle of the young lady who later, as a member of the congregation, wrote these impressions of the foundress. The Reverend James Maher was administrator of the Cathedral parish in Carlow where, contrary to expectation, the next Mercy convent opened. In his own benefactions and through his nephew, the Reverend Paul Cullen, then in Rome, later Cardinal Archbishop of Dublin, Father Maher consistently befriended the Institute during his long life. His niece's description of Mother Catherine tallies with Dean O'Brien's, which also belongs to the late 1830's. In fact, all glimpses of the foundress as she neared sixty confirm the impression she made on Sister Mary Catherine Maher of the Carlow community. An additional detail is given by another member of the congregation: "Her lips were thin and the mouth rather wide, but there was so much play of expression about it that it was her most agreeable feature."

Years of compassionate care of the afflicted had given mobility to her face, but the "feeling recollection of mind almost natural because wholly unaffected" that controlled her countenance to the "serene, cheerful, sweet religious gravity" was "index of a mind equally free from restraint and levity."

The death of a small shopkeeper in Carlow provided the circumstances that introduced Sisters of Mercy to the diocese of Kildare and Leighlin. Toward the close of 1836 Michael Nowlan left in the hands of his saintly bishop of legacy of £7000 for the poor. Bishop Nolan, only two years consecrated, was to live just long enough to make the bequest operative. Close to his clergy, including the priests of the college, where he himself had had a chair, he consulted them and found them in favor of bringing Sisters of Mercy to the town to administer the Nowlan funds. Dr. Andrew Fitzgerald, O. P., president of the college, offered the abandoned academy building on the edge of the campus for a temporary convent, and Bishop Nolan invited Mother Catherine to make the foundation.

Arrangements moved so fast that the new mission came as a surprise to the sisters. Negotiations for Cork and the dispositions of Bishop Kinsella had pointed to either diocese as the next likely field for the works of the Institute, but Carlow drew the first mission south of Dublin. How often in her preparations Mother

Catherine must have recalled the preparations for Carlow eight years before! Her nephews had become independent with James' coming of age, and their reckless spending and living were causing her real anxiety. The writer of the Dublin manuscript, referring to personal sorrow in the last years of Mother Catherine's life, remarks:

> During these years a great number of postulants entered . . . and we were accounted a very prosperous convent, but the foundress had plenty of sorrows . . . . The conduct of her nephews was most unsatisfactory. The youngest went to Australia without asking her advice or bidding her farewell and died there very soon; the two elder died of consumption brought on by reckless dissipation. She had by every means in her power striven to keep them in the right path and afterwards to reclaim them. How much she grieved for their errors few knew so well as I. They both died penitent.

The business of the new foundation certainly brought back memories of that earlier February and the kindnesses Dr. Fitzgerald had shown her nephews in their six years' residence at the lay school. It recalled, too, encouragement the now venerable Dominican had given her in the days when she was preparing to enter George's Hill novitiate.

"I never can forget," she once wrote to him, "all the animating lively hope that you created in my mind when we were rising out of nothing."

No one at the motherhouse nor at the Kingstown convent, for that matter, would have been surprised if the superior of St. Patrick's, Kingstown, had been summoned to take charge of the new mission, for each foundation thus far had been supplied from Kingstown. The selection, however, created as much surprise as the foundation itself. The sister designated to the office was, humanly speaking, indispensable to the motherhouse. She had managed finances at Baggot Street from the time the Institute began to shape into a religious congregation and recently she had been serving the foundress as assistant and secretary. More than that, Frances Warde had been an intimate of the McAuley children. With Sister Anne Agnes in her last illness and the boys untractable, Sister Francis' support was doubly sustaining. In fact, when Mother Catherine agreed to make the foundation, her sister secretary seemed least likely to be considered for it.

Another indispensable member of Mother Catherine's religious household, Ellen Corrigan (in religion, Sister Veronica), belonged to the familiar past. One of the early biographies identifies her as Catherine McAuley's personal maid at Coolock but, since Ellen was only eleven years old when the foundress sold the estate, such an interpretation of Sister Veronica's early connection with Mother Catherine is hardly warranted. Orphaned young, reared at Coolock and brought to Baggot Street when Catherine moved into the city, Ellen acted as confidential messenger to the foundress till old enough to determine her own future. After her profession as a lay sister, she was put in charge of the extern department of the House of Mercy where she gave particularly valuable service. Sister M. Vincent Hartnett, who entered early in 1837, gives us some insight into this service in the following words:

From their practical knowledge of business, the lay sisters were very valuable in carrying out the directions of the choir sisters in the House of Mercy, both as regarded needlework and the laundry; and they were also very useful in the extern department of the House of Mercy, which was very extensive and important and which existed in the convent from the very commencement.
The House of Refuge is composed of a considerable number of women, some of whom are candidates for admission and are waiting for a vacancy in the House of Mercy. These in the meantime attend daily in the room appointed for them, where they receive instruction or do whatever needlework is given them; and they receive partial or entire support as they may happen to require. Lodgings are also provided for them with some poor decent people in the neighborhood. The other divisions of these young women are governesses and servants who, having some little means economized, do not seek admission but attend daily until they are engaged by some of the ladies who apply for persons in their capacity. Many respectable persons have from time to time thankfully availed themselves of the benefits of both House of Mercy and extern provision.[1]

Early in February Sister Veronica developed typhus and died four days later. One of the sisters could have predicted then that Sister Francis would be superior of Carlow convent, for Sister Mary Clare Moore had observed Mother Catherine's reaction to bereavement. She invariably considered it a summons to greater generosity with God. As if to emphasize the call to sacrifice, death struck again taking Father Lubé's sister.

Sister Mary Rose Lubé continued to use her failing strength in the service of the poor, keeping her hands busy with the needle till the last hour of her life. She died March 11, 1837. One month later Mother Catherine set out in "Purcell's mail" for the pleasant college town where Michael Nowlan no longer sold delft in his little shop. The good he had done he not only took with him but left after him, for Purcell's coach carried missioners whose journeying had scarcely begun. There were young ladies in comfortable homes at Carlow that dark, wet April day, looking forward to comfortable years in comfortable homes, who would live their lives out in the hardships of foreign missions because of the passenger load Purcell's coach brought to town.

With Mother Catherine and her sister secretary were Sister M. Ursula Frayne, Sister M. Teresa White, and a novice, Sister M. Josephine Trenor. Useless for Father Maher to say, "We shall keep the first twelve to live and die here"! Sister Ursula was to cross the Atlantic on the first American foundation and, returning, set out again to make the first Australian foundation. There she would be startled one day by a visitor out of the bush, the pioneer Willie McAuley, not lost at sea as his relatives had supposed. He would bring his little daughters to a Mercy school on the other side of the world and one of them, growing up, would wear the Mercy habit and bear the foundress' name. If the future could have shown itself at the window of the jolting coach that day, Mother Catherine's personal sorrow would have lifted a little, but Sister Anne Agnes, left behind at Baggot Street, would not live the year out and the boys were farther from her than mere distance could contrive.

Among verses preserved at the Liverpool Convent of Mercy is a set composed by Mother Catherine a few days after her arrival in Carlow.[2] With no pretensions beyond amusing the sisters at the motherhouse, they assume unexpected importance in being the only extant first-hand source on the foundation. They are here quoted in part:

> About half past two we got into town
> And pass'd by our own house, where we should be set down;
> At least half a mile taken out of our way

In the midst of a crowd on a chief market day
We drove up to the inn but would not get out,
Nor had the coach room to turn about;
So there we remained, set up for a show,
Till a very kind person whom we did not know
Had the two first horses unlinked from the coach
So that nothing impeded our speedy approach
To a very neat convent prepared very nice.
The priest and the bishop were there in a trice
And conducted us on to our sisters in love
Who gave 78 kisses their fondness to prove
And the pleasantest dinner set out in good form,
All exceedingly good and pleasantly warm.
We had plenty of laughing and cheering and fun,
And music and singing when dinner was done.
The bishop and good Father Andrew at tea;
Soon after nine we all went away.
Ever since we are settling and running about
Some staying at home and some going out,
The new Sister Green is a very nice creature
Unlike to the old one in manner and feature.
Your "mother" has said now the fourth or fifth time,[3]
"Don't forget my best love in the midst of your rhyme."
Sisters Frances, Mary Teresa, and Grace,[4]
Beg also to get for their love a good place.
Write to me soon the poetical letter—
No matter how long, the more nonsense the better
I hope e'er long to write you another
And remain

Your fond and affectionate Mother.

"Sister Green," the postulant who entered at Carlow almost as soon as the sisters arrived, reminded the foundress that the pastor at Naas was still building a convent in the air. Rebecca Greene was the youngest of three children, all of whom became religious. She had a priest brother besides the sister to whom Mother Catherine referred. Their father, Major General Joe Greene, a liberal Protestant stationed at Naas Barracks in the British service, had married a devout Catholic. His elder daughter Jane had entered at Baggot Street but had to return because of ill health. Two weeks before the opening of Carlow Convent she re-entered at Tullamore and was recommended by Mother Catherine herself as possessing great "amiability and sweetness of disposition." She persevered in religion but lived only a half dozen years. "The new Sister Green," however, under the name Sister Mary Agnes, fulfilled all Jane's pious ambitions, going on the Naas foundation from Carlow and ending her life in the American missions.[5]

Sponsoring Mercy foundations became a kind of tradition in the Presentation Order. The hospitality which Mother Catherine describes here was repeated three months later in Cork and three years later in Galway.

Long before dark the Sisters of Mercy returned to their improvised convent across the college grounds.[6] If it deserved the foundress' versified description, the neatness resulted from lack of furniture and the superlative preparation centered in the ten-by-twelve chapel which the sisters readied for Mass with little difficulty. Bishop Nolan offered the Holy Sacrifice on the following morning and dedicated the convent to St. Leo, whose patronal feast is April 11. Not many hours of the day had passed before Mother Catherine's practicality began to operate. It was characteristic of her to enter on foundations without much provision for the sisters. Assurance that the work for the poor would be supported implied, she assumed, some arrangement for the sisters. As she said to Dean O'Brien when he represented to her the cost a foundation in Nova Scotia would entail: "You do not know on how little a nun can live."

Nevertheless, when any foundation had been undertaken, she did not leave the sisters without suitable provision for their state. As she experienced the extreme privation of their first days at St. Leo's, she consulted the sisters on the advisability of proceeding under such living conditions. Young, enthusiastic, and merry enough with a chair and bedless mattress apiece, they did not fail her hope. They would manage, they assured her. She nevertheless called Bishop Nolan's attention to the fact that no maintenance had been provided for the sisters beyond the old building and a few inadequate pieces of furniture. He gave her fifty pounds immediately and, not knowing that he would be dead in six months, promised an annual allowance of the same amount. He advised her, however, not to make his donation known lest it deter others from remembering the sisters' needs. Dr. Fitzgerald suspended rent on the old building until such time as the community might be able to pay a rental, and Mother Catherine left them a hundred pounds which she could ill afford. The missioners thus became assured of support while the charities were inaugurated.

The foundress was called back to Baggot Street before the end of the month by the serious illness of two novices, who fortunately recovered. When she returned to Carlow in May, she brought with her, at Father O'Hanlon's suggestion, Sister Anne Agnes. His hope that the mild air of Carlow would work healing was not to be fulfilled. In mid-June, in order to prepare for the Cork foundation, Mother Catherine returned to Baggot Street, where she was immediately confronted with trouble and sorrow. A third novice who had been stricken with typhus did not recover. Sister M. Aloysius Thorpe developed fever on June 21, the feast of her patron saint, and died nine days later. In the midst of this trial, matters at Kingstown came to a head. Mr. Nugent, the carpenter who made the coach house into a school, pressed for payment and the "shrewd financier"[7] in charge of the parish washed his hands of all responsibility. Unfortunately, none of the business had been carried on in writing and, though Mother Catherine now put a complete record of the oral transaction in the hands of her lawyer, the situation became increasingly uncomfortable.

These trials were the price of prosperity. The day Sister Aloysius died a postulant entered. The day she was buried four sisters were professed and two received. Since His Grace had set July 1 for the ceremony, Mother Catherine would not ask for postponement because of the funeral. A few days later another postulant arrived, but by then the foundress had left for Cork. Even though Sister Anne Agnes evidently had but a short time to live, Mother Catherine proceeded with the business of the new foundation, and it made it easier for her that Sister urged her to go. Sister M. Clare Moore, Sister M. Joseph Warde, Sister M. Vincent Deasy, recently professed, and Sister M. Anastasia McGauley were the appointees and Sister M. Teresa White went as Mother Catherine's traveling companion.[8]

Bishop Murphy had a delegation at the dock on July 6, 1837,

to meet the *Hercules* and bring the sisters to South Presentation Convent for Mass. Here Nano Nagle had founded the "Sisters of the Sacred Heart of Charitable Instruction" before Catherine McAuley was born and before Archbishop Murray had conceived his idea of "walking nuns." Here then the first active congregation of religious women in Ireland had anticipated both Relief Acts and reconstruction period and even the great social service movement of the nineteenth century. Those who had planned this reception planned better than they knew, for if there is ever to be a shrine to Nano Nagle it will be here where her genius lies buried. Her plans miscarried after her death and her institute withdrew to the cloister to become a nursery of charities. Among her foster children were these bonneted and cloaked[9] Sisters of Mercy who spent the first hours of their active mission in Cork at the convent once dedicated to "the Sacred Heart of Charitable Instruction." The spirit of Nano Nagle had never died, for another institute of charity[10] came to travel the lanes she had trudged, and now, as if her cloak had fallen on others still, the Sisters of Mercy left the cloister of "charitable instruction" to go again among the poor.

No. 4 Rutland Street, which became their home, still exists. If the neighborhood had fallen from some earlier state of grandeur in the foundress' time, it fails to show any evidence of it now. Only a feat of imagination today could conjure the well-appointed convent awaiting the Sisters of Mercy, July 6, 1837. Accustomed to "walking nuns," the people of Cork received the sisters with enthusiasm and understanding. No unfurnished cottage here, no abandoned school! No. 4 Rutland Street had been donated, furnished, and endowed by Miss Barbara Gould, a woman of many charitable interests; and a committee of ladies had the house in order and a luncheon ready for the sisters. Mother Catherine set aside some of the dainties for the sick poor. Visitations began July 8 with Mrs. Fitzgerald in Douglas Street.

Bishop Murphy called and appointed Sister Mary Clare Moore mother superior. She had been Mother Catherine's traveling companion on all the other foundations except Carlow and had served a term as superior of St. Patrick's, Kingstown. Yet her apprenticeship at Kingstown did not prepare her for the financial problem of her new position. Whereas Canon Sheridan manipulated for benefits to his parish, the Bishop of Cork would let the sisters make concessions to no one. He took upon himself not only the financial guidance of the new superior but of the foundress herself. His first injunction pertained to terms on which the community was to accept subjects. Having had no experience of like vigilance, the foundress accepted his recommendation as advisory rather than mandatory. Shortly afterward, therefore, she accepted a desirable candidate whose dower did not quite meet His Lordship's recommendation. Unfortunately for her, he was away at the time. On his return he reprimanded her sharply, construing her action as disobedience. She thereby came to learn what Brother Rice had learned before her: once religious came under Bishop Murphy's jurisdiction, his temporizing vanished and his administrative character asserted itself.

Sister M. Vincent Hartnett explains Mother Catherine's policy:

> Reverend Mother was deeply grateful to God for elevating her to the holy state of religion and enabling her to establish permanently those works for the relief and benefit of the poor. She was also anxious to extend to as many as prudence would permit the happiness she herself enjoyed; and therefore, to facilitate the entrance of those ladies who were anxious to become religious but the smallness of whose fortune would otherwise be an impediment, she curtailed the expenses usual at public ceremonies and quite did away with outfits ordinarily required at entrance.[11]

Bishop Murphy set October 25 for Sister M. Anastasia's profession and called the foundress' attention to what he considered an omission. The profession form for the Sisters of Mercy contained no distinguishing vow. Since the rule had not yet been confirmed, Mother Catherine accepted his suggestion that a fourth vow, "the service of the poor, sick and ignorant," be introduced. This change was sealed by approval in Rome, four years later.

Mother Catherine was again summoned to Dublin before the end of the month, this time at her niece's request. She took with her Sister M. Vincent Deasy and Sister M. Teresa White, leaving the latter in Carlow.

A great change had occurred in Sister Anne Agnes' appearance; yet the foundress' experience with consumptive patients made her think that Sister's illness still would be protracted.

Concerned for a novice's state of health, however, she wrote immediately to Sister M. Elizabeth Moore, then superior at Kingstown, to come in by train next day for "Sister Lance." Specifying that Sister M. de Chantal (McCann) be brought as companion, Mother Catherine unwittingly gave herself the opportunity of seeing for the last time the benefactress of Kingstown convent.

Sister Anne Agnes' request proved a real presentiment, for she died on the first day of the novena for the Assumption. Sisters of Mercy everywhere were in retreat. Such was Mother Catherine's regard for the rule that no exercise was omitted and all the sisters remained in retreat except the few who assisted with funeral arrangements. Sister Anne Agnes was the tenth Sister of Mercy to be interred in the Carmelite vault. Mother Catherine could not then know her double bereavement, but she saw her youngest nephew for the last time at his sister's deathbed. He went to sea shortly afterward and was not heard from again during his aunt's lifetime.[12]

Mother Catherine had planned to go back immediately after retreat to finish the business of the Cork foundation, but the Kingstown trouble and a new difficulty detained her. Their chaplain and friend of eight years, Father Burke, O.F.M., having volunteered for the African missions, was accepted. The Baggot Street institution therefore became dependent on the arrangements of Dr. Meyler, the parish administrator. Mother Catherine represented to him the multiple character of the charities and asked that a priest be assigned to take Father Burke's place. The request was refused, though one of the curates at the time, a Trinitarian, Father McDonogh, was much interested in the charities. Dr. Meyler created difficulties. He proposed a rotation system that threatened to deprive the women and children of the personal interest and consistent direction not only highly desirable but at times essential to their spiritual welfare.

The presence of regulars among parish curates was a relic of penal times. Adjustment had not yet reached a point where their services could be discontinued but had reached a point where parish clergy were conscious of awkwardness in the arrangement. That Dr. Meyler had some sensitiveness on that score becomes clear in a letter written by Mother Catherine a few months later.

Teresa Byrn became a postulant on the feast of the Assumption. Not many days later Mother M. Clare's elder sister, the artist, entered. With ten postulants at Baggot Street, Mother Catherine returned to the business of the Cork foundation, bringing with her Sister M. Cecilia Marmion. She left both the Kingstown and chaplaincy problems unsettled. A third concern, the stability of the Charleville foundation, began to intrude. Mother Angela had struggled along for several months, representing to Mother Catherine from time to time the hopelessness of her situation. A clergyman going from Charleville to Cork now called on the foundress, and left the impression that he had been asked to use his influence with her for permission to have the Charleville sisters go on some other mission. Mother Catherine was not pleased with the tenor of the visit, as Mother Angela learned.

Meanwhile the foundress sent a letter to her assistant back home.[13] The burden of its message was the chaplaincy situation, brought the more forcefully to her from the arrangement in Cork. For some time the sisters there had been obliged to go to Mass in the public church. The Reverend Theobald Matthew, their confessor, a Capuchin appointed by His Lordship, used his influence to procure daily Mass in the convent chapel through the courtesy of his own community.

"I would like to tell you all the little cheering things that God permits to fall in our way," Mother Catherine wrote Mother de Pazzi, "though it does not do so well for reading out as it might sound like boasting, but it has so happened that all our little ways are particularly liked here and our indoor and outdoor dress meet general admiration."

What scraps of comfort she lays out before the real business of the letter! The postscript is marked *private* and is the only direct evidence extant that Mother Catherine's calm could be ruffled. Taking up the subject of the chaplaincy difficulty, she admits: "It is constantly before me and makes me dread going home. I know it is not possible for me to have any more argument with Dr. Meyler without extreme agitation."

"I know the Bishop will be rather pleased than otherwise," she points out in the midst of her recommendation and ends, "Perhaps one third of what I have said will be more than sufficient, and this is the reason I dread the subject, because I find myself impelled to say too much."

So His Grace favored the arrangement that had prevailed for eight years, and she knew that he did! Yet, for reasons of his own, he left her to deal with Dr. Meyler.

Her concern was such as to excuse agitation; yet her admission betrays the natural temperament over which she excercised almost perfect control. Hers was a practical devotion to St. Francis de Sales. It accounts for the many references to him in her instructions to the sisters.[14]

Attended by the sisters he had so recently brought to the diocese, Bishop Nolan died of typhus fever on October 14. He had preached their August retreat. Mother Catherine in Cork heard of his illness through one of the clergy and wrote to Mother Francis for verification. By the time the superior at Carlow received the letter, His Lordship was already dead and Mother Francis prostrate with grief. Sister M. Teresa therefore replied, giving particulars and asking Mother Catherine to come to them as she had promised she would if they were in trouble. To this the foundress answered with a severe lecture on how bereavement should be supported.

As novice mistress she had said:

> The religious . . . should be calm and unmoved in all the occurrences of life, so that if she should hear of her nearest and dearest's being at the point of death, she should listen with all possible composure without showing any of those worldly unsubdued feelings which are quite contrary to the spirit of the true religious.

And Mother Francis had been one of those novices. "Sadness is an enemy of devotion," Mother Catherine had warned in those other days. "It undermines and destroys union with God, while it lessens the value of works performed in His Name. . . . View all the passing wants of this transitory life in the light of faith and love. . . . Give Him glory by faith and confidence as well as by fidelity."[15]

Mother Catherine's reply to Sister M. Teresa made clear that her promise did not apply to trials of God's direct willing. Death came from the hand of God. There were afflictions of another kind that Mother Catherine knew only too well. Such she had had in mind, she told Sister M. Teresa, "difficulties to which [Mother Francis'] new state exposed her, such as incurring the displeasure of her spiritual superiors without design, experiencing marks of disapprobation and not knowing why—bitter sweets incident to our state, and most of all requiring counsel and support."

On October 25 Bishop Murphy conferred the veil on the subject whose irregular dower had cost the foundress a sharp rebuke. His Lordship also received the vows of Sister M. Anastasia McGauley, the first Sister of Mercy to make the fourth vow. By this time Dr. Murphy's displeasure with Mother Catherine had completely evaporated. Henceforth the only reference His Lordship ever made to the foundress' financial indiscretion was by way of pleasantry. He referred to her as "the Sister of Divine Providence."

Two days before the ceremony Mother Catherine received word that Sister M. de Chantal McCann had typhus fever and was not expected to live. She therefore left Cork on October 26 and, though it must delay her arrival home, she stopped in Carlow to condole with the sisters on the sudden death of their saintly bishop. By the time she reached Dublin Sister Mary de Chantal was dead. Of this death the foundress wrote to Mother Angela:

Exactly the same fever which was sent by God to take the pious valued Bishop, Dr. Nolan, came, I trust, from the Divine Hand for her. She had quite a saintly death, continually repeating aloud: "My God, I love you. Forgive me and take me to yourself." The physicians were astonished.

Four years later Mother Catherine was still quoting Sister Mary de Chantal, this time for Mother Mary Anne's counsel:

I could not think any person with very cautious worldly views worthy to be admitted to holy profession. It is not a disposition to bestow gifts like benevolent persons in the world that bespeaks generosity of mind for the religious state; it is bestowing ourselves most freely and relying with unhesitating confidence on the Providence of God. When our innocent, yet very sensible Sister de Chantal was about to hand over all she possessed, making it impossible ever to command one shilling, her mother told her she ought to have some security as many persons were of the opinion that this house would not be established [i. e., permanently]. "What would you do then?" She answered: "Won't I have my sweet Lord?" And sweet He was to her indeed to the very last moment. Though we may not often have the consolation to meet such noble, universal disengagement as hers, yet a spirit directly opposite I humbly hope will never make its abode among us.[16]

From Baggot Street Mother Catherine went to Kingstown where she found Sister M. Elizabeth Moore also with symptoms of fever. Of this she told Mother Francis in a letter written November 22, but not till a month later did she disclose the injury she suffered the night she arrived at St. Patrick's.[17] To Mother Angela, more nearly her own age, she wrote revealingly:

"I . . . broke my left arm across the wrist and injured the sinews in the back of the hand so much that I am not likely to have the use of it for months, if ever."

She finally did tell Mother Francis of the accident but wrote optimistically:

I remained in care of an apothecary without taking off my clothes for two days, and as the inflammation was so great nothing could be done but apply leeches. I returned here and Surgeon White bound me up in boards. This is the twenty-first day. I have great hopes of soon getting my old companion on duty again and am happy to tell you from experience that a broken arm is by no means so distressing a matter as I always supposed. The want of its use is the chief inconvenience. However, take great care of your bones and, if you go through your convent before stairs are put up, be extremely cautious, for though not proportioned to all the lamentations we hear on such occasions, yet it gives a general shock to the frame that is not easily recovered.
No arrangement has been made for us yet as to chaplain . . . . We go to Westland Row every day . . . . Twelve couples start as gay as when traveling to Clarendon Street in our first happy days. Father McDonogh waits for us and we have three Masses and are home at nine o'clock.

So Carlow was to have a new convent, and it was already under way! Mr. Nowlan's brother and sister, learning of the sisters' situation, had supplemented their brother's benefaction. "The Sister of Divine Providence" truly knew wherein she trusted.

XXV

Multiplied Trial

LATE IN NOVEMBER of 1837 Mother Catherine wrote to Archbishop Murray's secretary, Father Hamilton, thanking him for a favor and concluding:

If it is not too much to ask, perhaps you would call here any time convenient for a few minutes. I think you could assist us in our present state without much difficulty.

But the matter was not to be so easily settled. If she could have foreseen that three years would pass before Dr. Meyler would consent to assign one priest to the chaplaincy at Baggot Street, she would certainly have written with more urgency.

Father Hamilton called. On his advice she had another interview with Dr. Meyler. The result was so perplexing that she wrote to Bishop Blake to know how to proceed further. He told her to lay the matter before His Grace, so she again wrote to Father Hamilton:

I am sure, Reverend Sir, you are disappointed to find our unpleasant business not settled. I wrote to Dr. Meyler the day you were here. We acceded to his will, promised forty pounds a year. He appeared perfectly satisfied at first, then complained of the salary but in the end said he would send Mr. Farrily. Three of those who were present considered all settled. In the evening I received a note to say the salary could not be accepted and that even if Mr. F—were satisfied Dr. Meyler would think it his duty to prevent him.
Mr. Lynch was sent on Monday to say Mass but not since. You told me, Reverend Sir, that we were to have Mr. Farrily entirely except his last Masses. Dr. Meyler said we were to have two. Of course, we

could not know whom to call on [in need] but even to this we assented, distressing as it is.
It is said that we all dislike the parish clergy—God forbid—and that we give freely elsewhere. Indeed, Reverend Sir, I should fear that God would be displeased with my ingratitude, did I not declare that Mr. O'Hanlon has been the most generous friend and that all he ever received for his nine years' constant attendance, often every day for a week preparing for profession, was thirty-two pounds in different sums from the sisters to get Mass for them—in all, the entire sum was £32 in nine years. The only apology I can offer for all this writing is that it comforts and relieves my mind to declare the truth where I trust I am not suspected of insincerity.[1]

Meanwhile, the sisters continued to walk to St. Andrew's daily for Mass. One of the novices,[2] herself a St. Andrew's parishioner, wrote of this experience, commenting on Mother Catherine's selflessness. With her arm in splints, she dressed unassisted except to ask the first sister ready to help her into her outdoor cloak. She hired two carriages for the sisters who were not well but she herself walked.

Until she broke her wrist, the same writer reports, she always carved dinner for the entire community. She did not sit down till all were served, yet she finished eating with the rest. If anyone referred to her "almost perpetual fast," she changed the subject lightly.

On Christmas Day, 1837, the Carmelite, Father Colgan, offered Mass in the convent chapel and, as if to compensate the community for their sacrifices, Divine Providence supplied such a dinner for the poor as had never before been given.

There were hundreds of guests, and not only was the large schoolroom filled but another large room below stairs. Besides this, a Christmas feast was given to the inmates of the House of Mercy, about seventy in number, in their large dining hall. To contribute to the happiness of her poor guests, [Mother Catherine] had the rooms tastefully decorated with evergreens, pictures and Scripture sentences appropriate to the time of Our Lord's Nativity; and she went about among the guests, contributing by her presence to the happiness of all. This was ever her practice, even when much afflicted herself, to strive all the more to make others happy. . . . She resolved to do as much as possible and leave the rest to God.[3]

Another bit of brightness on the closing year concerned two of her nephews. To Mother Francis she wrote:

It will give you pleasure to hear that James and Robert have been to see me, both respectable and going on remarkably well, living together and studying for the bar every day with real attention—Robert's pay increased . . . . Poor William would not be good. He is gone on a voyage to Demerara. Perhaps that may reduce his obstinacy . . . . James procured the vessel and settled with the captain in a manner I would never expect. He seems quite out of idleness and folly. [He and Robert] intend to go to London at Easter to make some of their terms. Robert will earn more at the press there.

Poor Willie, not yet sixteen years old![4] Mother Josephine Warde wrote of him: "He was the loved of all. His early wilfullness and the subsequent uncertainty of his fate were among [Mother Catherine's] keenest trials."[5]

Mother Francis received the letter in the midst of her own trials. A priest she had known from childhood had been raised to the episcopacy of the diocese to succeed Bishop Nolan, and His Lordship Bishop Haly proceeded to treat Mother Francis as if she were still a child. Since his character lacked the geniality that could have softened his attitude to paternal kindliness, his manner affected her much as the presence of a stern old preceptor in the family circle.

Early in 1838 Mother Catherine again wrote to Mother Francis. Since the first part of this letter gives a clear impression of the Kingstown and chaplaincy difficulties at their peak with the foundress' dispositions, it is worth quoting:

Convent, Baggot Street
January 17, 1838

My dearest Sister Mary Francis,

If I have inspired you with the melancholy view you take of our situation, I assure you that I did not intend to do so. We have just now indeed more than an ordinary portion of the cross in this one particular but may it not be the cross of Christ, which we so often pray to "be about us"? It has not the marks of an angry cross. There is no disunion, no gloomy depression of spirits, no departure from charity proceeding from it. The difficulties lessen every day. We get our poor inmates to confession by six at each time with Eliza Liston to bring them safe home and, please God, we will have all prepared for Holy Communion First Friday. We get an occasional charitable Mass and never go out on very wet mornings. I am sure Dr. Meyler would wish the matter settled according to his plan. We should have at least three priests and never know whom to call on as friend or chaplain and for this must pay or promise to pay 50 pounds per annum, which we really have not, independent of casual events. Mr. Delany, Sister de Pazzi's father, would contribute to pay a chaplain as we had before but not under the present circumstances. Miss McGuinness would also. I offered 40 pounds to Dr. Meyler and I now believe it was well it was rejected, for if we had not 20 to give at the end of the half year we would be suspected of withholding it and all the dispute would be renewed. Whenever I have the happiness of seeing Mr. Maher again, I will tell him and him only another strong reason why the proposed connection should be avoided if possible.[6]

I am not unhappy, thanks be to God, nor do I see any disedification likely to arise from the matter. Some think that after having Mr. Burke eight years we are not now easily pleased, and most of those who know why we go out seem to think we ought to have a distinct chaplain and only say Dr. Meyler is a little positive. This is the extent of it at present. It is humiliating, no doubt, a smart attack on self-importance, and if this part of it is well managed it must turn to good account. I humbly trust it will end very well.

Sister M. Teresa is in Kingstown "greatly tempted," she says, "to wish she was back with the Fathers in Carlow." There also we find a nice little cross, law proceeding for building the school, though we expressly said we could not contribute more than the ground, coach house, and fifty pounds from the bazaar. By giving that fifty pounds Mr. Sheridan says I am what he terms "committed" and he has left me in the hands of Mr. Nugent. I am hiding from some law person who wants to serve a paper on me personally and sent in to say he came from Dr. Murray. I am afraid to remain five minutes in the small parlor. This has caused more laughing than crying, you may be sure, for every man is suspected of being the process man and is kept at an awful distance by my dear [Sister] Teresa Carton. They make a demand of 450 pounds. I suppose we must sell Kingstown when Booterstown is nearly ready. Now you have the double cross, the cross of the diocese, out of it. All is consoling and animating, thanks be to God . . .

The last section of the letter tells of the activities at the parent house in behalf of the poor. In a week twenty trained workers had found employment through the House of Mercy office and twenty young women had been taken in their places. Donations for the charities tripled offerings formerly made by those enjoying the convenience of Mass in the convent chapel.

The saddest feature of the closing of the chapel is mentioned by the novice, Sister M. Vincent Hartnett. Many of the people who had been able to hear daily Mass in the convent chapel discontinued the practice because the parish church was too far away.

Though Mother Catherine sympathized with Mother Francis and her other superiors in their trials, she also knew how to interpret their problems in the light of individual temperament. She had a way of suggesting pointedly how a particular situation should be met. She came to look on Mother Francis' sensitiveness over Bishop Haly's attitude in terms of Frances Warde's own character. Referring to a visit from His Lordship some time later, the foundress wrote: "I could not describe the extreme kindness of Dr. Haly. He was afraid I would be uneasy lest the little arrangements he made should cause any unhappiness to you and he gave the most full and unquestionable assurance of deepest interest and regard. You have a true father in him."

Mother Francis, however, never felt comfortable in his presence and never recognized in his manner the fatherly regard that Mother Catherine described so confidently. Frances Warde had been given responsibility at an early age and had developed the aggressiveness that ability and experience bring out in certain characters.

When Georgina Moore was Mother M. Clare she wrote:

I mention Mother Francis because she was always with Reverend Mother even when a novice, so that some little feeling existed, as she never took her turn in the duties which other novices had. We had charge of the noviceship a week in turn, which she never took, and I remember some complained to Reverend Mother, but I believe it was necessary she should attend to other business, for Mother M. Anne was of such a retiring disposition that she could not bear to see strangers.

"Study the dispositions of all under your charge," Mother Catherine used to advise her young superiors, "and employ them according to their respective abilities."[7]

The positiveness of Mother Francis' character registered favorably or unfavorably with others according to their own temperaments.[8] In February a new trial befell her when one of the Carlow postulants died.[9] Remembering her grief over the death of Bishop Nolan four months earlier, Mother Catherine sent a most tactful letter, comforting yet exhorting to right religious dispositions under bereavement. The postscript is worth quoting for the glimpse it gives of the foundress' activity as she neared sixty: "I have been three hours out in the snow walking, so I am growing young—eight sisters in retreat and so much to be done . . ."

And almost immediately there was more to be done. Except for the trials in the home diocese, the year 1838 progressed with a great deal of prosperity. Many entered at Baggot Street, and there were no deaths. Father O'Hanlon secured a substantial donation for the House of Mercy, and Mother Catherine decided to erect a laundry as a means of support for young women out of employment.

Besides, a charitable woman in Booterstown provided for a convent there, and a committee of gentlemen, seeing what had been done at Kingstown, felt that charities under their management would be better off in the hands of religious. Though the benefactress, Mrs. Verschoyle,[10] was already dead, they proceeded with their plan, procured a house, and approached Mother Catherine for sisters to staff St. Anne's Convent, Booterstown. Since a number of subjects had entered in Carlow, she decided to withdraw Sister M. Ursula Frayne to take charge. Characteristically, she had left the problem of supplying sisters till the building would be ready, but now the building was almost finished and Mother Catherine must find a few companions for Sister Ursula.

"Charity sermon bad, chapel closed, bazaar unpromising," she wrote in the letter informing Mother Francis of Sister Ursula's withdrawal.[11]

Booterstown is an additional weight on my mind. I have endless difficulty in who will go and no animating circumstance except the earnest hope that God may receive some small portion of glory in the help given to His poor . . . . I have been there. It is quite finished and will have a good garden for the weak ones. I will find it difficult to add this charge to the present. When quite overwhelmed, I reanimate myself with the words of the dear saintly Dr. Nolan, "It is my lot."

Mother Catherine's anxieties increased with the illness of Mother Francis shortly thereafter and the reported illness of two sisters in Charleville, one of them the superior. "I suppose there was imprudent fasting," commented the foundress, "to which Sister Dunne is much inclined, you know."

If the new Kingstown superior, Sister M. Teresa White, was having difficulties, she kept them to herself, undoubtedly with heroic attention to one of Mother Catherine's favorite quotations from St. Francis de Sales, "If an action has a hundred faces, always look at the best."

Mother Catherine's usual optimism found plenty of support as the months passed. Mother Francis recovered. A new school and convent were going up in Tullamore; the Earl of Cork gave property for a new convent in Charleville, and Bishop Ryan of Limerick called at Baggot Street to secure a foundation for his episcopal city. In the midst of all the spring activity, English ladies arrived at No. 4 Rutland Street, Cork, to make a novitiate for a foundation in London.

There had been a three-cornered correspondence on the matter, first between Bishop Griffiths of London and Archbishop Murray and finally with Bishop Murphy of Cork. Since one of the three candidates had recently acquired a literary reputation that extended to Ireland, their Lordships decided that the Rutland Street house would be a better place of retirement than the motherhouse in the Irish capital. The decision either accorded with Miss Elizabeth Constantia Agnew's sentiments or was prompted by them, for on her arrival in Cork, May 4, she requested to be allowed to decline all visits from seculars. She and her two associates in "demi-religious" dress were met at the boat by Bishop Murphy's representative, Father Coffey, and were conducted to No. 4 Rutland Street where they immediately donned postulant's garb. After a few days, however, one of the three, who had come to be trained as a lay sister, returned to London to await the completion of Miss Agnew's and Miss Taylor's novitiate.

Though Mother Catherine was forced to reduce the number at the House of Mercy in Dublin while the laundry was under construction, on the whole the charities increased, and tranquillity marked the year 1838. Whatever spiritual travail the foundress endured, she mentioned her trials only to stimulate others to courage in their own.

"Thus we go on, my dear Sister Francis," she wrote in mid-May, "flourishing in the very midst of the cross, more than a common share of which has latterly fallen to my lot, thanks be to God. I humbly trust it is the Cross of Christ. I endeavour to make it in some way like His by silence."

Father Meyler had completely withdrawn the services of the priests at St. Andrew's! How much she felt the loss of the Blessed Sacrament at Baggot Street came home to her at Booterstown where the convent is annexed to the church in such a way that the main altar serves both the congregation and the community without infringing conventual seclusion.

"Pray fervently to God to take all bitterness from me," she wrote Mother Francis from St. Anne's. "I can scarcely think of what has been done to me without resentment. May God forgive me and make me humble before He calls me into His presence."[12]

Lighter moments came to the foundress from the heart of her own congregation. St. Anne's, Booterstown, gave her some of these in an exchange of verse on her feast day the following year. Sister M. Ursula wrote to Baggot Street in behalf of her little household:

My dear Reverend Mother, on this festive day,
Some lines in your honour I gladly would say,
But vain the endeavor: in vain do I try;
My muse is too humble for subject so high.
Though *louder* expressions of joy you may hear,
I'll answer for it—there's none more *sincere*
Than that of your children who with me unite
In begging the favour about which I write:
That you'll send Sister Celia, your representative here
And M. Aloysius to the sisters so dear
Before dinner today, as it would not be fair
To leave us here orphans and keep both Mothers there.
A pity it were that a day of such joy
Should bring with it a shade of alloy,
Which must be the case unless you will please
Grant us this favour, as you can with great ease.
If they come in the train, they'll be here in less time

By far, than I spend in writing this rhyme.
I know you will grant us this favour today
As on reading these lines I expect you will say:
"I cannot refuse them so just a request,
Then go back, my dear sisters, I think it is best;
Be merry and joyous in B town tonight
St. Catherine's day should to all bring delight."

And Mother Catherine replied:

My own dear child, you must eat, laugh and pray
Without Aloysius or Celia today;
And though you're not with us at this little fete,
We're planning to give you a very nice treat.
To this our sweet feast an octave we'll add
And give you a party will make your heart glad.
A nice picnic dinner just fit for the sod;
The white veils, in high joy will be off at a nod;
So merry a party I'm sure was ne'er seen
In parlour or drawing room, garden or green.
Kirwan will take them for about half a crown,
If you can contrive to let them lie down;
On the same day they could never come back;
'Twould spoil all the fun and break down the hack:
You can make up some pallets and place them all so
That we'd lie down together like pins in a row.
In the steamer to Cork we lay down all together
And slept mightily well without blanket or feather;
For the sake of our innocent pastime and play
We'll call Booterstown convent a steamer that day
And wonder there's half so much room on the sea.

After her return from the opening of the branch house at Booterstown, Mother Catherine began to lay plans for the Limerick foundation. In the midst of them she came to a conclusion: with the assignment of Sister Mary Elizabeth Moore to the superiorship, she was appointing the only sister left at the parent house who had qualities essential for governing. No further foundations could be made from the motherhouse because there were no "heads," as she expressed it. Yet among the postulants at the parent house the day[13] she put that decision in writing was Mary O'Connor, who as Mother M. Agnes would establish the congregation in London proper six years later and in New York within the decade.

One year after her second trip to Cork Mother Catherine set out again by packet. The sea voyage had been planned to give her not only an opportunity to confer with the English ladies for the Bermondsey foundation but to include a visit to Charleville in the overland trip north from Cork to Limerick. Her immediate destination therefore was No. 4 Rutland Street, but she was actually en route to Limerick with a traveling companion, the recently professed Sister M. Aloysius Scott, and the three sisters to begin the new foundation, one of them the novice Sister M. Vincent Hartnett. Before leaving Dublin, Mother Catherine warned the sisters not to address her in public by her religious title.

Father O'Hanlon had made a visitation of the Cork, Charleville, and Tullamore Mercy convents during the summer and had returned with an enthusiastic account of all three communities. The pastor of Charleville had also given a favorable report on Mother Angela and her household when he called at Baggot Street in July, but the foundress had some misgivings. Besides, she had promised Mother Angela a spring visit, which she had not been able to make.

An interesting little book, a collaboration, had issued from the Rutland Street house since Mother Catherine's fall visit. In her work among the poor of Cork Sister M. Vincent Deasy realized the value of a story Mother Catherine had related, probably at Baggot Street. She therefore asked the foundress to set it down for her. This Mother Catherine promised to do. Sister Vincent received the manuscript in February, 1838, and set about editing it for publication. It appeared under the title *Cottage Controversy*.[14] The author was the foundress herself.

By the time Mother Catherine and her party arrived in Cork the two English ladies had already received the habit under the names Sister Mary Clare (Agnew) and Sister Mary Augustine (Taylor). Beyond conversion to thc faith and some experience in a social service project in Bermondsey (South London) they did not have much in common. So little is available on Miss Taylor that it can be given in a sentence, whereas a volume could be written on Miss Agnew. In fact, she wrote several volumes on herself. Miss Taylor was a colorless individual with no remarkable talent and with a periodic disability of unexplained origin. Whatever the case, neither the inexperienced mother superior nor the foundress in her short contact clearly discerned. Because of Miss Agnew's place in the history of the congregation she must be dealt with at some length.

Sister Mary Clare Agnew's natural characteristics were so obscured by the culture of her class that she deceived even the foundress for a time. She had been sincere in affiliating with the Bermondsey project and she was in good faith in entering on a novitiate to found a Convent of Mercy in London. Apparently nothing in her noviceship showed up the characteristics that later controlled her life. Two circumstances contributed to the impression of stability she gave: she was a mature woman of social standing in a country where good breeding called for a particular reserve, and she had written a successful autobiographical novel. The character of the novel has significance in an analysis of its author. Both her training and her habits of thought gave Miss Agnew an unwarranted esteem for formalities, and her preoccupation with her personal history bred security in her own conceits. She therefore never acquired true self-knowledge, one of the fundamentals of spiritual life. Both Mother Clare and Mother Catherine at the time accepted her candor and social grace for the virtues she seemed to possess. On short acquaintance the foundress wrote enthusiastically:

> Sister Agnew is a delightful addition, every day more pleasing and amiable. She is evidently selected for a great work, always recollected but never solemn—no show of any kind, yet all that is valuable shows itself continually. She yields to the opinion of others like a little child and you find yourself irresistibly drawn to hers by the manner in which she submits. Had I met her as she is now ten or twelve years since, I might have been greatly benefited indeed, and even now she teaches me by her example what genuine meekness and humility are.

The community custom of encouraging talent further protected Miss Agnew from the type of discipline her character needed. Her artistic bent had been cultivated in several directions. She was a harpist and could play other instruments with some real talent. While in the novitiate, she not only wrote the third volume of her novel, *Geraldine,* but she did a set of sketches on the works of mercy with a running comment in four languages. Under some outside pressure her own bishop had requested the additional volume of *Geraldine* through Bishop Murphy. It must have been a discipline to comply, because novices then took active part in all the works of the Institute. Writing, therefore, had to be done in small margins of time between duties.

Some of the sisters in the congregation did not approve of Sister's using her novitiate experience to supplement the novel, but the foundress herself had no objection.

"I have known many who do not admire the third book of *Geraldine*," Mother Catherine wrote in reply to Mother Elizabeth's criticism, "though nothing ever exceeded its sale, not a copy to be had in Dublin."

The book of sketches was Sister's own idea. It was dedicated to Lady Clifford, a personal friend and a member of one of the old Catholic families in England. Though the author's name does not appear, the book must have been a gratification to the person who executed and assembled it. If illustrating the type of work to which Miss Agnew had committed herself and complimenting Lady Clifford were sufficient reason for its publication, it certainly had worth.

Altogether, the few days the foundress spent at No. 4 Rutland Street in the fall of 1838 were, to use one of her favorite words, "animating." The only impediment to progress was the Bishop's vigilance over dowries and his inquiry into the family connections of prospective subjects. No. 4 Rutland Street would already have outgrown its accommodations, if Mother Clare had been free to admit candidates. She had lived at the motherhouse for nine years, and knew, as the foundress herself expressed it, "on how little a nun can live."

The principal deterrent in the Cork situation was that even those who could meet His Lordship's terms hesitated to apply because the interview with Bishop Murphy was so formidable. Both Mother Clare and Mother Catherine regretted the situation, but the foundress would not interfere. The rule she had adopted gave the Bishop executive authority over the community.

In a letter written to Mother Angela a few months earlier she had warned, "Let us not forget that you and the community are subject to Dr. [Bishop] Crotty." In the same letter she mentions an effort in Mother Angela's behalf by "the monk, Mr. Reardon." Brother Reardon was one of the Irish Christian Brothers who had remained loyal to Brother Rice in the issue with Bishop Murphy.[15] The foundress' policy of concession to local conditions and her liberal interpretation of the jurisdiction of the local ordinary deserve study.

Confirmation of the rule three years later fixed the status of the congregation and brought the rule under control of the Holy See. The local ordinary, however, still has jurisdiction over pontifical institutes in matters pertaining to the government of his diocese and in certain matters connected with the welfare of the Institute and its members.[16]

XXVI

Harvesting the Sown

MOTHER CATHERINE and the sisters for the Limerick foundation arrived in Charleville on the feast of the Holy Name of Mary intending to spend a day and then proceed to Limerick on September 14, but the new foundation was not to be made, as planned, on the feast of the Exaltation of the Holy Cross. That day and the following, the feast of Our Lady of Sorrows, were well spent in stabilizing the Charleville foundation. In December she had written:

I am grieved to find such fainthearted symptoms among us . . . . Put your whole confidence in God. He never will let you want necessaries for yourself or children. It would afflict me and it would be a disgrace to our order to have a breakup.

She arrived just in time to prevent the "breakup."[1] That was a special feast of the Exaltation of the Holy Cross, for Mother Catherine's expectation of "a useful and flourishing institution in Charleville" began to be fulfilled. Her heart was heavy with foreboding on the feast of the Mother of Sorrows but light with hope nine days later on the feast of Our Lady of Mercy. The cornerstone for the new convent was laid that day on a site ideal for its purpose. The sturdiness of the building, which still stands, is indeed a symbol of Mother Catherine's prediction that St. Joseph's, Charleville, would eventually be "a strong branch." After the ceremony she and her companions set out, leaving Mother Angela and her little community truly reanimated in fervor. The travelers arrived in Limerick at eight o'clock in the evening, the feast of Our

Lady of Mercy, to establish the fifth convent outside the home diocese.

There is no foundation in the Institute like St. Mary's, Limerick. It was and is a hermitage, literally a garden enclosed, sown with eras of prayer and hushed with their peace. The foundress was impressed with its atmosphere a hundred years ago and the visitor today is struck with it. The door in the wall opens on timelessness. Timelessness rises from the unmarked graves beneath one's feet; it flows from the lancet windows of an ivy-covered ruin, void of glass for centuries, void of everything except the wall that still supports them, void of the church itself, for the sunlight that poured on St. Saviour's massiveness seven centuries ago has been pouring through the north wall windows for half as long, sunlight and lawn where monks and people once knelt, sunlight and gardens beyond—or quiet rain and peace. Ancient nobility, mitered monks, cowled priests, nuns, laity, and plague victims were buried on these grounds in periods of interment for close to a thousand years.[2]

The first religious house in the city occupied the site at the close of the twelfth century.[3] Not a vestige of it remained except the name "St. Peter's Cell," when the Sisters of Mercy entered its history in 1838. "Peter's Cell," as it was commonly called, had been a branch house of the Canonesses of St. Augustine; their convent church was dedicated to the Prince of the Apostles.

The ancient stone embroidery that separates the convent lawn from the convent gardens today is relic of another era. It is the north wall of a Dominican Abbey church endowed by the Prince of Thomond in the thirteenth century.[4] His tomb was on the north side of the chancel near the present cemetery plot. Today a statue of Our Lady of Lourdes, mounted on remnants of the old cloister piled up to support it, unintentionally marks the tomb of the princely benefactor who brought "the Fathers of the Rosary" to the city a half dozen years after the death of St. Dominic.

Two centuries of persecution accomplished the ruin of the abbey and secularized the environment, but nothing could alter the atmosphere. Efforts to restore the "Cell" to religious use in the nineteenth century thus far had been unsuccessful. In 1812 the Bishop of Limerick with the cooperation of Franciscan Fathers established the Poor Clares there but, after acquiring the property and erecting a convent and school, the community fell upon hard times and finally disbanded when their abbess died in 1830. Since the rule of the order made provision only for choir nuns in such an emergency, three lay sisters remained who managed the school and took care of cholera victims in 1832. Presentation Sisters came from Galway the following year to help in the aftermath of the epidemic.[5] Almost its last victim was one of the three lay sisters, Sister Catherine Shanahan, who died on her feast day in 1834. The Presentation Sisters withdrew in 1836, and the two Poor Clares, Sister Anne and Sister Mary, continued their charitable activites with the help of the laity. They were still in charge of "Peter's Cell" when Mother Catherine and her four sisters alighted at the only entrance to the grounds, a door in the east wall along an almost impassable road.[6]

Beyond the wall, north, south and west lay a vast slum of indescribable wretchedness. Mother Catherine gave an account of their situation to Sister M. Teresa White at Kingstown:

The approach is very bad, yet enough visitors have found a way passable to us. It is of but little consequence as we should often have to visit in the immediate neighborhood. We have found much more here than we expected, a very nice old convent enclosed by the walls of an abbey, a beautiful ruin. There is a most simple inviting tomb just opposite the cell I occupy. A holy abbess and a lay sister are deposited there, a very large weeping ash hanging over the grave. It looks delightful and excites meditation of the most consoling kind[7] . . . . The house is surrounded by trees and walking ground and all enclosed by fine old walls entirely lined with ivy. It is capable of being made a valuable institution if God will grant His blessing to our exertions. We are the third order who have made a trial—first Poor Clares, then Presentations and now Sisters of Mercy. God grant them the grace of perseverance . . . . We are saying the two Thirty Days' Prayers, one in the morning and one after Vespers.

I am sure you will unite with us in obtaining all the intercession you can. Get the sisters to invoke their patron saints and implore St. Teresa who loved foundations to intercede for poor Limerick where no seed has yet taken root.

Whether the merits of that other Sister Catherine (Shanahan, O. P. C.), martyr to the sick poor, pleaded in their behalf, whether St. Teresa "who loved foundations" interceded, or whether Our

Lady of the Rosary[8] herself intervened, the seed planted on the Feast of Our Lady of Mercy, 1838, and nurtured by Mother Catherine till the feast of the Immaculate Conception, did take root and, with God's blessing, did produce the valuable institution anticipated.[9]

Despite untoward conditions, several providential circumstances combined to favor the foundation. Preparations were in the hands of a committee directly responsible to His Lordship Bishop Ryan. Miss Heffernan, the principal benefactress, remained completely in the background, once she made over the necessary funds to the bishop. Though repairs were not quite completed when the sisters arrived, the furniture was exactly what Mother Catherine had specified to His Lordship. The two lay sisters and a secular teacher, Joanna Bridgeman, had the schools in excellent order, and the enthusiasm of Ellen Potter, a Limerick girl who had tried her vocation at Baggot Street, won support for the Sisters of Mercy. Ellen Potter had helped Sister Mary and Sister Anne set everything in order, and she was partly responsible for the number of laity who called on September 25, 1838, and promised their support. True, some came to say that their patronage lay with the Presentation Sisters who had settled at Sexton Street the previous year, but even this forthrightness had its merits. Patently, the Limerick people left no one in doubt of their allegiance nor bore anyone else ill-will because of it. If they were quick to say what they meant, they said it good-naturedly and could be depended upon to support it with the same clean-swept directness.

Ellen Potter's loyalty extended to a firm intention to join the group at "Peter's Cell." So effectively did she plead her cause the very first day that Mother Catherine let her stay. She deferred giving Ellen the postulant's cap, however, until His Lordship, who was away, returned.

Mother Catherine's experience with lay assistance on convent premises had prepared her for handling the committee. She so convinced the well-intentioned gentlemen of the sisters' efficiency in directing repairs that she not only rid the grounds of undesirable intrusion but kept the good-will and support of the committee members.

The worth of the Poor Clare lay sisters did not escape her. Afraid that years of independence might have impaired their religious character, she tested them during her three months' stay and found them desirable subjects. She then admitted them to profession in the Congregation of Mercy. The only difficulty they ever showed in adjusting was a disinclination to leave the grounds. Considering their years as cloistered religious, the foundress was amused and edified rather than displeased.

The morning after the Sisters of Mercy arrived, they went out to the parish chapel to Mass. Not till their return did they realize the consternation that had fallen upon Sister Anne and Sister Mary, who actually supposed that Mother Catherine had changed her mind about making the foundation.

The novice, Sister M. Vincent Hartnett, was professed on the feast of St. Raphael, a month after their arrival. She, too, had the advantage of the foundress' pre-profession instructions and she also left a record of her impressions. One of her observations might well be quoted here:

And in the midst of all those important and pressing occupations our venerated foundress was never seen in a hurry. She seemed to have nothing to attend to but the one matter in which at any moment she was seen occupied, and she performed that with the utmost quietness of manner, without the least impulsiveness or hastiness whatever. When any unlooked-for interruption interfered, she took that as tranquilly as the rest.[10]

The day after the profession ceremony Mother Catherine wrote to Mother Francis:

I cannot say when I shall be able to leave this foundation which, with much to excite hope and expectation, has still much, very much to contend with. It is quite novel to see those who have the smallest means most afraid to join. They are encouraged [in their attitude] by the priests who say if this breaks up, as two other communities have done, they would be nuns but what House could take them in without support, as they never could be regarded like full subjects. The friends of such as have property excite their fears that they [i. e., in the event of another failure] would be obliged to go where they might not like. Such a perplexing conflict as we have almost daily! . . . I cannot go for a full month. No person of less experience could manage at present, and I am very insufficient for the task. As to Sister Elizabeth, with all her readiness to undertake it, we never sent forward such a faint-hearted soldier. Now that she is in the field, she will do all interior and exterior work but to meet on business, confer with the Bishop, conclude with a sister, you might as well send a child that opens the door. I am sure this will surprise you. She gets white as death and her eyes like fever. She is greatly liked and when the alarms are a little over and a few in the House I expect all will go on well . . .

Mother Catherine's surprise over Sister Elizabeth's executive deficiency was matched by her surprise over Sister M. Aloysius Scott's equanimity. "I never knew her perfectly till now," she declared. "Sister Elizabeth often says she believes there is no mixture of human feelings remaining in her. So unalterably sweet and placid and unceasing day and night in her efforts to promote this object—she is everything at all times. How did I live so long with such a person and not know her? The sweetest we ever had could be a little disturbed particularly on occasions like this, but she is never moved in looks or manner."

Both sisters were young in years and young in religion. Sister Elizabeth had been professed in 1834, Sister Aloysius only a matter of months. "Nothing like foundations to bring forth character!" Mother Catherine concluded after a little more experience.

On the feast of All Saints, Joanna Bridgeman entered. After Sister Catherine Shanahan, the excellence of the schools at "Peter's Cell" must be attributed to her. Furthermore, she had been for some time associated with charities supported by her aunt, Joanna Redden, who maintained a Magdalen asylum as her principal charity. Aunt and niece now separated but were to work together again and separate again as Sisters of Mercy, the niece to go to the Crimea as a war nurse and return, the aunt to go on the American missions and die in California.

On the new superior's patronal feast, November 19, the House of Mercy opened, and Mother Catherine began to look forward to returning to Baggot Street after the ceremony of reception for the three postulants. "The Bishop has granted a remission on account of the necessity," she wrote. "Even the poor don't like the net caps but turn to the others . . . Every place has its own particular feeling which must be yielded to when possible." Shortly before leaving Limerick the foundress reported to Mother Francis:

I did not stay one day for rest or recreation but extreme caution was necessary in selecting sisters who were likely to make a steady, good beginning where there was so much to fear, and I trust we have succeeded: a Miss Bridgeman and Miss O'Farrell about twenty-four years old, [both] of as much mind and formed character as our darling Mary Teresa, and Sister Potter [who] was certainly designed for the Institute. [Ellen Potter's] ardent zeal for Limerick made her uneasy and restless elsewhere and her being on the spot with good connections and interest promoted the object very much, but we had some difficulties which required experience to manage. They are over, thank God, and I have great reason to think and hope that a lasting foundation is made.

The sisters were never to forget the reception. The crowd was too great to be accommodated and one clergyman, disappointed over the disappointment of some of his friends, helped them from outside the chapel to a place of vantage over the windowsill!

Mother Catherine waited till the feast of the Immaculate Conception to admit a postulant, then proceeded directly to Baggot Street. Kingstown convent had closed meanwhile and the sisters were back at the motherhouse. Though the work had been thereby lightened, the responsibility had been too great for Mother de Pazzi. Spells to which she had been subject occurred with increasing frequency during the foundress' absence. They were finally identified with epilepsy, which caused Mother Catherine fresh concern. That she did not relieve Mother de Pazzi of her charge occasions no surprise, for it is not the only instance of her using the weak to confound the strong.

Back in Limerick the new superior studied a letter written in verse that Mother Catherine had left for her guidance. It not only incorporates the foundress' creed for superiors of the Congregation of Mercy but it holds the mirror to her own executive virtues. Mother Elizabeth Moore showed the verses to Bishop Ryan. His Lordship read them and returned them with the succinct comment, "They should be written in gold."

They should certainly hang framed in the office of every superior of the Institute and they should be requoted whenever the character of the foundress of the Sisters of Mercy is taken under consideration.

My dearest Sister M______ E______
Don't let crosses vex or tease;
Try to meet *all* with peace and ease.
Notice the faults of every day
But *often* in a playful way,
And when you seriously complain,
Let it be known to give you pain.
Attend to one thing at a time;
You've 15 hours from 6 to 9.
Be mild and sweet in all your ways;
Now and again bestow some praise.
Avoid all solemn declaration,
All serious, close investigation,
Turn what you can into a jest
And with few words dismiss the rest.
Keep patience ever at your side;
You'll want it for a constant guide.
Show fond affection every day
And, above all, devoutly pray
That God may bless the charge He's given
And make of you their guide to Heaven—
The parting advice of your ever affectionate
M______ C______ M______

The following month Mother Catherine wrote another letter in rhyme, this to Sister Ellen Potter, one of the three received at the December 4 ceremony in Limerick. Addressed to a Mercy subject, it forms a kind of companion piece to that written for Mother Elizabeth. It epitomizes some of Mother Catherine's principal insistences: the passing of time, the obligation of using it for spiritual improvement, the maintenance of cordial charity among the sisters.

Something coincidental, if not prophetic, inheres in these lines written for Sister M. Teresa Potter. The year 1838 was literally her last full year on earth. The foundress herself did not survive her much more than a year.

Book Three

Fire Cast on the Earth

"The fire that Christ cast upon the earth is kindling very fast."
—MOTHER M. CATHERINE MC-AULEY, June 8, 1940

XXVII

Our Lady's Dower

LOOKING BACK over the century of Christian culture implanted in Britain by Columcille, "the Dove of Eire," Bede the Venerable referred to Ireland as "that peaceful nation always most friendly to the English."[1] A thousand years had passed since the historian's happy characterization, years of English repudiation, then disruption and persecution—the peace scattered, the friendliness obscured.

But a new era came at last with new missionaries to re-assemble the broken, to mortise and restore. What matter that the wronged must do the righting? This was the Christian pattern.

The year the Catholic Association made its first successful political effort toward Catholic Emancipation,[2] one of O'Connell's college classmates became Vicar Apostolic in the English Midlands—not that there was any political connection between Bishop Thomas Walsh and Daniel O'Connell nor any conscious collaboration, just that personalities in the great cause were moving into position.

Thomas Walsh, born of Irish parentage in London forty-nine years before had been brought to the Midland District while still a deacon. In 1818 when sixteen-year-old, Spanish-born Nicholas Wiseman was leaving England to attend the English College in Rome, just then re-opening, Father Walsh, already associated with Oscott College, became its president. Nine years later Catholic John Talbot succeeded his uncle in the Talbot title and estates, becoming the sixteenth Earl of Shrewsbury of Alton Towers in the Midlands.

The following year O'Connell was elected to a seat in the English Parliament; the truly remarkable Institute of Charity was founded in Italy by Father Rosmini;[3] and Father Nicholas Wiseman became rector of the English College in Rome as well as intermediary for all the English bishops. Seven years later Monsignor Wiseman and Bishop Thomas Walsh met at Wolverhampton and the two ecclesiastics who would consistently promote the Catholic revival had come together.

By then Lord Shrewsbury had discovered the brilliant if eccentric young Protestant architect, Augustus Welby Pugin, who as a convert would restore dignity and beauty to Catholic church buildings and, in collaboration with Bishop Walsh and the Cambridge converts, would do much to improve altar appointments and Church music.[4]

Wiseman already knew Ambrose Phillipps through George Spencer, the convert minister Bishop Walsh had sent to the English College. While in Rome these two converts had become friends of the little Italian Passionist, Father Dominic Barberi. All would meet again in the English Midlands.

Before Wiseman returned to Rome in 1836, he cooperated with O'Connell and Quin in founding the *Dublin Review*, through which Wiseman was to reach Newman. The two had already met casually at the English College in 1833, Newman Anglican of Anglicans at the time.

In 1839 Monsignor Wiseman was again in England. He found the Midlands alive with Catholic activity. Spencer had been made spiritual director at new Oscott, then recently built under Pugin's direction. Pugin himself was on the faculty as Professor of Ecclesiastical Art, supervising from that position the erection of a whole flock of church buildings. The most imposing of them all was the Birmingham cathedral, the first Catholic cathedral in England since the Reformation.

Among the buildings Pugin had under construction when the rector of the English College arrived in England in the summer of 1839 was what seemed an annex to Most Holy Trinity Church in Bermondsey, across the Thames from London proper. It was in reality a monastic building, the first convent to be erected in England since pre-Reformation days. So curiously does time deal with history that vestiges of an eleventh century Cluniac monastery[5] still stood in Bermondsey at the birth of those who finally established the new order.

Father Peter Butler, ordained December 17, 1831, had built Most Holy Trinity Church and had founded a religious order almost simultaneously, if the unstable little group of social workers who called themselves Sisters of Charity could be considered a religious institute. Miss Louisa Murray, a convert, and her servant, Elizabeth Boyce, began the work in a house next to the old chapel while the new church was being built. When the church opened in 1835, Father Butler turned the old chapel into a poor school. Miss Charlotte Collingridge and Miss Elizabeth Agnew[6] then came to his assistance. They were joined in a few months by Lady Barbara Eyre, who knew Miss Agnew socially.

With the arrival of the three recruits, Father Butler drew up a set of rules. Cells were improvised in the gallery of the old chapel, and a uniform was adopted, a plain black dress with a small white cap and veil. Elizabeth Boyce continued her services as a lay sister until Miss Murray found difficulty in adjusting to the new regime and withdrew to Norwich to continue social work again on her own. Elizabeth Boyce accompanied her. Miss Collingridge, unable to keep up with the physical pace, also withdrew. The two socialites were then joined by a Miss Mary O'Connor who took charge of the school, and Sarah Hawkins who replaced the "lay sister." Work was laborious, living conditions inconvenient and trying, but high motives sustained the workers and they persevered for several months, doing an immense amount of good. It was Father Butler who, seeing the need for a more stabilizing influence, consulted Bishop Griffiths on affiliating the group with the Sisters of Mercy. Small as the organization was, divergency in the piety of its members had already manifested itself in a tendency to a more contemplative way of life. This eventually produced an issue involving Miss Agnew. The only members of this group to persevere in religious life were Lady Barbara Eyre and Miss O'Connor.[7] Since Lady Barbara preceded Miss O'Connor in religion and lived eight years a professed religious, her identity as first English Sister of Mercy should be reverently acknowledged. She clung to her objective against all opposition and in spite of any sacrifice.

There are implications of mystery in the account of Lady Barbara's early life. She was "an eccentric and wayward character," writes the annalist and an anxiety to the Franciscan nuns who taught her, but they loved her and she them. Once when on her way to conclude an affair that would have brought her great misery, the record continues, she knelt in the carriage and said the Litany of our Lady. Unexpected difficulties arose, and she gave up the matter.

This evidence and the further statement that people flattered her for their own interest, furnish an impression of young Barbara Eyre. Apparently there was no predicting what she might do; and, since she was beautiful and full of generous impulse, there was no predicting what she might come to. Written into the account are devotion to the Mother of God, liberality, and attraction to social service. Much as she loved her worldly-minded mother, Countess Dorothy, her brother Francis, and her four younger sisters, she had a special love for her truly pious father, her eldest sister and her elder brother. The Countess was English and a Protestant. Francis Eyre was English with an Italian strain in his background. In fact, Barbara's paternal grandmother, Lady Mary, had been born of a marriage uniting two noble families, one English, the other Italian. She herself had been born in Rome. South European blood was strong in Barbara Eyre. It accounts for the impulsiveness so little understood by the English nuns.

Her father, Francis Eyre, had placed the girls in the convent school at Taunton in Somersetshire, to assure grounding in their Faith, and it is to the credit of the Franciscan nuns that Barbara's wayward tendencies not only remained in check but were finally controlled to a self-discipline so remarkable that the account of it reads like hagiography.

After leaving school, Barbara became her sister's companion on many missions of charity to the poor. Lady Charlotte would have joined the Franciscans at Taunton if she could have summoned the courage. Lacking it, she devoted her short life to good works, particularly among the sick poor. After Lady Charlotte's death in Paris, Lady Barbara spent several years traveling with her father, who himself died shortly after their return to England in 1827. His wonderful calm in the hour of death made an unforgettable impression on her, and the equally holy death of her elder brother shortly after he came into the title and estate determined her to seek admission among the Franciscan nuns. They told her kindly that she lacked the requisites for their order. She then wrote to Elizabeth Agnew (August 23, 1837) asking to be admitted among the workers in Bermondsey. She confessed her repugnances but depended on Miss Agnew's example and Father Butler's zealous charity to strengthen her. However unfit, she begged to be allowed to live and die at Bermondsey.

Her mother opposed her, threatening to disinherit her. Her friends discouraged her, and relatives dissuaded her tactfully on the ground of her frail health, but she arrived at the old chapel August 25, 1837, and lived the rest of her life at Bermondsey. She adopted the costume of the others, asking to be addressed as just "Sister Mary." She undertook the labors and endured the privations the program demanded, persevering during Miss Agnew's absence in Cork. She returned home only once, at the death of her mother. The countess had kept her word and had disinherited her eldest daughter, but the will was declared irregular, and Lady Barbara came into her share of the estate.

She gave Father Butler £1000 to erect the convent, which Pugin designed to fit the small plot of ground between the church and the street. He planned to attach the convent to the church through a room on the upper floor that would open on the main altar and serve as a tribune for the sisters.

Mention of the limited site recalls the history of the property transaction. A Protestant minister who admired the spirit of the young priest, Peter Butler, gave him a horse and carriage to attend the sick and dying poor in his parish. Shortly after the cholera epidemic the minister acted as intermediary in the purchase of church property. The owner later declared that, had he known the site was intended for a Catholic church, he would not have sold it "for a hatful of diamonds." If he could have foreseen that a convent would adjoin the church, without doubt his language would have been even more emphatic.

Before the English novices left the Rutland Street house in Cork, Bishop Murphy added the adjoining house to the convent property. The purchase puzzled Mother Clare who could have filled both houses with subjects if His Lordship were not so exacting on admissions. As it was, the community had ample room in the house Miss Gould had given them.

Bishop Murphy insisted that the foundress come to Cork for the profession of the English subjects, and His Lordship's insistences amounted to command. Fortunately, the Naas foundation, at last nearing reality, was to be made from Carlow. Mother Catherine knew that her time from August on would be devoted to the Bermondsey foundation.

Meanwhile, the see-saw business of re-opening the Kingstown convent preplexed her, and she was harassed by the peculiar defection of Miss McGuinness, the benefactress who had paid traveling expenses for the sisters on all previous foundations. Added to these trials, the illness and death of Sister M. Gertrude Jones weighed Mother Catherine with sorrow.

Excerpts from her letters during 1839 present these matters first-hand. On the feast of Epiphany she wrote to Mother M. Francis Warde:

I have come back to my corner after all are gone to bed to write a few lines to my poor old child . . . . We are exactly as you left us except that a new sister was concluded for this day from County Wexford. She comes in a week. I thought we should be without a postulant after the ceremony, not knowing anything of the expected one. She will not be twenty till next month—very pleasing and musical. It is striking ten. The fire is out and the windows are making an awful noise.

Apparently Mother Francis had been at Baggot Street for a recent ceremony. The wind storm developed into an island-wide hurricane. The following day the foundress wrote again to Mother Francis, telling her of the damage and concluding:

I fear the Kingstown business is going to be settled. I cannot wish the poor sisters to go there. They never shall except a private choir is made for them in the parish chapel, but I fear this will be done. *Do not say anything of it yet.*

The underlined warning in the last sentence proved to be discreet, for the business was not settled for a year and three months.

On Saturday January 26, the foundress wrote to Mr. Charles Cavanagh, her lawyer:

The sisters are just returned from Kingstown. Mr. Sheridan met them according to his appointment but said he thought there was a misunderstanding, that we would have to pay £470 before he would make the choir. This is very different from what he said to you.

This she amplified in a letter to Mother Francis:

Saturday—a new account about Kingstown. Mr. Sheridan told Mr. Cavanagh that if the schoolhouse were assigned to trustees for the children the debt should be paid and a choir made in the parish church for the sisters if they would return. Mr. Cavanagh agreed to this. Mr. Sheridan then wrote to me requesting two sisters would go out to select such portion of the church as was deemed necessary. Sisters Mary Teresa and Aloysius went on the day he appointed. After taking all their plan he recalled what he had agreed with Mr. Cavanagh and said in presence of Mr. Walsh that he never invited them to Kingstown and therefore could not be called upon to do what he heard was done for us in other places. I could not describe Mr. Cavanagh's surprise. He said Mr. Sheridan could not speak plainer [than he had done]. [Mr. Cavanagh] wrote expressing his surprise and shew'd me a copy of the letter. If it was to me he said it he would think it was my imagination. I think it would seem like defiance if we were to go now after the parish priest saying to two sisters in the presence of his curate that he never invited them. Sister Mary Teresa [White] could not avoid saying in reply that none of them liked to come. It is a perplexing business. Pray for me.

The foundress therefore decided to sell or rent the house as her April letter to the community lawyer shows:

May I beg to trouble you again about Kingstown? I hear of places letting all about and fear the season may pass with us. We want knives and many other things in the household way which must be quite spoiled there. Will you in charity conclude the matter for us?

But long before that—in fact, three weeks after the January 26 letter to Mr. Cavanagh, Mother Catherine wrote to him on a matter far more annoying than Canon Sheridan's hedging. Miss McGuinness was at last showing the "singular mode of thinking and judging" that "distinguished" her according to Dr. Blake's report from Newry, June 5, 1833.

The letter to Charles Cavanagh under date of February 14, 1839, runs:

Dear Sir:—I regret exceedingly being obliged to engage your time and attention so much but I cannot arrange this matter myself. Were it merely personal, I would soon put an end to it by giving Miss McGuinness what she now violently demands. She is acting in a most rude and unchristian manner. She called me a wretch twice before two or three and says I prepared a drink for her with something to stupefy her and sent it by Sister White, that you and I got her to sign the deed after she had taken this draught. This has spread through the House and may be productive of very injurious consequences.

Sister White's father has been appointed a stipendiary magistrate and is at present in town. I was thinking seriously of consulting him. Of course, he would take up very zealously such a charge brought against his child. Miss McG. seems to forget entirely that she is to observe any regulations. She interrupts our religious exercises, always saying that she acts by the direction of her lawyer, who she says, tells her she may go into every room in the convent, what no Religious Sister could do.

I will copy here what our Rule prescribes in reference to this case. It is signed and sealed by the Archbishop.

Chapter Eighth—Fourth Section

"As many shall be received in the establishment as the funds will admit of and no more, unless the subject bring with her a sufficient dower for her support in every necessary. Lodgers shall not be admitted with an exception in favor of a foundress or very particular benefactress."

Miss McG. wants to be a lodger without being either foundress or benefactress but that cannot be except we were permitted to violate our Rule.

If Miss McG. will give a release, I will propose (with permission) returning her £1000, though we never could consider a person giving 400 and paying her expenses eligible to be admitted as benefactress. It has been said here that Miss McG. has incurred damages by the manner she has spoken of the establishment before strangers. Her language indeed is dreadful. I am sure her poor head must be in a distracted state. Will you in charity to all make the above proposal, and I will get it concluded soon as possible?

About this time Mother Catherine had Sister M. Gertrude Jones removed to St. Anne's, Booterstown, where she died three months later. The foundress' appreciation of the character of this valiant soul became the subject of a letter familiar to every Sister of Mercy. Nevertheless, it deserves re-quoting. Under date of May 11, she wrote to Mother Francis from Booterstown:

My dearest Sister M. Francis,—our poor Sister M. Gertrude is no longer an inhabitant of this passing world. She died on Ascension Day. For the last year she has been chiefly confined to bed—fourteen weeks since she was removed here for change of air and chiefly in the hope that she could have the comfort of being present at Mass without many stairs to go up. No evident symptoms of death appeared until Monday last. She had every spiritual consolation. Mr. O'Hanlon came to her three times. Her dear remains were this morning deposited with her eleven Sisters in Religion. We hope to have them all home before another year.

Reviewing all the past, I regard poor Sister Gertrude as a martyr to the faith. The violent effort she made to embrace and practice it and the entire separation from all to whom she was ever known gave a shock to the whole nervous system which could not be recovered. Delighted as she felt with the Catholic Faith, she fancied all who faithfully observed it must be divine—hence she was disappointed. Yet for one moment she would not entertain the thought of returning lest there might be danger of losing it. Soon after her death, before I made any remark, Sister Mary Cecilia said, "Well, Reverend Mother, though poor Sister G. was sometimes very tiresome, I often thought she was like a martyr. She seemed every day to be offering great violence to feelings which were not in any degree overcome. All her mind turned to England and English manners. We could not converse so agreeably, cut out a cap, make a pudding or spread a plaster as they could in Bridgenorth, which she often said had every attraction under Heaven but the true Faith."

When describing the amiable and, as she used to say, exalted principles and disposition of her brother and his daughters, she seemed to think they were all lost for want of a knowledge of the Faith. This feeling was engraved on her heart by some supernatural means. Her case was an extraordinary one. God only can appreciate its value. I believe she may be truly said to have taken up her cross while in general we only carry it when it comes and keep it away as long as we can. I am certain her reward will be great. She suffered in mind and body for nine years from no visible cause but a rending of the heart from violent sacrifice of all the predilections of thirty-seven years. A vocation to religious life has its joys but her whole concern was the preservation of Faith and guarding against whatever would put it in danger, and she would not trust to her own perseverance if not shielded as she was.

Her countenance was sweetly composed in death, her teeth perfectly white, and not the slightest swelling in her feet—strong signs of not being in an unhealthy state of body. She expressed a strong desire to die on Ascension Day. Sister Monica and I were watching her. We had read all the last prayers three or four times and after eleven o'clock on Wednesday night concluded she would live a day or two longer as no change appeared. The instant the clock struck twelve, just at her door, she stretched out her arms and as if it were an immediate call on her to go, she settled her head and before we could read the departing prayers she was gone.

Certainly, as the foundress states, Sister Gertrude's vocation was extraordinary. She had had her own vision of the grail and she had had her own search. For over thirty years she waited, busying herself with charity to the poor. Expecting to continue work of the kind, she had brought a quantity of medicine with her to Baggot Street but found nothing familiar in her surroundings nor in the character of the charities. She arrived at the worst possible time, while the foundress was at George's Hill. The poverty and unrestricted asceticism practiced at Baggot Street appalled her, and conditions in the Dublin slums repelled her, but she would not withdraw. As the foundress implies, Sister seemed convinced that her salvation depended on her perseverance. Perhaps the English foundations, now about to be undertaken, owed their success to her eight years' unalleviated sacrifice.

XXVIII

Geraldine

In August Mother Catherine left Dublin on her fourth trip to Cork, this time to be present for the profession of the two English novices on the nineteenth. It became impossible to accommodate the numbers who wished to attend the ceremony. Invitations were therefore limited to the clergy, with a single exception in favor of Miss Barbara Gould, principal benefactor of the convent.

After characteristic temporizing Bishop Murphy finally agreed to release Mother M. Clare Moore for a year to help establish the English mission. Mother Catherine therefore appointed Sister M. Joseph Warde acting superior, and His Lordship confirmed the nomination.

The sisters left Cork the day after the profession, stopping at Charleville where they saw the new convent with its extensive gardens. In the soon-to-be-abandoned house on Clanchy Terrace Mother Catherine found none of the original group except the superior; yet others filled the places of those who had left. What the foundress had written the previous January of the Institute in general might be applied in particular to Charleville: "It evidently was to go on and surmount all obstacles."

The sisters proceeded to Limerick. Their carriage made its precarious way up the island road to the low door in the wall. The door opened. Soft, joyous voices made their own island in the quiet. If the dead could rouse, how startled to hear English accents!

Peace to you, Missioners of Mercy. Three centuries of wrong are buried here. Peace be to you. Stay in peace and go in peace. We bear you no ill-will.

Over five hundred poor children now attended the schools that Sister Catherine Shanahan had put under the National Board almost as soon as it came into existence. Others had entered into her labors. Her co-workers, Sister Anne and Sister Mary, were now Sisters of Mercy and the lay teacher whose skill matched Sister Catherine's was soon to enroll in the new community. In her death hour Sister Catherine, too, might have said, "It is expedient to you that I go."

Visitations, House of Mercy, and soup kitchen for the poor had been added to the charities. These had taken on the timelessness of the atmosphere, for they seemed to have been going on for centuries. And truly ages of service here!

Concerning the English sisters the community annalist wrote: "While here they excited much interest and many persons visited them."

Mother Catherine saw with gratitude that God was granting the blessings she had implored for "poor Limerick."

Sixteen hours of travel brought the party to Tullamore where they found everything in a state of transition. Over a year before, the cornerstone of a new convent had been laid on the eve of the feast of the Sacred Heart. Though Father O'Rafferty had given workmen "dawn to dark" superintendence, two serious delays intervened. Excavation revealed that they were building literally upon a rock, for there were only a few feet of top soil. Then just as the building was well under way, the January hurricane hurled the massive stone chimneys through rafters and flooring. The convent could not be ready for another year, though the chimneys, braced with iron, already rose anew from their bed of rock—the convent itself a promise in stone, which Mother Catherine transferred to words: "It will last for centuries."

How the five visitors were accommodated in the cottage already filled to overflowing is matter for wonder. Two postulants had entered after Jane Greene of Naas, a convert Miss Arabella Deverell, and Father Murtagh's cousin. In the meantime, at Mother Mary Anne's request Sister M. Teresa Purcell had been appointed mother assistant by Bishop Cantwell. If space were limited, work was not. Even English imagination could foresee greater progress.

Through the courtesy of Father O'Rafferty the party went from Tullamore to Carlow by carriage. There a new convent awaited them. Poplars and evergreens, for which the foundress had a special preference, had been planted before the building went up. The grounds therefore already had an aspect of beauty. Carlow convent had the distinction of being the first building erected as a Convent of Mercy. The sisters had much to tell their visitors, for on the feast of the Visitation of Our Lady the previous month they had left the old academy where some still slept on mattresses on the floor. After blessing the convent, His Lordship Bishop Haly said Mass for them in the new chapel. Dr. Fitzgerald said a second Mass immediately afterward, and Father Maher offered a third. These friends of the community now did their utmost to honor Mother Catherine and "the good ladies" Dr. O'Rafferty had brought from Tullamore, for thus the parish priest at St. Joseph's invariably referred to the sisters.

During their stay Bishop Haly offered his daily Mass in the convent chapel, and Dr. Fitzgerald gave a series of religious conferences. "The English sisters were particularly pleased with the energy of the venerable, fervent old Dominican," the community annals state, and were impressed by the bishop's holiness, "his great urbanity and kindliness."

The Carlow novitiate, too, had increased in number, with Father Maher's niece one of the new members. Though but a postulant at the time, she was to write her recollections later as community annalist:

The impression made on us young people by the expected visit of our graver sisters was a fear that we should be under some particular restraint while they were with us, for we had had a vigorous lecture to act religiously, politely and affectionately. After a few hours, however, we liked our new acquaintances very well. Mother Clare had a strikingly meek look and manner. Sister Mary de Sales was very pretty and lively, eager to help us recreate gaily. The other sisters were not young but ladylike. We thought them eccentric in their attitudes at prayer. We excused ourselves for so thinking by saying they were English converts. In after years they proved to be eccentric indeed.

Reverend Mother McAuley was liked by all except one postulant in whose stocking she had observed a hole on a previous visit. She was up at the first call every morning and joined in all our exercises, taking the place usually occupied by the mother assistant. She spent much of her time conferring with the professed sisters [four including the Carlow superior] as a foundation to Naas was in contemplation. I think what pleased us most in Reverend Mother McAuley was the absence of a manner telling "I am the foundress." She was cheerful and motherly with all of us and looked very devout at her prayers. The morning of her departure she asked Mother Francis if she might take two or three twists of bread off the refectory table as she and her companions would be six hours on the road, the old stage-coach being the quickest mode of conveyance. Her request for the bread was made with a natural sincerity that seemed to say it was quite good enough. Mother Francis offered to have a luncheon prepared, but it was declined.

The Presentation *Annals* tell of a visit paid their convent by the Carlow superior and her guests. Since the foundress is not named, Mother Francis probably called on the day Mother Catherine took the Cullen girls, Anne (recently received under the name Sister M. Paula) and Ellen, a postulant, to see their father, Gerald Cullen[1] of Craan, who was then sick. Mother Catherine's visit proved profitable to the Carlow novitiate; impressed by her words of congratulation to Mr. Cullen on having daughters in religion, a third, Catherine, entered later.

The room that Mother Catherine occupied during her stay in the "new convent" has become an oratory where Mass is said on occasions.[2]

En route to Dublin the sisters stopped to look in on the convent Father Doyle at last had ready for the sisters.[3] On the eve of the feast of Our Lady of Mercy Mother Francis would bring Sister Mary Joseph Trenor[4] as superior, Sister Mary Catherine Meagher and Sister Mary Agnes Greene to stay, and the novice Sister M. Angela Johnson to help temporarily.

"While the stagehorses were changing at Naas," Mother Catherine wrote encouragingly to Mother Francis, "we looked in at the sweet little convent from the window. It is a nice spot, the walks and shrubs neatly arranged."

Naas parish had been under the patronage of St. David from the Norman invasion till Father Doyle built the new church in 1827. To distinguish it from the Protestant St. David's he called the new edifice "Our Lady and St. David's." The convent, however, was named simply St. Mary's.

Father Maher's niece describes the departure from St. Leo's. "All wept, but the excitement and imagined importance of a foundation soon stopped the flow of tears." Dr. Fitzgerald took Mother M. Francis Warde and Sister M. Joseph Trenor in the bishop's carriage on the afternoon of September 23. They carried a valuable little parcel of manuscripts, containing a copy of the rule and ceremonial and a few religious treatises. One of the manuscripts was signed and dated by the postulant who transcribed it: "April 5, 1839—Pray for Sister Anne Cullen, Convent of Mercy, Carlow."

His Grace called on the English missioners when they arrived at Baggot Street. He then set October third for the profession of Sister M. Francis Xavier O'Connell and Sister M. Anne Frances de Chantal Markey. Mother Catherine wrote to Mother Francis in Naas:

If any good chance would bring you to me the evening before, after all your ceremony ended [i. e., the blessing of Naas convent] what a comfort it would be to have you once more one of the number, and if we had a hope of your good bishop, that indeed would be cheering. Perhaps Dr. Fitzgerald and Father Maher [would come], but I suppose this is all too much to think of. . . . On our ceremony day we expect to have 45 sisters at dinner. You and child [companion] would make 47 at tea.

How charmingly persuasive the mother foundress could be! And how gratifying to her the spirit at St. Mary's, Naas, if the original can be judged by the present!

The English sisters had had to give up hope of being in Bermondsey by September 24, for the convent was far from completed. Mother Catherine therefore planned to take them to Newry after the October profession that they might receive the blessing of "the truly sanctified" Dr. Blake.

There the party enjoyed the hospitality of the Poor Clare nuns who conducted a school in the hostile North. Poor Clare convent records have the following account of the visit:

Previous to the founding of the Sisters of Mercy in Bermondsey, London, an application was made by the foundress of that order to our Right Reverend superior, Dr. Blake, to permit her to visit this convent accompanied by the sisters who were in preparation for this great work,

Mother Mary Clare Moore, Sister Mary Clare Agnew, author of *Geraldine, a Tale of Conscience*, and Sister Mary Augustine Taylor. They arrived here on Saturday, October 5, and remained until Wednesday morning, during which time they not only joined in the general exercises of the community but made particular enquiries concerning our conventual observances and choir ceremonies. Our Reverend Mother Abbess presented them with a manuscript copy of Asseline's *Discourses,* not then in print, also a copy of our different ceremonials and one on the manner of life of the Béziers nuns. The good religious in return, with very grateful expressions for the hospitality they acknowledged to have received, presented an invaluable book, the life of our holy foundress St. Clare, in French, the life of Mother Mary of the Cross, and the lives of the lately canonized saints.

After their return to Baggot Street Mother Catherine brought the sisters to George's Hill Presentation Convent. Her enthusiasm over the visit is well known. "They were delighted and so was I," she wrote to Mother Francis the following month. "I said I would kiss the chairs and tables but by some mistake I kissed a grand new chair in the parlor. However, I managed as Ducky Mary Quin used. I took it [the kiss] back and brought it up to the old rush chair I used to sit on in the noviceship."

About this time Father Richard Colgan of the Calced Carmelites, then on his way to Rome, proposed translating the rule into Italian to accompany a petition for its confirmation. He advised Mother Catherine to prepare this petition to the Holy Father and have it signed by the respective superiors of her foundations. He further recommended that she solicit letters of endorsement from bishops who favored her Institute.

She informed Bishop Blake of Father Colgan's visit and received a characteristic letter in reply:

Dear Reverend Mother,—instead of hesitating a moment I would wish to comply at once with every request that comes from you and particularly when the request is that I would recommend your petition for the approbation of the Holy See. In complying with such a request, I am sure I could not say too much in praise of your Institute or of the intrinsic excellence of the rules and constitutions or of the perfect adaptation of these to the great and peculiar duties of your community or of the strict observance by which they are carried into effect. But as the sincere friend of your Institute I think it my duty to suggest rather the regular and most approved mode, usually adopted on such occasions, of having your petition sanctioned and corroborated by the joint request and signature of your venerable Archbishop. Whatever is asked in that way, if it be at all reasonable, is usually, and almost as a matter of course, granted. I give this advice because, from my experience in such matters, I believe it to be the best I can offer.

I was much gratified in hearing from the Reverend Mother Prioress of St. Clare's that you and your venerated companions on your late visit to Newry are all well after the journey. That you and they may always be well and daily receive an increase of every good and perfect gift of God is the sincere wish, dear Reverend Mother, of

Your faithful servant in Christ
M. Blake.[5]

Simultaneously with Bishop Blake's letter came a reply from Bishop Ryan of Limerick. Other letters of endorsement arrived in response to the circular Mother Catherine had sent: one from the Primate, Archbishop Crolly, who knew the work of the Carlow and Limerick communities, one from Archbishop Murray, others from Bishop Kinsella and Bishop Murphy. In London she would add Bishop Griffiths' to the collection.[6]

The foundress' follow-up letter to Bishop Haly of Carlow, written the day before she left Ireland, contains a brief survey of the development of the Institute:

Dear and Respected Lord,—I took the liberty of sending you a little circular which I was directed to forward to the bishops in whose dioceses a branch of our Institute was formed. Perhaps, my Lord, I should have explained the nature of the application more fully. In the year 1830 our venerated Archbishop obtained permission from the Holy See for three of us to serve a novitiate in a Presentation Convent with intention to add the visitation of the sick and charge of distressed women. In 1835 our progress was represented, and the Pope then imparted to us his approbation and benediction. The bishop prepared our rule, and finding it after due trial well suited to our purpose, we now seek its final confirmation in form of a petition from ourselves, a memorial or request from His Grace and all the recommendation we can obtain from other prelates. The Primate has given his in very gratifying terms and Doctor Kinsella has enclosed me a letter to His Holiness, though we are not in either diocese. We take all our documents to London on Monday next and trust you will be so kind to add the tribute of your approbation.

Dr. Haly sent his endorsement direct to the Cardinal Prefect of the Sacred College of Propaganda. His Lordship wrote a highly commendatory letter doubly forceful from his having two distinct foundations in his diocese, a fact that deserves notice; for, though the foundress kept the houses in the Dublin area filial to the motherhouse, she permitted independent houses in the neighboring diocese.

Enough publicity had been given the projected mission in Bermondsey to stir up an angry reaction against the sisters. After the journalistic fashion of the day, English newspaper accounts were colored—in this case with prejudice. It therefore required more courage to undertake the journey than casual preparations admitted.

On the eve of departure Mother Catherine wrote:

I need not tell you all the difficulties I have to meet in getting away from this poor old charge, which would and will do as well without me. The six travellers leave dear Ireland tomorrow, all in tolerable good health and more than tolerable spirits,—Sister Agnew rejoiced, Sister Taylor in rapture and their mother [Mother M. Clare Moore] all animation, Sister M. Cecilia greatly improved and Sister Mary Teresa smart as a lark. I have my list of songs prepared for the journey. . . . The little excitement of my going will last a few days—I trust only a few.

We have had long and most kind visits from our poor Bishop [Archbishop Murray who had not been well], a cordial leave-taking and fervent prayers for safe return. Nine Masses are to be offered for us tomorrow, thank God. I am sure Mr. O'Hanlon is a little alarmed at the angry things which are said in the English papers. He gave me ten thousand cautions yesterday.

So much "for reading out"—in postscript, however, Mother Catherine pleaded with Mother Francis: "Get all the prayers you can for poor me."

Whatever anxiety the foundress felt, she acted according to character and proceeded in the same sprightly tenor as her letter.

The outdoor dress at the time could hardly be distinguished from the conservative dress of elderly women. To avoid attracting attention to their Catholicity, still much in disfavor, Mother Catherine resorted to a custom familiar and dear to her when she lived among Quakers. She requested the sisters to call her "Friend Catherine." That spared them anything like the embarrassing situation of the Cork journey when Mother Elizabeth Moore suddenly addressed her "Kitty," as Dr. McAuley invariably did.

They set sail from Kingstown and, after a rough passage on the Irish Sea, entrained at Liverpool and arrived in London after dark the following evening.

Though no angry mob beset the sisters, untoward circumstances of a less spectacular kind awaited them in Bermondsey. Since Father Butler lay dying on November 19, 1839, it was believed, the sisters found their way from the railway station to the bastille-like quarters Mr. Pugin had under construction. England is never at its best in late November, and all of Pugin's buildings thus far had been churches. Bermondsey convent was a sort of architectural hybrid. Mother Catherine had asked Father Butler to have two rooms finished. Six were finished but in such proportions as to disconcert rather than comfort. On the narrow plot of land between the church and street the rest of the vast building spread out in two directions. Closing out the night, they seemed to have brought the whole London damp within. Mother Catherine later wrote of the "up to the ceiling" windows: "I could not touch the glass without standing on a chair." Marooned as they felt in the one furnished room, they made the best of their situation, ate the supper Father Butler's sister had prepared, and retired to awake to a busy day.

His Lordship Bishop Griffiths called, pressed £50 into the foundress' protesting hand, and promised to come the following day to offer Mass and bless the convent. Foundation Day for Bermondsey, therefore, is the feast of the Presentation of Our Lady.

Since the highlights of the journey and of the first weeks in London appear in Mother Catherine's correspondence, her letter to Mother M. Elizabeth Moore, because of its greater detail, is included here:

Convent of the Sisters of Mercy
Bermondsey, London
December 17, 1839

My ever dear Sister Mary Elizabeth,

I know you are anxious to hear from me but not more than I am to write to you a full account of our journey and the progress we have made in our new undertaking. We sailed from Kingstown on Monday evening the 18th of November at 6 o'clock in the *Queen Victoria,* arrived in Liverpool at half-past six next morning, were conducted to the Mersey Hotel where breakfast was ready, laughed and talked over the adventures of the night, particularly my traveling title changed from your Kitty to "Friend Catherine"—an improvement, you will say—proceeded in the train most comfortably and reached London in very good time. Just think a moment: what extraordinary expedition! We dined in Baggot Street on Monday and arrived in London time enough to take refreshment, say our prayers and go to bed early on Tuesday night—very different from our travels in Ireland. We were sixteen hours going from Limerick to Tullamore.

The convent is built in the old, heavy, monastic style. It will not be finished for another year nor dry in three years, but our unceasing engagements have contributed to preserve us from the bad effects of a damp house. Indeed we have been "busy bodies." The Bishop called the day after we arrived. He was exceedingly kind, said the Irish Sisters must be entertained by him and insisted on giving me a fifty pound note. In vain he was assured that all was provided which we were accustomed to. He would not be refused. He is remarkably gentle, his appearance between Dr. Blake and Dr. Murray—wears a gold chain and large cross outside his dress and wears purple stockings. His Lordship celebrated Mass and blessed the convent on the Feast of the Presentation. He also appointed Thursday last, 12th of December, for the Reception of six who have been waiting with pious anxiety more than a year. The Bishop left everything to me and, as the test of their sincerity was not to be questioned, we concluded that it would be well to get all into religious order first.

On the morning of the ceremony the church, which accommodates four thousand, was crowded to excess. Tickets had been circulated by the Bishop's direction and none that we would call poor was invited. The seats next to the sanctuary were filled with nobility: the Countess of Newburgh, Countess Constantia Clifford, Lady Bedington, Dowager

Countess Newburgh, Lady Petre, the Miss Cannings, Mrs. Weld, Mrs. Maxwell—you'll be surprised that I remember all these titles but they are the particular friends of Sister Agnew and familiar visitors. Some are of the immediate family of one of our new novices of whom you shall hear a description.

At eleven o'clock a grand High Mass commenced. The organ and choir are considered very fine. After Mass the hymn *O Gloriosa* was performed and we advanced from the entrance leading to our convent. The Bishop wished the ceremony to be last lest any of those high persons should be late. Procession: Sister Mary Teresa carrying an immense cross, Sisters M. Cecilia, M. Clare Agnew, M. Augustine Taylor, one by one to make the most of a few, Mother Mary Clare and her valuable assistant, "Friend Catherine" or your Kitty with their six postulants following. All were admitted to the sanctuary. The altar is the highest I ever saw—nine steps—two platforms, the Bishop at the top in very rich episcopal dress. Kitty had to go up and down eighteen times, three times with each. Indeed I might have said "poor Kitty!" First the Lady Barbara Eyre, daughter of the late and sister to the present Earl of Newburgh, about Sister Agnew's age, has been a beauty —very dignified appearance; humble and pleasing; wore a full court dress worth a hundred guineas, besides valuable diamonds. Her train went below the last step when [she was] at the top. Next, a Lancashire lady, not young, very nice and amiable;[7] the next one from Gravelines, young; a fourth, London, about thirty—and two lay sisters,[8] all desirable. Thirty-six priests—sermon preached by Doctor Maguire, explaining the nature of the order and the spiritual and corporal works of mercy. You would think the Bishop performed the ceremony every month. He did not make one mistake and pronounced every word most audibly. Nothing could exceed the joy manifested by all at living to see the Institute established.

The situation of the convent is exactly what Kilmainham is to Dublin, only this a better neighborhood.

Amongst the visitors after the ceremony we had our *friend* Miss Lizzie O'Reilly and Miss Granger, sister to Mrs. Thomas Farrell, who claimed Irish acquaintance with Kitty in the most gracious manner. There is great work here for the poor sisters, two large hospitals, Guy's and St. Thomas', four workhouses, endless converts. The people are delighted. Miss Birch of Manchester Square enters next week, young and very nice, Miss Best of Bath soon after—every application is referred by the Bishop to Kitty, who is major domo.

The following note from Her Majesty's hairdresser will amuse you:

"By desire of the Countess Constantia Clifford,[9] Monsieur Trufitt will wait on the Sisters of Mercy at nine o'clock on Thursday morning to adjust a court headdress."

Lady Barbara was my charge on that morning. I went to her cell and said in a disguised voice, "Please, your Ladyship, Monsieur Trufitt is come." She was at the other side of her bed and did not see me and answered, "Take down that box with my feather and diamonds." When she discovered her mistake, she was sincerely distressed and said: "Oh, what shall I do? Is it to Reverend Mother I have spoken thus?"

Indeed they all have, thank God, a nice sense of religious respect. Yet we cannot avoid preferring our sweet Irish sisters everywhere and Sister Augustine, though such an attached Englishwoman, says she loves the Irish sisters more.

Mrs. Agnew, Sister's mama, is a most delightful woman.[10] Though she is sixty-eight years old, you could never think of age when conversing with her. Her residence is Brighton. She came to remain in London for a few weeks on her daughter's arrival, is most affectionate and delighted to see her child so happy. A younger daughter and one married are all the family. They are also very kind and evidently astonished to find such mild Irish nuns. Mrs. Agnew, particularly pleased with the young lady superior, acknowledges she did not expect her daughter would meet such a companion in the South of Ireland. The Marchioness of Wellesley[11] wrote a most kind note, regretting she was prevented by severe cold from visiting the convent but would take the first opportunity of doing so. The poor Sisters of Mercy are great persons. Lady Barbara is Sister Mary de Sales.[12]

I do not admire Mr. Pugin's taste. He has put the windows up to the ceiling. We could not touch the glass without standing on a chair. Sister M. Cecilia has not been quite well since we came. I suppose we shall return in about a month or five weeks. When Sister Agnew's cards come out, she will send you a set. You heard of them—"The Spiritual and Corporal Works of Mercy, illustrated with etchings by a Sister of Mercy."

How I long to hear of you and dear community, your ceremony and new additions. You will write me a long account, a letter that I may show to all. Will you remember that? Give my love a thousand times to dear Sister Vincent and M. Teresa and all my very dear sisters, particularly Sisters Mary and Anne. I could wish this moment with all my heart that I were with you and them even for a little time. I had a letter from Baggot Street lately. All are as I left them but I believe they would not tell me were it otherwise. I am often weary of myself. Farewell, my ever dear child. May God preserve and bless you. Pray for your fondly attached Kitty.

M. C. McAuley

The postscript reveals one of Lady Barbara's charities, a new dress for every little girl in the school:[13]

Remember me to Reverend Mr. Fitzgibbons and Mr. Nash. We have High Mass every Sunday. I like the Irish piety better. It seems more genuine though not near so much exteriorly.

You may judge how unceasingly we have been employed. Besides the spiritual and temporal preparation for the sisters we had to prepare dresses for two hundred poor girls of the school who were to attend the ceremony. Will you remember to return my most grateful and respectful thanks to your bishop for the very kind and valuable letter His Lordship sent me?

No account of this ceremony would be complete without the anecdote featuring Lord Augustus Fitzclarence, first cousin to the young queen.[14] In arranging the reception to follow an eleven o'clock High Mass Bishop Griffiths may have been considerate of the late comers but certainly not of the early arrivals. Some guests had come as early as nine o'clock. From the number of carriages waiting, the whole neighborhood knew that something unusual was taking place at Most Holy Trinity Church.

Short-staffed in the household and unprepared for the length of the ceremony, the sisters returned to the convent in mid-afternoon to find all the fires out. At any time of year their predicament would have been discomfiting but the heavy December rain outside conspired with the Puginesque atmosphere within threatening social calamity, for no ceremony had ever drawn so many and such distinguished guests. The sisters were forced to explain their embarrassment to those invited to lunch. Lord Fitzclarence created merriment by setting himself up as master fire-builder. Rivalry arose among the gentlemen and supplied considerable entertainment as the young nobleman defended his claim. His joviality literally and figuratively warmed the atmosphere, making the tea hour an unforgettable occasion.

Such was the "mob" that crowded around the sisters—gentility, their hands raised not in execration as had been threatened, but in benefaction, for the charity begun in the old chapel was now extended through their generosity. Yet Bermondsey foundation did become the center of trial to the young Institute, for here Mother Catherine contracted the cold that began her final illness and here she suffered the first rift in the congregation, a subtle attack on the very fundamentals distinguishing her work. Coming from persons aiming at religious ideals, it called for great patience, firmness and tact. It had its purpose, too, for the Institute, since in combating it, the foundress wrote a forceful exposition on the Mercy ideal with its reciprocal flow of action and contemplation. She included a warning against misinterpretation and corruption of the true spirit of her congregation. The Bermondsey community holds this precious manuscript.

Though the eight and a half finely written pages contain no unimportant sentence, the following excerpt has been made for its nuclear character:

> We ought make account that our perfection and merit consist in acquitting ourselves well of our duties so that, though the spirit of prayer and retreat should be most dear to us, yet such a spirit as would never withdraw us from works of mercy. Otherwise, it should be regarded as a temptation rather than the effect of sincere piety. It would be an artifice of the enemy who, transforming himself into an angel of light, would endeavour to withdraw us from our vocation under the pretense of labouring for our advancement. We ought to give ourselves to prayer in the true spirit of our vocation, to obtain new vigor, zeal and fervor in the exercise of our state, going on with increasing efforts . . .

The first evidence of the new spirit passed before the foundress' notice under the guise of fervor. It did not immediately disrupt because time is the fostering element of insidious evil.

Mother Catherine returned to Dublin aware of a meticulous something in Sister M. Cecilia Marmion that had not been there before and of a more marked simplicity in Sister M. Teresa White. Had Sister Teresa already penetrated the superficiality of the Bermondsey mother assistant or was the refinement of simplicity an unconscious reaction to formal overtones already intruding in Bermondsey convent spirituality? Whatever the case, Mother

Catherine became conscious of divergent interpretations in Sister M. Cecilia and a greater unanimity with Sister M. Teresa White.

Referring to the personal sufferings of Mother Catherine during her two months in Bermondsey, Sister Teresa wrote:

Our dear mother had a miserable time of it, being almost constantly ailing. I always thought the Bermondsey foundation was the beginning of her death-sickness, for she was never perfectly well afterward. Being a great lover of holy poverty, she would never allow the least attention to be paid to her more than to any other sister. . . . While she was very ill in London, I prepared her breakfast and brought it to her. Because I brought the best I could get—white sugar, china tea-pot, and cream-ewer—she said, "My heart, why did you not bring me a little tea in a mug as you would to a poor person?" Scarcely had she spoken when the tray upset and everything was spilled on the bed. Then she said pleasantly, "Now you are punished for not remembering that your old mother is only a poor nun." She had other trials in London. Even now there was on the part of one of her companions a tendency towards the introduction of novelties. This, to my mind, never shows a sensible head. I often heard our poor mother say: "Destroy the simplicity of our Institute and it is gone."[15]

Before many months passed, even the novices, who became Sister Cecilia's charge in March, realized that their mistress did not have the foundress' singleness of vision. One of them has left a record of Mother Catherine's intervention. As in the instance of Mother de Pazzi's physical handicap, the foundress did not remove Mother Cecilia from office but managed by patience and, at times, prompt revision. The novice mentioned, later wrote the Dublin manuscript. On the subject of the new spirit and its source she reports:

Until the year 1839 Reverend Mother had enjoyed good health. She always suffered from rheumatism in her head and now and then, but certainly not often, had sick days when she caught cold from being out in rain, but when she left us to begin the foundation at Bermondsey she seemed likely to live many healthy years. This first of Pugin's convents was built most inconveniently and she got cold immediately on her arrival. The London air was uncongenial to her but moreso still the spirit of one of the sisters. This lady who all through life—when a Protestant, when a convert secular, when a Sister of Mercy, and when no longer so—was consistently actuated by the desire of concentrating everyone's admiration (and, if possible, affections) on herself, could not live without manoeuvering. She contrived to create a misunderstanding between our foundress and Mother M. Clare [the writer's sister], which though of short duration was very painful to the former, who loved her younger sister fondly. She contrived to make Mother M. Cecilia Marmion discontented with our customs and bent on making changes, also a fret to our dear superior . . .

When Mother Catherine returned from Bermondsey, she filled all the offices of the discreets. . . . I fancy she thought Mother M. de Pazzi too austere a mistress of novices and named her mother assistant. The sister who replaced her, however, showed how little she had of [the foundress'] spirit and how much of the spirit of change. The practice of silence during the five minutes preceding our common duties was not observed on recreation days. I was directed to observe it. A professed sister spoke to me. I made a sign of silence. She drew Mother Catherine's attention to the circumstance. Now, Reverend Mother when displeased with any of us usually called us by our surnames.

She called me over and said, "Pray, little girl, why did you not answer Sister Mary Teresa?"

I told her.

"You are not to attend such commands in future. Madame Marmion shall make none of her improvements here while I live," and she laughed and chatted with us till the next duty.

Soon afterward she went into the noviceship and saw a very pretty green card on which were written extracts from the fifth chapter of our constitutions with some other directions, concluding: "If any of the professed sisters should require the services of a novice she shall apply to her mistress." Mother Catherine took down the card and wetting her handkerchief, effaced the paragraph. About half an hour later the mistress of novices was observed with tearful eyes, and there were no more improvements while [the foundress] lived.

If these measures seem drastic, much was at stake—how much the same writer points out: "[The foundress] disliked the spirit of change which possessed some of the sisters under pretense of seeking greater perfection, saying that if they adopted the practices of other orders it was making out that ours was not required by the Church."

XXIX

Presentiments

BACK IN DUBLIN Mother Catherine, hampered by increasing debility, took up her burden of activity and sorrow. Her last meeting with Robert McAuley had been painful. Already in an advanced stage of consumption, he persisted in a course of conduct that his guardian could not approve, and she had left for England displeased with him. When he realized that she would return too late to grant him pardon for the anxiety he had caused her, he grieved.[1] Though the knowledge of his repentance consoled her, his deathbed message tore her affectionate heart. A year later she was still reminding Mother Francis, who had known him from childhood: "Robert's last wish was that the sisters would pray for the repose of his poor soul."

One of her first letters after her return from England expressed warm gratitude to Mother M. Elizabeth Moore for a message of condolence. She congratulated the Limerick community on an accession of subjects. Five ceremonies of reception had taken place in little more than a year. "I suppose Baggot Street may retire," she wrote, "and I suppose also that the foundations will soon be made from you and others," she added hopefully.

In this letter she injected a note of counsel so causally that no one would suspect the source of her observations, those final weeks in Bermondsey: "May our Blessed Redeemer dwell with you in such a manner as will shield you from everything that could be any drawback—above all, from particular attachments and aught that could produce jealousy, coldness or party spirit. I have no fears for you on the subject, but I have a conviction on my mind of its fatal consequences." She closed with the news of "a prevailing influenza among the poor of Dublin and great poverty."

To Mother Francis she wrote on January 30, two weeks after her return from London:

I have been chiefly confined to bed since my return, not down until yesterday, first an infection for which I was obliged to have a physician [by Father O'Hanlon's order[2]] and then my old mouth complaint to a great degree which has kept me on infant's diet more than ten days.

I received your letter in London. As to what you said of the application to Rome, I did exactly what was marked out for me, a petition from the "Mother House," a memorial from the Archbishop of Dublin praying a confirmation of the rule to which his approbation is attached, and letters of recommendation from the bishops in whose dioceses branches of the order were established. This has been most fully executed. The letters were as favorable as they could be. I am sure Mr. Maher feels sufficiently interested in our regard to do all in his power. A private letter to his nephew[3] would have even more effect than one obtained through influence or entreaty and I am certain he has done whatever he thought would promote success . . .

I do not know how my poor Sister Mary Clare will be disposed of. She is superior in London until the 22 of August. On that day Sister Agnew takes her place. I am sure they will be anxious to keep her if Dr. Murphy consents. The Bishop of London said he never saw such maturity in so young a person, that she had judgment in her countenance. She is, thank God, perfectly indifferent where or how she shall be.

Baggot Street was not to retire. During the foundress' absence Father Lacy of Wexford had attended a reception in Carlow (January 8, 1840). There he spoke optimistically of an interview he had had with Mother Catherine in behalf of a foundation for the southeastern corner of Ireland. While still convalescent, the foundress received an appeal from the vortex of Catholic activity in England.

Her reply to Bishop Walsh of the Midlands left Dublin under date of February 4:

My Lord, I have the honor of receiving your esteemed letter and would feel great happiness in co-operating to the full extent of my power in the accomplishment of your desire. If two persons who manifested a vocation for the religious state were sent here, one year and three months would finish the time of probation for a new Institute. They could then return accompanied by one or two well acquainted with our regulations. The pension for each during the novitiate is twenty-five pounds per annum. If circumstances required a reduction, it would be made.

Perhaps, my Lord, the persons in view would rather not come to Ireland but join our Sisters on their arrival in Birmingham. This would save expense, and having the ceremony of reception at home might produce a pious excitement that would animate others to follow. Whatever you think best suited to the views and inclinations of those who are disposed to promote the object shall be met in every possible way. My Lord, as to building, I beg leave to suggest the advantage of not doing so on a very limited scale. We should hope that an establishment in Birmingham would be productive of others. Your convent should have at least twenty cells, 10 feet by 7, a small window, and a door made so close to the partition wall as to leave a sufficient space for the bed's head; a noviceship about 18 feet by 14, a community room, refectory, and choir, each 25 feet by 19; a good room for infirmary and a small reception parlour. It is very desirable there should be only two floors above the basement story. The refectory should be close to the kitchen—all executed in the plainest style without any cornice; cheap grates and stone chimney pieces. This could be completed in ten months and would not cost more than a small building where ornamental work would be introduced.

My Lord, if you would think it better merely to commence the preparations for building and to hire a small house for beginning, perhaps the people would be induced to contribute more freely to its completion but it should be commenced, My Lord, as the Sisters would not feel happy except they had a convent in prospect. The convent in Bermondsey is not well suited to the purpose. The sleeping rooms are too large, the other rooms too small, the corridors confined and not well lighted. All the Gothic work outside has made it expensive. A plain, simple, durable building is much more desirable.

Earnestly begging that you will give me and community a place in your charitable remembrance, I have the honor and happiness to remain

My Lord, with great respect your obedient servant

In Christ

Mary C. McAuley[4]

Malignant typhus showed itself in Ireland early in 1840. By March it was marking many for death, among them little Sister M. Teresa Vincent Potter in Limerick, a sister in Cork, and at the motherhouse the second of the three Marmion sisters.

Mother Catherine had never been busier: Archbishop Murray,

promising financial assistance, had requested that she re-open the Kingstown house; Bishop Walsh wrote that he would send English girls to Dublin after Lent to be trained for the Birmingham foundation; negotiations for a Convent of Mercy in Galway had been completed and the sisters to go already designated—Sister Mary Teresa White as superior, Sister M. Catherine Leahy to stay. When Mother Catherine selected the sisters for this foundation, she had the firm intention of withdrawing Sister Mary Teresa after six months, but she reckoned without Father Daly, of whom she said after a little experience, "He is the greatest master we ever met."

Bermondsey had taught Mother Catherine Sister Mary Teresa's value, though as far back as May 1838, when Sister was in the difficult Kingstown charge, the foundress wrote of her: "She is never troublesome, never complaining of anything or pressing me to go to Kingstown, and all with her are most happy, even my perverse Teresa Byrn." Back from London, Mother Catherine observed to Sister Mary Clare Augustine: "Sister M. Teresa has most of my spirit, and I trust more to her guiding the Institute than to any other sister."[5]

One wonders what provoked so positive a declaration from the foundress. An intimation of death? Some presentiment she certainly had, for in the very letter[6] telling Mother Elizabeth that she would loan Sister Teresa to Galway for six months, Mother Catherine lists her first complete cabinet. "His Grace came here on the sixth to make the appointments: Mother M. de Pazzi, assistant, Sister Aloysius, bursar, Sister M. Cecilia, mother of novices."

Of herself she wrote: "Every day I am weak at some time"; and, referring to a request made by Mother Elizabeth, "It would add fifty miles to my travelling who am journeying fast enough out of this world."

Before leaving for Galway, the Dublin infirmarian could match if not surpass Sister M. Teresa's Bermondsey experience with the foundress. When Sister M. Catherine brought chicken to her patient, she received a strong lecture on poverty, and Mother Catherine "absolutely refused" to touch the delicacy.

Before going to Galway Mother Catherine committed herself to a foundation in Birr where a schism had occurred. At the death of the local pastor, Catholics had hoped for the appointment of their much loved curate, Father Crotty. When Bishop Kennedy disappointed them, they withdrew to a chapel where Father Crotty continued to serve them. In an effort to mend the rift, His Lordship replaced his appointee with the popular Dr. Spain, highly regarded by the Irish people for his part in "the battle of the tithes," but the people were confirmed in their schism and would not respond even to Dr. Spain. Father Spain summoned Father Theobald Matthew,[7] a Capuchin just rising to fame through his amazingly successful Total Abstinence Society. The acclaim that he received throughout Ireland gave the Birr pastor hope that the humble Franciscan would win his parishioners back to the Church. However, Father Matthew failed. On the subject of temperance they would listen to him but on their grievance against the bishop they would listen to no one.

"Bring the Sisters of Mercy," counseled the celebrated preacher, whose connection with the Cork community has already been mentioned. "They will instruct the children and the battle will be half won."

Father Spain wrote to Mother McAuley, who consulted Father Matthew, with the result that she agreed to do all she could to end the scandal. In her own words, "The Reverend Mr. Matthew made me promise that immediately after Galway I would endeavour to make up a branch for Birr where the unfortunate Crottys have done so much to injure religion. He said that they must be truly spiritual souls confiding entirely in Divine Providence as there is no foundation fund."

Since there were hardly a dozen families attending the church in Birr, the parish priest could offer nothing but his house, which he promised the sisters for a convent. There is no better example of Mother Catherine's complete trust in Divine Providence than this last of her Irish foundations. With the re-opening of Kingstown and the commitment for Galway, the number of professed sisters at the motherhouse would be all but exhausted. The parish priest at Birr had no resources, and the foundress had never had less. Of her financial situation at this time the London manuscript says:

Just then by the misconduct of a person to whom she had entrusted a considerable sum of money, she experienced heavy losses which she felt the more keenly as she had always shown him especial kindness, and even after this ingratitude she did not diminish the exertions of her friendship for his unhappy family.

The convictions Mother Catherine poured into her correspondence with her other convents during the remaining months of her life were coined from her own spiritual experience: "The Lord and Master of our house and home is a faithful provider. Let us never desire more than enough. He will give that and a blessing." And again to the same house:[8] "We have ever confided largely in Divine Providence and shall continue to do so."

In the spring of 1840 a priest, transferred to St. Andrew's, afforded much comfort to the foundress and her community at Baggot Street. Some arrangement about Mass had been made, as Mother Catherine's reference to Sister Francis Marmion's death shows:

We got permission to have the community Mass celebrated in the infirmary. Although she appeared to us insensible, all her uneasiness ceased immediately after the Elevation. She turned on her side, got into a quiet sleep and remained till quarter before two when her pure gentle self expired. The last Sacraments were administered on Saturday.

Whatever else Mother Catherine confided to Mother Elizabeth has been torn off. The top of the next page continues "—was strongly manifested during her illness. Nothing more was done for us."

Yet Father Meyler had officiated at a reception ceremony and had been interested enough in the growth of the Institute to visit Birmingham convent, then being built. On the ceremony Mother Catherine had reported to Mother Elizabeth: "Dean Meyler, gracious as possible, M. C. McAuley, a very good child, smiling and praying alternately, attended at table."

The new clerical friend at St. Andrew's is mentioned in a comforting letter written to Mother M. Elizabeth on the feast of St. Joseph. Mother had reported the critical illness of Ellen Potter, whose full religious name, "Sister Mary Teresa Vincent de Paul," Mother Catherine had used for the first line of some verses early in the year.

No words could describe what I felt on reading the first line of your letter. Though accounts from Carlow were as hopeless, I fear much in this case. This dear, sweet, innocent creature—you will indeed have a child in heaven. God will support you in this great affliction. His Holy Will be done. If He calls her away, it will be to shield her from some impending evil or to exercise your patience and to try do you love Him as much when He takes as when He gives. Some grand motive must actuate all His visitations. . . . May God bless and preserve you and grant you all humble, cheerful submission to the Divine Will.

Two days later, after word of Sister's death, Mother Catherine wrote again:

This has not been done in anger. Some joyful circumstance will soon prove that God is watching over your concerns, which are all His own, but without the Cross the real Crown cannot come. Some great thing which He designs to accomplish would have been too much without a little bitter in the cup. Bless and love the fatherly Hand which has hurt you. He will soon come with both Hands filled with favors and blessings.

Since Limerick had the only community cemetery at the time, Ellen Potter's burial established procedure for other interments. The description of her funeral called forth reference to Father Mulhall, the new curate at St. Andrew's:

My ever dear Sister M. Elizabeth,

Your last letter was a great comfort to me. When I read it in the community room, all exclaimed, "I don't know who would not like to die under such circumstances." . . . It was indeed a heavenly ceremony, moreso than any reception or profession. It was like a grand entrance into Paradise . . .

Mr. Mulhall, a very spiritual priest removed to Westland Row, came to see us on the death of our dear Sister M. Francis [Marmion] and said, "I congratulate you. You have or will soon have another friend in heaven. How delighted to be forming a community there!"

I asked him would it be wrong to hope that it was now formed.

He answered, "What are they here for but to prepare for heaven? They ought to go as soon as they are ready, to make room for poor souls that are in daily danger. There is no other way for carrying on this holy traffic so as to meet the designs of God. It is His own Divine plan."

This good priest is quite a comfort to us.

A sister present when Sister M. Vincent Potter died made this comment on the foundress' humble wisdom:

Dear Reverend Mother often dwelt upon the lesson herein given. Sometimes she would say, "In a few years there will be as many in this room as there are now, though not one of us will be present. The works will go on just as now but done by other sisters." Again, "Let us not think any one individual necessary for carrying out the work of God; no one is necessary."[9]

During Easter week, on April 29, the four English postulants arrived to make a novitiate for the Birmingham foundation. Three days later Mother Catherine left for Galway. It was already May. She took as her traveling companion the new superior's young sister, Sister Mary de Sales White. Like Cork, Galway had several flourishing religious communities and, like Cork, Galway was a thriving coastal city. Unlike Cork, however, Galway faces the west and takes its manner from its outlook. Beyond the Corrib and the Claddagh, beyond the shoulder of Connemara and the Aran Islands, three thousand miles of ocean stretch. Proudful, taciturn, incisive—Galway bears the centuries better than most of the "chief haven" towns[10] of pre-penal Ireland. Conceding nothing, forgetting nothing, Galway City under the appearance of apathy teems with activity and wears a repose that has no kinship with patience.

Father O'Hanlon accompanied the founding party. They stayed overnight in Tullamore. The old convent had been enlarged by merging it with the house next door—a very temporary arrangement, for the new convent was close to completion. They next stopped, by Father O'Hanlon's arrangement, at Loughrea where the Carmelite nuns received them.[11]

At Baggot Street and at Tullamore there had been much light conjecture as to whether the founding party would sleep on boards and eat Carmelite fare. They did neither.[12] Though the foundress had the privilege of occupying the prioress' cell, it was hospitably dressed for the occasion. Retiring to rest, Mother Catherine thought of her beloved dead lying in the Carmelite vault at St. Teresa's. Close upon the thought of these dear dead came the conviction that she herself would go soon, not to be buried in the Carmelite vault, however, but in the ground, "like the poor." Whenever the foundress thought of death for herself in her few remaining months, she visualized a burial plot, and since Limerick had the only community cemetery at the time, she referred frequently to the fresh grave under the willow tree close to the north wall of old St. Saviour's. She began to plan a cemetery for Baggot Street.

On the cover of a notebook in which Mother Catherine did transcribing during her last months, she wrote aspirations and reminders of the dead. The mottled surface offered spaces for inscription, and on the front appear the following prayers:

> All for the honor and glory of God . . . Incline unto mine aid, O Lord . . . O Lord, make haste to help me . . . Lord Jesus, have pity on me . . . My God, I am humbly sorry for having offended Thee . . . Open our mouths to bless Thy holy Name . . . Save us, O Jesus, or we perish . . . Lord, grant me the grace of a happy death . . . Lord, have mercy on me . . . Mother of God, pray for me . . . St. Joseph, pray for us.

On the back:

> E. and J. McA . . . O. and M. Conway . . . J. Conway . . . Cath., M. T. McA . . . Mary McAuley . . . W. Callaghan . . . Cath. Callaghan . . . J. Byrn, Anne Byrn . . . Rev. F. Armstrong . . . Rev. J. Nugent . . . Rev. D. Burke . . . Rev. T. Carroll . . . O blessed Jesus, grant me grace to learn of Thee to be meek and humble of heart that I may be united to Thee and find rest in Thee . . . Mortify in me, dear Jesus, whatever displeases Thee and render me according to Thy Heart's desire.

These inscriptions, which might be easily overlooked, reveal some of the foundress' most intimate thoughts.

From Loughrea the sisters were driven to Galway in carriages, arriving after considerable delay on the road because of a broken wheel. They looked in at the house[13] selected for their convent and went on to spend the night with the Presentation Sisters. Nearly thirteen years had passed since Sister Mary Louis Tighe's reception day. The Presentation novice had grown into a stout middle-aged nun whom Mother Catherine would not have recognized except that Sister hurried forward to greet her. Catherine McAuley, too, had changed from the modishly dressed social worker into the religiously-garbed foundress on her ninth founding mission. Though she was unaware of it, the consultor of the Sacred Congregation had already cast his vote in favor of confirmation of the rule of her congregation.[14]

A Mrs. Martyn, who had been chiefly instrumental in providing the means that brought the sisters to Galway, remained in the background. Her charity was to be rewarded in the vocation of her daughter, for Elizabeth Martyn later became a Sister of Mercy.

The day after their arrival the sisters took over the Lombard Street house and did what they could to give it religious character. "I expect a new convent will be erected for them very soon," Mother Catherine wrote after they had settled.

Since the Galway community *Annals* have been written in retrospect, the principal sources on this foundation are the foundress' letters and the research of Mother M. Teresa Austin Carroll twenty and more years later, while many of the pioneer sisters were still living.

By the first week of June Mother Catherine could tell Mother Francis that four postulants had entered and that there would be fifteen within six months except that the financial condition of the Galway foundation required a dower sufficient to support each sister.

The foundress' characterization of Father Daly was accurate: "Reverend Mr. Daly is guardian. . . . He is most generous but has not the means proportioned to his undertakings and is always engaged in too much."

"There is really no money among the people," she added, "all high consequence in poverty." As evidence she mentioned the difficulty "an estated gentleman" had to meet the dower for his daughter and the small amount of ready money available to another estated gentleman "who commonly drives four horses to his carriage."

"We said our two sweet Thirty Days' Prayers, the one to Our Saviour in the morning, to the Blessed Virgin in the evening. We did this also in London. My faith in it has increased very much."

Before the prayers had ended, one of the postulants, Mary Bourke of Ower, contracted typhus and died. Mother Catherine describes her death:

> She was a little heavy on Monday week like a slight cold, on Thursday was prevailed on with difficulty not to get up. On Sunday night at eleven o'clock the last Sacraments were administered and yesterday, Tuesday,

the ninth day, her death expected, sinking all day. . . . Four physicians are attending. They visit four times a day. She is greatly esteemed and respected and so closely connected with many around that it is quite a public matter.

This letter to Mother Elizabeth was interrupted by Sister's death. It continues:

This morning at quarter past three o'clock she expired. She died most happily, in fervent sentiments of gratitude to God. . .
We are founding on the Cross now indeed—only eight days since she was forced to stay in bed, not thinking herself seriously ill. . . . I never saw a person who seemed to have a more amiable disposition, never thought of the religious life till she heard of the Sisters of Mercy coming to Galway and embraced the inspiration the moment it came. She was most pleasing and quite a lady in manners and appearance enjoying the gay world in all its fashion to the week of our arrival. God has certainly accepted her offering and she is—I have no doubt—gone before Him received and professed by Himself. I traveled a hundred miles to meet this cross and another has traveled after me. Sister Aloysius is very seriously ill, appearance of rapid decline.

But the bursar at the parent house was not to die yet. She would weather the Birr foundation as superior for three years and when all the schismatics had returned to the fold, her work would be completed.

The postulant Sister Mary Bourke had a different history. When she saw that the foundress was distressed at telling her the seriousness of her illness, she exclaimed, "O darling Reverend Mother, what were we created for or what is our existence prolonged for but to attain a happy death?"

As Mother Catherine later remarked, "Her affectionate manner proved how perfectly her mind was prepared and how sweetly resigned she was." And the foundress might have added: her actions proved her generosity and love of God, for she left her dower that another without one might take her place. Applications for admission came in such numbers after her death that she seemed to have gained influence with Him who had "received and professed" her.

On Corpus Christi Christina Joyce of Mervue entered—

the first Christina we ever had and quite as pretty as Christina White . . . a sweet postulant, a second Mary Teresa McAuley in look and manner, all ardor, sighing for the bleak winter to be cold and wet . . .

Her family were going to travel, and although she would have seen the Pope in all the religious splendor of the Holy City, she entreated to be left at home, having determined to join us as soon as possible. In writing she communicated her ardent desire. Her mama is very pious and on their return they visited the sisters in London, were very much pleased and soon gave consent.

We had our reception of three on Thursday last. The Bishop wore grand ornaments just arrived to him from France, which he said he would not wear till our ceremony.

Our postulants have names new to us, Miss Joyce, Christina, Miss MacDonnell, Ismena. Miss MacDonnell, nineteen years old, plays the harp and sings. Miss Curran, a novice, plays and sings remarkably well, all sacred music.

The noviceship is very nice, the table fifteen feet long with twelve drawers, grey carpet; community table seven feet, six drawers, grey carpet, rush chairs, piano; choir, beautiful crimson cloth carpets, seats like Baggot Street as Sister M. C. and M. T. wished; refectory tables full as long as Baggot Street, close to the kitchen but very convenient to the choir and community room. Thank God they are comfortable before I leave them . . .

Your next letter will be to Baggot Street where it will find me, please God, Monday next. We shall be immediately preparing for our reception there. The English postulants are quite impatient for the votes. God bless you and all.[15]

Mother Catherine was not to have the pleasure of a visit to Limerick, for she had been summoned home through a message of Father O'Hanlon direct to Father Daly. In explanation to Mother Elizabeth she wrote:

Reverend Mr. Daly had a letter from Mr. O'Hanlon which he would not show me but informed me that I was to return immediately. Our places are engaged for Sunday. In Mr. O'Hanlon's letter he promises Mr. Daly that if I am not detained longer I should return in a few weeks. You may be certain Galway will never see me again but from Limerick. I do think it would be very well for me to come to Miss Joyce's reception, which will be in September, my own favorite month.

Our ceremonies in Baggot Street, reception of English sisters and profession of three will be about the fifth or sixth. I would then set off for Limerick direct and most certainly keep them waiting in Galway as long as Mr. Daly would have patience. You would like him very much though he is the greatest master we ever met. I really could not leave this without his full concurrence except I were to become angry or stiff.

All reasoning and entreaty were fruitless. He said, "You shall not go. Not a vehicle in Galway should carry you.[16] I will not suffer the foundation to be injured." This makes me fear he has a melancholy account as he so quickly assented. I shall be truly glad of the excuse to return in order to get to you and my dear Sister Vincent.

I thank God for your wonderful progress, and I comfort myself thinking I shall so soon see them all and everything about you will look so beautiful. The only disappointment I fear is that the Bishop may be at the sea. I would be very sorry not to see him. You remember he was there when we arrived first in September, '38. All unite with me in love to you and Sister M. Vincent. I will write from Dublin on Tuesday or Wednesday next. May God forever bless you, my dear Sister M. Elizabeth. Absence has much increased my affection for you. Even the new sisters here are sorry for our mutual disappointment this time—I have talked so much of it.

But Mother Catherine was not to go to Limerick in September either. How she accepted the disappointment is exposed in her July 28th letter to Mother Elizabeth, which also reveals the state of her health and the situation at the parent house.

I had a very fatiguing journey, traveled all night. . . . I had not been well for a month before I left Galway and have still a cough and bad appetite. . . . I could not recollect any circumstance that inflicted such painful disappointment on me as not going to Limerick before my return and I suppose it is for this very reason I was not permitted to go, because I desired it too ardently. I rejoice now at my mortification, for it was a real one. . . . The English postulants are quite strangers to me. They were only three days here before I left. They are all that is promising, [having] every mark of real solid vocation, most edifying at all times and at recreation the gayest of the gay. So far they seem to have corresponded very faithfully with the graces received, as each day there appears increased fervor and animation. The sixth has arrived since I came back. They renew my spirit greatly—five creatures fit to adorn society coming forward joyfully to consecrate themselves to the service of the poor for Christ's sake. This is some of the fire He cast on the earth—kindling. Mr. Hardman, the father of one of them, is the chief contributor to the convent now erecting. It is getting on rapidly, and we hear he is on the spot every day rejoicing at its progress. His child, about twenty-one, is as nice and pleasing as you can imagine. A few days after he proposed building the convent his daughter got the vocation as a reward of his generosity.

May God bless the poor Sisters of Mercy and make them very humble that they may not be unworthy of the distinguished blessings God has bestowed upon them. If one spark of generous gratitude exists in the first-born children, they will labor to impress humility and meekness by example more than precept, the virtues recommended most by our dear Saviour and chiefly by example. The Bishop has promised to receive the English Sisters but has not yet appointed the day. It looks quite extraordinary to see the refectory without a vacant seat after all we have parted in life and death.

To Sister M. Teresa in Galway, who had met the English girls, Mother Catherine gives a more detailed account:

Miss Edwards, who came while I was in Galway, is a sweet creature, quite refined, simple and interesting; Sister Mary Ann Becket a prime pet with Mother Cecilia is very gentle and all that is desirable; Sister Juliana Hardman very satisfactory— all her doubts and fears have passed away; Sister Ann Wood very amiable though not so pleasing as others from a natural disposition to silence and too much reserve; Sister Lucy Bond greatly improved, not near so much of the wild English girl.

They are most interesting, two so playful that they afford amusement to all at recreation. One, about twenty, thinks she will be best suited for superioress of Birmingham; makes up most amusing reasons. Mr. Colgan came to the community room at recreation yesterday evening. He called her Mother Eliza, and she affects to think that all is now confirmed. We get a delightful description of the convent. Dr. Murphy and Dr. Meyler have seen it. Indeed it could not be too nice for the first inhabitants that God has destined for it. May He continue His blessings to them.[17]

In yet another letter[18] the foundress turns the spotlight on the most distinguished of the Midland subjects, Mary Ann Becket, reputedly a collateral descendant of the holy bishop of Canterbury: "Sister Becket, a convert of high connections, is quite equal to Sister Moore in arts and sciences, languages, painting," and she could have added music.

In her correspondence with her superiors Mother Catherine had a way of mentioning trials in the same running-comment manner of relating incidents. As a result, no strong impression of discomfort carries. Yet she had plenty of the gnat-like afflictions that make any day a battleground for virtue of a high order.

While she was away, contractor and workmen took the opportunity to suspend work on the laundry. On her return they harried her by manipulations that show how undeveloped business principles were in the horse-trading era. No wonder the contractor had been able to underbid all others! Two years before she reported to Dr. Fitzgerald, who had recommended Mr. Mullins:

Mr. Mullins has undertaken to build the laundry and I was greatly surprised to find his estimate five hundred pounds less than one we got and two hundred less than any other.

Now she was forced to put the matter into the hands of her lawyer:

Dear Sir:

I enclose you a copy of the two notes I wrote to Mr. Mullins, which he terms "graciously offensive." Inasmuch as he has made himself a very principal party, complaints must necessarily be addressed or referred to him. The man called a contractor could not alter the most glaring defect without his permission and repeatedly said he "got enough to starve on" by the engagement.

My first note was occasioned by receiving three messages from Mr. Mullins requesting I would give directions for the waterpipes—not clearly saying that it was not part of the contract work, but that I "wrote so well." This inclined me suspect and when I decidedly refused to give the order, Brophy told me that it was an extra charge. I then wrote to Mr. M—, and next day the work was begun. Immediately after my second note the man was taken away, bed and all in two hours. The keys have been given us. All the time I was away this man was constantly among our poor people and even more troublesome when the Sisters were there, saying he was not to go away till all accounts were settled. It is an unkind, unjust transaction. I have good reason to say so.

I send the copy with the remarks I made at the time.

Dear Sir, your grateful
M. C. McAuley

Mother de Pazzi's illness, mentioned so often as increasingly troublesome, had an aspect that puzzled Mother Catherine, clouded the atmosphere in the community circle, and tried the foundress when she herself was in poor health. The Dublin manuscript gives an instance:

Poor Reverend Mother's patience and humility seemed to increase with her trials. A sister whom I know she loved and trusted more than the others was afflicted with severe illness which injured her mental much more than her bodily powers so that she became inconceivably melan-

choly and captious. Reverend Mother, too large-minded herself to understand a groundless jealousy, indeed any jealousy at all, tried in vain to find out what was the trouble. At last one morning when I was drawing at lecture, then given in the Bishop's Parlour, I was left last, not finding it convenient to rise. Reverend Mother, who knew this Sister often spoke to me, said, "Sister Mary Clare, what ails Sister?"
Now it would not have answered at all to tell her Sister's grievances so I only said, "Reverend Mother, I wish you would sit in the community room as you used to do when it was down stairs."
She answered that she could not on account of her failing strength but she wished we would sit with her—and there was room enough, for there were but four of us in the community, including the mistress of novices. She told me to bring down the paint box. In the community room I found Sister, who asked me with some warmth what had detained me. I told her that Reverend Mother wished us to sit with her and that she ought to bring down her desk, but she refused, saying she could not speak to Reverend Mother if sisters her juniors were to be constantly present. I went back and said to Reverend Mother, "It will not do for us all to sit here, so, if you please, I shall take away my things. You should ask only Sister ———."
About an hour later I met Sister quite radiant, her desk in her hand. Reverend Mother had complained of loneliness and asked her [to go down]. So Sister M. de Sales and I escaped the visitors and poor Sister gave less annoyance for a while.

On August third Mother Catherine wrote to Bishop Walsh to tell him that Archbishop Murray would give the religious habit to the English subjects the following week. In designating a day on his busy program, His Grace granted permission for the sisters to come out of retreat on the tenth for the ceremony.

Two days later an English priest arrived with two young ladies. Since they had been unable to learn the exact date of the reception, they came early in order not to miss it. They registered at The Shelbourne, already distinguished for just the right conservatism and character.[19]

This hotel is conveniently near Merrion Square and Baggot Street. More than once Mother Catherine mentions it in her correspondence, since lay people coming a distance for ceremonies registered there. In fact, the last bequest to the Institute during the foundress' life came from a widow residing at The Shelbourne.

The English postulants received their religious names with the habit. John Hardman's daughter retained her own with the usual prefix *Mary;* Anne Wood became Sister M. Xavier, Lucy Bond Sister M. Vincent and Elizabeth Edwards Sister M. Cecilia. Miss Polding, who had arrived on the feast of St. Magdalen, was named Sister Mary Magdalen, and Miss Borini who came to the reception and stayed became Sister M. Angela. These last two were received at the December ceremony.

Lucy Bond and Elizabeth Edwards had kept the noviceship lively. Yet it was Sister Mary Xavier Wood with "a natural disposition to silence and too much reserve" whose success with classes of converts later elicited a characteristic remark from Father Dominic Barberi.[20]

XXX

Filiality to Our Lady of the Americas

SOMETIME during 1839 or 1840 the Reverend Richard Baptist O'Brien, recently appointed to work in the vicariate of Nova Scotia, called at Baggot Street.[1] Though assigned to his new duties in October 1838, he had spent months trying to find clergymen to accompany him. After Mother Catherine's death, he made known through the *Halifax Register* that the foundress of the Sisters of Mercy offered to bring sisters to Nova Scotia at a time when he could not locate priests willing to undertake the mission.

When he represented to her the difficulties, she so effectively disposed of them that only his own unfamiliarity with his new territory kept him from accepting. By summer, 1840, Mother Catherine was definitely planning on a North American mission. In her July 27 letter to the new superior at Galway she mentioned Bishop Fleming and referred to the postulant he had sent from Newfoundland to prepare for his mission.[2]

In the summer of 1840 also, the matter of confirmation of the rule moved along favorably in Rome. The news trickled through, as her August 5 letter to Mother Francis shows:

> You say Dr. Cullen might call during retreat. I would, of course see him. . . . I am not surprised at what you say as to the confirmation of our Rule. We have been led to expect it all the past month, but these matters seldom go on so rapidly at the Holy See. It is, however, certain that the process of examination has been gone through and most strong promises made for the conclusion. A priest coming to Ireland was asked could he wait a few weeks to carry it with him. Yet I suppose all possible interest and attention may be necessary to prevent its being delayed.

The accuracy of Mother Catherine's information can now be known from the Sacred College of Propaganda Fide archives. In July Cardinal Polidori had placed all the documents before the Sacred College with the vote of the consultor, Most Reverend Paul Gavino Secchi-Murro of the Servants of Mary.[3] Calling attention to Roman approval given the Mercy Institute in January 1835, the consultor wrote:

> The spirit of the Institute and the particular object that it proposes has already merited the most distinguished praises of this Sacred College, enhanced by the sovereign pleasure of the Holy Father who declared it worthy of his paternal affection and prayed for the Divine Benediction which has made it increase and prosper with such honor for the Catholic Church and with much fruit for civil society. There only remains, therefore, to recognize the fitness and perfection of the Rules . . . because nothing else stands in the way of the entire and formal approval of the Holy See that has been at this time cordially and with suppliant insistence requested by the Archbishop of Dublin, by the Vicar Apostolic of London and by other Bishops of Ireland . . .
>
> Both for the wholly evangelical doctrine taught in [the Rules] and for the maxims of solid piety inculcated and for the spirit of the most perfect charity manifested in them, they are worthy of every praise and therefore merit the highest approbation of this Sacred Congregation . . .

On the monastic character of the constitutions, the most reverend Servite Father made an observation of special interest in the light of the later practice of the Sacred Congregations. The consultor's statements, presented as an opinion, are prefaced accordingly:

> It is, I believe, to be observed with pleasure that, departing from the custom lately introduced in new religious institutes of women, of establishing a motherhouse, electing a superior general,—in short, of founding a quasi-monarchic state resembling religious orders of men, it is declared instead that the houses of the new Institute of Sisters of Mercy will be respectively under the authority and jurisdiction of the diocesan bishop—a provision which is more in conformity with the ancient and more common discipline of the Church and more fitting to the nature of this type of institution and more expedient to preserve good order and to maintain in it the regular discipline.

A further observation by the most reverend consultor has found corroboration in the subsequent history of the congregation. He points out the inadequacy of the constitutions accompanying the rule:

Constitutions cannot be said to be complete when they lack those positive prescriptions for observance of rule which are so necessary for religious communities, especially of women, whence to remove doubt, disquietude and perplexity of soul in subjects, to moderate within certain limits the authority of superiors and to avoid as much as possible those differences that give place to suspicion of arbitrariness in whoever presides—so easy where either the law is silent or motives are not known . . .

A few will be supplied through good traditional customs and with good management of superiors seconded by perfect obedience of inferiors. Since the Rules are most excellent and since on these principally must fall the approval of the Holy See, it does not seem that the grace [of confirmation] ought to be delayed. By means of a few introduced additions, they can re-issue satisfactory constitutions.[4]

The most reverend consultor might have found something of the superior general in a letter Mother Catherine wrote to Mother Mary Anne Doyle late in August. It begins to the point:

I had a letter this day from Limerick. Sister Elizabeth says you are about to send two sisters to learn the Examination System—indeed she speaks as if you were to be one. Surely not! I suppose you will never be one of the appointed teachers, though you might oversee. Would it not be better to try to get a well-qualified Monitress from the Model School until your sisters know the method . . . . I do not think they permit anyone to attend the Model School in Dublin except those who are settled with them for the purpose and remain all day, paying a certain fee. . . . I need not add that you have this house at your command if you think of Dublin.

With the death of the foundress the following year this type of legislation and vigilance from Dublin completely disappeared.

Disappointed again in her plan to visit Limerick, Mother Catherine wrote Mother Elizabeth the reason. Sister Mary Agnes O'Connor and Sister Mary Frances Boylan were to be professed on the feast of Our Lady of Mercy. In order to reach Galway in time for the reception, she would have to go direct. A difficulty had arisen over the proposed visit to Limerick anyway, for Father Croke wished Mother Catherine to call at Charleville and see the new convent, which was now occupied. To visit both convents en route to Galway would not be feasible.

"Traveling charges are to be remitted before we move," she told Mother Elizabeth, adding, "Indeed the Galway founders have been very generous in this and every other way." As for Baggot Street, she tells Mother Francis: "I have been obliged to guard against any increase of expense since Miss McGuinness withdrew her aid."

Mother Francis was trying to place a sister with a small dower. Dr. Fitzgerald objected to receiving her in Carlow because there were already several members of her family in the Carlow community. She could not be taken at Baggot Street because finances there were low, nor in Galway for two reasons. She must have not only sufficient dower but "must be educated in modern style, not as a teacher." The prohibitory phrase shows with what little regard teaching was held at the time. "High consequence" would have none of it. Referring to Father Daly's requirements Mother Catherine said:

> He objected to a very nice young person to whom an uncle left £300, because previous to that she was for a few months at a most respectable dress and millinery warehouse in Clare Street. He said the County Galway people would find out anything and that it would be a certain injury.

Mother Catherine suggested Birr. Unwilling to wait for the Birr foundation, Mother Francis inquired about Charleville, but Father Croke with his new convent proved as exacting as Father Daly.[5] This correspondence about placing little Miss Maher went on for a period of months. In it can be discerned again the supervisory authority of the foundress.

Before setting out for Galway Mother Catherine received a letter from Bishop Griffiths "asking for two professed sisters to forward some views" that he did not fully explain, but, as she expressed it, he asked "the favor so much in the name of God that it would be impossible to refuse, though very distressing and inconvenient."

His "views" never materialized, since typhus invaded the convent shortly afterward and the recruits had to substitute for the sick. "Besides the poor schools and the ordinary visitation of the sick and dying," Sister M. Vincent Hartnett records, "the sisters visited Guy's and St. Thomas' Hospitals and four workhouses."[6]

Late in September Mother Catherine left Dublin with Sister M. de Sales and little Sister Teresa Mary White, sometimes called "Sister Teresa, the less." Sister Teresa had been in Booterstown recuperating from "one of her low tedious fevers." Just then Mother Catherine was thinking of putting her in charge at Birr.

"At present I cannot fix my mind on any as head but little Sister White," she told Mother Francis. "[She is] very faithful to her vocation and well versed in all our ways. Tell me what you think of her for such a purpose. I fear a little tendency to party spirit which yet remains would be a great impediment."

The foundress has left her own description of the ceremony:

> Mr. Matthew arrived at the church in Mrs. Reddington's carriage, three more of her carriages following close with different members of her family, all to compliment him. We came next: the two beautiful postulants and my poor self in Mr. Joyce's carriage; Sisters Mary Teresa, M. Catherine and Teresa Mary in Mr. MacDonnell's carriage; Sister de Sales, M. de Chantal and a lay sister in the bishop's carriage. Miss MacDonnell had a white dress from Dublin, so made up as to turn into a cope. We saw it all in pieces before we left. Her good family would do anything for religion. Miss Joyce had white satin with lace deep over. Both wore white wreaths on their hair.
>
> The sermon was delightful. Mr. Matthew has become quite eloquent since I heard him before. The convent was crowded after the ceremony, all anxious to see him. The families of both sisters supplied a grand dejeuner.[7]

This time Mother Catherine did get to Limerick and remained for several days. She expected to stop in Carlow also but was summoned home by a message that Father Butler was at The Shelbourne waiting for the promised sisters.[8] She saw Sister Mary de Sales White and Sister Mary Xavier O'Connell on board *The Queen* at Kingstown the following Monday. At parting, her motherly heart counseled her to accompany them, but her good judgment kept her from doing so.

"Thank God, I am at rest again," she wrote after the sisters' departure, "I think the name of another foundation would make me sick, but they say I would get up again. Indeed the thought of it at present would greatly distress me. On this late occasion I traveled one hundred miles a day, which is very fatiguing except on the railways."

Yet before the week was out she was seriously planning to take the six English subjects to Limerick after their profession. In another month she would go to Carlow to discuss the Wexford foundation and to bring back the bursar, Sister M. Aloysius Scott, who was to be superior at Birr. "She is so much beloved by all," the foundress wrote of her, and the Carlow annalist recalled:

> She was just recovering from a severe attack of hemorrhage [when she came]. We could not fail to observe that delicate health did not prevent her from being constantly and usefully employed. She remained here about three months and took great pains to teach the sisters painting, illuminating and fancy needle work, all of which she herself executed very neatly. She also helped train the choir.

Houses of Mercy had opened simultaneously (September 24) in Galway and in Carlow. Mother Catherine had seen the one and had brought back a uniform of the type used in Galway. She would now see the other.

During the month she wrote the letter to the Holy See[9] that she had been advised to send as a follow-up on her petition for confirmation of the "Rule of Our Blessed Lady of Mercy." She represented the development of the Institute in the intervening months, mentioning two added houses and giving the new total of fourteen houses and one hundred forty-two sisters.

So "ill-fated" Kingstown had re-opened.

Kingstown continued to be a cross. With the re-opening of the house, new financial problems arose and fresh difficulties, giving force to Mother Catherine's qualifying term "ill-fated." The writer of the Dublin manuscript, who managed the house for the first weeks, hints at the blunders of her successor and the imprudence of the school sister:

> The school at Kingstown opened directly on the street so that seculars could enter it without any sister's being aware except her who taught

there, nor even had she been willing could she at all times communicate the entrance of a visitor to the local superior. Unfortunately the school sister was most liable to err in such a position. The local superior with a multitude of virtues had no talents, and her mistakes proved almost as troublesome as the other's faults.

By the end of October the serious illness of her nephew and ward James McAuley brought her regularly to Kingstown where he lay, as she expressed it, "in the last stages of decline." The sisters attended him during the day and a young man cared for him at night.

"Pray and get prayers for him," she begged Mother Francis. "He is really pious, wished the priest to visit him frequently and receives Holy Communion as often as persons in his state can. . . . He is quite cheerful and speaks of his death most happily. This is great consolation. . . . My earthly joys are cut down, thank God, but the joys of my state are many and I feel the most lively gratitude."

When typhus took two of the Bermondsey sisters, Mother Catherine paid a high tribute to Mother M. Clare Moore in a letter to Sister M. de Sales White: "May God preserve my poor Sister Mary Clare," she wrote. "I know she will not give herself rest while able to stand."

Such was the spirit of "the first flock." Their pace had been set by the cholera epidemic that came close upon their reception of the habit. Referring to epidemics of typhus, the foundress said consolingly:

Your constitution on [one] occasion and Mother Mary Clare's on many others proved not to have any predisposition for fever. Whatever God pleases, a fever and His Love—what better? But it is most pleasing to Him that we use all prudent precaution. To act otherwise would bespeak confidence in our prepared state which we have but weak foundation for. Duty only should bring us in the way of contagion.

No change here since we parted save that I do not see my dear Sister Mary de Sales dusting and polishing all about the altar on Friday. I am pleased to hear you are refectorian. I believe you never had that office before. Sister Juliana will take great care of all your little brushes, etc. You know when she leaves you will be returning, if Almighty God is pleased to confirm our arrangements. Any alteration He wishes will be our joy and delight.

To Mother Francis she wrote:

What a scene of trial we sent them to! This is the way of God's Providence. I suppose all will go on well to show us that what we think a drawback will be followed by greater progress. If they should have a new foundation, it will not be without the cross.

Before going to Carlow Mother Catherine sent a report to Bishop Walsh on the Birmingham subjects with an account of expenditures for the half year. On the subject of the horarium her letter says:

I give you a copy of our distribution of time, My Lord, which has been found well adapted to the duties of our order. It is contained in our observances, not in our Rule, and therefore subject to any alteration that place or circumstances might require.[10]

As far back as 1838 the Wexford mission had been talked of, and now it was to be a reality. Two years before, while on the Limerick foundation, Mother Catherine had informed Sister M. Teresa White, then in Kingstown: "A Wexford priest told a Cork priest that our sisters are going to Wexford immediately. Indeed I believe he said they were going to be there in a week positively. I think they will wait for me. I am so experienced now in such affairs that it would not be well to go without me."

But now, two years later, they were going without her, for the Birr foundation, probably the most difficult she had made, was to be undertaken immediately after Christmas. Her visit to Carlow in November served several purposes. She brought with her Sister M. Juliana Hardman who had "that kind of cough which a little change of air often removes." She went over the plans for Wexford and she taught in the pension school that had been opened the previous year. At the time English and French were the principal subjects. A dancing master came regularly to supplement the sisters' work in preparing young ladies to take their place in social life. Later, music and drawing were added to the curriculum.[11]

Again the annalist supplies telling comment:

We saw with regret that the health of our revered foundress was breaking greatly and [observed] that she took but little care of herself. The benefit school being open, she gave instructions in it. She also brought a present of four veils for the professed sisters. The gossamer used until then was set aside and nun's crape substituted to wear in the convent. Mother McAuley observed that the gossamer was "too like a bit of millinery."

She reclaimed the veils later, however, because Dr. Fitzgerald did not like them. Always compliant when possible, she was particularly disposed toward the venerable Dominican who had befriended her Institute from its infancy. His recent ill health made her even more considerate. "You know he has strange notions and must be humored," she remarked.

Mother Catherine continued to advise Mother Francis on the Wexford foundation.[12] Her practical sense of the value of advertising comes out in a correction she took the trouble to make when the Dublin papers published the arrival of the Sisters of Charity in Wexford.

I immediately sent the following, which will appear tomorrow—"The beloved and venerated Dr. Keating, Catholic bishop of Ferns, has brought a branch of [the Order of Mercy] into the town of Wexford from the flourishing establishment in Carlow."

Practical sense of another kind dictated the advice on clothing and furniture suitable to the poverty of their state:

There cannot be any objection to your wearing the cashmere cloaks if you prefer them. I believe the sisters everywhere think they have a more religious appearance. It must be difficult to preserve them nice-looking in winter. The frequent cleaning in Dublin would soon make them look very bad. I hope most sincerely Mr. Lacey will not furnish the convent in a worldly style. But a few days since I heard the "fashion of Naas" spoken of.

One of the Wexford benefactors[13] who had been calling at Baggot Street for some time is mentioned in the same letter:

I hope you have the happiness of seeing the truly charitable Mr. M. Devereux. He was so kind to call on me and as usual it was not a mere visit of compliment. He always brings what Sister Teresa calls "good luck." Mr. O'Connell came next day with five pounds and an unknown with ten pounds. We remark something of this kind always after Mr. D—'s visit.

She reminds Mother Francis for the second time that something must be done about removing the designation "Orphan

House" from the building where the Sisters had begun works of Mercy in Wexford.[14]

In postscript she informed Mother Francis:

> We go to Birr by Tullamore. I did not know it was so near till we got an invitation. [We] sleep there on Saturday, the 26th, and go into Birr [a matter of twenty miles] St. John's Day after our devotions.[15]

In the meantime Mother Catherine wrote to Sister Mary de Sales White, whose brother lived in Carlow:

> The founders leave Carlow for Wexford this day [vigil of the Immaculate Conception] and Sister Susan goes from this to join them tomorrow as she was designed for Wexford. Two enter tomorrow, Miss MacDonnell and Miss Vigne, a convert—both well educated and young, 18 and 23.
>
> I shall now feel very anxious to hear of the Holy Profession of your dear religious namesake [Sister M. de Sales Eyre]. Give her my most affectionate regards and tell her the best prayers I can say shall be offered for her.
>
> When I went for Sister M. Aloysius to Carlow I saw the doctor. He was very well and all his family is well, so near an increase that Mrs. White could not venture to the convent. Their little Margaret is quite a smart pupil at the pension school—in deep affliction for getting a bad judgment the day I was there.
>
> All well in Galway. They are beginning to press us now for Westport.[16] We must refer that matter to Father Daly. It gives me great consolation and relief to find Carlow so prepared to divide. I think they will now keep it up. Liverpool is expected to be the next. In about another year Limerick will be starting. Cork could step out but Dr. Murphy will be slow and sure. Sister M. Aloysius looks remarkably well. She will be a nice little mother superior.

"Be sure to give my most affectionate love to your namesake in religion," she repeated in one of her numerous postscripts.

Sister Mary Francis de Sales Eyre was having a difficult time. As the year of her novitiate drew to a close, Mother Clare decided that Sister would be unequal to the sacrifices entailed in religious profession. The absolute divestment of possessions peculiar to solemn vows then prevailed in the Institute from the foundress' George's Hill training. The greatest sacrifice Lady Barbara Eyre would have to make at profession inhered in the complete detachment implied. All her life she had been accustomed to gift-giving and liberal benefactions of her choice. On the matter of gift-giving Mother Catherine was to express herself in another connection.

> It is not a disposition to bestow gifts like benevolent persons in the world that bespeaks generosity of mind for the religious state; it is bestowing ourselves most freely and relying with unhesitating confidence on the Providence of God.[17]

During the months of her novitiate Lady Barbara had not shown enough detachment to convince Mother Clare that she could persevere. In fact, Sister hoped for an adjustment that would allow her to continue certain charities, but no concession could be made. Meanwhile, her profession was deferred. Her social connections, the amount of her correspondence, the care of her health and, most of all, her love of self-directed almsgiving caused her superior serious concern. Her natural reserve also presented a difficulty for Mother Clare. In an effort to dissuade her from continuing in religion Mother worked constructively, pointing out the amount of good Sister could do as a lay social worker and the advantages of the secular state for one whose health required special care. Unimpressed by such representations, Lady Barbara struggled to face the divestment that she must make if she would "live and die at Bermondsey."

XXXI

A Way with Schism

FROM TIME TO TIME Mother Catherine betrayed how ineradicable was the impression Bermondsey convent had made upon her. Before leaving for Birr, she sent Father Butler an acrostic in verse requesting him to enclose part of the cloister used regularly by the sisters. In the Irish Midlands the foundress was to endure more severe cold than Bermondsey's chill, and the severity of the winter in Birr would confirm in her the sickness now carrying her to her death.

Philanthropic by nature, Mother Catherine had the eye of a utilitarian rather than a poet. Her tastes were conventional, her outlook metropolitan. All her life had been spent in the Irish capital under conditions that fostered practicality. Her verses are narrative, didactic, philosophical even, but hardly lyric. Yet her descriptions of St. Mary's, Limerick, prove that she was not devoid of lyric expression. Indeed, it is hard not to be lyrical about St. Mary's.

"I have been speaking so romantically of Limerick," she wrote Mother Elizabeth, "that the English Sisters [for the Birmingham foundation] asked would it be possible for them to see it after their Profession, should they succeed."

Then the practical asserted itself:

> This is a long look-out till next August. I at first answered that it would not be possible. Sister Mary Cecilia [mistress of novices] begged to say it would and that Limerick was the only convent so many could visit as the traveling by boat would be only thirty shillings [round trip] and no coach would carry them elsewhere. Stopping at Shannon harbor would make it two pounds each. This they seem to think no difficulty.

If nine went it would be £18. Ought I to sanction such application of money as if it were found on a hill? The rational and irrational powers have been contending ever since the thought was suggested. They discoursed as follows:

R—Would not so much money accomplish some good and useful object?

Ir—Perhaps that money would not be forthcoming for any other purpose but lie doing nothing.

R—Would not a visit of such distance tend to dissipate the fruit of their meditations before and after Profession?

Ir—Seeing a branch of the Institute so short a time formed now fully and regularly established might rather serve to strengthen their pious resolution and animate their hopes for what they were about to undertake.

R—Could they not be told of it? Surely they would not entertain any doubt.

Ir—What we are told by unquestionable authority inspires confidence but what we see confirms it.

R—Where would they lie down at night?

Ir—Anywhere.

R—They could not get into the refectory.

Ir—They could get in but it would be difficult to get out. I admit there would be more fun than feeding.

Now, after all this nonsense I was seriously thinking of a great improvement that might be made in the refectory if the wall was removed and the passage added to the kitchen with the door of the kitchen opening into the refectory. It would make a great addition though it appears little now—or if the kitchen wall were also moved and a little from the kitchen also added. . . . Look at it with all your brains and you will soon make a great improvement. We find the kitchen opening into the refectory most convenient.

And again to Limerick:

We have this moment received your sweet fruit and flowers. I seldom see any so fragrant. The offering of genuine affection has everything to enhance its value. I am looking at them now and think the roses have some unusual shade, and such bright purple and rich yellow flowers! . . . Everyone who came in since I began said, "Oh! the sweet smell—where did you get all the lovely flowers?" and when answered "from Limerick," I think they fancied them somewhat out of the common way.

This excerpt contains the only reference to the colors of nature in all Mother Catherine's extant correspondence, though she often mentions gardens—i.e., lawns with flowers, trees, and shrubs. Yet the color of the Irish countryside passed seasonally before her eyes in her journeyings by canal and by coach the breadth of Ireland and crosswise to the south: hawthorn appliqued along the roadside, whin running its sun-gold brook fashion down the rough-meadowed hills, appleblossoms recklessly escaping patterned espaliers, rose-petaled dogwood proclaiming summer, fragrance of woodbine up the boreens,[1] knobs of bog cotton embroidering fustian stretches of turfland, eyelets of scarlet poppies on the wheatfields, heather bleeding ecclesiastic purple in high places, everywhere the little rouge-kissed Celtic daisies and somewhere unexpectedly the blue sky fallen on a field of flax. The kaleidoscopic aspect of nature north, east, south and west did not escape Mother Catherine, but the dark procession of human misery absorbed her.

The "merry sun-muted sound of harness bells" on the tinker's "shaggy piebald cob" might arrest the casual traveler; an artist's eye[2] might find pleasure in the sight of the barefoot tinker girl herself with "wild hair and clean complexion," her tartan shoulder-shawl and other bright clothes indicating "the magpie nature of her mind"; but the experienced social worker in the nun saw only the magpie mind and untutored soul.

The December landscape was bleak enough by holiday time, 1840, as the usual Christmas charities busied Sisters of Mercy in the twelve convents of their Institute. What the foundress would call "pious excitement" gave an air of the unusual to activities at "poor Baggot Street," for the Birr founding party were to leave the following day on their new mission—the bursar Sister M. Aloysius Scott as superior, Sister Rose Lynch, and a postulant Anna Maria McEvoy. Little Sister Teresa Mary White had come back from Limerick to be Mother Catherine's companion. Mother Catherine could not know, of course, that she was presiding for the last time over festivities for the poor at her own St. Mary's, and, much as she spoke of death in her last months, it probably did not enter her thoughts on this busiest of Christmases. September was her favorite month for its number of Marian feasts, but Christmas was her favorite day. Her tender love of the Divine Infant reborn dominated all other religious sentiments and imbued the charities with special joy. The holly that delighted her decorated every department of her great house.

Heavier bells than the tinker's smote the chill air of St. Stephen's day as the coaches ran their charted cross-country course. The tinkers' bells were silent. Wintering close to their forges, the tin-pedlars beat out bright new pans to wheedle shillings from wary housewives on the next twopenny mending run. The brown road unwound in the pale sunlight under the horses' sure-footed team-work, and the carriage came to a stop before the head inn of a town on the rim of the Irish Midlands. Mother Catherine knew Tulla-more well by now, though less than five years had passed since she had visited it to make her first foundation.

On preparations for Birr she had informed Mother Elizabeth:

> I wrote to Mother Mary Ann asking could she let five go to sleep on Saturday 26 and could our devotions on Sunday, breakfast and visit to the new convent be over by twelve o'clock and two post carriages be ready to start for Birr. I prayed her to answer quickly, plainly and briefly.
>
> She writes as follows: "Cead Mille Faulte"—good dry lodging, entertainment for man and beast, coffee for teetotalers, Mass at 8:00, breakfast 9/2, visit the new convent at 10:00, two first-rate chaises from head inn at the door at 12:00, refreshments with the P. P. of Eglish (Father Murtagh) half way, arrive in Birr 4:00 p. m., no fog till 5:00. Dear Reverend Mother, affectionately yours.
>
> Sister Aloysius heard this read with great surprise. She did not suppose there was so much life in that quarter. If she had not read it, she would be certain it fell out of my poor head.

The foundress' own account of the new mission is given by letter. On the feast of the Holy Name Mother Catherine wrote to Mother Francis, still in Wexford:

> I am anxious to write to you from my strange habitation. How many new beds have I rested in! When I awake in the morning I ask my-self where I am, and on the last two or three foundations I could not recollect for some minutes. This is a good old house, delightfully situ-ated with fields or garden all around it, though as close to the main street of the town as Baggot Street is to Little James Street, yet quite remote from all other buildings—walls or hedges in every direction. It

must be particularly healthy. Just now it appears like a fine summer day. Ten or twelve sisters could be very well accommodated. There is one fine room nearly as large as our first schoolroom, now our community room.

Sister Aloysius is remarkably well. I firmly believe that Father Matthew has been the agent of her final recovery, as he has prayed so much for the Birr foundress. The first good was done by taking her out of the doctor's hands and sending her to you.

Our journey here was quite free from fatigue. We traveled to Tullamore on Saturday, got good sleep. Sunday morning devotions and breakfast over by ten, we went to the new convent to which a passage has been made through the garden of the old. It is a beautiful edifice, a grand tribute to religion, an ornament to the town. I had no idea of its extent. The stairs, which are the finest I ever saw, were not even planed when I was there last. The community room with rich stucco work is a little larger than our old community room. Dr. O'Rafferty complained of the center piece for a hanging lamp and desired the superintending man to order a vine wreath around it with leaves much raised. The choir or chapel is in preparation and will be nice indeed. There are two reception rooms about the size of Baggot Street parlor; novitiate 24 feet, infirmary the same; community room and thirty cells, store rooms, and closets. Water is brought through the entire house by conductors so that a pipe may be put anywhere. The schoolrooms are very fine and connected to the convent. The entire concern is a great sight from the canal boat. One of the little foundresses, Sister M. Rose, said she thought it was a palace.

I am sure God is preparing a distinguished place in heaven for the generous, excellent man who has erected it. If I said more, it would not be too much. It will last for centuries.

We got two post carriages at twelve o'clock and stopped for dinner with our dear friend Father Murtagh, parish priest of Eglish, within four miles of Birr. Our own parish priest, Dr. Spain, Dean and Vicar General, with one of his curates was invited to meet us—four priests and five sisters, a teetotaler entertainment, coffee served immediately after dinner. We arrived here before six, said our two Thirty Days' prayers and went to rest. On Monday I saw five or six ladies, one a candidate, Miss Egan, 24 years old, a fine young person educated at Thurles convent. Mr. Egan is said to be the chief earthly author of the convent and indeed it would appear so but not a word on that subject. He keeps seven clerks, some of them brothers to the curates.[3]

We got two turkeys, a leg of mutton, and a bowl of butter, provision for retreat which is now happily over. We get a choir made us next week and an appointed place in the church, which is so near that we will not require cloaks or bonnets.

Your patient was up before 5 and did not breakfast till after 10. She has risen at 5/2 every morning since we arrived; looks remarkably well.

After Mass the Vicar said, "My dear people, I have a present to make you. I have a New Year's gift for you, the most gratifying a pastor could have. I present you the Sisters of Mercy, who by their example and pious instruction will draw upon our town the blessings of heaven. I recommend them to your respectful attention and I beseech God to bless them and you."

We had great laughing at breakfast saying he might have tried us a little longer, not to make a present of us so soon.

We have not met any poor Crottyites yet but expect to see them soon, for they are most unhappy though still obstinate—the common punishment of rebellion in religion. The unfortunate Crotty is indefatigable in his evil works. He is joined by Mr. Carlile who was one of the commissioners of education. They have the same church and preach the same doctrine that "nothing is to be feared but popery." This speaks well for National Education. Had Mr. Carlile found it likely to injure the Catholic Church, he would not have abandoned it.

Our postulant is quite a different person here from what she was in Baggot Street, useful in every way. Nothing like foundations for rousing us all! God Almighty bless you, my dear Sister Mary Francis, and grant us all grace to keep the holy resolution we made in our retreat. I will expect a long letter for this.

The sureness of Mother Catherine's perception in educational matters shows here. Her own education among Protestants, her years of experience with schools and school methods that had caused her to use her influence toward withdrawing Catholic children from the government-supported Kildare Place system also gave her insight into the value of National Education as organized under the bill of 1831. Both she and Dr. Murray[4] endorsed it from the beginning, though many another in similar positions opposed it till years of practice proved its worth.

On Mr. Carlile Mother Catherine further remarked: "If I can judge of a countenance, his spiritual influence will not be extensive." Here, too, her estimation proved correct.

Birr convent exists today as a school. It still has the fields and garden that drew forth Mother Catherine's delighted comment. The parlor and choir on opposite sides of the main door facing the "garden" have become classroom and school office. The sweet-toned bell that used to call the sisters to prayer still hangs at the top of the staircase just outside the room once occupied by the foundress. This room is now an oratory containing two of the original choir prieu-dieux designed by Mother Catherine. Even without the prieu-dieux the room has a shrine-like atmosphere. A wide view still extends across the rustic garden to the Cam Cor[5] and beyond, where open fields follow the stream along toward Castle Ross. The street lies to the left outside the garden wall. Here, too, is a garden enclosed and here, close to the summit of her own soul's journey, the foundress laid her campaign of mercy against the ranks of schism.

The sisters were surprised to learn that the short street bounding the garden wall had no name. To the amusement of the others, one of their number proposed naming it *Baggot Street*.

Summer-like weather favored them their first week in Birr, but on January third a blizzard swept out of the bogland, covering roads with snow and ice. Intense cold closed in and persisted for several weeks. The sisters proceeded undauntedly in the work of reclaiming souls, for vicissitudes of weather were mortifications Mother Catherine had taught them to utilize. If the evil that possessed Birr was to be cast out by prayer and penance, the penance must follow lines of duty. The foundress' letters prove that several varieties burgeoned from their surroundings and their labors, though she wrote lightly, even humorously of them.

"My dear Sister Mary Cecilia," she addressed the mistress of novices back in Dublin. "Here we are surrounded by Newfoundland ice, obliged to keep hot turf under the butter to enable us to cut it."

Newfoundland would be the next foundation after Birmingham, she then believed, for Bishop Fleming's protégée, Mary Anne Creedon, would complete her novitiate and make her profession in the spring. What a long lonely trek to the end of *her* soul's journey! Sister Francis Warde, already on her third Irish foundation, would travel alone across American prairies, but Sister Francis Creedon would be in time the only Sister of Mercy on the remote island of Newfoundland![6] Yet no amount of hardship was to withdraw her from the mission field for which the foundress trained her, and the flourishing community in that other St. John's to the north stands witness of her courage and perseverance.

"Tell Sister Francis," the letter goes on to say, "I am obliged to take hold of some person to keep me up. Sister Mary Rose and I walked one mile and a half yesterday in all the snow to visit an unfortunate family who were followers of Crotty."

Though neither foundress nor missioner knew at the time, Sister Rose's hardihood was to win for her a place on the Newfoundland mission.

The account resumes:

Our excuse for going uninvited was that they had a son twenty-six years old killed by a fall from a house. We were pretty well received until a Crottyite lady, who probably saw us going, arrived. Looking deeply at me, she said, "We are all sinners." I bowed as low as Sister Vigne does dancing "Sir Roger." It was snowing greatly, and she seemed resolved to wait till it would cease but finding us disposed to wait her out (I made this known by settling our seats close to the fire and talking about Father Matthew and the pledge) our lady retired. I did all I could to waken the poor people to a sense of their state. They both promised to come to us but I fear they have been too long in a perverse state to hope that one visit would produce effect. Schismatics for eight years!

They had been deluded by the false charity of the unfortunate fallen priest who used to distribute among them all that was collected at the church, though not his to bestow. . . . He was only curate and in opposition to his pastor would give out the money in this way.

They are all replenished with the perverted texts of Scripture. I asked them would it not seem that St. Paul feared we might mistake such conduct for charity when he said, "If you give your goods to feed the poor, *etc.*" I asked did they not think Our Blessed Saviour had tender charity for the poor and yet when He dwelt among them in our mortal state He did not take any money to give them or remove them from their poverty, which made them dear to Him and which He made choice of for Himself; that when they were constantly about Him He did not think of relieving their wants till He feared lest they should faint but was ever attending to their spiritual necessities, only mindful to prepare them to share in His own glory, teaching them to bear their short trials and afflictions in submission to the Divine Will and promising them all the treasures of Heaven forever and ever. I asked them was

He not master of all the wealth of this world. Did He not love the poor in a particular manner? Was He or Mr. Crotty the best judge of what was good for them and did He not desire to do all that would make them happy here by the gifts of His holy grace and hereafter by a share in His Kingdom?

They were moved a little. What an awful thing is the loss of grace! A perverse spirit seems to hold the heart and force it on to ruin.

We had our retreat very happily, shut up reception rooms, retired upstairs and went through all our exercises most regularly; made the Renovation of Vows in the public church witnessed by thousands to the great delight of Mr. Spain. Sister Aloysius was up that morning by mistake at half-past four and fasting till ten, up at our usual hour every morning since we came and out on the mission almost every day. She has been with a desperate Crottyite who struck the priest. She was very successful, made him cry heartily. Her appetite and spirit are remarkably good . . .

I have a little secret to tell you. Don't proclaim it. I have my morning cloak on for a petticoat, the end of the sleeves sewed up to make pockets. All my wardrobe in washing—I came home yesterday with at least a half yard deep of mud and melted snow, and I have not a cold in my head. I was out five hours. Hurrah for foundations! They make the old young and the young merry. . . . I got my dear Mother de Pazzi's letter on Saturday. Tell her to keep Sister M. Clare [Augustine Moore] close to the register.

Give me a true and faithful account of your charge, to each of whom give my most affectionate love. I often wish I had dear Sister Lucy Vincent [Bond] to dress the evening fire, which is sometimes forgotten.

Butter, milk and bread Dublin price, tea higher, meat much cheaper (good for four pence), all turf [fire], manners very like Dublin, no Irish [spoken], three minutes to four! God bless you all.

The formal renovation of vows mentioned so "happily" in this letter was the last ceremony of the kind performed by the foundress.[7] On Mother Catherine's regard for it Sister M. Vincent Hartnett made this observation:

Reverend Mother used to take delight in renewing her vows and she strove to inspire the sisters with the same feeling, exhorting them to do so frequently.

She regarded the retreat in the last three days of the year, at the close of which the solemn renewal is made by all, as a privileged time of devotion. She encouraged the sisters to make the most of that time so as to stir up their gratitude to the Divine Spouse of their souls and to make their act of renewal on the first day of the year in a manner worthy of Him and expressive of their heartfelt gratitude.

"When at first we make our vows," she would say, "we are not so well acquainted with the extent of that Infinite Goodness to whom we engage ourselves forever; but as each succeeding year brings new proofs of His love, we ought at each renewal to evince the joy and confidence which the experience of His ever increasing mercies must inspire."

That such were her feelings was evident by her manner of reading the Act [of Renewal] and of pronouncing the *Te Deum* at the end of the ceremony.[8]

Before Mother Catherine wrote to Mother Cecilia again, she had heard from Father O'Hanlon in behalf of Mary Ann Becket who had not persevered with the other English girls for the Birmingham foundation. Perhaps she had entered too soon after her conversion. Whatever doubts and scruples assailed her drove her temporarily back to her former religious sect where she found that she could never again feel at home. Beset by new spiritual distress, she returned to the convent confessor.

There is coincidence if not foreshadowing in Mother Catherine's concern for Mary Ann Becket while at Birr, for Mary Ann was to return to Baggot Street and replace Sister M. Rose on the Birr mission.[9] From mid-January till mid-April Mother Catherine's correspondence with the mistress of novices of the parent community carries references to the progress of Miss Becket through her trial of spirit. Few knew better than Mother Catherine the travail of spiritual birth.

"Poor Miss Becket most anxious to return. . . . I feel very much for her and wish I knew what to do. . . . Should poor Miss Becket return, you will act exactly as Father O'Hanlon directs. . . . Miss Becket has gone to her friend in England, quite reconverted to the Catholic faith."[10]

The friend in England was Mary Ann's spiritual director, the convert minister Reverend George Spencer[11] who had been educated for the priesthood under Dr. Wiseman at the English College and who was already spiritual director at Oscott when Bishop Wiseman arrived there in the fall of 1840.[12]

Through Mother M. Anastasia Becket's connections with the

Catholic renaissance in England, Birr convent has a distinctive character.[13]

By mid-January the foundress could already tell Mother Cecilia: "Our mission goes on very well. Some of the old obstinate party are preparing for confession."

The rest of the letter gives community news and notes of general interest as well as further progress of the new foundations.

Sister M. Aloysius is perfectly at home as the most vigilant clever manager I have met in some time. I never knew till now the loss she must have been to her father's large family. We put our candles under a bushel. She is in excellent health, has departed from her Carlow rules, is up at five o'clock and out visiting in the snow when she would have been in bed at Baggot Street; Sister M. Teresa cheerful and active, always employed, takes two cups of tea overflowing, three pieces of bread, no chops, but good appetite; Sister M. Rose as usual, Sister Anna Maria most zealous . . .

We are now here nineteen days and have been to the parish church every morning but one, not attended with any inconvenience. On the first Sunday of the month we had our usual morning exercises: Thirty Days' Prayer, lecture, Office for the Dead all before Mass, breakfast 10/2, no distress or injury to old or young. Our expected postulant still lingering, her father crying here on Sunday . . .

I had a letter from London. . . . My dear Sister Mary Clare wishes most anxiously to return to her old home [Baggot Street] when she leaves Bermondsey and begs me to petition Dr. Murphy, which I suppose would be quite unavailing. She says they are doing so well in Cork that she is not required, and it would be a great comfort to her and to us if he would let her return to her favorite home. . . . I had a most amusing account from Limerick of their bazaar, two long letters having at the end "to be continued"; letter from Galway, all well, an increase expected; Wexford taking the lead. A Wexford newspaper says: "The most visible change has taken place in our town since the arrival of the Sisters of Mercy."

My clothes are not dry yet, the morning cloak still as a substitute, and the sleeves for pockets keep me in mind of John Gilpin's belt with the two jars meeting behind—no fire drying here, for the turf ashes spoil anything. Flannel never dries in frost.

We have two great comforts here, excellent bread in Dublin household form and pure sparkling spring water. I have not had one moment's indisposition and S. M. A. laughs at the stirabout that broke her tooth.

I am beginning to cherish the Primate's opinion that "too many women living together engender troublesome humors of mind and body."

Sister Aloysius just called me with a great iron sledge in her hand. She saw through a small aperture a long room; instantly broke through a slight partition and discovered a spacious apartment full as large as our present community room [in Baggot Street]. It has three windows and a cornice skirting the grate and chimney piece. The bishop when residing here, not requiring so much room gave it up for oats and hay, getting up by a ladder to one of the windows. It will make six fine cells. She is now making out a House of Mercy from stable and coach house. I never cease thanking God for giving me courage to bring her into action, and she is delighted.

We hope our little choir will be nicely furnished. We have got a table like that in the noviceship—as well made—chairs the same color, no cane or rush to be got. They are stuffed and covered with black Saxony cloth.

Mr. Egan, father to the sister we expect, goes to Dublin on Monday. If he visits the convent I hope he will meet every attention, see the House etc. Speak of his daughter as sister. Be very gracious.

In another letter to Mother Cecilia the foundress warns: "Don't say a word of any difficulty about Miss Egan where it could be mentioned outside. Mr. Egan has a sister in Dublin who knows every priest in half the world."

Mother Catherine's letter to the lay sister, Sister Teresa Carton, who had sent a bundle of Dublin newspapers, begins with gratitude and anecdote:

Your affectionate letter was truly acceptable to me. The delightful speech of Mr. O'Connell was quite a treat. We teetotalers may rejoice now indeed. I never liked anything better than I now like a good drink of water. My health is remarkably good, thank God. Our long fast agreed well with all. Sister Aloysius feels strong and takes the most active part. She was out for hours when the weather was severe; came in wet but got no cold.

Sister Mary Rose afforded us great recreation yesterday evening. She and Sister M. Teresa had been visiting an old man who deserted his religion. He is becoming quite penitent. He said to Sister M. Teresa, "Well, since the first day I saw you I never had you from my thoughts. You are the most heavenly young woman I ever met." In another place they were standing together when an old sinner said, "Well, if God did not send His ministers to convert me, sure He sent His little ones." They could scarcely keep from laughing when they looked at each other. In another place a woman who came from a neighboring cabin to look at them said, "Such pretty little jewels—as fair as an egg!"

This is a very fine day. We had good light this morning at six o'clock. I am rejoiced to hear our laundry is improving. I am sure my dear Sisters will leave nothing in their power undone. . . . Do not be uneasy about me; I have all my wardrobe. I made the most of it for amusement. Sister Aloysius will be extremely obliged to Sister Mary Clare [Augustine] if she will find her a sketch of the tabernacle soon as possible. God bless you, dear.[14]

On the long fast that agreed so well with all, the Birr community annalist says:

Mass being at eight o'clock in the church, there was difficulty in carrying out the usual distribution of time. It became necessary to have spiritual lecture at 7 o'clock. Young sisters up since 5:30 (or 5:15, if vigilatrix) found it somewhat trying to proceed from meditation and Office to the cold community room and sit hemming dusters and the like by the light of a few tallow candles. It required all the charm of their first introduction to Rodriguez to make them forget their surroundings and enter on a new world of thought!

Mother Catherine did not imply any mitigation of cold in mentioning January 19 as a fine day, for her letter to Sister M. de Sales begins: "With all around me covered with snow and my poor fingers petrified I will endeavor to write a few lines to you and my dear Sister M. Xavier."

In spite of her protestations of good health in her letters to Dublin the note of eternity is struck in this letter: "I hope to have the happiness of going for you, should God be pleased to spare me till then."

On the work in Birr she wrote:

You have heard of the injury done by the apostate Crotty. We meet many who have not been present at Mass for ten or twelve years and in almost every poor family there is still a deluded member who through some evil infatuation follows the unhappy man; though about three years since when he yielded to remorse he told them publicly that he was leading them astray, but soon returned to the destructive work again. All the poor souls receive the Sisters with affection and confidence. Sister Aloysius has succeeded in bringing several of the unfortunate schismatics to seek reconciliation . . .

The Bishop resides forty miles distant. He is, I fear, no great patron of nuns. It was from his diocese the Ursulines came to Galway. The Presentation branch that succeeded them are not likely to remain . . .

Mother Catherine's conjecture on Bishop Kennedy proved correct.[15] The letter to Sister M. de Sales continues:

Most dashing accounts from your old town—[16] Sister Francis attracting all around her—the orphan house preparing—the wings to be raised equal to the front and twenty cells with corridors all around—House of Mercy in one wing, orphan house in the other—one hundred a year secured for this purpose. Mr. R. Devereaux is most generous. I expect the next letter will announce a third [postulant]—no addition to poor Galway yet. I feel great tenderness for that branch as the youngest until I leave this. Sister Mary Teresa's House of Mercy is doing great good, thank God. Mr. Daly says there are no nuns like his own. I had a letter from him in which he says, "Now remember, I tell you in time that you must bring Mary de Sales to the Profession."

Limerick goes on fast. We are invited to Ennis but indeed we are come to a resting place—no more from poor Baggot Street, though I think before you return we shall have seven new sisters to fill up the places of those who will go to Birmingham.

This is called the tableland of Ireland, very fine light air. . . . My fingers are very cold and stiff.

Two weeks later Mother Catherine was still adverting to the cold: "I am so frozen, so petrified with cold that I can scarcely hold the pen."

Late in January ecclesiastics converged on Dublin for the consecration of new St. Andrew's on Westland Row. Among them was Bishop Wiseman of Oscott who had not been in Ireland since his childhood. He called several times at Baggot Street, said Mass there on the feast of the Purification and again, and came a third time to give the sisters a conference. He was, of course, particularly interested in the novices for the Birmingham foundation.

"Poor Sister de Pazzi has been very ill," Mother Catherine told Sister Teresa in Galway. "Sister Cecilia had three Bishops to entertain on Sunday and five yesterday, Drs. Crolly, Murphy, Ryan, Kinsella and Wiseman from Oscott. She is delighted with Dr. Crolly and Dr. Wiseman. Dr. Meyler accompanied the latter.[17]

"Some remarks have been made on my being twice absent during the novitiate of the Birmingham Sisters. English Bishops think Superiors ought to be with their charge."

How much the remarks affected the foundress can be inferred from the rest of the letter and from her procedure. "I would have left immediately on receipt of Sister Cecilia's letter," she said in writing to Sister Francis, "but had promised the new postulant to read and explain part of the Rule for her, at which I will work diligently to help poor Sister Aloysius, who cannot speak much."

To Sister Cecilia herself Mother Catherine explained:

On receiving your last letter, I commenced writing to say I would be home on Monday next, but Sister Aloysius was greatly agitated. . . . We have spoken quietly and rationally on the subject and she is satisfied I should return Monday week. . . . I will not write again except any disappointment occurs. The coach leaves here at eight o'clock and arrives at the Hibernian Hotel, Dawson Street, at half past six.

So Bishop Wiseman must wait till August to meet the foundress.

The letter to Galway carried an enclosure for Sister M. Louis Tighe, suffering under family bereavement: "I feel very much for my poor Sister Tighe. She was most fondly attached to her sister. Send the enclosed."

On the tide of memory came the recollection of other friendships, the dearest of her many loved connections. The letter concludes:

I will not expect a letter from you till I return to our old dear habitation where I shall never again see all my dearly beloved Sisters but all strange faces. Someone has said that the first separation (from kindred and friends) was a joyful sorrow but that separations in Religion are bitter sorrows. What must it be to me who never met one unkind Sister. This is a gloomy subject.

But she immediately touches the gloom with light: "We will all meet in Heaven. Oh, what joy even to think of it! God bless you, my very dear Sister Mary Teresa. Give my affectionate love to dear Sister Mary Catherine and each of the happy flock."

This letter must have remained a consolation to Mother Teresa White, for she and the foundress never did meet again in this world.

Before Mother Catherine left Birr, Mother M. Aloysius' successor in office had entered. Susan Egan solved the problem of farewell to her father by attending Anna Maria McEvoy's reception on the feast of the Purification and staying on as a postulant. The incident introduces little Mary Agnes Egan whose conduct on this and another occasion shows the spirit of this future Sister of Mercy.

While converting his rectory to receive the sisters, Father Spain had delegated twenty-four year old Susan Egan and a pious widow, Mrs. Coghlan, to arrange furniture and make other housewifely preparations. When the missioners arrived, they found a few loyal parishioners. Susàn Egan and her little sister Mary Agnes were among them. Mrs. Coghlan was in the kitchen basting a turkey. Susan had had no intention of bringing Mary Agnes but found it impossible to resist her pleading.

"There will be no seat for you, dear," she argued. "There are barely enough chairs for all."

"No matter," the youngster replied, "I'll bring my own little stool."

At this Susan capitulated, and Mary Agnes, carrying her little stool, went around by Mill Lane and arrived in time to see the sisters. One can believe that it was not forgetfulness but foresight that caused her to leave the stool at the convent.

Nevertheless, she was not admitted to the February reception, and indeed few were, as it was held in the little convent chapel. When Mary Agnes called early in the evening to accompany her sister home, Mother Catherine told her that Susan had decided to stay. Mary Agnes refused to leave. No amount of emphasis on the need of giving the information to her father budged her. She stood with her back braced to the door, evidently under the impression that she might be forced out bodily. Finally Mother Catherine wrote a note to Mr. Egan. The tangible message had the psychological effect and Mary Agnes set out, undoubtedly taking the short route home.

She was to come back next day, sent to apologize on her knees to Mother Catherine. And she was to come back to stay fourteen years later on the feast of Our Lady of Sorrows, a sad little Mary Agnes whose much loved father had died in a train wreck.

XXXII

Reverend Mother

LEAVING Sister M. Teresa White in Birr, Mother Catherine set out by coach at eight o'clock on the morning of February 10, and arrived in Dublin shortly after six o'clock in the evening. In her absence Mother de Pazzi had turned more and more to Sister M. Clare Augustine. The two were at the stage stop in Dawson Street to meet her. Because of the extra week in Birr the foundress had had to abandon the plan to stop over in Naas "to gratify Sister Trenor." Besides, she had developed a sciatic or rheumatic condition in her right side, which crippled under the cold.

"I could scarcely do justice in description to the kindness of the coachmen," she wrote to Mother Aloysius.

> The first from the time we left Birr at every stage was quite compassionate to me, offering to carry me into the inns to get to a fire, really uneasy about me. When changing, he recommended me to the second who was equally kind, and neither sought any payment. I mention this as I never met anything of the sort before.
>
> When we arrived in Dublin, my weak side was stiff and I was quite bent or shrunk in size. A car was waiting for me with a very small man as driver. The good coachman said, "Is this little man come for this little woman?" . . . I was not able to laugh then but we all have laughed plenty since.

In spite of the cold in her side she went almost immediately to Booterstown to see her nephew.

"I have seen the Sisters in Booterstown," she wrote on February 13. "Their poor patient is much changed. Kingstown is too far till the noise of the wheels is out of my head."

The mild weather that set in immediately after her return from Birr fostered rather than warded off colds. By Sunday Mother Catherine herself had a heavy cold, and the following week influenza began to spread in Dublin. The foundress was put on the infirmarian's list by order of Father O'Hanlon, but she evaded the doctor.

"I am doctoring myself," she told Mother Francis . . . "Mr. Time taken into account, [she was in her early sixties] I am doing very well. I do think that a cough has made a resting place with me and will be a usual visitor in future. I am now going to hide from the doctor who is gone up to four influenza patients."

How sick she was is revealed in her pre-Lenten letter to Sister M. de Sales, which she accomplished with great effort.

"My dearest child," it began, "I have felt quite anxious to write to you and my dear Sister M. Xavier but my old cough has made me so nervous that I could not nor cannot now write distinctly. You must read with patience. We have imported the London influenza."

The rest of the letter exposes Mother Catherine's purpose in writing it, a practical exhortation on the spirit of Lent.

Now my dearly beloved child, I hope you are exceedingly cautious as to the fast of Lent.

Remember Obedience! Leave every other sacrifice, and you will be far more mortified in taking what you do not like than in abstaining from [food]. You have not sufficient strength to fast. Take a good collation in the morning, the usual allowance here and some light supper. Take a crust or something if you have a long walk [on visitations]. Sister M. Xavier will, I know, take care in this particular. I lay this obligation on you.

How rapidly the days, weeks, and months are passing, another month ended that seemed but a few days begun. If we have not forfeited the friendship of Almighty God but have been trying to love Him more and more and to serve Him faithfully, they were blessed days for us. Oh, let us endeavor to use these days as we should wish the past to have been. Let us enter into the spirit of the Church making this a truly penitential season, mortifying the pride of self-opinion, performing all with a humble heart, keeping the first Lenten admonition engraved on our heart: "You are dust and unto dust will soon return"—our poor bodies only, but our precious immortal souls after passing through these few years of pilgrimage, pain and sorrow will, if we are faithful, soon enter on the joys of a blissful eternity.

The simplest and most practical lesson I know, my dear Sister Mary de Sales, is to resolve to be good today but better tomorrow. Let us take one day only in hands at a time, merely making a resolve for tomorrow. Thus we may hope to get on taking short careful steps and great strides. God bless you, my dear children. Pray fervently for your ever affectionate mother in Christ.

M. C. McAuley.[1]

This advice, written on the eve of her own last Lenten season on earth and undoubtedly approved by the spiritual director of the Institute, the Carmelite prior Father O'Hanlon, has a special message for all Mother Catherine's spiritual daughters. The postscript should not be overlooked, for it implies a harvest of interior mortification: "Do all you can to comfort my dear Mother M. Clare. I will not expect to hear from you during Lent except something should make it necessary, but you shall hear from me."

One of Sister M. de Sales' companions in religion gives further information on the foundress' practical advice:

Reverend Mother often emphatically impressed on the sisters' minds the necessity of a punctual attendance to every duty in a religious community, [exhorting against] not attending one day because a sister felt faint and absenting herself another on account of some little pain or ache.[2]

Yet Mother Catherine's concern for the health of the sisters caused her to anticipate Mother Cecilia's visit to Birr, which had been planned for May to assist with the public reception then scheduled. Consulting Father O'Hanlon, she found him not only agreeable but insistent. She explained to Mother Francis:

She was very weak and had some complaints similar to the last which poor Sister M. Francis [Marmion] had and it being the same period of the year, we became a little superstitiously affected. An unexpected favorable opportunity offered and I sent her to Birr. As we had designed that she should go to assist at their ceremony in May, I had not so much difficulty to surmount, all having a strong objection to move merely for health.

And in her other correspondence, she amplifies:

My poor Sister M. Cecilia would have been delighted to go to Tullamore, but Mr. O'Hanlon said what I knew, of course, that there was not room. To me it would be great relief, for Sister de Pazzi would never make the least objection, for what reason I know not, but she objects to a move anywhere else. When Carlow was mentioned for Sister Aloysius Scott as near her native air, Sister de Pazzi cried and grieved, begging she would be sent to Tullamore. I believe she believes there is more of our first fervor there than elsewhere. It will amuse you to hear that when she and I have a little [disagreement] it is followed by a wish that she was in Tullamore.

Father O'Hanlon's paternal interest included all the houses of the congregation. As the foundress expressed it, "His care and anxiety for us all increases everyday. He said yesterday 'This is my fourteenth year among you.' "

To Mother Cecilia she wrote:

Father O'Hanlon came yesterday and advised me to take off the cloak and drive out to Booterstown. Today I have done both, though half an hour before I would not have cut two inches off for pattern, I felt so afraid of making a patient of myself again. I think I am much better, not coughing much. He was delighted I sent you away and says you will get strong, fit. He was angry, exceedingly angry when told of Sister Aloysius' keeping damp clothes on and charged me to tell her it would not be pleasing to God. This has spared me the pain of scolding as I intended. Such a mild admonition would never proceed from me on such an aggravated occasion.

I brought Sister Justina in today [from Booterstown] and of course recreation followed. I have been a most attentive person ever since, read lecture, heard and corrected reading at one o'clock, got into many of the secrets of your holy office and acquitted myself like anything but a beginner.

Though in serious decline, the foundress' own health continued, as she expressed it, "variable." She had suffered so long from inflamation of the mouth and stomach and had surmounted every physical impediment to activity by sheer force of will that it was hard for her to believe her condition critical.

One of the sisters who lived with her at Baggot Street made this observation:

She uniformly excluded herself in everything that might seem like indulgence or appear to claim a privilege, though her health was much weakened by her assiduous labors and great austerities. It was only while suffering from her broken arm that she dispensed herself from carving for the whole community and she resumed the practice as soon as she was able. This duty she performed standing, no matter what amount of fatigue she had gone through during the day, and it was only after she had helped everyone at table that she herself sat down to her very scanty meal. A few minutes were all she allowed herself for dinner, so that she had always finished as soon as any at table. . . . Her cheerfulness was such that her almost perpetual fast was rarely noticed and, when it was alluded to by anyone, she would playfully turn the subject of conversation. Ultimately, however, it impaired her constitution and made her less able to recover from the series of colds she caught on the occasion of going to the new foundations.[3]

Finally Father O'Hanlon insisted that she see a doctor. She wrote depreciatingly of his diagnosis:

Five minutes in a room with a window ever so little open brings on an hour's coughing with great expectoration. Mr. O'Hanlon particularly requested I would consult Dr. Stokes. I have seen him twice. . . . My right lung is diseased. I have now less confidence than ever in the faculty, and you know my stock was small enough. I do not think my lung is affected. . . . If my lung is actually engaged, the progress will not be checked, and the fact of no debility—not half so much as I have had when my gums were inflamed—shows that it cannot be. . . . I here humbly confess that my chief motive just now is to show that one of the most distinguished among our medical professors may be mistaken and that we should not immediately take up their opinions.

Solicitous as Mother Catherine was for the health of the sisters, she did not like them to be health-conscious. Probably because of the early death of her sisters, Mother Cecilia inclined to be so. Mother Catherine's own attitude had developed from her two-fold experience, close association with members of the medical profession through those in her own family and years of practical nursing. Ready to make every allowance for debility, she was nevertheless quick to detect mere fuss. She gave in to Mother Cecilia's dislike for canal travel on the return trip from Birr, to the great discomfort of herself and companion as it developed; yet when the mistress of novices was making a fuss at Liverpool a few weeks later, Mother Catherine settled the matter with a sentence. According to the Birmingham annalist:

The voyage went on fairly until the Sisters had to quit the vessel and seat themselves in a shallow looking boat to row across to shore. All looked dangerous then and Mother M. Cecilia showed great signs of alarm. Reverend Mother McAuley, perceiving her emotion, quietly remarked: "Don't make such a to-do, child; if you go to the bottom, we shall all go."

In this case, the water-route was the only way to their destination, and if Mother Cecilia was to arrive at all, she must go by open boat.

Despite Sister M. Clare Augustine's criticism of the food at Baggot Street, Mother Catherine laid great stress on sufficient food and had every sympathy for poor appetite. Fresh air, a contented mind, and simple diet were important factors in health, she believed, and change of atmosphere, reasonable activity and good appetite were antidotes for ordinary ills.

Whatever she might say to Mother Cecilia directly, to Mother Aloysius she wrote:

> Will you make my poor Mother Cecilia strong? Do not confine her too much. Milk, coffee and crisp thin toast might help her appetite. I cannot eat my toast except it is very thin and well toasted. Want of appetite is troublesome to ourselves and others.

Though she herself seemed to have a special love for each sister, which she showed with every mark of motherly affection, she deplored anything bordering on the inordinate. Observing in some of the novices a too human attachment for Mother Cecilia, she rightly judged that the mistress of novices had not sufficiently discouraged it.

These defects she pointed out in some verses run off prose-fashion in her first report from the novitiate to the mistress:

> You were disappointed at no poetry from Birr in all the fine air. Perhaps you would like a little now you are there. No doctor now is to be seen, no bottles either blue or green, no sofa pillows, stool or screen. The doctor called the day you went. To help to get you through this Lent a box of pills and bottle, big enough to carry in a gig. He'd like they should be sent by post, the carriage sixteen pence at most, but as no customer was found, he took them back quite safe and sound.
>
> I'd wish to shield you next from love except what takes its flight above. A sister whose last tie is broken on this subject thus has spoken: Oh never, shall my heart with any creature share a part, though it was said by ancient bard that not to love was very hard, and in truth he must confess not to be loved was nothing less, but it is worse than all he'd

prove to be deprived of what we love. Yet do you not know full well, my dear, such love should never enter here. By many pangs you've learned to know it ever ends in pain and woe. These things, my dear, do not forget. Let none again e'er see you pet and, lest an angry dart should strike, in future love them all alike.

I am rejoiced to hear of Father Birmingham's recovery. I could not make up my mind to his dying this time. Sister Lucy Vincent asked me to write to you immediately. NO! All send fond love. Give mine to each, share and share alike.

God bless you and make you a good child of your affectionate mother.

M. C. McAuley

To relieve the criticism of an entirely personal application, the foundress suggested that Mother Cecilia share it with the professed sisters at St. John's. In this she lived up to her parting advice to Mother Elizabeth Moore on the office of mother superior. When possible, attention should be called to faults "in a playful way." She also lived up to her own counsel, "now and again bestow some praise." In the very next letter she confessed that it was difficult not to respond to "darling, heavenly little Sister Margaret Dwyer. I never met in this great world a sweeter little dove," she wrote, "all animation, candor and good sense. Mrs. Dwyer comes often, declaring she would not submit to any such regulation [as the control of visits]. We are obliged to submit."

And in a month's time she reported:

I have all that is satisfactory to communicate to you. The sisters of the noviceship are truly edifying and admirably formed so far as they are advanced. You have great reason to rejoice and to return many thanks to God for blessing your humble efforts. It is my greatest happiness to be with them. Their tempers are regulated so that they seem always prepared for humiliating remarks, which you know I am not sparing of. It comforts me more than I can express to find them so initiated in the real spirit of their state. May God continue to bless them.

I am doing my share regularly, thank God, novices and postulants in turn, the Rule every evening with scolding and coaxing—the lay novice very promising, little Mary Lawless dancing in and out of the habit, which is made, and the once doubtful Sister Teresa [McDonald] most rationally happy. . . . I was very much pleased with your note to her. It was exactly what I like. Is not this miraculous? An old torment even tearing notes and letters to pieces. I read it out for all and took great pains to do it justice.

We commence the Thirty Days' Prayer on Thursday in place of the Psalter [said during Lent], the substance of petition that God will graciously direct all the arrangements to be made for the establishment of the convent in Birmingham.

Five years had passed since Mother Catherine relinquished charge of the novices, years of spiritual experience and expansion —one might almost say of culmination. Regrettably, these novices made no notes, though the Birmingham *Annals* say of Mother M. Vincent Polding: "To the last she delighted to recall the days of her noviceship and the instructions of our venerable foundress, which she had faithfully treasured in her memory."

During Lent Mother Catherine received the joyful news that Lady Barbara Eyre was to be professed.

"We expect Sister Mary Clare from London 26th April," she told Mother Francis. "Four will be professed Easter week, so she will leave eight black veils. Lady Barbara Eyre, thank God, will be one of them. She found it difficult to relinquish *all,* and no other terms would be acceded to."

Close upon the Lady Barbara's decision to relinquish all came news from Frances Gibson of Eaton House, Liverpool, and Mary Ann Becket of Enville, Staffordshire. The former had finally summoned courage to leave her father and mother; the latter had reached a plateau in her spiritual struggle. What blessings fell upon the English missions from Lady Barbara's self-conquest remains for the records of eternity to expose.

To Miss Gibson Mother Catherine wrote under date of March 28, 1841:

I have been favored with your very pleasing communication and am delighted at the near prospect of receiving you as a member of our community. Your note to Sister Juliana excited great pity. What pain indeed it must give you to wound the affection of your very estimable parents, who make this generous sacrifice for God's glory and your happiness. It is a great triumph over nature. The grace must flow from our Divine Redeemer who came on earth not to bring delusive enjoyment which we call peace but a heavenly sword sharpened on the cross to cut those dearest ties that have such a strong hold on the heart and thus to draw all to Himself: You who in obedience to His call will enter into His immediate service and your respected parents who cooperate with His designs by not placing an obstacle in your way.

Two weeks later the foundress enclosed Miss Becket's note in a letter to Mother Cecilia with the comment: "I know the note from Miss Becket will be consoling to you. I wrote to express the great pleasure it gave me. Thanks be to God, she seems now out of danger."

As for Lady Barbara, she assigned her tangible wealth, with the exception of a few personal bequests, to religious purposes, principally to erect a hospital in St. John's Wood, London, and to help complete St. George Cathedral, Southwark. Though she laid in a supply of clothing, she soon relinquished that also under the spirit of her profession.

The story of Sister Mary de Sales Eyre's life as a professed religious is a story of self-conquest.[4] Since she did not live the decade out, it belongs properly to the foundation period of Bermondsey convent. As a novice she had been punctual in all her religious excerises and exact in conforming to directions, hard as she found them at times. As a professed religious she retained the strict regularity of her noviceship and began a crusade of self-discipline that seemed to leave no natural inclination unchecked. She entered into all the works of the congregation, reduced the visits of friends and relatives to the rare-occasional, discontinued her personal correspondence and applied herself to cultivating a love for the meanest and poorest of supplies needed by a religious.

After five years of effort to perfect her religious life by every unobtrusive means she knew—undeviating fidelity to the horarium, a strict regard for silence, devotion to the classroom and to the service of the sick poor as assigned—she had a premonition of death. She said nothing at the time but used her energies to continue unflaggingly the course she had been following. Sleeplessness now beset her. Yet she rose with the call and moved with the community, carrying out obediences as if her strength could not give out. Though not strictly obliged to the Lenten fast, she observed it in all its rigor from year to year and, since no visible difference showed in her always frail appearance and no diminution of activity resulted, Mother Clare Moore permitted these evidences of fervor in the religious whose vocation she had so seriously doubted. But Mother Clare was mistaken here, too. When it finally became clear to her that Sister de Sales' exertions were drawn from no store of health, however meager, but were rather the result of superhuman effort, she brought in a physician. The doctor pronounced sister's condition hopeless, ordered her to bed, and told Mother Clare that death was very near.

Sister submitted to all the doctor's prescriptions with the obedience that had marked her entire religious life.

An early instance of this exact obedience had occurred on her reception day and was witnessed by the foundress herself. When royal hairdresser had retired, when diamond tiara and necklace had put the final touch to her Ladyship's natural beauty and perfect grooming, the foundress surveyed the bride of Christ with some misgiving. Accustomed as she was to the styles of the early nineteenth century, which she herself had relinquished but a few years, she heartily wished that some of the yardage in the flowing train had been used for her Ladyship's throat and shoulders. Selecting a rich lace scarf from the wardrobe supplied by the Newburgh family, Mother Catherine suggested that milady wear it into church. In the same vein of pleasantry that had existed between the two throughout the morning, her Ladyship laughed it aside nor could any amount of coaxing persuade her that the foundress was entirely serious.

Before the ceremony, however, Mother Catherine said to Mother Clare Moore, already appointed superior, "Give this to Sister and tell her to put it on."

She obeyed with such simplicity that any personal preference seemed completely and instantaneously obliterated.

After the doctor's pronouncement Sister Mary de Sales Eyre determined to draw from the remaining weeks of her life their utmost spiritual resources. She declined all visits except those of her superior and the sister infirmarian. She seemed so satisfied to remain in her narrow cell that Mother Clare made no effort to remove her to the more spacious infirmary. Too sick to read, she prayed, kissed her crucifix, and said her beads which she loved. She directed no attention to her suffering, with the result that a tumor in her arm went unnoticed till it enlarged the bone.

With care she outlived the doctor's prediction long enough to suffer deprivation of the one comfort left her. Father Butler, her spiritual director for over twelve years, died while she lingered. He had been severe with her, the community *Annals* say, but she depended on his direction and was obedient to it. However much she felt, she showed no grief but became more recollected. As days passed she no longer asked, "How long do you think I can live?" as she had done from time to time with apparent joy. All her spiritual vision seemed trained on one outlook: whenever and whatever God pleases.

An instance of her detachment must not go unmentioned. When Mother Clare reminded Sister that her family should be notified of the seriousness of her condition, she replied with evident sincerity: "It will be time enough when I am dead."

Mother Clare nevertheless sent word to the young Countess of Newburgh, who came immediately. The tenor of the visit showed her that she was not expected to come again. Disturbed by the dismissal, she complained to Bishop Wiseman. He went to the convent to secure Mother Clare's permission for further visits, only to learn that the request had come from Sister herself. He then asked to see Sister and was brought to the sick room where he gently remonstrated with her.

"All my religious life," she told him, "I have had to work hard for detachment and I do not wish to be distracted now."

She died Friday of Easter week, April 13, 1849, and was interred under the high altar of Most Holy Trinity Church[5] eight years almost to the day of Mother Catherine's jubilant writing of what might well stand as her epitaph: "Lady Barbara—at last a humble Sister of Mercy."

On the eve of the feast of St. Catherine of Siena, Mother Catherine's own feast day, the last of her sister's children but one died. Since she believed Willie McAuley lost at sea, the foundress accepted this bereavement as final. "He is in a most heavenly state of mind," Mother Catherine had written the week after Easter, "imploring God's forgiveness and quite happy." To Mother Francis who had known him from childhood and to Dr. Fitzgerald who had influenced his spiritual life Mother Catherine sent an account of his death:

My poor dear James is in eternity. He died like a saint. Though parched with thirst, he would not take a drop of water without making the Sign of the Cross or let his pillow be moved till he said some little prayer. He never was impatient for five minutes, though six months without being up one entire day. He received the Holy Viaticum every eighth day and lived to the last eighth so as to receive two hours before he expired. He would never let the crucifix be removed from a table at his bedside even when his uncle came. Tell this to Dr. Fitzgerald. It will give him pleasure to find that the religious impressions did not pass away. You will pray fervently for him, I know.

I have nothing now to draw me for one hour from my religious sisters where all my joy on earth is centered. Every year's experience of their worth attaches me more strongly, and I am as ardent for new ones as if I were beginning. I suppose that is the spirit of my state, and my first children, Sister de Pazzi excepted, seem to have it also.

Thank you for the nice St. Catherine. We had no folly here on her day, so many in retreat. Indeed, I was very glad.

And if there had been no retreat, she would have entered into the spirit of the day despite her personal bereavement. Fortunately seven were in immediate retreat, three for profession, among them her godchild little Sister Camillus Byrn, and four to be received. The double ceremony would take place on May 4.

On May 6 Mother Catherine left for Birr, taking with her the new Sister Mary Aloysius [Cowley]. Father O'Hanlon accompanied them, not to stay but expecting to return to Birr for the reception on Ascension Thursday. Meanwhile, however, Mother Elizabeth Moore petitioned him to come to Limerick, so he left the honors of the Birr reception to His Lordship, Bishop Kennedy, who presided, and to the eloquence of Father Matthew. Mary Ann Heenan and Susan Egan were received in the public church, the former under the name Sister Mary Joseph, the latter as Sister Mary Vincent.

Jane Frances Gibson of Eaton House, West Derby, entered during Mother Catherine's absence in Birr. She was not unknown in the Dublin novitiate, for Juliana Hardman's sister had married into the family and Fanny had visited the Hardmans at Handsworth in Birmingham.

The novices had looked forward with special interest to the arrival of this first subject from Liverpool. Rumors that a Convent of Mercy was being planned for that industrial city had reached Ireland. Though the foundress had not been consulted, the rumor had basis in the manoeuvers of certain clergymen.

"I have been told two or three times that you are going to Liverpool," she informed Mother Francis in March, "and Sisters of Charity also," she added. "Matters with you are not closed or you would tell me," she concluded.

It was not hard to trace the rumors. Dr. Youens, Vicar General for the recently formed Lancashire District, was not only a friend of Father Maher in Carlow but a particular friend of the Gibsons. When he heard that Father Gibson's sister had definitely settled on going to the Mercy novitiate in Dublin, his hopes soared, and he optimistically looked about for a suitable piece of property in Liverpool. Frances Gibson's original intention had been to join the Birmingham community when it materialized. A desire to make her novitiate under the foundress herself became so strong, however, that she decided to follow Juliana Hardman's example and go to Dublin. This information reached Carlow early in the year. Since Dr. Youens depended on Father Maher's experience and influence, Mother Francis knew of his project but was in no position to report on it. When Miss Fanny actually arrived and a bequest made the purchase of a Mount Vernon property possible, Father Maher entered the plans with real enthusiasm. He had watched the progress at Carlow with fatherly interest and had developed what Mother Catherine described in Mother Francis as a "genuine ardor and a kind of real, innocent, pious anxiety to be engaged in such works."

That he had some sense of circumventing the foundress, however indeliberately, gains support from his avoiding Baggot Street. Early in June Mother Catherine told Mother Francis, "I heard yesterday that Father Maher was in Dublin lately. It grieved me that he did not call."

Her next remarks should have reassured anyone eager to reserve the Liverpool foundation for Carlow: "I look forward with fear and trembling to my Birmingham journey. I have really got a surfeit."

How sincere she was appears in her reaction to Bishop England's visit in behalf of his American mission. "Have you heard of the great rage for missions?" she asked Mother Aloysius, "the bishops of foreign districts going about to get all the religious sisters they can."

Dr. England from Charleston [South Carolina] celebrated Mass here this morning and gave a most animated exhortation. In a loud voice, he said: "Fear nothing. Follow Paul in peril, pestilence and famine that you may be his glorious associate for time and eternity. The moment you get into his path you feel as if in heaven."

After breakfast we assembled all the troops in the community room from all quarters, laundry, dining hall, everywhere. By chance two were in from Kingstown. We made a great muster. The question was put by His Lordship from the chair: Who will come to Charleston with me to act as superior?

The only one who came forward offering to fill the office was Sister Margaret Teresa Dwyer. This afforded great laughing. I had arranged it with her before but did not think she would have courage. His Lordship was obliged to acknowledge that we are poor, dependent on the white veils and caps. We certainly look like a community that would take time to come to maturity, reduced to infancy again as we are.[6]

About the time Mother Catherine's early June letter reached Carlow the Rule of the Sisters of Mercy was confirmed in Rome. News of it came first to Father Maher through his nephew the future Cardinal, Dr. Paul Cullen. The decree[7] issued later under date of July 5, 1841, stated: "His Holiness in an audience on June 6, 1841, approved it [the Institute] unreservedly and benignly confirmed the Rules and Constitutions . . . as stipulated."

Meanwhile Mother M. Clare Moore had returned to Dublin "too much infected with the precise," as Mother Catherine described the change in her manner. Dr. Murphy came from Cork to meet her, not only as a point of courtesy but to make sure that Dublin would not claim her. He calmly included her sister in the recruiting of his forces.

"He adds," wrote Mother Catherine in some dismay, "what I have no recollection of—that I promised the second Sister Mary Clare to do some wonderful things. I dare not venture to contend with him."

Mother Clare had hardly left London when difficulties arose.[8] Before the end of July the foundress confided to Mother Francis:

Having heard from a priest some unfavorable reports of Bermondsey, I wrote to Mr. Butler begging him to tell me the real state. I this moment received the enclosed. Read it and send it again to me when you are writing. Two left under angry circumstances—I believe are enemies. Sister Agnew is fond of *extremes* in piety. This is her greatest error. She wrote to me in the greatest alarm about a most trifling matter. If you and I were to write on such subjects, we would never be done.

The day after Mother M. Clare Moore left England, the new superior had Sister Mary de Sales Eyre appointed to the office of Mother Assistant, and it is to the latter's credit that she preserved not only her vocation but the true spirit of the Institute through all the weathercock changes introduced while Sister Mary Clare Agnew directed the community. The first departure from fundamentals came in the announcement that henceforth the sisters might choose between action and contemplation. Those attracted to works of mercy applied themselves to the service of the poor; those pursuing contemplation spent more hours in chapel than the horarium, rightly interpreted, allowed.

The inspired lady's love of order went so far as to impose the same level for books during spiritual exercises, and she had several ingenious devices for making tall sisters seem shorter and short sisters seem taller. In the refectory, her originality overthrew the ancient monastic order of seating. She required her religious to sit facing the wall from the inside of the cenaculum tables—an aid to recollection that had escaped the genius of Sts. Benedict, Dominic, and Francis and even the Carmelite reform.

The new Reverend Mother finally applied to the bishop for permission to establish Perpetual Adoration in Bermondsey Convent of Mercy, basing her request on personal revelation. In view of the fact that the Rule was already confirmed, the bishop had no power to grant such a permission. In refusing, however, he made no reference to Rome. He counseled simplicity, hoping, no doubt, to guide the deluded lady to self-knowledge. But Miss Agnew was under the most blinding influence, pride of conceit. After alienating the community with strictures they had no real obligation to heed, she found her position untenable and had the inspiration to withdraw to the Trappistines.

Both spiritual director and bishop advised against the change only to receive importunity and the disclosure of further revelations. To these His Lordship did not reply. Miss Agnew's final letter gave evidence enough of self-delusion. She interpreted His Lordship's silence as consent and announced her departure, directing the money funded under her worldly name as well as further profits from her published works be used for the sick poor visited by the sisters. She hoped to supply through the exercise of her talents the £15 required for postulancy expenses at the Convent of La Trappe in Dorsetshire. She promised to return the clothing she wore away but requested to keep the print of St. Clare that had been hanging in her conventual cell. With that studied gesture Miss Agnew stepped out of Bermondsey parish history.[9]

XXXIII

Upstream with the Catholic Revival

DURING JULY Dr. Edward Pusey of Oxford called at Baggot Street on his own initiative. The new convent building at Handsworth had become part of the Catholic interest, and whatever was of Catholic interest was of interest to the Tractarians. Already widely known as an antiquarian and philosopher, Dr. Pusey had joined the Tractarians but recently. At this time he was just beginning to exert the influence that was to make him father of a new Anglican school of thought.[1] Indirectly through his influence many converts came into the Church; yet he himself fulfilled the foundress' estimate of him and remained an Anglican. As early as 1841, when his greatest work lay ahead, Mother Catherine observed in him the defect later remarked by those reviewing his long life in retrospect: his intellectual powers were historical rather than logical.

Though she saw in him, too, the gentleness for which he was known among his friends, her description implies a slight impatience with his lack of logic:

We had a long visit from Mr. Pusey, Professor of Oxford whose new opinions have created so much interest. His appearance is that of a negligent author such as some of the poets are described. His manner is most pleasing. His countenance is not expressive of a strong mind but in conversation he does not betray any imbecility except the wanderings of all Protestants. He says they must get back their title *Catholic*. He expressed his firm belief in the Real Presence and says we are a safe, sound branch from the old root with many encumbrances and superfluous practices, not of importance in any way. The Greek

Orthodox is another sound branch and his own, the reformed Catholic branch, is a third. He was extremely guarded not to say anything which might offend and he apologized for once calling the Pope Bishop of Rome or Romish Bishop. . . . Dr. Pusey has invited himself [to the profession of Birmingham subjects].

Mother Catherine had had too much experience among Protestants to wish to talk religion with Dr. Pusey. She preferred to meet him on the ground of antiquity, but the best examples of illumination the convent possessed had been lent to Carlow. For once Mother Catherine might have wished that Sister Clare Augustine were slower. Early in Lent she had complained to Mother Francis, then waiting for the Dublin Register as pattern for St. Leo's artist, Sister M. Cecilia Maher:

Sister Mary Clare is a character not suited to my taste or my ability to govern though possessing many very estimable points. She teased and perplexed me so much about the difficulty of copying the two pages that I was really obliged to give up, unwilling to command lest it should produce disedifying consequences. She said it would take the entire Lent. Indeed you can have no idea how little she does in a week. As to a day's work, it is laughable. She will show me three leaves, saying "I finished these today"—three rose or lily leaves!

Shortly, however, she wrote in another strain:

Sister M. Clare is working indeed at the Register. She is quite ashamed to leave it unfinished. I hope to get a safe way of sending it to you for Sister M. Cecilia to copy what she likes.

And now it was in Carlow when she could have used it. The following week she wrote to Mother Francis:

As we shall want all our little exhibition for the ceremony I hope you can send the Register. I felt a great want in not having it to show to Dr. Pusey, the Oxford professor who spoke of illuminated works. Those little affairs are a good fill-up and spare the trouble of talking much.

Though Dr. Pusey did come to the ceremony accompanied by his little daughter, Archbishop Murray engaged all his visiting time, so there was no need for the Register.

In accord with Dr. Wiseman's advice, given during his February visit, Mother Catherine had had the Birmingham novices invite Bishop Walsh to receive their vows. He replied with enthusiasm, promising to bring his coadjutor to preach at the ceremony.

"I sent Dr. Walsh's letter to our Bishop," the foundress wrote in mid-July. "Returning it, he says, 'This is indeed a high honor to all concerned.' "

But they were not to be so honored. In the meantime, Bishop Walsh and Bishop Wiseman had been summoned to the continent on business so secret that not even Dr. Griffiths of London could locate them. If he could have done so, he would have been disturbed indeed, for Dr. Walsh and his coadjutor were in Belgium negotiating to bring the Passionists to England. Among the opinions on which Dr. Griffiths and the Midland Bishops diverged radically was this matter of introducing foreign orders into England.

So the two had proceeded with discretion. How right they were in their mission the future would disclose, for the Passionist with whom they were carrying on their business was the Passionist later appointed to the foundation, Father Dominic Barberi.

By the second week of August the two bishops were back in London. Dr. Walsh wrote requesting Dr. Murray to replace him at the ceremony. Since Sister M. Juliana's father was at the point of death, according to doctor's belief, Archbishop Murray set the profession date for the following week.

Meanwhile, Sister Frances Gibson's eldest sister had died. The foundress reserved the information till after retreat and decided to take Sister to England as traveling companion to see her family in Liverpool.

The Liverpool foundation had its price in sacrifice. Frances Gibson's short postulate had been necessarily rigorous. Though Mother Catherine stressed grooming as a point of religious decorum, she did not wish the sisters to be fastidious. Sister Frances' first duty temporarily reduced to unsightliness her beautiful hands; she had to clean, trim, and polish sixteen oil lamps. Her imperious manner was checked by the foundress herself through a little drama that shows the novice mistress in Mother Catherine.

Sister was once sent on a message to the foundress, who was then in the community room.[2] The postulant sped along the corridor, arrived before the closed door, and knocked vigorously. The hurried footsteps and knock identified the messenger for all within. Mother Catherine herself rose and opened the door. She dropped a deep curtsy, took the astonished postulant by the hand and introduced her as "Her Grace the Duchess of Knock."

Divorced from her attitude at recreation, isolated anecdotes from the training period of postulants and novices show an edge of severity. Letters to the mistress of novices and the foundress' remark about the inadequacy of Sister M. Clare Agnew's religious formation show that Mother Catherine expected the postulate and novitiate to bring religious to a platform from which to proceed after profession. Toward the end of her life, too, Mother Catherine realized that most of the novices would leave the motherhouse on mission as soon as they were professed. She knew that they themselves would soon be the superiors and novice mistresses of her congregation. That she did not fail to discern Frances Gibson's worth, a remark made to Mother Francis reveals: "She is a treasure to religion, a sweet, docile, animated creature, all alive and delighted with her duties."

Bishop Brown was beginning to make it clear that he wished the Liverpool Convent of Mercy founded from the motherhouse. Toward the end of July Mother Catherine gave Mother Francis a hint of this:

> A few days before Dr. Youens came to Dublin our Sister Gibson had a letter from Dr. Brown, her bishop, who seemed to wish to make arrangements here for Liverpool. If he has had any consultation with Dr. Griffiths of London or Dr. Walsh of Birmingham, they would endeavor to impress him with the feeling that establishments in England ought to be made from the motherhouse, as they attribute to that want whatever little difficulty has been found in Bermondsey. Certainly in that instance more experience was required to take down some of Sister Agnew's self-importance as to opinion and bring her well through a novitiate, but the case in question is a very different one. The sister you offer as superior is to remain and her dispositions are well suited. . . . If our little plans could be favored, perhaps we might sail together after our ceremony. I think you will do well to send the enclosed note to Dr. Youens.

Under date of August 3, Mother Catherine summarized the whole matter for Sister M. Teresa White in Galway:

I have had a writing business about the Liverpool foundation. Dr. Youens, a most pious respectable English clergyman, has been making some arrangements for it in Carlow as he knows Mr. Maher. Dr. Brown, the Bishop, wishes to treat with the motherhouse and I fear my poor Sister M. Francis will be disappointed as she has such genuine ardour and a kind of real innocent pious anxiety to be engaged in such works.[3] I am sorry and still hope she may be chosen—hence I have manifested all the indifference that Mr. Daly admires so much and have given seven lines of writing in reply to a sheetful, ever praying that God may produce the effect He most desires.

On August 18 Mother Catherine again heard from Dr. Youens. On August 19 the six Birmingham subjects were professed and Frances Gibson was received under the name Sister M. Liguori. The following day Mother Catherine drew up her will and that evening, accompanied by the Carmelite prior and Father Gaffney, the sisters set out for Liverpool. She planned to leave Mother M. Cecilia Marmion on the new foundation until Sister M. Juliana Hardman became somewhat experienced for the office of mother superior. On this decision she remarked to Mother Francis:

Sister M. Cecilia, you know, is a general favorite. Perhaps there never was a more beloved mistress of novices. They call the noviceship paradise though the best discipline is kept up. Her going away will make it easier for any novice or postulant to be moved. Indeed it will be another great blow to poor Baggot Street which has passed through many sorrows. The sweet little Scotch sister said to me, "What shall I do when Mother Cecilia is gone?"

As foundations multiplied, Mother Catherine referred again and again to the importance of the office of superior. Her correspondence shows how much prayerful concern went into such appointments.

"My dearest child," she wrote to Mother Teresa White, "pray most fervently next month and get all the prayers you can that God may direct me in making arrangements for Birmingham. I am a little perplexed. . . . All are truly good religious, but I am at a great loss about a superior. I do not know what to do."

And to Mother M. Aloysius:

I hope you are getting in love with your charge. It was a great mistake to think that my wish for St. John's[4] was to release myself from my responsibility. No indeed! I think it a sweet occupation. The spirit of penance alone would take me from it. When I see my poor effort for their improvement blessed with success, I think none so happy as I am. . . . Take care of yourself and be a good mother superior. You could not be a better thing at this side of the grave.

In this connection members of the congregation will find it of timely interest to observe the matters on which the foundress exerted jurisdiction. The sisters' school in Birr had drawn all the children from Father Crotty's classrooms. In an early August letter Mother Catherine reveals the astounding fact by contrast: "We calculate that 600 children in the archdiocese receive daily tuition from the sisters. . . . Birr going on well, 450 children at their school. All have left Mr. Crotty's."[5]

When Birr authorities made some objection to her affiliating all Mercy schools with the National Board, she instantly defended the community practice:

I am very sorry to find any displeasure existing toward the Education Board. Ever since the decision of the Cardinals it is regarded with additional confidence and Dr. Murray its chief patron. This is the peace to be prayed for. . . . Prayer will do more than all the money in the Bank of Ireland. Let us pray well and never grow weary.

Yet in another instance Mother Catherine advised the superior in Birr to use whatever discretion was required to keep the Vicar from considering her a mother general or, as she expressed it, a "mistress general." The foundress' discrimination between local considerations and community rights deserves study in the light of the original draft of her rule and of canonical norms established since.[6]

Birmingham was the first foundation made after confirmation of the rule. Again Mother Catherine gives the account:

We had our ceremony on Thursday and sailed on Friday, got here about four o'clock on Saturday, had scarcely time to put on guimps when we were summoned to the choir where the Right Reverend Dr. Wiseman in full pontificals recited the *Te Deum,* said a few animating words and concluded with fervent prayer for the aid of Almighty God.

The convent is beautiful and fully furnished for twenty sisters. The ceiling of the choir is blue and gold with the word *Mercy* in every type and character all over it. Mr. Pugin would not permit cloth of any kind on the rooms—rush chairs and oak tables but all is admirable, so religious that no want can be felt. The whole building cost but three thousand pounds. I would say six without hesitation. . .

Mr. Pugin had redeemed himself with Mother Catherine. By following exactly the general directions she had sent, he executed a convent that satisfied the foundress.[7]

The letter to Mother Francis continues:

Father O'Hanlon came with us. We were most happily circumstanced travelling, nine of us and Father Gaffney, who was our guardian angel. Dr. Brown, Bishop of Kilmore, who was going to Leamington, joined us. Mr. O'Hanlon most kindly went to London to bring Sisters de Sales and Xavier to me. . . . Old Mr. Hardman whose death was expected has rallied wonderfully. They are a most holy family.

The sacrifices John Hardman poured into this last of his benefactions, the Convent of Mercy, can be told in part. Not only had he donated the land and paid for the building and furnishings, but he gave up his home and moved to adjacent property to supervise every detail of the work going on.[8] He included a children's home to accommodate orphans he had been supporting.

Mother Catherine took Sister Mary Juliana to visit him and the joy of their meeting after so many months and under such happy circumstances undoubtedly contributed to his temporary recovery.

The Birmingham convent *Annals* say:

Her visit gave him great pleasure, and he expressed himself much gratified to find from her conversation that the sisters of her institute were fully prepared to carry out all the charitable and benevolent works he had laboured so perseveringly to forward. He admired exceedingly her zeal and self-sacrifice.

Mr. Hardman's granddaughter, Lucy Powell,[9] entered the following week and Sister Mary Juliana's elder sister entered the following year.

Any account of the Birmingham foundation should pay tribute to its second benefactor, John Talbot, the sixteenth Earl of Shrewsbury.

The Hardman archives contain a letter from him on the matter of building the convent, which proves that he had hoped to be co-benefactor in its erection. Mr. Hardman, however, who had set his mind on being sole donor, suggested that His Lordship establish an endowment as his share in the charity. Though the latter preferred to share in building the convent, "Good Earl John," as he was widely known, wrote Mr. Hardman from Italy that he would cooperate either way. He economized by living much of the year away from his estate, palatial Alton Towers in Staffordshire, in order to build churches and engage in other charities in the English Midlands during the period of Catholic restoration.

His generosity in contributing £2000 for the maintenance of the convent is memorialized in the chapel and in the refectory.[10] As multiplied as the word *Mercy* in the ceiling, the Talbot coat of arms inlay the chapel floor, and four mullioned windows behind the transverse table in the refectory contain the coats of arms of the two ecclesiastics and the two Catholic families that figured in bringing Sisters of Mercy to Handsworth: Bishop Walsh, Bishop Wiseman, John Talbot, premier Earl of England, and John Hardman.

Few changes have been made in the convent building. Sisters of Mercy today can therefore pray in the last Mercy chapel enriched by the prayers of their Mother Foundress and blessed through the presence of Cardinal Newman.[11]

Before the month had run out, Mother Catherine knew that her health was slipping irrevocably. On August 30 she informed Bishop Brown of Galway that it would be impossible for her to attend the profession of Sister Mary Joseph Joyce, as she had planned, and on September 6, the day Sister M. Juliana Hardman became mother superior,[12] the foundress wrote Sister Teresa Carton the letter that, read in retrospect, indicates her awareness that the convent infirmary at Baggot Street would claim her remaining days.

The letter to the lay sister, who was to outlive her by nearly fifty years, concludes: "It is strange, my dear Sister Teresa, to write so much about myself and give such trouble."

The "trouble" pertained to directions on how the infirmary was to be prepared. The bed was to be cut down.

You will try to have this done exactly. Make the person read it well. He will think the bed too near the ground, but it is to be. . . . Move your bed to where Sister M. Clare's is and clear out your corner for mine where I will not hear the noise of the street. I will want a fire. When I think of the day you will get this—I suppose the eighth—[13]

The rest of the page is torn away, probably to supply the design to the carpenter. "When I think of the day you will get this—I suppose the eighth"—that sentence prosaically referred to the amount of time the carpenter's job would take.

The Birmingham *Annals* comment:

Reverend Mother McAuley's health became a source of great anxiety to those who were well aware of its decline. Her cough was very trying to her during her stay at Handsworth, and her weakness and debility were evidently on the increase but, as she was ever calm, joyous and hopeful, the sisters in general did not realize the critical state she was in at the time she left them.

Eleven years had passed since that other feast of Our Lady's Nativity, the day she had set her face and her will toward the Presentation novitiate against her natural inclination and preference. Birmingham now had the fourteenth Mercy foundation and the fifteenth would be planned in Liverpool on her way back to the motherhouse.

During that first week of her favorite month the foundress began to suffer the last phase of her final illness: "I have been very weak and sick for the last 12 or 14 days," she wrote to Mother M. Aloysius in Birr. "I did not intend to write until we changed quarters, but your account of Father Toohey has distressed me. You may be sure we will pray most fervently for him. . . . I shall be most anxious to hear."

Details on the home journey are given in a letter to Mother Francis:

I received your note about half an hour before we left Birmingham. We had a weary passage from Liverpool; kept three hours waiting for water and did not arrive in Kingstown until nine o'clock. The poor sisters had comfortable tea for us. We rested there until twelve o'clock.

Sister Xavier is much improved, Sister de Sales just the same, poor skin and bone. I had with me the young novice, Sister Gibson. She has had great family afflictions, her poor papa now in London after some severe operation and her mama's letters such as 'tis wonderful she could bear. Never did I see a vocation so proved. Dr. Youens, who is an intimate friend, had her mama to meet us at his house. We dined with him as the packet did not sail till near eight. He brought us to look at the place where he intends to build a convent. It is very well suited, quite close to the town with three good approaches to it. The present house he says will remain for a House of Mercy. . . . He seems quite ardent in the matter. He sent a sister in my absence for that foundation, a Miss Consitt, a very nice person indeed.

We "dressed for dinner" so he and some of his priests have now seen the full costume which they like very much.

Bishop Brown . . . arranged with Dr. Youens to proceed as Dr. Walsh did "to have English subjects prepared in the motherhouse."

The Liverpool foundation would be made, after all, from the motherhouse and, though they could not know it as they viewed the site of the new convent on Mt. Vernon, two of its superiors were present. Sister Mary Liguori Gibson later succeeded Sister Mary de Sales White as mother superior.

Close to the fourteenth anniversary of the opening of her great house Mother Catherine crossed its threshold inward for the last time. "Poor Baggot Street" was indeed "reduced to infancy," as she had said, but it was the infancy of regeneration.

"I am quite renovated by a delightful addition to the flock," she had told Mother Francis during the summer.

On Wednesday last the first Scotch sister . . . came, twenty-two years old, most interesting. This sweet sister was never out of Scotland before. The variety of accent is now quite amusing at recreation. On Wednesday a very nice niece of Dr. Murray's [comes], Miss Elizabeth Murray of County Wicklow, the daughter of his youngest and favorite brother. . . . She [resembles] the Bishop.

Mother de Pazzi's sister, eighteen years younger, had entered on the feast of the Assumption and Marianne Consitt from Liverpool on the last day of August.

The new spiritual children who came to greet her would cross the threshold outward, some of them passing over thousands of miles of ocean to multiply mercy on the earth. The variety of accent that so pleased her would become a medley and the color of the faces of her spiritual daughters would include the black, the yellow, and the brown. All this lay in promise in the fresh young faces before her as she set her own face toward eternity.

What pleased her most was the spirit of the congregation that no amount of diversity had altered. As she expressed it to Mother M. Elizabeth Moore:

> All are good and happy. The blessing of unity still dwells among us, and oh, what a blessing! It should make all things else [i. e., hardships and difficulties] pass into nothing. All laugh and play together. Not one cold, stiff soul appears. From the day they enter all reserve of an ungracious kind leaves them. This is the spirit of the order indeed, the true spirit of Mercy flowing on us, that notwithstanding our unworthiness God never seems to visit us with angry punishment. He may punish a little in mercy but never in wrath. Take what He will from us, He still leaves His holy Peace and this He has graciously extended to all our convents. Thousands of thanks and praises to His holy Name![14]

Fortunately Mother de Pazzi's health had been exceptionally good through much of the year 1841, for complete charge of the Dublin convent and its charities now fell upon her. Fortunately, too, she had had considerable experience during Mother Catherine's absences, particularly after the bursar and mistress of novices had also left the motherhouse. In the spring the foundress had written of her:

> Mother de Pazzi is the most active, busy person you could see, general provider for both Houses and laundry superintendent. I have not seen her for half an hour in the Bishop's Parlor since you went.

And again:

> I do not know if she ever sat down [at all] till dinner [at four o'clock]. She certainly has a great deal of worldly matters to attend to every day. . . . [She] is remarkably well, thank God.

Even the "Foundation Circulars," as Mother Catherine called her round of letters to her other convents, fell to the mother assistant after a day or two.

On the feast of Our Lady of Mercy, the day after the foundress' return from England, she wrote several notes, each the urgency of charity—one to the sisters in Birmingham to assure them of her safe arrival, one to her first associate, Mother Mary Anne Doyle, in behalf of Sister M. Justina whose health remained frail, and a letter of condolence to the sisters in Birr on the death of a priest devoted to the poor. Short as these letters were, they required effort, and the one to Tullamore has a particular pathos if it is read with her own state of health in mind.

My dear Sister Mary Anne,—I am going to give to you a little trouble or rather beg you to accept it. A dear, much valued sister in a most delicate state thinks she would receive benefit from change of air, which has been prescribed for her. Mr. O'Hanlon, our ever dear good Father, would go with her on Monday next if you can admit her. I need not recommend her to your tenderness. I know she will experience every mark of affection, though a stranger. All expenses, of course, will be defrayed. Write me a line immediately that we may have her ready. She is one of the last professed, Sister M. Justina.

I received your letter in Birmingham and will reply to it soon. I am going to propose myself as deputy to Dr. O'Rafferty in the guardianship of your convent. Your good bishop was much mistaken as to property here. We have ever confided largely in Divine Providence and shall continue to do so.

God bless you.

Your ever affectionate
M. C. McAuley

Thenceforth the foundress went about the business of preparing for death as she had gone about all the business of her lifetime. Orderly by habit, she proceeded from day to day of these last six weeks preparing the way for her successor.

On Saturday, October 2, she wrote encouragingly in answer to a letter from the diffident new superior in Birmingham:

I am most happy to hear that the little affairs at St. Etheldreda's go on so well. . . . I have great consolation in reflecting on the arrangement we have made. Every day I feel a strong conviction that it was the best mode of proceeding. The only thing that embitters it a little is the recollection that it gives pain to you. . . . I shall be looking most anxiously for a long letter, though not deserving, as I am so often heard exclaiming against them. I am quite certain of hearing that all goes on happily and that each of my most dear sisters will give her whole heart to the good work in which God has engaged them with a pure intention of pleasing Him, and my own dear Sister Juliana will do all in her power to fill the place allotted to her and will pray fervently for those animating graces which will lead us on in uniform peace, making the yoke of our dear Redeemer easy.

I kept for the last what I know you will like to hear, that every person who has seen me since my return thinks I look much better.[15]

With such assurances she cheered all around her as well as the sisters on mission. Two days later she wrote equally cheerfully to the sisters in Birr, chiding Sister M. Vincent Egan (four months a novice) for not praying-in more subjects to enlarge their little religious family and sweetly scolding the members of that little group for not writing to her. The whole tenor of the message evinces the motherly solicitude she had for this foundation.[16] Marking the letter specifically "Monday, feast of St. Francis Assisi," she begins as if the feast may have provoked thoughts of her poor little "flock" in Birr:

I was thinking of my poor children in Birr during the night at different times, though I had quite enough sleep. I made a kind of resolution to write this day, and although the duty is now Mother de Pazzi's, yet I must keep my nocturnal resolution.

I am comforted by the recollection that poor Father Edmond [Toohey] was not a frequent visitor. You would feel the loss so much more. I suppose you will often see Father Frank Healy—not too often, for you will all be better engaged. I hope Father Frank will be as great a favorite with the poor as his predecessor. I am sure he will.

What is my dear Sister Vincent doing? She ought to have great grandchildren before this. We met in Birmingham a most pious nobleman, Lord Clifford. He told us that he was asked for advice in a case of some difficulty. His Lordship had replied: "Let the offended or afflicted person repeat three Hail Marys three times a day for eleven days." The desired effect was produced. Now, my dear Sister M. Vincent must not be offended but ought to be afflicted. Let her reflect on her loss until she becomes somewhat afflicted. She will then be a proper client in this case and will obtain the benefit so often experienced and even very lately.

Why do they never write a line to their grandmother? Sister Vincent, Sister Maria, my own conquest Sister Magdalen or my old own child Sister M. Rose. It is but just punishment for their neglect that their generations do not spring up.

Birmingham is very promising—Sister Juliana appointed superior the second week we were there, Sister Cecilia to be home before Christmas. This is the best arrangement we ever had, pleasing to bishops, priests and to all but the dear amiable poor soul who is now Reverend Mother.

Pray who gave you such a false account of me? I am just as you saw me.

So the news that she had failed physically was traveling! The rest of this letter contains an important sentence. Not only does it carry an intimation of death, but it probably holds the key to the discrepancy between her advice and her practice on the matter of corporal penance.

"Pray fervently that God may grant me the grace of a holy penitential preparation," she wrote, "and the grace of a happy death."

This sentence seems to have been written under debility or emotion, for the penmanship widens uncertainly.

Throughout her religious life she had urged upon her sisters the practical penances arising from their laborious duties. The foundress' appreciation of the religious state was such that she exerted all her teaching skill to impress her spiritual daughters with the transformation effected by the virtue of religion, saying that one act in the religious state had a singular value differing from the merit of works of charity and piety accomplished by others of the Faith or out of it.

In illustration she told of the piety of one of her Protestant friends[17] who used to seclude herself and make a long, prayerful preparation for the Lord's Supper as commemorated in her church. The religious, she would say, should make each day's work a preparation for the next day's Communion so that, if it should happen that the time in the morning were shortened, her preparation was already made.

Though she protected the secret of her own mortifications, circumstances have revealed that toward the end of her life she adopted penitential practices not in accord with her recommendations. The explanation seems to lie in the concluding sentence of this last letter to Birr. For some time she had been unable to engage in the duties of the Institute as formerly. Debility and preparation for new missions as well as days of travel and further days of inauguration had deprived her of much of the type of work that used to fill her time. Exhausting in their own way the new duties certainly were; yet they lacked much of the penitential character of works involving nursing and teaching.[18] Under Father O'Hanlon's direction she therefore supplemented the new fatigues with spiritual practices suited to her role of foundress; and now with death before her she continued them as preparation for the greatest of all transitions.

In the lower left corner of this final letter to Birr she wrote cryptically: "This is now called St. Mary's. Your child is St. John's" —a meditation for her "poor children in Birr" then and thereafter.

On the feast of "the little Poor Man" she also wrote a note of felicitation and encouragement to Sister M. Joseph Joyce whose profession she had been unable to attend.

> My very dear Sister Mary Joseph—how sincerely, how joyfully I congratulate you on the completion of your ardent hopes and wishes. What a sweet and blessed union you have formed! Now it is that you must prove your love and gratitude by going hand in hand with your Divine Redeemer—nothing to interest you but what relates to His greater glory. May He grant you every grace and blessing and make you one of His dearest and best beloved. Pray for your ever affectionate
>
> Mary C. McAuley

And a month, almost to the day, before her death she sent a short letter to Mother M. Francis Warde on defects in the translation of the rule. The personal part of it says:

> I have felt the last bad change in the weather very much. Father O'Hanlon brought your affectionate note. I humbly hope I am done with travelling for some time. If ever any poor sinner got a surfeit of it I have. . . . God Almighty bless you.[19]

An adjustment letter to the Booterstown committee on the fifteenth of October and two notes to her lawyer the following week on the legacy left by Mrs. Ryan of The Shelbourne complete Mother Catherine's correspondence.

Sometime during October she fastened together the last sheaf of her papers and turned completely to the business of a "holy penitential preparation" for death.

The "Act of Consecration"[20] written out long before was reaching the hour of final fulfillment:

I consecrate to Thee my heart; receive it as an acceptable sacrifice. I conjure Thee to preserve and unite it to Thine, for with Thee I desire to reside all the days of my life, to live in future unknown to the world and known only to Thee.

To Thee I consecrate my will . . . my understanding . . . my memory. I consecrate to Thee my body. Purify it more and more and render it worthy of being the temple of the Holy Ghost. O Jesus, I now surrender it to Thee. Dispose of it according to Thy blessed Will. I submit freely to all mortifications, infirmities, sickness, sorrows, and death. . . . I consecrate to Thee, sweet Jesus, all that I might possess in earthly goods, authority or influence. All is Thine. Dispose of me as Thou pleasest. I consecrate to Thee all that I can—joys, sorrows, life and death to testify to Thee my love and, as far as I am able, to induce all hearts to love Thee. Mercifully vouchsafe to receive me. I am now resolved with the help of Thy Grace, O my God, to be Thine without reserve or division and to serve Thee with lively devotion to the last hour of my existence. Amen.

To the novices she had said: "Should we live to be a hundred, each day should be more perfect." What she thought of living to be a hundred she had registered elsewhere:[21]

What is this poor miserable world but a place of sorrow and continued disappointment? God be praised it is not our fixed abode, only the weary road that leads to it. Oh, what would we do if in place of seventy or eighty years God had appointed three or four hundred for our journey?

She was not to have the seventy even, and if she could have the three or four hundred she had shown clearly what she would do.

Two years before, when a clergyman had asked for an account of the Institute, she submitted the following:

I would find it most difficult to write what Mr. Clarke wishes, for the circumstances which would make it interesting could never be introduced in a public discourse. It commenced with two, Sister Doyle and I. The plan from the beginning was such as is now in practice, and in 1827 the House was opened. In a year and a half we were joined so fast that it became a matter of general wonder. Dr. Murray gave his most cordial approbation and visited frequently. All was done under his direction from the time we entered the House, which was erected for the purpose of charity. Dr. Blake and Reverend Mr. Armstrong were chiefly concerned, received all the ideas I had formed and consulted for two years at least before the house was built. I am sure Dr. Blake had it constantly before him in all his communication with Heaven, for I never can forget his fervent prayers when it was in progress.

Seeing us increase so rapidly and all going on in the greatest order almost of itself, great anxiety was expressed to give it stability. We who began were prepared to do whatever was recommended and in September, 1830, we went with dear Sister Harley to George's Hill to serve a novitiate for the purpose of firmly establishing it. In December, 1831, we returned and the progress has gone on as you know. We now have gone beyond a hundred in number and the desire to join seems rather to increase. Though it was thought the foundations would retard it, it seems to be quite otherwise. There has been a most marked Providential guidance which the want of prudence, vigilance, or judgment has not impeded, and it is here that we can most clearly see the designs of God. I could mark circumstances calculated to defeat it at once but nothing, however injurious in itself, has done any injury.

This is all I could say. Loss of property has been supplied; the death of the most valuable sisters passed away as of no consequence. The alarm that was spread by such repeated deaths did not prevent others crowding in—in short, it evidently was to go on and surmount all obstacles, many of which were great indeed, proceeding from causes within and without.

One thing is remarkable, that no breach of charity ever occurred among us. The sun never, I believe, went down on our anger. This is our only boast. Otherwise, we have been deficient enough and far, very far from co-operating generously with God in our regard, but we will try to do better, all of us, to repair the past.[22]

Organizing her papers had brought back the financial concern that had harried her from the beginning. She well knew now that her "folly," as Dr. James had dubbed the great house, had no security but Divine Providence.

The Dublin MS states:

She was greatly harassed by pecuniary difficulties,—in fact, so much so that she feared the community might be obliged to disperse. Next to Mr. Cavanagh the most useful friend she had was Sister M. de Pazzi's brother, Mr. Bernard Delany. She always liked him very much and had great confidence in his business talents and discretion, and he fully justified it. He spared no pains to serve us, and if things are all right with us now, as I believe they are, much of it is due to his activity and liberality also.[23]

On the feast of All Souls Mother Catherine became bedridden. One incident from this last week was supplied to Mother M. Teresa Austin Carroll by Mother M. Liguori Gibson of Liverpool. Going past the infirmary door one morning and seeing it ajar, the novice Sister M. Liguori put in her head to inquire for the patient. Invited in, she threw her arms about Mother Catherine and burst into tears, saying impulsively, "O Reverend Mother, stay with us. What would the order do if you died?"

She had many long years to remember the answer: "My child, never say that again. If the order be *my* work, the sooner it falls to the ground, the better: if it is God's work, it needs no one."

XXXIV

Martinmastide, 1841

MARTINMASTIDE is a bright little season set almost midway in November's deepening somberness. Literally it extends from the death day of St. Martin of Tours, November 8, to his burial day, November 11, observed by the Church as his feast day. In passing, Martin the Bishop has left a bit of color on the faded year, a thin gold line of demarcation: Martinmas summer on the land, Martinmas tenure on the calendar.

As for Martinmas itself, Ghéon says: "It is an autumnal feast of hope. On St. Martin's day we taste the wine of the last gathering; we build fires of leaves on the hills; outstanding claims are settled, leases renewed . . . so that the past is closed, the future opened up."[1]

Mother Catherine had lived the spirit of Martinmas from year to year, for the eve of this feast brought the anniversary of William Callaghan's death and this Martinmas would be the eighth anniversary of Sister Mary Teresa McAuley's last day on earth. What the foundress' thoughts were as the first week of November ran out cannot be known, but those whose names she had inscribed on her mottled note book were certainly in her prayerful remembrances. Her calm procedure reflected the spirit of the "Act of Resignation" she herself had composed some time before:

> My God, I am thine for all eternity, teach me to cast my whole self into the arms of Thy Providence with the most lively, unbounded confidence in Thy compassionate, tender pity. Grant, O most merciful Redeemer, that whatever Thou dost ordain or permit may always be acceptable to me. Take from my heart all painful anxiety;

suffer nothing to afflict me but sin, nothing to delight me but the hope of coming to the possession of Thee, my God, in Thine own everlasting Kingdom. Amen.[2]

The state of her health in the early days of November has been charted by Sister M. Clare Augustine Moore.

An abscess had formed internally; her debility was most painful so that to walk from room to room fatigued her. She coughed incessantly; her appetite was gone; she could not sleep. The highest medical advice was procured but it was useless and she knew it, but she took all that was ordered and submitted to all the little alleviations in the way of diet which the sisters presented to her, though a foul taste with which she was constantly afflicted prevented any comfort from them. This was perhaps the reason she accepted them, for when she was ill after her return from Bermondsey she lectured the infirmarian for buying a chicken and absolutely refused to touch it . . .

Besides the internal abscess she had a hideous ulcer on the lower part of her back, brought on by the use of haircloth and a large chain. This she had concealed. Her brother, how I know not, became aware of it and wanted to see it, which she refused to allow but consented to let Sister [Teresa Carton] who slept with her in the infirmary dress it. Sister told me it was almost as large as the palm of her own hand, with green matter in the middle.[3]

During her last few days Mother Catherine still served herself in every possible way, permitting the lay sister to do only what she herself could not manage. Thus Sister Teresa alone saw and dressed the ulcer that some instrument of penance had opened in the foundress' back. One can imagine Dr. James' annoyance could he have known the cause!

On Monday, November 8, as a measure toward recovery she was anointed so unexpectedly that the sisters did not put on their church cloaks according to custom. It may be that Father O'Hanlon came prepared to anoint her and proceeded without much opportunity for the sisters to observe the usual formality. On Tuesday, after Dr. Stokes' visit, Mother de Pazzi realized that the foundress' condition was critical.

The following day she directed Sister M. Ursula Frayne to notify the superiors of their other convents. "Dear Reverend Mother," the message ran:

With feelings of the deepest and most bitter regret it devolves on me to announce to you that our very dear and much beloved Reverend Mother is considered to be past hope of recovery. May Almighty God in His Infinite Mercy prepare us all for the heavy affliction that awaits us.

Mother de Pazzi had already notified Mother M. Elizabeth Moore, who through a set of favoring circumstances had been able to come immediately. Bishop Ryan himself was about to leave for Dublin. He not only granted her permission to go but accompanied her. He first, however, exacted a promise that she would return to Limerick, no matter what developed, for he feared that, in the event of the foundress' death, she would be retained at the motherhouse.

On Tuesday, unaware of the crisis in the foundress' condition, His Lordship sent word that he would return to Limerick the following day. Sorrowfully Mother Elizabeth took final leave of Mother Catherine. Her obedience had visible reward. When Bishop Ryan learned that the foundress was dying, he allowed Mother Elizabeth to stay. She later wrote the circular letter that gives an eyewitness account of Mother Catherine's last days. This she sent to the superiors who had been her companions at Baggot Street before they were assigned to missions.

At the Tuesday visit Dr. Stokes told Sister Teresa to watch Reverend Mother carefully since the abscess would soon burst and its rupture would be the immediate forerunner of death. The patient suffered acutely throughout the day. Sometime during the long night of pain she got up and the rupture occurred, leaving her so weak that she had to call Sister Teresa to help her back into bed. Thus in the early morning hours of November 10, Martinmas Eve, Mother Catherine entered the last stage of her illness.

Very early the next morning she sent Sister Teresa Carton on a practical errand. At two o'clock in the morning the patient wanted a quantity of brown wrapping paper and some cord—in fact, plenty of cord.

These first directions were so casual that the lay sister proceeded quite as if Dr. Stokes' warning had never been spoken and as if "the dreaded lesion" had not occurred. Yet she as well as her patient knew that some preparation for death was going forward. Within the curtains of her bed Mother Catherine wrapped a package. The sounds were familiar to Sister Teresa. Mother Catherine had wrapped many a package and many a package Sister Teresa had wrapped for her or had helped her wrap—in broad daylight. This experience was different. Apprehension filled the curtained space where Sister sat bolt upright in unaccountable fright. Then the familiar voice spoke softly, and Sister, reassured, emerged from her bed to another errand. She was to go to the kitchen, stir up the fire, put the package in, and turn her back till the flames had entirely consumed the parcel. Mother Catherine's directions became imperative: "I forbid you under obedience to open it or look at it while it is burning."

Terrified by the emphasis, Sister stood motionless.

Sensing dread, Mother Catherine asked gently, "Would you be afraid, dear?"

Poor Sister Teresa's fear rushed into words: "Oh, Reverend Mother, I would be afraid I might look."

The foundress had permitted two other sisters to attend her during the day, Mother M. Elizabeth Moore and the recently professed novice, Sister M. Vincent Whitty.[4] Mother Catherine now made a decision.

"Well, call Sister Mary Vincent," she conceded. When Sister Vincent came down, the foundress repeated the instructions, being specific about drawing red coals over the parcel after consigning it to the fire.

The two descended to the kitchen and Sister Teresa dutifully kept her back to the fire while it did its work. Did Sister M. Vincent smell the haircloth burning or see the charred evidences as she banked the fire again? To Sister M. Clare Augustine she hinted of haircloth but to the Passionist Father Vincent Grotti,[5] under whose direction she later made a retreat, she revealed the contents of the package. He not only released her of any obligation to preserve the secret but said that it should be made known. "Tell the vision to no man," he quoted, "till the Son of Man be risen from the dead."[6]

Mother M. Elizabeth Moore, referring to the incident, merely states that Mother Catherine's boots were burned. It would have been like Mother Catherine to dispose of the worn boots she would never use again, but the foundress would have made no solemn prohibitions over a pair of well-worn shoes. Something she wished forever concealed was in the package, and the witness says: "instruments of penance" and shoes "studded with sharp nails."

As far back as 1835 Mother M. Clare Moore observed that Mother Catherine had difficulty in walking, though she gave herself no exemptions from the long Kingstown visitations. Had her boots been made intentionally uncomfortable?

According to Mother Catherine's own statement, the sisters had been making cloth shoes under Sister M. de Sales White's inspiration, having them capped and soled by the local cobbler.[7] It would have been easy for her to introduce a penitential addition, though between convent shoemaker and local cobbler the boots could have been uncomfortable enough without any ingenious planning.

About four o'clock in the morning she asked to have her bed moved to the center of the room as she would soon want air. How well she knew! How many deathbeds she had attended!

Before Mass she sent for the sisters and spoke to each. Over and over she repeated: "Preserve union and peace," and over and over she promised: "Do this and your happiness shall be so great as to cause you wonder."

For each, too, she had a special exhortation or comment. To Sister M. Genevieve Jarmy who was in her seventy-second year, she spoke of the joy of dying, revealing for her encouragement her own ineffable joy in these last hours. She told Sister M. Vincent Whitty and Sister M. Agnes O'Connor[8] that they would accomplish much for God's kingdom. She affectionately summoned the six-months professed little Sister M. Camillus Byrn, whom she had mothered from earliest infancy, and soothed her: "Kiss me, my darling, and go away but don't be crying. I shall see you again."

And so one by one she greeted them and they passed, individuals but symbols, too, representing their sisters elsewhere in Ireland and in England and all those others to come, the hundreds and the thousands to the tens of thousands. One legacy for all: union, charity, peace, wondrous happiness—and a message for each down to the last.

Then the foundress said quite in her old manner that it would comfort her to see the sisters again in their church cloaks, since through inadvertence they had not put on their white cloaks for her anointing on Monday. At eight-thirty, Mass began there in the infirmary with Mother Catherine on her deathbed surrounded by her white cloaked Sisters of Mercy.

"If thy whole body be lightsome . . . the whole shall be lightsome," the Gospel ran, "and as a bright lamp shall enlighten thee."

"Blessed is that servant whom, when the Lord shall come, he shall find watching: amen I say to you, he shall set him over all his goods."

"My truth and my mercy shall be with him . . . "

After Mass Mr. Cavanagh came and she confirmed her will.

"I think her agony commenced about eleven o'clock," Mother Elizabeth recorded. "She spoke very little. . . . Cautious as she was of bringing herself into notice in health, she was still more so in sickness, waiting on herself even in her last agony, preserving to the last moment the same peace and serenity of mind which so eminently distinguished her through life; omitting not an iota of what was essential and totally disregarding all but what was of moment."

Sister M. Vincent Hartnett's memoir points the source of this great peace and serenity of mind: "Reverend Mother told us not only to obey the Will of God but to love it with our whole heart and soul."

During the day Dr. James, his wife and daughters came, Mrs. Macauley to remain in loving devotion to the end. Dean Meyler and the new Father O'Carroll from St. Andrew's called, Father Walsh from Kingstown,[9] Dean Gaffney and the faithful Carmelite prior, so glad of his fourteen years of service to the Institute of Our Lady of Mercy.

When Dr. Stokes came in, she saved him any pronouncement by giving her own:

"Well, Doctor, the scene is drawing to a close."

At five o'clock she asked that the candle be placed in her hand, thereby dedicating the remaining three hours of her life to the Divine Will.

"We commenced the last prayers," Mother Elizabeth wrote. "When I repeated one or two she herself had taught me, she said with energy, 'God bless you!' "

Mother Elizabeth does not specify those she selected but the prayer that had blessed Catherine McAuley's early childhood must have poured blessings on these final hours. As far back as she could remember she had heard it. She had said its aspirations with the striking of the hour, and she had incorporated it in the prayers of her Institute. It could not fail her now. The hand that held the candle, the clock now striking must summon those pleading changes: "Jesus, Jesus, Jesus, have mercy on us . . . help us . . . strengthen us . . . comfort us . . . make us steadfast . . . enlighten us with spiritual wisdom.

"Jesus, Jesus, Jesus, grant us grace to fear Thee . . . to love Thee . . . to call on Thee for help . . . to direct our lives to Thee. . . . O Blessed Redeemer, keep us continually mortified here, that, purified by the fire of Thy Love, we may, when we depart out of this world, enter immediately into the everlasting possession of Thee."

The prayers of all her life rose now to bless her passing.

"When we thought the senses must be going," Mother Elizabeth continues, "and that it might be well to rouse attention by praying a little louder, she said, 'No occasion, my darling, to speak so loud, I hear distinctly.' In this way she continued till ten minutes before eight o'clock when she calmly breathed her last sigh."

And the witness who had attended many a deathbed concludes: "I did not think it possible for human nature to have such self-possession at the awful moment of death."

One evidence of self-possession that tradition has preserved, Mother Elizabeth does not mention:

"The sisters are tired," Mother Catherine observed. "Be sure they have a comfortable cup of tea when I am gone."

Almost a year to the day Mother Catherine had written of Father Matthew:

> We passed through populous towns on fair and market days without hearing one angry voice—men, women, and children dressed [up] and all so peaceable and happy. This proves to us what the special grace of God can produce, though bestowed but on one man, yet so as to go forth among millions.[10]

Of herself, too, might be said: "The special grace of God bestowed on one shall go forth among millions."

In that other November also she had related of the sister who now succeeded her in office:

> We expect St. John's [Newfoundland] will come about in May or June. I announced that whoever could take tea without milk should go there as superior, milk being very difficult to procure. Mother de Pazzi commenced this morning and has declared herself so far an efficient candidate.[11]

Mother de Pazzi's jesting had its kernel of truth. She had no real intention of volunteering for Newfoundland nor of qualifying for superior anywhere. Mother Catherine's absences had given her more experience of the latter than she cared for. Now, however, the irrevocable absence had come, and Mother de Pazzi could never again follow the foundress with letters of petition to return. The burden of office was hers alone.[12]

Mother M. Teresa arrived from Galway at midnight, too late to hear again the voice that was like no other voice she had ever heard. She whose spirit, according to the foundress, was so like her own had the privilege of helping to prepare the body for burial.

"I never met anyone like her," Mother Teresa told Mother Austin Carroll years later. "She was rather tall . . . and had a queenly air. . . . Her appearance was very remarkable. There was something about her so kind yet so discerning that you would fancy she read your heart. If you came to speak to her on the most trifling matter, although occupied with the most important affairs, she would instantly lay all aside and give you any satisfaction in her power."[13]

She was laid in state in the chapel that had cost her so much suffering. Draped in black now, it was the jewel case for her precious remains. The calm so characteristic of her in life beautified her in death. The poor whom she had served, benefactors who had supported her charities, the clergy she had reverenced—whether they befriended or opposed her—came, paid their respects in their different ways and went. The illness of Archbishop Murray and the necessity of preparing a cemetery on the convent grounds deferred the interment till Monday.

His Grace appointed her devoted friend Bishop Kinsella to represent him. His Lordship consecrated the burial plot outside the chapel corridor and officiated at the Mass. The sad little Face of the Infant looked out from its place above the altar where He stood on His Mother's knee, clasping His heart to His breast. His Mother, communing, her vision fixed on the near scene, supported her Child with her right hand and extended the other holding her heart aglow. These had hung framed over the altar when Catherine McAuley, Lady of Mercy, conducted her charity center for the poor, when in resignation to the Divine Will she absented herself to make a novitiate among the Sisters of the Presentation, when as the first Sister of Mercy she returned with her companions to cooperate with the arrangements of Divine Providence by training missionaries for the home field and finally for remote parts of the world. This representation of Divine Compassion had been the picture of her choice when, an heiress, she devoted herself to the poor. How much more it meant to her as a religious Sister of Mercy!

Her funeral Mass was sung at eleven o'clock on Monday, November 15, the old feast of the Patronage of Our Lady. The veil of the Sister of Mercy was then lowered over the foundress' face; the casket was closed. Bishops, priests and white cloaked sisters bearing lighted candles passed along the chapel corridor and out to the new little cemetery where Mother Mary Catherine McAuley, according to her expressed wish, was laid in the ground, "like the poor."[14]

> O God, Who dost manifest Thine almighty power most chiefly in sparing and showing mercy: multiply upon us Thy mercy: that as we hasten towards Thy promises, Thou mayest make us partakers of the heavenly treasures. Through Our Lord Jesus Christ, Thy Son, Who liveth and reigneth with Thee in the unity of the Holy Ghost, God, world without end.
>
> Prayer for Mass of Tenth Sunday after Pentecost

Notes

PREFACE

1. E. H. A., "Catherine McAuley, Foundress of the Sisters of Mercy," *The Golden Hour,* X (September, 1929), 142-146.

2. Sister (or Mother) M. Vincent Hartnett (Anna Maria) entered the Baggot Street Convent from the same parish (St. Andrew's) on February 5, 1837, went on the Limerick foundation in September of the following year and was professed on October 24, 1838. She became superior of the Roscommon foundation. Her biography of the foundress was published in 1864. She died the following year.

3. Sister Mary Catherine McAuley died on September 11, 1952, at Convent of Mercy, Kyneton, Victoria, Australia.

CHAPTER I

1. W. E. H. Lecky, *Leaders of Public Opinion in Ireland* (New York: Longmans, Green and Co., 1912) II, 48.

2. Denis Gwynn, *The Second Spring* (London: Burns, Oates, 1942), p. 1.

3. Cf. Myles V. Ronan, *An Apostle of Catholic Dublin* (Dublin: Browne and Nolan, 1944), pp. 32-34.

4. Cf. note 1 of Chapter V for the history of Liffey Street chapel (St. Mary's) on which James McGauley worked in early manhood.

5. The London MS is the source of these quotations. The London and Dublin MSS were the work of two sisters who became at separate times members of the Congregation of Mercy. The younger of the two, Georgina Moore, joined Miss McAuley in the first years of the South Dublin charities and took the name of her elder sister, Mary Clare, when the Baggot Street project became a religious institute. As superior of Bermondsey community Mother Mary Clare spent most of her life in London. Shortly after the foundress' death she wrote the memoir I designate as the London MS. It became an integral part of the Bermondsey *Annals.* The elder of the two sisters, Mary Clare Moore, an artist, met Miss McAuley in 1829 but did not associate herself with the Baggot Street charities until a half dozen years after the Institute became a religious community. She spent most of her convent life at the parent house under the name Sister Mary Clare Augustine. In 1864 she wrote a memoir from her own experience and from direct contact with early members of the community and others who had known Catherine McAuley. I refer to Sister M. Clare Augustine's memoir as the Dublin MS. This manuscript belongs to the parent community. Another

Moore portfolio, also the property of the Dublin community, results from correspondence between Mother M. Clare Moore and her sister when the latter was planning her memoir. Five letters, averaging about 1500 words each, were written by the former from London during 1844 and 1845. The August 23, 1844 letter characterizes Mrs. Mc(G)auley as a "philosopher above form."

6. Whether the Stormanstown House of today is actually Catherine McAuley's birthplace is questionable. The Protestant rector of Santry in the last quarter of the nineteenth century has left the history quoted below. From it one might deduce that the foundress of the Sisters of Mercy had been born in the old mansion. Still, the description of the present house here given does not entirely tally. Therefore, its age remains a question. Mrs. Drew, wife of the present owner, states that the building was 200 years old in 1956.

> Stormanstown House, erected in the early part of the seventeenth century, stood a short distance southwest from the present house; tradition describes it as a noble mansion covered with tiles, numerous spacious apartments. In the latter part of the last century it became ruinous; one gable about 40 feet high was standing in 1823, when it was taken down, and the materials used in the erection of the present house by William Leslie Badham, Esq., who in 1843 sold his interest to the Courtney family from whom it passed by sale in 1880 to the present (1883) owner, Philip Barrington, Esq. The present house is a comfortable slated mansion of three stories high, situated on a rising ground and commands in front an extensive view of the Dublin and Wicklow Mountains. A small plantation surrounds the house and the garden lies to the northwest. Broken pieces of marble, tiles, etc., are frequently dug up in the back lawn on the site of the old house. (*History and Description of the Santry and Cloghran Parishes* by Benjamin Adams, D. D., Rector of Santry.)

7. In the early biographical sketches of Catherine McAuley, both 1778 and 1787 are given as the year of her birth. From the record of her father's will, the year 1787 must be discarded because James Mc(G)auley's will was made on July 18, 1783, and proved on August 2 of the same year.

The year 1778 is used in a sketch of Mother McAuley by the Very Rev. Dominick Murphy of Cork (*Dublin Review,* March 1847). Whatever the source of his information, deviating as it did from contemporaneous records at George's Hill and at Baggot Street, Dr. Murphy considered it reliable enough to repeat seventeen years later when he expanded the Review article for his *Sketches of Irish Nunneries* (1865).

Meanwhile, Mother M. Vincent Hartnett's biography of the foundress had been published (*The Life of Reverend Mother Catherine McAuley,* Dublin: John F. Fowler, 1864). She gives September 29, 1778, as Catherine McAuley's birth date.

8. Dyer (*British Popular Customs*) gives several instances of house garlanding as a sign of Michaelmas cheer within doors and calls attention to the custom of beflowering houses for the election of a mayor, since the new mayor assumed office on Michaelmas. Both Urlin and Walsh (cf. bibliography) refer to the Irish custom of killing a sheep to be distributed among the poor. Urlin states that the Michaelmas alms was a tribute of gratitude commemorating St. Michael's coming, sword aflame, to the aid of St. Patrick on one occasion. Walsh characterizes Irish Michaelmas as a "festal day of joy, plenty, and universal benevolence." Adding to Urlin's information on election customs at Michaelmas in England, Walsh gives this further note: "There is a pretty and delicate fancy still prevalent in some parts of England, that at midnight on Michaelmas Eve the bracken puts forth a small blue flower, which withers and falls before dawn."

9. Whatever Catherine McAuley's age at the time of her father's death, Geor-

gina Moore, one of her first and closest associates in the Baggot Street work, makes this assertion:

> She imbibed early impressions of piety from her father, who was very exact in all religious duties and was in the habit of assembling little children in his house to teach them the catechism, but he died while she was yet very young. . .

St. Thérèse is credited with a similar remarkable recall of a childhood experience. In *Collected Letters of St. Thérèse of Lisieux,* edited by Abbé Combes and translated in 1949 by F. J. Sheed, Soeur Thérèse is quoted as saying (p. 223): "I remember perfectly my journey to the Visitation of Le Mans at the age of three." Abbé Combes supplies the note: "Easter Monday, 29 March, 1875—Thérèse was in fact only two years and three months."

10. July 18, 1783: Sir William Betham *Genealogical Abstracts Prerogative Wills,* XLIX, 26 (Public Record Office of Ireland).

CHAPTER II

1. On June 24, 1784, Elinor Mc(G)auley leased a new brick and stone house nearer Dublin and sold it to Dr. Huson Bigger, June 20, 1787. Maps of Lord Drogheda's estate recently received at the National Library of Ireland may, when catalogued, give some clue to this house, which was bounded on the east by the Earl's estate and on the west by the road leading out to Stormanstown House. No reference to the three years spent here exists except in the Memorial at the Registry of Deeds Office in Dublin.

2. Queen Street in St. Paul's parish was a relatively new street in a district built up during the previous century. Elinor Mc(G)auley took the lease on No. 52 Queen Street, June 6, 1787, and sold it on August 13, 1796. It had been the residence of a Mr. Francis Conway, possibly a family connection.

3. Sister M. Catherine Maher, Carlow annalist.

4. The house at 28 East Arran Street has been demolished but the old Apothecaries' Hall and the house at 34 Mary Street still stand.

5. William Armstrong twice served the Hall as governor and intermittently held other honorary positions.

6. "By a lease dated March 6, 1792, the Apothecaries' Hall acquired premises in Mary Street for a term of 96 years." (Registry of Deeds Office, Dublin.)

7. From 1787 to 1815 William Armstrong is listed at 34 Mary Street. In 1815 the number 42 is given in accord with an adjustment of property numbers.

8. Anne Conway Byrn's eldest daughter Catherine eventually became a Dominican nun under the name Sister Mary Raymund (spelling taken from the Dominican records, Drogheda). Her part in helping to establish Catherine Mc Auley's work appears in its proper place in the text. Catherine Byrn's sisters became Sisters of Mercy. Ann, called in religion Sister Mary Margaret, entered the Bermondsey community. Teresa, Sister Mary Camillus, came to the New York foundation in 1846, and died a member of the Baltimore community. The letter here quoted is in the Bermondsey Convent of Mercy archives. About Dr. Owen Conway, Sister further says: "His father, who amassed a great fortune by honorable industry, gave him the education and profession of a gentleman."

9. Israel Read, surgeon to the Meath Hospital before 1795, member of the Royal College of Surgeons of Ireland, resided at 38 Molesworth Street according to *Wilson's Dublin Directory,* 1783, p. 91. He took indentured apprentices. To be one of his successful apprentices assured entrance into the social life of the period. (C. A. Cameron, *History of the Royal College of Surgeons in Ireland,* pp. 110, 122, 276, 342, 343, 396, 397.)

10. Cf. note 1 of Chapter V.

11. The Psalter of Jesus has fifteen sets of petitions, each having nine aspirations of the Holy Name of Jesus and all incorporating a plea of mercy.

CHAPTER III

1. Georgina Moore in the London MS.

2. Constantia Maxwell marshals an amazing number of witnesses in her *Dublin Under the Georges* (London: Faber and Faber, Ltd.) and *Country and Town in Ireland under the Georges* (London: George G. Harrap and Co., Ltd., 1940). The quotations in this chapter are made from pp. 84 and 87 of *Dublin.*

3. Dublin MS.

4. "Dear Reverend Mother's love for holy poverty, great and eminent as it was, never led her into doing what might be offensive to her neighbor or might tend to lower the dignity of her holy state in the opinion of seculars. This she impressed, also, on the sisters both by word and example. She would not suffer any patching or mending on the exterior dress, whether for the convent or outdoor, that might be calculated to excite contempt in the minds of secular observers; she put no bounds to the humble nature of all other clothing. Her own other clothing was always of the meanest description and no more than was barely enough and that repaired as long as it was possible to keep it together." Mother M. Vincent Hartnett, *The Life of Rev. Mother Catherine McAuley,* p. 96.

Also see Chapter XXIV for the paragraph on this subject which appeared in the copy of the rule that Mother Catherine herself wrote.

5. Séan O'Faoláin, *An Irish Journey* (London: Longmans, Green, 1940), pp. 292, 294.

6. The Duke of Devonshire, Lord Lieutenant of Ireland in the mid-eighteenth century, advised Handel that Dublin would give a more amiable reception to his art. Handel, therefore, brought his *Messiah* to the Irish capital to present it publicly for the first time. Dublin more than fulfilled His Grace's expectations. When shortly after the death of Handel, the first English-born George married Charlotte of Mecklenburg, Court patronage of music was assured into the next century, for this George became "the third of England." He was an accomplished organist and his consort Queen Charlotte had been taught by one of the Bachs.

7. London MS.

CHAPTER IV

1. Warren Hastings resigned in 1785 and returned to England.

2. John Armstrong McAuley, Mother Catherine's grandnephew (died May 14, 1949), was named not for his grandmother's foster father, William Armstrong, as might be supposed, but from his father's regard for the Reverend Edward Armstrong. (A letter to the author from J. A. McAuley's sister, Sister Mary Catherine McAuley, Convent of Mercy, Kyneton, Victoria, Australia.)

3. Private letter of Anna Maria Doyle (Mother Mary Anne), Carysfort Park Convent of Mercy archives.

4. Mr. Callaghan's will, January 27, 1822, begins: "I, William Callaghan, formerly residing at the Apothecaries' Hall, Mary Street."

5. Hayden and Moonan, *A Short History of the Irish People,* (New York: Longmans, Green & Co., 1927; Dublin: The Educational Company of Ireland, Ltd.), p. 427.

6. *Ibid.,* p. 428.

7. James Carty, *Classbook of Irish History* (London: The Macmillan Co., 1943), III, 101.

8. *Ibid.,* p. 99.

9. Hayden and Moonan, *op. cit.,* p. 429.

10. Wolfe Tone did not live to be executed.

NOTES

CHAPTER V

1. Bishop Donnelly's *A Short History of Some Dublin Parishes* (Dublin: Catholic Truth Society pamphlets), p. 11, quotes the Edgerton Manuscript (1749), British Museum, on St. Mary's:

> A chapel in Liffey Street was built in 1729 by collections made among the R. C.'s of that parish, forwarded by the industry of John Linegar, who was registered priest thereof in 1704. This chapel, though small, is neat, altar railed in, steps ascending to it of oak; fore-part of the altar covered with gilt leather, and name of Jesus in glory in the midst. On the altar is a gilt tabernacle with six large gilt candlesticks and as many nosegays of artificial flowers; the altar-piece, carved and embellished with four pillars, cornices and other decorations gilt and painted. The picture of Conception of the B. V. M., to whom the chapel is dedicated, fills the altar-piece; and on each side are paintings of the Apostles Peter and Paul. Opposite the altar hangs a handsome brass branch for tapers; near it is a neat oak pulpit, on the sounding-board of which is a figure of a gilt dove, representing the Descent of the Holy Ghost. In said chapel is a small sacristy, four decent confessionals, two galleries, several pews for better sort, and two sprinkling pots of black marble in chapel yard.

In an "Appendix" (pp. 22, 23), Bishop Donnelly says:

> "The Reverend John Linegar, a curate in St. Michan's was appointed first parish priest of St. Mary's. In the published "List of registered Popish Priests" in 1704, he already appears as P. P. of St. Mary's, but this was only to meet the requirements of the law and had no canonical significance as a Catholic parish had not come into existence until four years later.
>
> "For the first ten years of his administration he was compelled to celebrate Mass and conduct religious services for his parishioners in a hired room in Mary Street, but about the year 1729, as stated in our manuscript, he began to collect funds and build a commodious chapel in Upper Liffey Street, which served its sacred purpose for nearly one hundred years. The old building has disappeared but the site is at present (early twentieth century) covered by a new store belonging to Messrs. Bewley and Draper of Mary Street, of exactly the same dimensions. It runs behind the houses on the west side of Liffey Street from No. 21 to 26.
>
> "Part of the furniture of Liffey Street Chapel was transferred to the Pro-Cathedral, Marlborough Street, at the time it was opened, notably the pillars and cornices here described, which now form the handsome super-structure of the side altars, and also the painting of the Immaculate Conception, which for full half a century hung behind the high altar of the Pro-Cathedral but eventually had to make way for the artistic stained-glassed window that now occupies the space. The picture, however, is preserved in the Archbishop's House, Drumcondra. The holy water font in the south portico of Marlborough Street Pro-Cathedral belongs indeed to Liffey Street but could not have been one of the sprinkling-pots here referred to, as the inscription on it gives the date 1760, eleven years subsequent to the date of the manuscript."

Liffey Street Chapel was closed in 1826 when the Pro-Cathedral finally opened. It had been under construction for ten years. The chapel pulpit was sent to Mother McAuley whose Baggot Street house was being built. Though her father had been dead for over forty years, there were those who remembered that he did the woodwork in St. Mary's. The corniced altarpiece pillars, his work also, now frame the Blessed Virgin's statue at the Pro-Cathedral, for statue and pillars were transferred to the new St. Mary's.

2. The original letter, written October 23, 1867, to Mother Clare Moore at Bermondsey, is in the Bermondsey Convent of Mercy archives, now held at Lourdes Mount Convent of Mercy, Kent.

3. London MS.

4. Mother M. Clare Moore (London MS) gives the following account of Catherine's connection with Father Betagh:

> Being thrown so much among Protestants, she read assiduously the best controversial works and went often for instruction to the Very Reverend Father Betagh, whose learning and piety made everyone revere his words and who was also an able controversialist; hence, her visits to him caused some to think that she had been a Protestant.

5. In a letter written from Birr, January 21, 1841, to the mistress of novices at Baggot Street, Mother McAuley, referring to names, begins a sentence, "Finding I had Teresa in confirmation." In other words, she gives the impression that she learned her confirmation name through some source. The fact that she did not remember it implies that she was extremely young when confirmed.

6. St. *Michan* is pronounced Mĭsh'an.

7. Father Daniel Murray had previously met Mary Aikenhead in her native city, Cork. He again met her in 1808 doing social service work among the poor in Dublin, and he resolved to include her in his plan for an active congregation devoted to charity.

8. Nano Nagle had been pioneer in the effort to establish an active congregation in Ireland, only to have her congregation diverted to restrictions of the cloister after her death.

9. William Callaghan leased Coolock House and grounds, July 27, 1803, and bought "part of the Town and lands of Coolock containing 22 acres with all houses and buildings thereon," April 26, 1809. (Registry of Deeds Office, Dublin, reference 607-354-417041.)

CHAPTER VI

1. James McAuley sold the estate after Robert's death in 1840.

2. Sister Mary Raymund (Catherine) Byrn declares herself incompetent to speak with finality on the subject of Dr. William Macauley's Orange interests. His granddaughter, Sister Mary Catherine of Australia, without being directly interrogated, supplies among casual reminiscences on her father this positive evidence: "He was a very spoiled child as he was the youngest and his mother died when he was quite young. His father took him everywhere with him, even to the Loyal Orange Lodge, and he could repeat the Orange toast. The only words I remember are 'knee-deep in Popish blood.'" (Letter to the author, January 12, 1947.)

3. Dublin MS.

4. Private letter, Bermondsey Convent of Mercy records.

5. In a letter to her sister (Sister Mary Margaret Byrn, Bermondsey Convent of Mercy) Sister Mary Raymund wrote, October 23, 1867: "I used to feel indignant at the plainness of our beloved father's appearance and manners being censured by those who might with advantage have taken a lesson from him in refinement."

6. Data on Sister Mary Raymund (Catherine) Byrn are supplied through the courtesy of the superiors of the Dominican Convent, Drogheda, where Sister spent the greater part of her religious life. She died on December 19, 1869.

7. Dublin MS.

8. Mother M. Clare Moore's September 1, 1844 letter to her sister, Sister M. Clare Augustine Moore, at Baggot Street.

9. London MS.

10. After long negotiation the Dublin Sisters of Mercy have finally (1955) succeeded in purchasing Coolock House.

11. Derry MS.

12. Father Michael Bernard Keogh was appointed to Baldoyle in 1818 (Capuchin records, Dublin).

13. W. J. Fitzpatrick, *Irish Wits and Worthies* (Dublin: James Duffy, Sons, and Co., 1873), p. 189.

14. October 23, 1867 letter to Mother M. Clare Moore.

15. London MS.

CHAPTER VII

1. The Dublin MS says of him: "He, if not a pious, was undeniably a determined Protestant."

2. In recalling childhood memories to Teresa Byrn, Willie McAuley wrote on July 9, 1884: "I see Mr. Callaghan's sharp features."

3. "She had then no expectation of the large fortune that afterwards was hers, but her benefactor had once spoken of leaving her a thousand pounds, and she thought if she had that, or even a few hundred, she would hire a couple of rooms and work for and with her protégées. The idea haunted her very dreams. Night after night she would see herself in some very large place where a number of young women were employed as laundresses or at plain work, while she herself would be surrounded by a crowd of ragged children, whom she was washing and dressing very busily." (Derry MS)

4. "Rev. Mr. Nugent . . . with an ardent zeal devoted himself to the task of Mr. Callaghan's conversion, which he at last happily accomplished and received him into the Church the night before his death." (Sister M. Raymund Byrn, letter cited.)

5. Ronan, *An Apostle of Catholic Dublin,* p. 132: "The reconstructed stable-chapel of 1700 had done duty for 110 years."

6. "Dr. Murray gave his most cordial approbation and visited frequently. All was done under his direction from the time we entered the house, which was erected for the purpose of charity. Dr. Blake and Rev. Mr. Armstrong were chiefly concerned, received all the ideas I had formed and consulted for two years at least before the house was built." (Letter to Mother M. Elizabeth Moore, January 13, 1839.)

7. St. Mary's had been Archbishop Troy's mensal parish.

8. Referring to the Star of the Sea Church (1872), Bishop Donnelly says: "Application for a site was made to the landlord, the Honorable Sidney Herbert, and, with the latter's usual liberality, it was promptly granted. . . . He walled in property for schools and leased it to the parish priest and the Archbishop for a term of 150 years at a rent of *one shilling* per annum." (*A Short History of Some Dublin Parishes.*)

9. Dr. Armstrong was withdrawn from St. Mary's by Archbishop Murray himself at the death of Archbishop Troy. Archbishop Murray, Parish Priest at St. Andrew's from 1811 to 1823, was requested to retain his position by some whose reasons he could not easily disregard. He therefore applied to the Holy See for permission to make a mensal parish of St. Andrew's also, St. Mary's having been created such under Dr. Troy. The permission granted, Archbishop Murray established Father Armstrong as administrator through the following letter (Donnelly, *op. cit.,* Part VII [1910], p. 149) addressed to Father McDonogh, senior curate at St. Andrew's:

Dear Mr. McDonogh,

Several religious friends of mine on whose judgment I place much reliance strongly urged me to retain the parish of Townsend Street for reasons which

I could not but think of considerable weight. I stated these things to the Holy See, the answer from which has been favorable, and I am still to continue your Parish Priest. As I cannot, however, give the same personal attendance as formerly, I must endeavor to supply the deficiency.
I have given my collection and rooms to Mr. Armstrong who will in return give to the chapel that attendance which my other duties will no longer allow me to bestow. This will give to your society in the chapel house an addition which, I trust, you will find in many respects highly agreeable. Mr. Armstrong will prepare to take his place among you as speedily as possible, and I have no doubt but he will meet in Townsend Street with the same brotherly affection that he deservedly experienced in Liffey Street for so many years.

Always most truly yours,
D. Murray

Cumberland Street
28 July 1823

Father McDonogh, a Trinitarian, became a staunch supporter of Catherine McAuley and her associates. In fact, for a while, he was the only friend the Sisters of Mercy had at St. Andrew's chapel house.

10.

Presentation Convent
Galway, Eire
April 20, 1948

My dear Sister M. Bertrand,

Reverend Mother asked me to send you any information I know regarding Sister M. Lewis (Fanny Tighe).
It is a pleasure for me to do so as I happen to belong to the same parish she lived in, where her memory was revered by the older generation as she taught catechism in the parish church, Newcastle, when she was at home.
My father, on his first visit to me after my entrance, asked me to show him Miss Tighe's grave although he had only heard of her, as he was not born when she entered. It shows what an impression she made on the simple country people . . .
With very best wishes,

Yours sincerely in J. C.
Sister M. Bridget

Sister Frances Tighe, called in religion Mary Lewis, daughter of Thomas and Catherine Tighe, was born in the parish of Athenry and Newcastle, County Galway, in the Archdiocese of Tuam, was baptized and confirmed. She entered this Convent on the 3rd May, 1827, took the habit of this Congregation on the 6th of November 1827, being 29 years of age. She made her Profession on the 3rd day of November, 1829 in the Chapel of this Convent of the Presentation. . . . She died on Sunday, 7th May, 1876, being the Feast of the Patronage of St. Joseph, to whom she had always a special devotion. At the close of her long and wearisome illness of two years, she earnestly pleaded with St. Joseph to come for her on the above day, and at 5 a.m. she calmly expired just as the duties of the day commenced. R. I. P. (*Annals*—Presentation Convent, Galway.)
The above is all that is written in the *Annals* concerning her but as I lived with the nuns who knew her, I remember hearing them speak of her as a very holy, zealous nun who had a bright, happy disposition. Her patron in religion was St. Aloysius but, as the name was already taken, she got the other form of his name, spelled either *Lewis* or Louis.
Before her entrance into religion, a good part of her time was spent in Dublin where her aunt lived. It was then she became acquainted with your

holy Foundress who hoped she would remain with her and assist her in carrying out the good works she was planning, but Sister M. Lewis was anxious to enter a convent immediately and got to know the Presentation Sisters of Galway through her first cousin, Sister M. Peter Tighe, who had joined this community a few years previous. The convent was in its infancy then—only 12 years founded.

Sister M. Bridget

11. "The solicitation of some friends induced her to visit the Convent of the Sisters of Charity, Stanhope Street, it being supposed that their co-operation might be of use to her in directing the proposed institution. But to herself it was evident that this could not be, and the more information she acquired concerning the government and general management of the House of Refuge, the more she became convinced that the principles on which it was conducted were utterly incompatible with her design. The only consequence of these visits was therefore to confirm her in her resolution never to admit the interference of a non-resident committee and never to close the doors of the institution against anyone because she had experienced its protection before." (Derry MS, section headed "1824, 1825, 1826.")

12. Dublin MS.

13. The Derry manuscript is the most specific of the unpublished memoirs. It is patently the work of an efficient sister secretary to Mother Mary Anne (Anna Maria) Doyle, first of Catherine's associates in the Baggot Street project, or by someone close to her in the work there. Comparison with Mother Mary Anne's extant correspondence rules out its being her own, but she died at her last foundation, Derry, where the manuscript was preserved.

14. The Bermondsey community owns two lengthy letters written by the foundress' nephew, William Montgomery McAuley, as he signs himself: July 9, 1884, and September 15, 1885. In the first, addressed to Teresa Byrn, then Sister Mary Camillus of Baltimore, Md., he gives, with some reminiscences aimed at establishing his identity, an account of his wanderings, his settling in Australia, his marriage, and the difficulty he had had trying to re-establish connections with Ireland in the hope of laying claim to what remained of the family estate. The second, written also from Tomahawk Creek, Irrewillipe (Victoria, Australia), is addressed to Ann Byrn, Sister Mary Margaret of the Bermondsey community. It is patently a reply to her letter telling him of Sister M. Camillus' death. In this letter Willie gives further details of his experiences, other reminiscences of Baggot Street, and some facts about his family apparently in answer to questions from Sister Mary Margaret's letter to him. The first letter carries a note appended by Sister M. Camillus for her sister, Sister Mary Margaret.

15. "Grandfather McAuley (Willie) wrote his life while at our home (I was a child then) . . . . He lived with us for the eight years of his life after his wife died. . . .When he died, his daughter, Mrs. Emily Maude Yorke, took the manuscript. . . . She told me once that white ants got at the manuscript so she burnt it." (Excerpts from letters written to the author by Mrs. William McAuley O'Leary, Kundabung, N. S. W., January 13, 1946; April 20, 1947; November 6, 1949.)

16. Dr. James McAuley's daughter Emily married a Mr. Tanner, but Emily McAuley Tanner was younger than Willie and Teresa. Coolock House was sold when Willie and Teresa were seven years old.

CHAPTER VIII

1. "She was also much devoted to schools and while in the world visited them as much as she could." Private letter of Anna Maria Doyle (Mother Mary Anne), Dublin community archives.

2. Mrs. Fitzherbert.

3. Warburton, Whitelaw and Walsh, *History of Dublin,* pp. 847, 852-854 cited by Very Rev. Myles V. Ronan, *An Apostle of Catholic Dublin,* p. 35.

4. W. J. Fitzpatrick, *Life, Times and Correspondence of the Right Rev. Dr. Doyle* (Revised edition, M. H. Gill and Son, Dublin, 1880), p. 227.

5. "On account of her Protestant connexion she was supposed to be a Protestant and was initiated into their method of inducing Catholic children to attend under the idea that there would be no interference with their religion while at the same time the work of proselytism was slowly, silently but successfully carried on." (Derry MS)

6. "This lady (Mary Macauley) was far from participating in the disapprobation with which her husband and brother regarded the matter. She had indeed no precise idea of the nature of the benefits her excellent sister prepared to confer on the poor, yet she would frequently speak of the delight she hoped to experience in seeing the poor enjoying the comforts of that great house, but she did not live so long. Her health, which had long been precarious, now hopelessly declined." (Derry MS, "1827.")

7. Dr. James William Macauley, whose town house was at 58 Upper Leeson Street, died January 12, 1873. His will was proved the last day of the same month. (Public Record Office of Ireland.)

8. Sir George, who died in 1940, was the only son of Lieutenant George W. Macauley, one of Dr. James McAuley's nine children. In maturity Dr. James adopted the spelling of the family name used by his children. Nina Macauley Grimston, of Willingdon, Sussex, Sir George's only sister, has kindly supplied me with data on her father's family.

9. Father John McCormick was chaplain to the Carmelite nuns at Blackrock. He died in 1841, age 68 years. It is significant that Mary Macauley was reconciled to the Church shortly after mid-July. Undoubtedly Father McCormick had solicited the prayers of the Carmelite nuns whose patronal feast is July 16.

10. Kilmainham means literally "St. Maignend's Church," for a monastic church stood on the site in pre-Norman times. St. Maignan had been abbot of the monastery at Killmaignend (Kilmainham) in the seventh century. The Royal Hospital at Kilmainham (now occupied by the Civic Guards) was erected in 1680-1682 on the site of the Priory of Knights Hospitallers, which succeeded the Celtic Abbey. The Priory was suppressed by Henry VIII in 1541. Bishop Donnelly reminds us that a relic of the ancient priory survives integrally in the present building: " . . . at the time of the erection of the Royal Hospital (1680), the walls of the Priory Church were the only remains above the ground, and the mullions of the antique eastern window were so well preserved as to form the tracery of the existing chapel window, the only visible surviving relic of the Priory of the Knights Hospitallers." Donnelly, *A Short History of Some Dublin Parishes,* Part IX (1911), pp. 209-210.

11. On the subject of the foundress' own devotion to the Mother of God, Sister M. Vincent Hartnett later wrote:

> The devotion of our beloved foundress to the ever blessed Mother of God was most tender and filial and she looked on the privilege of having our Institute under her protection as one of the highest we could enjoy. All feasts of the Blessed Virgin she observed with great solemnity and holy joy; and she impressed the same upon the sisters and in fact promoted devotion to the holy Mother of God wherever she could. She always gave out to the community the novenas previous to the feasts of the Blessed Virgin and she solemnized with the utmost devotion that especially of Our Lady of Mercy. That solemnity, moreover, she arranged for an hour when the inmates of the House of Mercy could attend and, to excite devotion the more, she had the altar decorated and the devotions accompanied with music. The entire

month of September she devoted to special pious exercises. She said the Thirty Days' Prayer in behalf of the entire Institute. This custom has since been continued in all the Convents of Mercy. The feast of the Dolours of our Immaculate Mother was one of special veneration with her also. Compassionating and sharing in heart and affection the sorrows of the holy, sinless Mother of God, she sympathized deeply with what she had it not in her power to alleviate. She used to call September the month of the Blessed Virgin. The devotions of the month of May were not then generally practiced.

On every feast Reverend Mother was sure to note the virtue or mystery which the Church commemorated, drawing instruction from it for the sisters and holding up for imitation the virtues of her who, next to our Divine Lord, is the most perfect model of every virtue. She showed how our honour and love of her ought to emulate that which God Himself deigned to manifest towards her and that we ought to give proof of ours by imitating her and endeavouring to make all under our care imitate her likewise. We ought to make known to them her virtues so as to excite them to admire, love and follow her. Then she would remind the sisters that if all are bound to love and honour the holy Mother of God, how much more we who are her own chosen children, bearing her name and that of her sweetest attribute, Mercy! Reverend Mother never wearied extolling the Blessed Virgin and, though her words were very simple, they were so fervently and sweetly expressed, and her whole heart so spoke in them, that they animated all who heard them to a renewed zeal and devotion. (*The Life of Rev. Mother Catherine McAuley,* pp. 114, 115.)

CHAPTER IX

1. Charles Cavanagh was introduced to the charity by the first chaplain, the Reverend Daniel Burke, O.F.M.

2. Father L'Estrange and Father O'Hanlon were alternately Prior and Provincial of St. Teresa's, Clarendon Street. The former, O'Connell's friend and confessor, was responsible for the interest the O'Connells took in the Baggot Street charities.

Father Francis Joseph of St. Teresa (Francis) L'Estrange was born in Fleet Street, Dublin, in 1788, was professed in Granada in 1805, returned to Ireland in 1810, went to Rome in 1821, was Prior at St. Teresa's, Dublin, 1826-29; Provincial 1829-32; died at Cobh, County Cork, September 6, 1833, where he had gone for his health. He was appointed Provincial July 25, 1829, by letter from the Father General in Rome at the recommendation of his predecessor, Father Raymund O'Hanlon.

Father Raymund of the Virgin of Carmel (Redmond) O'Hanlon was born in 1789 at Kill, County Kildare, was Professed at Granada, Spain, January 2, 1807. The war with Spain returned him to Dublin before ordination. He was ordained by Archbishop Murray in December 1809 and stationed at St. Teresa's. He was made Prior of St. Teresa's in 1820, a position he retained till 1823. He was Provincial from 1826 to 1829; went to Rome for four months in March 1830; he became Prior at St. Teresa's again in 1832 and remained so for several terms till 1849, after which he was Provincial and Prior alternately till 1856. He died in 1864.

(Data from the Carmelite Monastery records at St. Teresa's, Clarendon St., Dublin, were supplied by the Very Reverend Michael Moylan, Casa Generalizia, Rome.)

3. September 13, 1844 letter from Mother M. Clare Moore to her sister.

CHAPTER X

1. During the imprisonment of Pope Pius VII by Napoleon, Monsignor Quarrantotti, Secretary of the College of Propaganda, planned to grant England the privilege of veto on appointment of English and Irish bishops. O'Connell supported the Irish bishops in their opposition, and a clerical committee set out for Rome to explain the Irish position.

2. Rev. William Meagher, *Commemorative Oration of the Most Rev. Daniel Murray with Historical and Biographical Notes* (Dublin: Gerald Bellew, 1853), pp. 8-12.

3. This is probably "Missie Rice" mentioned later in Catherine's correspondence. Unable to learn whether the child had ever been baptized, Catherine had the sacrament administered conditionally.

4. "The House of Mercy continued to be a weighty charge, as it always must be until some description of industrial occupation suited to the majority of the inmates can be procured. Many of the poor girls were able to do the needlework kindly and charitably sent but the greater number were not capable of doing it, and in the short time they continued in the house they had so many other things to learn that they could not become proficients. The average length of residence was about four months during which they should be instructed in the duties of religion and, in many cases, prepared for the sacraments, sometimes even first Communion, so that even some of those who could contribute to their support by needlework were not able to devote all their time to such occupation. In consequence, the sisters had to make great exertions among and through their friends to support so many claimants—generally sixty." Hartnett, *The Life of Rev. Mother Catherine McAuley,* p. 89.

5. "She began to suffer greatly from an apprehension that her charitable projects could never be realized on account of the expenses they would necessarily entail; but she was encouraged by the exhortations of the Rev. Mr. Armstrong who then suggested, among other and higher motives of consolation, that a good subscription for the purpose might be easily raised as the institution was situated in such a fashionable neighborhood.

"This trial afterwards frequently recurred, though at intervals, and she had need of all her fortitude to bear up against it. Yet, putting her trust in God, whose aid she continually implored by fervent prayer, she resolved to continue what she had begun and leave this issue to Him." (Derry MS)

6. Actually there was a similar institution under Protestant patronage next door. Opposition came first from Catholics who resented the combination of circumstances that had given this stranger an advantage over them. As the writer of the Derry MS avers, "It was a galling thing to many that one who had been born their inferior in rank and fortune should now occupy a more influential position than rank or wealth had procured for them."

7. The original letter signed by Archbishop Murray is in the Mercy archives at Carysfort Park. The term "House of Mercy" was corrected to read "House of Mary of Mercy."

8. *Letters of Mary Aikenhead* (Dublin: M. H. Gill and Son, 1914), p. 19.

9. Father Armstrong's picture may still be seen at the parent house in Dublin.

10. "In his last illness [he] was devotedly tended by Catherine McAuley until he closed his eyes in death." (Bishop Donnelly, *History of Dublin Parishes.*)

11. "Mr. Armstrong . . . said if we were a religious community it [the chaplaincy plan of 1837] could not be attempted and he was deeply afflicted on his deathbed that we were not so established." (Excerpt of a letter written from Cork by the foundress, October 3, 1837, to the Mother Assistant at the parent house.)

12. Quotation from a letter used by Father Meagher (cf. note 2 of this chap-

ter) in his appended notes to the published form of his month's mind sermon on Archbishop Murray (pp. 117-118). Though the signature has been omitted, internal evidence identifies the writer unmistakably as Sister Mary Raymund Byrn, O. P.

13. "The Very Reverend Dr. Armstrong was the great friend and advisor of our dear Foundress and had rendered her many services with the Archbishop who loved him as a most holy and zealous priest and esteemed him in a particular manner." (London MS)

The subject of Father Armstrong's advice is further amplified by Mother M. Clare Moore, writer of the London MS, in a letter to her sister, Sister M. Clare Augustine Moore, September 2, 1844: "He had been the greatest friend of Archbishop Murray and might reasonably expect His Grace's friendship for an undertaking in which he was so much concerned; yet his last advice . . . was not that she should confide in Dr. Murray but most emphatically again and again he repeated: 'Do not put your trust in any human being, but place all your confidence in God alone,' prophesying almost that all human aid would fail. She often told me this when oppressed by care."

CHAPTER XI

1. Dr. Armstrong bequeathed £50 to furnish a dormitory.

2. Rev. Francis N. Korth, S. J., in an article entitled "Secular Institutes" (*Review for Religious,* X [1951], 296-301) traces the rise of this type of religious organization and tells of the favorable recognition given it by Pope Pius XII through the Apostolic Constitution, *Provida Mater Ecclesia,* February 2, 1947. Clearly, Catherine McAuley was ahead of her time.

3. This is the first extant letter of Catherine McAuley.

4. Letter from Mother M. Clare Moore to her sister, August 23, 1844.

5. "On the twenty-second of June, 1828, Miss Frances Warde was associated to the pious labours of the institute, though rather as an amateur in good works than as one who meant to give up the world for the service of God's poor; for though she resided pretty constantly at Baggot Street, she did not assume the black dress and plain cap of the resident members but went out to drive and visit her friends till the following November." (Derry MS)

6. The Dublin MS adds *The Suffering of Christ.*

7. London MS.

8. The Carlow College lay-school records were opened to review by the courtesy of the present college authorities in 1946. The data herein given were culled from "judgment books" and bursar's lists of the period 1829-1836. The latter were in three sections under dates 1827-30; 1831-33; 1834-36. The McAuley boys do not appear in the next list, 1836-39. These records inadvertently disclose the influence that changed the spelling of the Macauley boys' surname.

9. The anecdote about Dr. Fitzgerald's displeasure over Willie McAuley's taking the name *Dominic* at Confirmation and of Dr. Fitzgerald's exclamatory remarks was supplied by Willie's daughter, Sister Mary Catherine McAuley of Kyneton, Victoria, Australia. Sister Mary Catherine also supplied her father's attitude toward Dr. and Mrs. James McAuley (letters to the author January 12, 1947, and October 26, 1947, respectively).

10. Mother Mary Anne Doyle, mentioning Dr. Macauley's death, writes of the boys: "They were received into the Church the year following by the Chaplain, Rev. D. Burke, in the Convent Chapel." (Private letter, Carysfort Park Convent archives.) Since she was in the House, her authority is not to be questioned. Mother M. Austin Carroll states that James and Robert were baptized in Carlow, William in the convent chapel.

CHAPTER XII

1. "That same day, November 22, the Archbishop gave permission for the visitation of the sick, which Miss McAuley requested at the suggestion of Miss Doyle." (Derry MS)

2. Mother M. Clare Moore's letter of August 28, 1844, gives this information on visitation of the sick before 1830: "We used to visit Sir P. Dunn's Hospital daily, or any time we liked; besides, the poor in their own houses." In the September 13, 1844, letter she says of the time after September 8, 1830: "We were left very disconsolate. We had certainly enough work to keep us from fretting, for besides school, which was more laborious under the old system, we had very many poor sick with Sir P. Dunn's Hospital, the Incurables' at Donnybrook and the Lying-in Hospital at the Coombe to attend."

3. The Derry MS gives the same details on dress: "The community then adopted an outdoor costume: for winter a coarse grey cloak with a hood, a black silk bonnet and muslin veil; in summer the cloak was replaced by a black rock-spun shawl."

4. Dublin MS.

CHAPTER XIII

1. "On Christmas day the first Mass was celebrated and a plentiful dinner of roast beef and plum pudding was provided for the children that attended the school." (Derry MS)

2. "The Reverend Mr. Kelly, who was P. P. of Townsend Street, kept us a year and half walking to Clarendon Street every day—poor women and children—after Mr. Armstrong's death." (Excerpt from Mother McAuley's letter from Cork to her Mother Assistant, October 3, 1837.)

3. Source material on the Reverend Matthias Kelly, administrator of St. Andrew's, 1826-1831, is from Bishop Donnelly's account of Dublin parishes. The personal references are from the Dublin and London MSS and from a letter of Mother M. Clare Moore to her sister at the parent house, August 23, 1844.

4. Certain titles for the clergy are more commonly used in Ireland and England than in the United States—e. g., *Dr., Canon, Dean.* A century ago in these countries a priest was frequently referred to as "Mr." or "the Reverend Mr.— ————," a relic of customs in Penal times.

5. Something of the love the Mother Foundress had for the Heart of Divine Mercy and the Virgin Mother's heart of perfect human compassion is reflected in this painting.

6. Mother M. Austin Carroll refers to the celebrant as the Rev. Mr. W. ————————. Father Kelly's curate (first rank) was the Reverend Patrick Woods, devoted to Father Kelly's interests and sympathetic with his opinions.

7. Mother M. Austin Carroll's account of the dedication sermon and ceremony is followed because Mother M. Austin's source was Frances Warde, who was present.

8. "The costume adopted for the resident members was a wide round dress of black valentia, confined at the waist, made in one from the throat to the ground, with full, wide sleeves; plain lace cap with black muslin lining, having a very high caul and an open quilling around the face." (Derry MS)

9. Of this Mother M. Vincent Hartnett says: "Before the Archbishop left the house he nominated Rev. Daniel Burke chaplain and directed that the chapel be opened to the public. Rev. Mr. Burke [he said] should commence his duty by celebrating Mass [there] on the following Sunday, the feast of Pentecost, which that year was the 7th of June." (*The Life of Rev. Mother Catherine McAuley,* p. 50.)

10. "On the Octave of the Ascension of Our Lord the chapel was dedicated by the Archbishop under the invocation of Our Lady of Mercy." (Derry MS)
11. Letter from Mother Mary Anne Doyle to Sister M. Clare Augustine Moore.

CHAPTER XIV

1. August 23, 1844 letter.
2. Fitzpatrick, *Irish Wits and Worthies,* p. 189.
3. "*The Following of Christ* was one of Miss McAuley's favorite books, also Blythe's *Paraphrase on the Seven Penitential Psalms;* her prayerbook was entitled *Devotions to the Sacred Heart of Jesus.*" (London MS) Her favorite chapters of the *Following of Christ* were the thirtieth of Book III, and the eighth of Book IV. *Devotions to the Sacred Heart,* translated by Rev. Joseph Joy Dean, has long since been out of print.
4. September 1, 1844 letter.
5. Margaret Dunne was sent to Dr. Blake by Miss O'Grady's uncle, Father McCormick.
6. The Stanhope Street Refuge originated as a lay charity. Secular who supported it invited the Sisters of Charity to cooperate, apparently with the understanding that the work would proceed under the policy and patronage of the committee of ladies already in charge.
7. "I was not in Baggot Street from June '29 to June '30, so that I know the occurrences of that year only from hearsay." (Mother M. Clare Moore's letter of August 28, 1844.)
8. Meagher, *Commemorative Oration of the Most Rev. Daniel Murray,* p. 6.
9. On an occasion when Dr. Murray had mixed punch for Dr. Troy, the latter remarked, "it is like yourself—too silky." (Fitzpatrick, *op. cit.,* p. 184.)
10. Meagher, *op. cit.,* pp. 117, 118.

CHAPTER XV

1. Data on the Reverend Daniel Burke, O. F. M., were supplied from Franciscan records at Killiney, Dublin, through the courtesy of Father Provincial, October 5, 1948.
2. The Derry MS gives an account of the part this clergyman took in the discussion the day the chapel was dedicated, of the letter here mentioned, and of "reverses" that followed.
3. Fitzpatrick in *Irish Wits and Worthies* quotes Dr. Reynolds approvingly on "the truly sanctified" Dr. Blake.
4. "This spring (1830) a school for young ladies was opened in the refectory, but it proved a signal failure and the very few pupils it ever contained dropped off within the year." (Derry MS)
5. Carolina Murphy, daughter of Dr. Robert Murphy and Elizabeth Wilmore, was born September 29, 1812, and baptized the same day by Rev. J. McEneiry. (Data from St. Mary's, Killarney, records.)
6. Annie Frances Delany (80 years old in 1950), a member of the Delany family, remembers Mary Delany's brother and younger sister who died in the late nineteenth century. The Delanys have excellent records covering a period of two hundred years. Their estate at Castle Durrow has been in the family for nearly two centuries. (Data secured through Rev. Joseph Clohosey, St. Kieran's College, Kilkenny, and Sister Mary Dympna of the Kilkenny Presentation Convent.)

7. "She bequeathed certain legacies for charitable purposes but most unaccountably forgot the institution of Mercy, so that the sisters reaped no temporal reward for this good work, which included in its performance the exercise of a great many virtues." (Derry MS)

CHAPTER XVI

1. September 13, 1844 letter.
2. September 13, 1844 letter.
3. "She loved to pray before the Most Holy Sacrament, and finding that in Carlow they said after the mid-day prayers one of the beautiful effusions of love at the end of the *Soul United to Jesus* she liked them so well that she began to use them herself. After a month, however, she ceased this devotion, and when I asked her why, said that if she added prayers herself some very devout successor would add more, till especially in poor convents, the Sisters would be incapable of the duties of the Institute and we should end like the Presentation nuns, after Miss Nagle's death, in being enclosed. Still she told me she always used these prayers herself and advised me to do the same." (Dublin MS)
4. Elizabeth Harley's father, John Harley, paymaster of the 47th Regiment, apparently married twice, for her brother John (Lieutenant of 47th Regiment) was killed in the battle of Vitoria (1813) at the age of 19. Another brother Robert, born December 13, 1829, served in Africa and in British Honduras. His mother had six brothers in service, one naval, five military, surname Gray. Robert advanced to Brigadier General and was knighted. He was governor of British Honduras when the Sisters of Mercy arrived to make a foundation in Belize. He retired in 1884 and died in South Kensington in 1892. (Military data from the Colonial Office Library, Downing Street.)
5. "They were professed in the habit of the Presentation nuns, which much resembles ours in all but coif and the smallness of the guimp, which is round and made of linen, double. The habit also is serge with broader pleats round the figure. After the ceremony, however, they assumed the coif, which it had been agreed should be worn by the Sisters of Mercy in future, the idea of which was borrowed from the Carmelite coif. They put on our usual black bonnets and cloaks and returned to the convent." (Derry MS)
6. September 13, 1844 letter.
7. Dublin MS.
8. Rev. H. C. Luynes was a Parisian of Irish parentage. He had been educated at the University of Paris and had studied law but decided to devote his life to religion. He entered the Theological Seminary of St. Sulpice in 1825 and was on his way to the American missions when he stopped in Dublin. He began his work on the American missions in Kentucky. After Bishop Flaget brought the Jesuits there, Father Luynes joined the Jesuits and later came to New York where he may be said to have spent the rest of his life, connected principally with St. Francis Xavier's Church and College. He arrived in New York the very year the Sisters of Mercy came from Baggot Street to establish a mission. Father Luynes lived for a short period in Brooklyn and in Troy and traveled through Mexico and Chile in 1849 to collect funds to finish the church and college. (*New York Herald*, Monday, January 21, 1878.)
9. "Easter week (1830) the annual bazaar was held in the Rotunda and was very productive though patronized chiefly by Protestants. . . . The usual bazaar at Easter was not held this year (1831)." (Derry MS)
10. "Four young persons named Catherine Hazlitt, Mary Davis, Eliza McMahon, and Hannah Fulham were admitted with the intention of becoming lay sisters. They were placed much on the same footing as those destined for choir nuns, ate at the same table and passed the time of recreation together. This, it

was soon found, would not answer, and as the two first though well conducted did not seem to have a true vocation they were otherwise provided for; Mary Davis was dismissed for some reprehensible levities." (*Ibid.*)

11. "Nor is it the mere form of words to say that she loved the meanest offices, for she exercised them in preference to all other, taking pleasure in appearing before seculars with her hands all black, the more so if she perceived that it made them consider her a menial to the community. She suffered with the utmost sweetness, patience, and resignation . . ." (Derry MS)

12. London MS.

CHAPTER XVII

1. George's Hill Presentation Convent records.

2. Since this memoir was written at Mother M. Austin Carroll's request with the purpose of using it as a source for her biography of Mother McAuley, it probably perished with other reference material. The Sisters of Mercy of the Union, through the foresight of Mother M. Carmelita Hartman, R. S. M., first Mother General, have the written testimony of an eyewitness that Mother M. Austin Carroll's trunk with all its contents was burned after her death. This document is in the community archives at the General Motherhouse. (Bethesda P. O., Washington, D. C.)

3. Private letter of Mother Mary Anne Doyle held by the parent community.

CHAPTER XVIII

1. "¿Adónde vas?" . . . she asked him on December 9. "Pues sábete, mi benjamin amado, que yo soy la siempre Virgen Santa Maria, Madre del Verdadero Dios; . . . en él mostraré y daré todo mi amor a tí, a todos los nacidos en estas tierras y a todos los amadores miós que me invoquen y en mí confien; porque soy vuestra piadosa Madre."

And on December 12 when he was trying to evade her:

"¿No estoy yo aquí que soy tu Madre? ¿No estás bajo mi sombra? ¿no soy yo tu salud? ¿No estas por ventura en mi regazo? ¿Que más has menester?"

José A. Romero, S. J., *Breve Historia de Las Apariciones y Culto de Nuestra Señora de Guádalupe* (Villa G. Madero, D. F., Basilica de Santa Maria de Guadalupe, 1945), pp. 7, 10.

2. In 1945 Pius XII "proclaimed Our Lady of Guadalupe patroness of America, with the title *Empress.*" (C. J. McNaspy, S. J., "Empress of America," *Review for Religious,* XIV [1955], 113.)

3. Most congregations of women devoted to active work had arisen in France to combat the evils of oppression there, to stem the tide against religion, and to reclaim those who had fallen away.

4. Notes at St. Maries of the Isle, Cork, on several of the early sisters seem to be the work of Frances Warde's sister who entered in 1833, went on the Cork foundation in 1837, and succeeded Mother M. Clare Moore as superior in 1839. These notes state that Brother Rice directed Mary Jones to Catherine McAuley.

5. The pattern for the Mercy coif was borrowed from the Carmelites according to Mother M. Clare Moore, but the manner of wearing it shows Mother M. Augustine's influence. Had Mother McAuley insisted on a black guimp, the resemblance to the Charity habit would have been more marked. Sisters of Mercy who have not seen Mother Catherine's own coifs (one preserved by the Dublin community and one by the Limerick Sisters of Mercy) would not recognize the description here given.

6. Mother M. Clare Moore (Bermondsey records).

7. Hartnett, *The Life of Rev. Mother Catherine McAuley,* pp. 138, 139.

8. Mother M. Augustine was trained to religious life at Bar Convent, York, by Mary Ward's sisters (Institute of Mary). In 1822 Archbishop Murray brought a foundation of the Institute of Mary to Dublin. In Ireland these sisters are called "the Loreto nuns."

9. "At nine unless there was a second Mass, a spiritual lecture was read to all the sisters assembled, according to their standing in religion, in noviceship and community room." (Derry MS)

10. In sending an horarium to Bishop Walsh of Birmingham (Nov. 6, 1840) the foundress appended this note.

11. Because of the long period of persecution in England and in Ireland few spiritual reading books for religious were available in English in the early nineteenth century. Translations were therefore made and transcribed by members of new congregations. Recalling the original reason for oral reading, Reverend Augustine Klaas, S. J., advocates a change. Cf. "Attend to Reading," *Review for Religious,* July 15, 1950 (College Press, St. Mary's College, St. Mary's, Kansas).

12. The novenas made in choir include one for the New Year and one before each of the following feasts: Purification, St. Patrick, St. Joseph, Annunciation, St. Catherine of Siena, Pentecost, Sacred Heart, Assumption, Nativity of Our Lady, Our Lady of Mercy, Guardian Angels, Presentation of the Blessed Virgin, Immaculate Conception and Christmas.

CHAPTER XIX

1. The parent community later reverted to this precedent, abandoning the traditional bridal gown and veil. Some other branches of the congregation have followed their example.

2. Hartnett, *The Life of Rev. Mother Catherine McAuley,* p. 74.

3. September 13, 1844 letter.

4. London MS.

5. August 26, 1845 letter.

6. Mother Catherine discarded the olive-colored outdoor cloak and adopted a black, hooded going-out cloak. The discarded cloaks were used indoors for protection against the early morning chill of an unheated chapel. Mother Catherine's chapel cloak, relic of the days of the Ladies of Mercy at Baggot Street, is preserved by the Limerick community.

7. August 26, 1845 letter.

8. Rev. Roland Burke Savage, *Catherine McAuley* (Dublin: M. H. Gill and Son, 1949), p. 150. Section 1 of Chapter 9 covers the subject of the 1832 cholera epidemic in Dublin.

9. Sister M. Clare Moore.

10. The first interments on the Carmelite register are listed "House of Mercy, Baggot Street." Others are abbreviated "O. M." or "O. Mercy," thus establishing the initials long in use among Sisters of Mercy.

CHAPTER XX

1. Hartnett, *The Life of Rev. Mother Catherine McAuley,* p. 90.

2. It is said that Anne Moore had been unable to meet the dowry required of another congregation. That contention seems to be supported by the fact that shortly after Mother Catherine accepted her on Dr. Blake's recommendation he turned over to the community £700 in Grand Canal stock recently bequeathed to him.

3. Father Gaffney later became a Jesuit.

4. Meagher, *Commemorative Oration,* p. 118.

5. Dublin MS.

6. Hartnett, *op. cit.*, pp. 92-93.
7. *Ibid.*, p. 93.
8. Cf. Chapter X.
9. Mother M. Clare Moore in the London MS.
10. *Ibid.*

CHAPTER XXI

1. Rev. Clement R. Orth, *Approbation of Religious Institutes* (Washington: Catholic University of America Press, 1931), pp. 132-133.
2. A few months before Catherine McAuley opened her girls' poor school on Baggot Street, Brother Rice had opened a poor school for boys on the north side of the city.
3. Translation of Italian documents from the archives of the Sacred College of Propaganda Fide has been made by the Very Reverend Monsignor T. G. Mulqueen, S. T. D., principal of Catholic Central High School, Troy, New York. Translation of Latin documents from the Sacred College has been made by Sisters M. Gonzaga and M. Berchmans, R.S.M., Latin department.
4. London MS.
5. "The Rotunda Gardens and Assembly Rooms . . . here concerts, masquerades, cardparties and balls were held, the entertainments given during the winter being described by Malton as 'the most elegant amusements of Dublin.' " Constantia Maxwell, *Dublin under the Georges,* p. 96.
6. Loreto Abbey, Rathfarnham, still has on record the name of little Kate McCann, admitted to the boarding school October 22, 1832. The fact that her name does not appear on the Children of Mary list indicates that she was resident a relatively short time. Notes at St. Maries of the Isle, Cork, reveal that the child died of whooping cough.
7. Donnelly, *A Short History of Some Dublin Parishes,* Part IV (1907), p. 161.
8. London MS.
9. Later Archbishop of Nova Scotia.
10. Some of these novices had the foresight to take notes on the foundress' instructions. One of them made a collection and prefaced it. This manuscript will be mentioned in its place.
11. Hartnett, *The Life of Rev. Mother Catherine McAuley,* pp. 116, 167-168.

CHAPTER XXII

1. "She lost a great part of her uncle's estate because of an informality in his will. She loved poverty and obscurity and would not face the publicity a lawsuit would entail. There is every reason to believe that she would have been successful in her claim." (Tullamore *Annals.*)
2. *Ibid.*
3. Hartnett, *The Life of Rev. Mother Catherine McAuley,* p. 106.
4. A roadway ran through one section of the ground floor!
5. Catherine Macauley was received on July 3, 1834, and professed on October 22, 1836.
6. London MS.
7. *Ibid.*
8. Hartnett, *op. cit.*, p. 108.
9. These instructions with other notes Sister M. Teresa collected before she left the motherhouse have been edited by the Albany Sisters of Mercy with the permission of Tullamore superiors. (*Retreat Instructions of Mother M. Catherine McAuley,* Westminster, Md.: Newman Press, 1952.)
10. Cf. Archbishop Murray's advice quoted in Chapter XIX.

CHAPTER XXIII

1. *Letters of Mary Aikenhead,* p. 66.
2. August 23, 1844 letter.
3. The Poor Clare community had disbanded after the death of their Prioress, December 19, 1830, and the Presentation Convent of Sexton Street did not open till May 8, 1837 (Limerick Presentation Convent *Annals*).
4. London MS.
5. *Ibid.*

CHAPTER XXIV

1. Hartnett, *The Life of Rev. Mother Catherine McAuley,* p. 95. (Sister M. Vincent Hartnett entered four days before the death of Sister Veronica Corrigan.)
2. Sister M. Teresa White's younger sister (in religion, Sister M. de Sales) became first superior of the Liverpool convent. Copies of verses hitherto uncovered lay among other records there.
3. "Mother"—the sister assigned to direct a newly arrived postulant in minor matters of procedure.
4. Grace Trenor, the novice Sister M. Josephine.
5. Sister Mary Agnes Greene went on the Arkansas mission in 1850 and later joined the New Orleans community, where she died December 7, 1903.
6. Twilight arrives late and merges slowly with a pale night at this time of year in Ireland.
7. Cf. Bishop Donnelly's estimation of Canon Sheridan, quoted in Chapter XXI.
8. Mention of Sister M. Teresa White brings up the circumstance that there were two sisters by that name, Sister M. Teresa of Jesus, professed in 1835, and Sister M. Teresa White, professed in 1837. The former, born in Carlow, had a sister in the community, Sister M. de Sales White, professed in 1839. The second Sister M. Teresa White remained in the congregation only thirteen years.
9. "We did at first wear shawls in summer, for our trains were very short. Before we got the religious habit we always wore them in summer, and in winter grey cloaks bound with black, then the olive cloth. Our sleeves too were very narrow, but just before the cholera we began to wear black stuff cloaks with hoods. I was much more than a year professed when we got the merino cloaks lined, without hoods, and fastened up the front, for summer, and then the cloth cloaks were made in the same way. A fresh alteration—trifling—was made when we were going to Cork. I remember Dr. Blake objected to our wearing the coif in the streets and thought a little English cap would look very neat, but this Reverend Mother would not yield to." (Mother M. Clare Moore, August 25, 1846 letter.)
10. The Irish Sisters of Charity came to Cork in 1826. Of their work Mother Catherine wrote to Mother Angela in Charleville: "The Sisters of Charity in Cork have been but five in number and a lay sister for ten years. It is wonderful all they do and they are not all in good health . . ."
11. Hartnett, *op. cit.,* p. 95.
12. Willie's daughter, Sister Mary Catherine McAuley, says that her father left Ireland after his sister Catherine's death, and he himself in a letter to his cousin Sister M. Camillus Byrn (cf. Chapter XI) recalls the room in which Sister Anne Agnes died. Teresa Byrn was evidently present also.
13. The October 4, 1837, letter is preserved in part with Bermondsey papers.
14. In the collection of the foundress' counsels, published under the title *Familiar Instructions of Mother McAuley,* Mother Catherine refers to forty spiritual authorities, nearly all of them beatified or canonized. The greatest num-

ber of references are to St. Francis de Sales. Next in recognition are the Carmelite mystics St. Teresa and St. Mary Magdalene de Pazzi, with St. Paul and St. Ignatius receiving about equal notice in third place.

15. Hartnett, *op. cit.,* p. 103.

16. July 24, 1841 letter.

17. On the foundress' first return from Cork in July she had fallen down a flight of stairs at the motherhouse. (Cf. July 27, 1837 letter to Sister M. Elizabeth Moore at Kingstown.) She was close to sixty years of age and probably suffered from impaired vision.

CHAPTER XXV

1. December 19, 1837, Archiepiscopal archives, Dublin.

2. Sister M. Vincent Hartnett.

3. Hartnett, *The Life of Rev. Mother Catherine McAuley,* pp. 138, 139.

4. Sister Mary Catherine McAuley writes of Mother Catherine's youngest ward: "Dad . . . was, on the whole, a very quiet man, an inveterate reader and a hard worker. . . . For the thirty years that I knew him well he was a total abstainer and went to daily Mass, even serving the priest when there was no altar boy. . . . He looked so reverent and venerable." (Personal letter to the author, October, 1947.)

5. Sarah Warde, Frances Warde's elder sister, entered in 1833 and remained at the motherhouse until taken on the Cork foundation in 1837. She remembered Willie McAuley well. Given the name Sister Mary Joseph at reception, she was commonly called Sister Mary Josephine after she went to Cork.

6. Father Maher of Carlow used to say Mass at the convent in Dublin when in town. He had been in Dublin the previous week. Called back suddenly to Carlow, he received a humorous letter from the foundress on the money that might be due him for his services if anyone could figure out the financial regulations. Since Father Maher's services were always gratis, only the philosophy underlying the message should be taken seriously. "You will excuse me, I am sure," the letter ran, "for taking this little advantage, for you know that although I should be simple as a dove I must also be prudent as a serpent, and since very little good can be accomplished or evil avoided without money, we must look after it in small as well as in great matters."

7. Quotation from a notebook of sayings and sentiments of the foundress, St. Maries of the Isle, Cork (*Maries,* old genitive correctly written without an apostrophe; pronounced *Mary's*).

8. "Mother Francis Warde, a true apostle of the Order of Mercy, has just begun for the fourth time all the toil and labor attending the establishment of a Convent of Mercy; you are aware, I suppose, that she was not in office in Pittsburgh for better than a year. . . . Will you believe it? I did not know Mother Francis when I first saw her. She is greatly changed in appearance . . . quiet and subdued, indeed almost as quiet as yourself. Upon my remarking it to her, she said that it was time for her now to look old and careworn, her charge in Pittsburgh had been so heavy and accompanied by many trials." (Letter of Sister M. Camillus Byrn from Houston Street Convent of Mercy, New York, to Mother Mary Anne Doyle, Easter 1851—Derry Mercy archives.)

9. This postulant had been in delicate health. Mother Catherine had tried to dissuade her from entering but admitted her at the Bishop's request. She is buried on the Presentation Convent grounds.

10. Mrs. Verschoyle was the Catholic wife of one of Lord Fitzwilliam's agents. When widowed, she carried on her husband's work with Lord Fitzwilliam's tenants and did a great deal of charity for the Catholic poor.

11. The custom of inviting a noted preacher to a particular church and taking up a collection in behalf of some charity had been for years favored by both Catholic and Protestant authorities. The amount collected on these occasions often ran into hundreds of pounds.

12. June 16, 1838 letter.

13. August 23, 1838 letter.

14. In 1883 it was re-edited from New Orleans by Mother M. Teresa Austin Carroll and was published in New York under the authorship of Catherine McAuley. The only known copy extant is in the archives of the Sisters of Mercy of the Union, General Motherhouse, Washington, D. C.

15. From the designation in the Apostolic Brief, *"Fratres Monachi,"* Brother Rice's followers were commonly referred to as "monks." Brother Michael Reardon (spelled *Riordan* in Cork community records) is not to be confused with Brother Austin Reardon, through whom Bishop Murphy established the Presentation Brothers.

16. The form of agreement between the parent house and the Bishop of a diocese covers eight essentials.

Agreement

The Sisters of Mercy who compose this foundation and who are sent out from the parenthouse, ————, leave that diocese to place themselves under the protection of the Right Reverend ————, Bishop of ————, subject to the following conditions:

first, that the Right Reverend Prelate, as soon as they have placed themselves under his jurisdiction, become the guardian of their rule, constitutions and customs, as at present existing, and by his canonical authority give force and vigor to their observance;

second, that the Right Reverend Prelate shall not introduce new practices of devotion or charity, however excellent in themselves, or abolish any of those already established, as experience has amply demonstrated how admirably they are adapted to the attainment of the sublime end of this holy Institute, the sanctification of the members, and the spiritual and temporal advantage of their fellow creatures;

third, that the Right Reverend Prelate shall provide the sisters with a house suitable for the purposes of a convent so that the observances imposed by their rule may be practiced with decorum and attended to with that order and exactness which the sound of the bell insures in all the houses of the congregation;

fourth, that the Right Reverend Prelate shall by the appointment of a chaplain secure to the sisters daily Mass in the convent or nearest church;

fifth, that the Right Reverend Prelate secure the sisters a moderate revenue such as will maintain them in that simple mode of living which as religious suffices for them;

sixth, that in the admission or dismissal of subjects the sisters be allowed the exercise of that liberty to which they are entitled by the rule, constitutions and customs of the congregation;

seventh, that besides the ordinary confessor the Right Reverend Prelate will appoint an extraordinary director to whom the guidance of the sisters in the spiritual life shall be confided but that neither of them shall be authorized to interfere with the external observances, customs or duties of the community;

eighth, should these conditions be agreed to, the sisters consent to leave the convent of ———— and establish themselves in the Diocese of ———— and to promise on their own part and on that of their successors to persevere with fidelity in the duties of their holy vocation and in obedience to their ecclesiastical superior, the present Bishop of ———— and those who shall succeed him in that See.

NOTES

CHAPTER XXVI

1. "We left Cork on the twelfth intending to stay in Charleville and go to Limerick on the Exaltation of the Holy Cross, but I found I could be more useful there than perhaps I have ever been. There was danger of all breaking up and my heart felt sorrowful when I thought of the poor being deprived of the comfort which God seemed to intend for them. I made every effort and praised be God, all came round. The first stone of a nice convent was laid on our dear festival, the 24th, and leaving all in joy and happiness, we proceeded to our present abode on the same favorite day." (Letter from Limerick, October 12, 1838, to Sister M. Teresa White at Kingstown.)

2. Seven bishops, an archbishop, the Prince of Thomond himself, and eminent Irishmen of the Abbey period were buried here in the early centuries of the Abbey church. (Rev. M. H. McInerny, O. P., *History of the Irish Dominicans*, pp. 502-506.) Of the marked graves, the Poor Clare Prioress and three poor Clare nuns were interred in the early nineteenth century. Unclaimed bodies of victims of the 1832 cholera epidemic lie buried between the walk and the convent wall.

3. Rev. John Begley, *Diocese of Limerick, Ancient and Medieval,* pp. 377-378.

4. *O Heyne's Irish Dominicans,* edited by Rev. Ambrose Coleman, O. P., pp. 52-53.

5. May 1833 to April 7, 1836. (Galway Presentation Convent *Annals.*)

6. This door was permanently closed and inscribed in 1879. A street cut through to the west side of the grounds made possible a more satisfactory entrance.

7. The weeping ash is gone. In its place stands the gravestone of Mother M. Elizabeth Moore, the sister Mother Catherine brought with her to be superior of the Limerick Convent of Mercy.

8. The Flemish oak statue of Our Lady of Limerick is a representation of Our Lady of the Rosary dating from the Dominican Abbey period. Its history is given in an article by the archeologist, Rev. Michael Moloney, *Religious Houses in Medieval Limerick,* p. 25 of the centenary booklet (Convent of Mercy, 1838-1938).

A legend credits an apparition of Our Lady to seventeenth century Limerick. Part of the old city wall still stands on convent grounds. The passage of the Mother of God from the Cathedral (St. Mary's, now Protestant) to the Dominican Church, thence to St. Francis outside the walls, accompanied by St. Dominic, St. Francis, and five other celestial beings, is given no interpretation. Two separate accounts also exist of a mysterious light that passed over the city during the Cromwellian siege, one account from within the walls, one by a Cromwellian diarist in the enemy camp. The same date, July 13, 1651, is attached to each. (Rev. Dominic O'Daly, O. P., *History of the Geraldines,* edited by Rev. C. P. Meehan, pp. 52-53.)

9. The Limerick community not only carries on the usual works of the congregation, but they have supplemented their works of mercy to include the training of subjects for Mercy missions in Africa. The flourishing charities at St. Mary's well support the foundress' judgment of what would eventuate, "if God would grant His blessing."

10. Hartnett, *The Life of Rev. Mother Catherine McAuley*, p. 167.

CHAPTER XXVII

1. Carty, *Classbook of Irish History,* p. 145.

2. The Waterford election.

3. "It promised the Bishops in England full freedom from that outside interference they had found so paralyzing in attempting to develop their Districts."

Denis Gwynn, *Father Luigi Gentili* (Dublin: Clonmore and Reynolds, 1951), p. 71.

4. "Going into Catholic chapels what did I see? . . . artificial flowers under glass shades . . . brackets painted with sham shadows supporting nothing; and vestments who can describe? In the music gallery soprano and contralto soloists publicly emulating each other, lady vergers in feathers collecting the offertories. . . . Even Bishop Milner's own chapel, he the Catholic pioneer of the revival, not exempt." Denis Gwynn, *Lord Shrewsbury, Pugin and the Catholic Revival* (London: Hollis and Carter, 1946; Westminster, Maryland: The Newman Press, 1946), p. 19.

"Administer baptism out of an old physick phial; reserve the Blessed Sacrament in *dirty cupboard;* say Mass in vestment made out of an old gown; burn gas on the altar; have everything as *mean,* as pitiful, as shabby as you please; hire Protestant performers to sing; *leave out every ceremony in the ritual . . .*" (*Ibid.*, p. 56.)

5. "The west gateway was standing in 1777, and the last remaining portions of the abbey were demolished in 1805—namely, the north gate and adjoining buildings." Rev. L. J. Bourdelot, *The Story of the Catholic Church in Bermondsey* (London: Burns, Oates and Washbourne, Ltd., 1923), p. 23.

"Charles Knight in his *Walks around London* writes: 'It is a curious circumstance that within forty years after what remained of the magnificent Abbey of Bermondsey had been swept away a new conventual establishment rose up . . . in a large and picturesque pile with its stately church, fitted in every way for the residence and accommodation of thirty or forty—the convent of the Sisters of Mercy.' " (*Ibid.*, pp. 24-25.)

6. The Agnews had held an English title through four centuries.

7. Mary O'Connor received the habit from Mother McAuley December 12, 1839, and died November 1, 1840, of malignant typhus contracted from nursing the sick poor.

CHAPTER XXVIII

1. Father Maher's nephew, brother to Father Paul Cullen, then in Rome, later Cardinal Archbishop of Dublin.

2. I heard Mass in this oratory on July 29, 1946.

3. This building is now the Primary School, the present chapel a reconstruction of the original school.

4. On the petition for confirmation of the rule the superior of Cork Convent of Mercy and the superior of St. Mary's, Naas, both signed themselves Sister Mary Joseph with surname. Yet both are commonly referred to under the feminine form of the name, *Sister Mary Josephine*.

5. Sacred College of Propaganda Archives.

6. In a letter to Mother M. Angela Dunne, January 20, 1841, Mother Catherine refers to an endorsement from Bishop Cantwell also. This letter is not at the Sacred College of Propaganda. Bishop Cantwell had been in Rome from April to October and may have sent his letter through another channel.

7. Jane Latham (Sister Mary Xaveria) had been a member of a French community in Gravelines for a number of years. She brought with her Susan Weller who became Sister Mary Vincent at this reception. Both were dismissed the following year. The former later affiliated with Miss Agnew when she attempted to found a community. By singular coincidence Jane Latham was buried on the convent grounds at Maryvale. Old Oscott became a Convent of Mercy on November 11, 1851, after Newman and the Oratorians vacated.

8. Sister Teresa Boyce and a convert, Sister Joseph Hawkins, outlived the professed sisters, Sister Mary de Sales Eyre and Sister Mary Ursula O'Connor. Sister

Joseph's mother, present on this occasion, thought she saw an aura of light above her child's head. She was so much impressed by the experience that she entered the Church.

9. The Eyres and Cliffords were related.

10. In a letter written December 26 to Mother M. Angela Dunne of Charleville Mother Catherine says: "Mrs. Agnew is quite an accomplished person of very dignified appearance and benevolent mind; is half Catholic, yet I fear she will let the time pass without doing what is essential. . . . She is fondly attached to our Religious Sister and says she had from infancy such a noble, candid disposition, so perfectly disinterested and so unquestionably sincere that she never could continue to oppose her. Yet she regrets very much that she would not wait for this *fancied* change into the Catholic Church. Her fixed home is Brighton but she came to stay in London a few weeks in order to see her daughter frequently. At first she came privately but seeing we were more respectable than she expected came ever after in her own carriage to the public entrance."

11. At her special request the sisters were to attend the Marchioness of Wellesley during her last illness.

12. In the letter to Mother M. Angela Dunne Mother Catherine says of Sister M. de Sales: "Lady Barbara's example will be extremely useful. She has commenced in the most edifying manner, a model of humility and conformity."

13. Another of Mother Catherine's letters quoted on page 159 of Sister M. Vincent Hartnett's memoir amplifies this account: "You may be sure the poor habit makers had a busy time. Worldly dress had also to be prepared and net caps, bibs, and tippets for two hundred poor girls of the schools who were to attend the ceremony."

14. Lord Augustus was eighth of nine children born to William IV and the actress Dora Bland. At the death of William IV in 1837 his niece Victoria came to the throne.

15. Letter to Mother M. Teresa Austin Carroll, *Leaves from the Annals of the Sisters of Mercy* (New York: The Catholic Publication Society, 1883), II, 58.

CHAPTER XXIX

1. Robert McAuley died during the first week of January, 1840, and was interred in Glasnevin cemetery on the feast of Epiphany.

2. Father O'Hanlon recognized immediately the seriousness of Mother Catherine's illness, ordered her to bed, and insisted that a physician be called. The doctor confirmed the Carmelite Prior's judgment.

3. Father Paul Cullen, future cardinal.

4. This is one of the letters from the sheaf of material recently added to Birmingham convent records through the courtesy of the Hardman family.

5. Dublin MS.

6. March 14, 1840.

7. Father Matthew and a Quaker companion established the Total Abstinence Society as a measure against conditions among the poor. Catholics and Protestants alike supported the movement, which spread to England and the United States. Salem, Massachusetts, has a statue of Father Matthew commemorating his visit there in 1849. (William J. Gurney, "Temperance Movement Instituted by Irish Priest Almost 100 Years before Alcoholics Anonymous," Boston *Pilot,* July 26, 1952.)

8. St. Joseph's Convent of Mercy, Tullamore.

9. Hartnett, *The Life of Rev. Mother Catherine McAuley*, p. 121.

10. Helen Landreth, *Dear Dark Head* (New York: Whittlesey House, 1936), p. 174.

11. The building which then housed the Carmelites later became a Convent of Mercy. A new primary school, staffed by Mother Catherine's spiritual daughters, now occupies the site.

12. Mother Catherine wrote a rhymed letter about the journey, the only extant first-hand record. The Liverpool community possesses the entire sixteen stanzas, three of which follow:

"Stopped at Mount Carmel on the way
And passed a most delightful day.
  Dear, simple nuns!
Had lamb and salad for our dinner—
Far, far too good for any sinner,
  At tea hot buns.

Got use of the superior's cell
And slept all night extremely well
  On my soft pillow.
When lying down on my nice bed
I thought how very soon this head
  Must wear the willow.

Next morning we had Mass in choir
And, to our very heart's desire
  Our own dear Father.
Then we had breakfast warm and neat,
Both tea and coffee, eggs and meat.
  Whiche'er we'd rather."

13. The cathedral now occupies this site on Lombard Street.

14. The Most Reverend P. Gavino Secchi-Murro, Sacred College of Propaganda Fide, March 3, 1840.

15. June 30, 1840 letter to Mother M. Francis Warde.

16. There is no doubt that Father Daly could effect this impediment to her leaving, for he was chairman of Town Commissioners.

17. This second paragraph is from the July 30, 1840 letter to Carlow.

18. June 8, 1840 letter to Mother M. Francis Warde.

19. Elizabeth Bowen gives a vivid impression of the Shelbourne's character in her book, *The Shelbourne* (London: George Harrap and Co., 1951). Thackeray wrote part of his *Irish Sketch Book* there in the early 1840's (pp. 13, 14); George Moore used it for a setting for one of his novels toward the end of the century (pp. 109-111, 119); Yeats later sat in its "majestic drawing room" and read his poems to his friends (p. 192); and, most important of all, the new Irish Constitution was drafted in the "lofty first-floor sitting room, No. 112," with its outlook on the Green (p. 178).

20. These young ladies were professed just in time to assume classes for the converts who poured into the Church through Bishop Wiseman's influence. Men who were timid about approaching the other nuns flocked to quiet, reserved Sister Mary Xavier Wood. The sisters, who were all in their early twenties, began to question the propriety of their conducting convert classes for men. Sister Mary Xavier took her problem to the little Italian Passionist, then giving a retreat at Birmingham convent. At the next conference Father Dominic began: "My sisters, some of you have doubts about the propriety of instructing men. Oh, instruct da poor men, my sisters; instruct da poor men! If da community were young and handsome, it might be different, but for *you*—oh! for *you* der is no danger. You are all too ugly far."

NOTES

CHAPTER XXX

1. Father O'Brien had been asked to go to Halifax to inaugurate a college for boys. He became the first president of what today is St. Mary's University. St. Mary's has been staffed by Jesuits since 1940.

2. It is interesting to learn from Bishop Fleming's own correspondence that he brought the Sisters of Mercy to Newfoundland, first American foundation, expressly to conduct a private school for girls of "the more wealthy and comfortable classes." Mother McAuley not only sanctioned such schools in Ireland but had taught in the Carlow pension school while visiting there. Archbishop Howley quotes Dr. Fleming: "I sent . . . under the care of the sainted foundress, the late Mother McAuley, a young lady . . . that she should return to me after her profession, together with such other ladies as should be inspired to accompany her, to found a Convent of Mercy at St. John's and open a day-school for such as could pay for their education, a school where children may be taught the elegant and fashionable accomplishments of the day and at the same time have their young minds properly imbued with the principles of religion." Very Rev. M. F. Howley, *Ecclesiastical History of Newfoundland* (Boston: Doyle and Whittle, 1888), p. 370.

3. The Servite Order, dedicated to Our Lady, was founded in Florence, Italy, in 1233. Its members follow the Rule of St. Augustine in a partly active, partly contemplative community life.

4. It is noteworthy that a movement to remedy the defect has recently gained widespread attention in the congregation.

5. "Little Miss Maher" finally entered in Kinsale (1845) and went on the Ohio foundation as superior in 1858. There she did distinguished service by stabilizing and preserving the community through unusual and prolonged trials.

6. Hartnett, *The Life of Rev. Mother Catherine McAuley*, p. 161.

7. By a curious re-arrangement, the scene of the first Galway Mercy reception is now part of the present convent. When the Pro-Cathedral was erected on the site of the first Convent of Mercy on Lombard Street, the sisters were given the church and rectory for chapel and convent. The convent has been extended on both sides of the church with rooms connecting the various buildings in labyrinthine fashion. The church Mother Catherine mentions in this letter is today the convent chapel.

8. The foundress left Sister Teresa Mary temporarily in Limerick, "almost native air." She returned to Baggot Street to accompany Mother Catherine and the founding party to Birr. After the foundress' death she went again to Limerick convent and from there retired to secular life.

9. For the discovery of this letter in the Sacred College of Propaganda archives the congregation is indebted to the historian, Brother J. D. Fitzpatrick of the Christian Brothers of Ireland.

10. The horarium and notes in the foundress' handwriting run:

5/2 [i. e., 5:30] Rise
6 Assemble in choir—*Angelus, Little Hours, Meditation*
7 Make up cells, etc.
7/2 Mass
8/4 Breakfast
9 Lecture
9/2 Prepare for school, visitation of sick, or instruction of adults
10 These duties entered upon
11 3/4 Particular examen, visit to the Blessed Sacrament
12 *Angelus* and Acts of Faith, Hope and Charity, Litany of Jesus
4 Dinner
5 *Vespers,* Litany of the Blessed Virgin
5/2 Lecture

6 Angelus, Matins and Lauds, Litany for happy death
6 3/4 Supper
7 Recreation
9 Examen, Litany of Saints, morning meditation prepared
10 All in bed

Sisters engaged in the visitation of the sick are exempt from any choir duty from 10 till 4 but all in choir at Office and all attend lectures. The rosary is said by obligation but no time marked. It is often said going on the visitation.

11. The classroom in which Mother Catherine taught is today the community room.

12. With Mother Catherine's endorsement Mother M. Francis took Sister M. Teresa Kelly as superior for Wexford and for the foundation Sisters M. Gertrude Kinsella, Aloysius Redmond of Wexford, and two lay sisters. Sister M. Cecilia Maher was Mother Francis' traveling companion.

13. Mr. Richard Devereux was present at St. Michael's Convent of Mercy, Wexford, for the Golden Jubilee celebration in 1881. Three other persons who had known Mother McAuley personally were also present: Father Roche, Father Lacy and Dr. Furlong.

14. St. Michael became the patron of the Wexford convent when the sisters moved to Summer Hill, September 29, 1842.

15. Consequently Birr convent was called St. John's.

16. Westport was founded from Carlow after Mother McAuley's death.

17. Letter to Mother Mary Anne Doyle, July 24, 1841.

CHAPTER XXXI

1. Boreen: mountain road.

2. Bryan MacMahon, "The Cat and the Cornfield," *The Sign,* XXXIII (1953), 22-26.

3. This and the preceding sentence are introduced from later letters.

4. This does not imply that Dr. Murray stood alone in his attitude, but that as Archbishop of Dublin his endorsement exerted wide influence.

5. The Cam Cor (literally "Crooked Weir") meets the Brosna which flows into the Shannon.

6. "The two ladies who accompanied Miss Creedon to found the convent were Miss Lynch (Sister Mary Rose) and Miss Freyne (Sister Mary Ursula). These latter returned to Ireland in November, 1843, leaving the sole charge of the institution on the shoulders of Sister M. Francis. [The author's footnote tells that Miss Lynch later retired from the Order and settled in Toulouse, France, whereas Sister Mary Ursula went on the Australian missions and died "full of merits and good works."] For nine months, during a period of great trial, did she alone maintain the existence of the Order when, owing to some untoward circumstances, the Bishop was all the time undecided as to whether the convent should be preserved or suppressed. The indomitable perseverance of Miss Creedon triumphed. Day after day, week after week, month after month, she went regularly through all the routine of convent discipline—rang herself to prayer, to meditation, to refectory, to choir; performed by herself the Office, the spiritual lecture, the visit; attended the sick, taught the school—in a word, continued every practice just as if there were a whole community under her charge." Howley, *Ecclesiastical History of Newfoundland,* p. 374.

7. A picture of this church, in which Mother Catherine made her last public renovation of vows, appears among the illustrations. The cornerstone had been laid on August 1, 1817, and the church completed on August 1, 1824.

8. Hartnett, *The Life of Rev. Mother Catherine McAuley*, pp. 117-118.

9. Mother M. Anastasia Becket became mother assistant in Birr convent

shortly after her profession in 1844 and remained in that office until she succeeded Rev. Mother M. Vincent Egan in 1860. Mother Anastasia died on April 9, 1905. Her brother's son, a Protestant minister in America, the Reverend Percival Becket, was the only other member of her family who became a Catholic.

10. This last reference is taken from Mother Catherine's February 13 letter to the Reverend Mother in Birr.

11. Birr convent has a piece of the Honorable George Herbert Spencer's Salvation Army sash.

12. Father Spencer himself was approaching a spiritual transition. Before the end of the decade he had become a Passionist.

13. Father Spencer remained Mother M. Anastasia Becket's lifelong friend. Years later, Cardinal Newman himself closed a little known but remarkably characteristic letter to her with the statement: "I shall be much pleased at anything you are kind enough to tell me about Father Spencer." (Matthew Russell, "A Batch of Letters," *The Irish Ecclesiastical Record,* No. 356 [August, 1897], 98,99.) Father Spencer made his first visit to Birr to preach at Sister's reception. He stayed several days. A Mr. Bennett of Thomastown, who had sons at Oscott, claimed Father as his guest and the Bennett family, father, mother and seven boys, became devoted friends of Father Spencer's protégée thereafter. Three of the seven later became priests for the English mission (Liverpool diocese). One of them declared that his inspiration came at Mary Ann Becket's reception. At any rate, two of them arrived in the family drawing room after dinner dressed as nuns, to the amusement of the family and the entertainment of their guest. The historic crucifix in the cloister of the new convent, built under Mother Anastasia's direction, came to the community through Father Spencer's connection with the Passionists; for Father Vincent Grotti, who succeeded Father Dominic Barberi in the office of Provincial in England, gave the crucifix to the convent as a relic of St. Paul of the Cross who had used it on missions. It was the handwork of a Passionist lay brother; the head of the corpus has hair and the corpus itself is a moving representation of the torn Body of Christ.
Mother M. Anastasia Becket's influence, moreover, brought that astounding personage Dr. Gentili of the Order of Charity to give the first preached retreat the Birr community enjoyed. As Luigi Gentili, a brilliant young Italian lawyer, he had achieved every worldly end he set himself even to securing a title. He suffered the first thwart of his career through contact with the English Catholics in Rome. Humbled by the erratic Benedictine Bishop Baines, Vicar Apostolic of the Western District, Gentili turned to the Institute of Charity, then recently founded by Father Rosmini. As a member of the Order of Charity Father Gentlli became a prominent figure in the Catholic renaissance in England. On the occasion of the retreat Father Gentili went over the grounds and en couraged Mother Anastasia to proceed with plans Pugin had made for the proposed new convent. She had hesitated to adopt them because of the expense involved in so ambitious an undertaking. She decided, however, to act on Father Gentili's advice, and it developed that certain remarks he made to her proved prophetic. Birr convent in the Irish Midlands thus neighbored the great Catholic resurgence in the English Midlands.

14. Two months later the foundress wrote to Mother Teresa in Galway:

> Thank God, the poor deluded souls are returning fast and preparing to approach the holy sacraments. Little Sister M. Teresa is following them everywhere and begs we will unite in the Thirty Days' Prayer during April for the conversion of the apostate leader. I must write to moderate her zeal. I am really afraid she would speak to him if they met in any poor place, which would be exceedingly wrong.

15. The strain that showed in Bishop Kennedy a few years later was already at work, had undoubtedly been working on him for some time. After the Crotty-

ites returned to the Church and their leader left Ireland, the sisters fell victim of their bishop's misinterpretations. Not only in their work of reclamation did they make reparation for the poor curate but also in suffering with forbearance, as he had not done, the strictures of his scrupulous bishop. Perhaps the merits of their patience brought the wayward Crotty back to the Church. At any rate, the testimony of Dr. Richard B. O'Brien of All Hallows', Dublin, stands as evidence of the poor man's final penitence. Only the intervention of Archbishop Murray relieved the Birr community of the injustice laid upon them. Not many months after the misunderstanding cleared, the mental disease that had been afflicting the good prelate became evident.

16. Jane White (Sister Mary de Sales) was born at Fairy Lawn, Wexford, in 1813; her elder sister Amelia (Sister Mary Teresa, superior of Galway Convent) was born in 1809 at Kiscarry House, Carlow.

17. This sentence and the one preceding it are excerpted from the February 3 letter to Mother M. Francis on the same subject.

CHAPTER XXXII

1. February 28, 1841.
2. Hartnett, *The Life of Rev. Mother Catherine McAuley*, p. 85.
3. *Ibid.*, p. 137.
4. This account of the religious life of Sister Mary de Sales Eyre is drawn from the Bermondsey convent *Annals,* written during Mother M. Clare's term of office.
5. The thought that she would escape the pomp attending funerals of her relatives had always pleased her and the prospect of being interred among the Sisters gave her joy.
6. All the professed sisters of Dublin were, through necessity, either at Kingstown or Booterstown.
7. "Decree enacted in a general session of the Sacred Congregation of Propaganda on July 20, 1840. . . . Given in Rome from the palace of the Sacred College of Propaganda the fifth day of July in the year 1841."
8. Mother M. Clare left Bermondsey June 14, 1841. As arranged during the foundress' stay in 1839-1840, Sister Mary Clare Agnew then became mother superior.
9. Miss Agnew did not stay the year out at La Trappe. She nevertheless gained the support of Bishop Baines and later of Bishop Baggs in fresh ventures. Her ability to summon confidence from such sources would be surprising in almost any other period of ecclesiastical history. English bishops at the time, however, were struggling with the great problems of adjustment in the years between Emancipation and the restoration of the hierarchy. The influx of converts had their place in the rehabilitation, and most of the bishops were glad of their services. In fact, because of the position and outlook of the old Catholics, their Lordships in many instances were obliged to depend on the new.

Miss Agnew made three efforts to rejoin the Sisters of Mercy. After her sojourn with the Trappistines she applied to Baggot Street and was rejected. She then induced Bishop Baggs to secure a foundation from Bermondsey with the intention of giving her charge. Fortunately, Mother M. Clare Moore, who had been recalled to the superiorship of Bermondsey convent, learned who had initiated the idea and declined making the foundation. His Lordship had the naïveté to assure Mother Clare that he would require a fresh novitiate of the ex-Trappistine. His prospective superior, however, spared both him and Mother Clare further discussion by setting out for Rome with Jane Latham who had been dismissed from Bermondsey convent in the fall of 1841.

In Rome, with Cardinal Acton's support, Miss Agnew founded a community that distintegrated. Returning to London, she established another house only to have her associates disband. She then applied to St. Edward's Convent of Mercy,

founded from Baggot Street in 1844. Rejected there, she appealed to Cardinal Wiseman who asked the community to reverse their decision. They regretted to disappoint His Eminence but refused to admit Miss Agnew.
A letter to Baggot Street written by Mother Mary Anne Doyle from Derry (founded in 1843) says: "I suppose dear Reverend Mother has heard that Miss Agnew is gone to Rome . . . to get changes made in the Rule. She was most pressing to get it from me, but I would not give it."

CHAPTER XXXIII

1. In 1843 Dr. Pusey wrote his treatise, *The Holy Eucharist a Comfort to the Penitent,* which temporarily cost him the right to preach in the Anglican Church.
2. Mother M. Teresa Austin Carroll, *Leaves from the Annals of the Sisters of Mercy,* (New York: The Catholic Publication Society Co., 1883) II, 363.
3. How well Mother Catherine knew her young protégée! The aggressiveness that the foundress terms "pious anxiety" was not always so charitably interpreted in Mother Francis' long, fruitful missionary career. Bishop Haly of Carlow was only the first of many to oppose her. Nor were her associates in Baggot Street the last to react to her unfavorably, for Mother M. Teresa Austin Carroll records of Mother M. Angela Fitzgerald, a superior in one of Mother Francis' own foundations: "It was an added trial to one of her affectionate disposition that at that time and for many years afterward she could not like Mother Warde, though she always showed her the greatest respect." *Ibid.,* IV, 518.
Father Albert Foley, S. J., in his *Bishop Healy: Beloved Outcast* (New York: Farrar, Straus and Young, 1954, p. 172), describing Bishop Healy's association with the Sisters of Mercy in the chapter "His Dear Daughters" says of their superior: "Mother Warde ruled her community in the fashion of the mitred abbesses of old."
4. This is ambiguous, for the foundation to St. John's, Newfoundland, was expected in the late spring. Though St. John's, Birr, has been called her favorite mission, Archbishop Howley, who was nine years old when the Sisters of Mercy arrived in St. John's, says: "There is a tradition of the Order that Mother McAuley herself intended to come to Newfoundland to found the house here had not death taken her away." (*Ecclesiastical History of Newfoundland,* p. 371.)
5. Letter written August 3, 1841, to Mother M. Teresa White.
6. Cf. Chapter XXIV where Mother Catherine quotes as final authority "the Sacred Canons and Apostolical Constitutions."
7. Its only defect has been remedied. Originally, cells occupied the ground floor off the corridor leading to the chapel. Separating walls have since been removed and a chapter room has been provided to the left with windows opening on the chapel. Rooms to the right have become offices. The chapter room can now extend chapel accommodations when necessary.
In Birmingham convent the corridor just above the one that leads to chapel ends with mullioned windows opening directly on the rood of the rood screen. Pugin was almost fanatically insistent on a rood screen for all his churches. In this case the arrangement is particularly happy, for the sick and infirm may attend community exercises by pushing apart the quaint windows opening on the chapel. Mother Catherine's idea of seemliness with regard to the chapel has been described by Sister M. Vincent Hartnett:

> The choir and chapel she kept in nice devotional order, appropriately but not very richly decorated; and she took the greatest pains to prevent noise or any want of decorum. She wished that everything in the immediate neighborhood of the Most Holy Sacrament should breathe the air of reverent piety and that it should never be disturbed by quickness of movement or a rustling of garments. Hence the sisters were directed to enter cautiously and noiselessly.

> When saying the Office, though she wished all to do so distinctly and audibly, she would not allow one voice to be distinguished above another. (*The Life of Rev. Mother Catherine McAuley,* p. 117.)

8. When Mr. Hardman lay dying, his bed was moved where he could see the convent chapel. Death came during the novena for the Assumption when the sisters were in retreat. Mr. Hardman, therefore, had the consolation of being attended by the little Passionist Father Dominic Barberi, the retreat master, and by three Sisters of Mercy, members of his own family. His favorite aspiration had always been: "Have mercy on me, O Lord, according to thy great mercy." Though he had asked to be buried like the poor, circumstances gave a religious splendor to his funeral that his poor coffin and uncarriaged cortège could not dim. Moved to the convent chapel the night before his interment, the casket was borne the following morning to his parish church, St. Chad's Cathedral. Clergy chanting the Office for the Dead fell in line behind the casket, and mourners followed in such numbers that the solemn procession resembled a cortège for the obsequies of the great.

While in Birr the foundress had written the following to Sister M. Juliana Hardman, then in the novitiate at Baggot Street:

> As your good mother must be anxious to know the result of her inquiry will you, my dear, write immediately to say that the person she refers to may be admitted to Mass "on account of her infirmity" and whoever is really necessary to afford her assistance, but this permission cannot extend to any member of her family except there is a part of the chapel distinct from what the Sisters are to occupy. We always have discretionary power to admit an individual occasionally to Mass but not to give them an established liberty to attend. Mark particularly that it is in consideration of her infirmity that we give the general permission.

After Mr. Hardman's death, this "good mother," Barbara Ellison Hardman, came to live at the convent as a benefactor. Limiting her needs to essentials, she spent her income on charity. After over twenty-six frugal and beneficent years she died on February 18, 1872. During these years she was called affectionately "Mother de Chantal."

9. Lucy Powell (Sister Mary Joseph) was received at a public ceremony in St. Chad's Cathedral, December 6, 1841, while Mother M. Cecilia Marmion was still acting superior. Mrs. Powell (nee Hardman) happened to sit next to a curious but critical Protestant who whispered to her unidentified neighbor: "I did not think people could be found now-a-days who would make such fools of themselves." With some spirit Mrs. Powell replied *sotto voce*: "That fool is my daughter." Dr. Wiseman's sermon, which followed, enlightened Mrs. Powell's neighbor on the wisdom of this particular type of folly.

10. The Mercy design can still be traced in the choir ceiling, though it has been repainted, and the refectory windows are still intact. Largely through Hardman generosity, a church was erected in 1846-1847 on the convent grounds to accommodate the numbers of converts that poured into the Church through Bishop Wiseman's preaching and the sisters' follow-up instructions. St. Chad's Cathedral was the nearest church to Handsworth at the time. Consecrated in 1847, the convent church did not round out the century. It was bombed beyond rehabilitation in World War II. The original chapel, only a few yards away, lost only its stained-glass windows.

11. While working on records at Birmingham Convent of Mercy, I had the privilege of occupying the cell that had been Mother Catherine's in August and September, 1841. I also spoke with a senior sister, since deceased, who had been present in the chapel as a novice when Cardinal Newman addressed the sisters. Her comment is worth recording: "He seemed feeble as he went up the aisle, and he spoke so low that I had to strain to hear him. I remember only his words re-

minding us that there is nothing in life but to love and serve God. He made me think of John the Evangelist in his old age."

12. Mother M. Juliana gave one outstanding evidence of her Benedictine training while superior of Birmingham Convent of Mercy. When the House of Mercy opened in 1845, she secured Bishop Walsh's permission to organize a group of lay workers as oblates. Those who stayed permanently became Franciscan tertiaries. The oblates not only helped in the House of Mercy but also went on catechetical missions with the sisters.

13. This letter is postmarked "September 8" from Birmingham.

14. Easter Monday letter, 1841.

15. Birmingham convent did not long retain the name of the English saint whose statue adorns a niche outside the building. It became St. Mary's when the motherhouse became St. Catherine's (after the foundress' death).

16. Birr *Annals* state that because of the financial situation brought on the parish by schism, the foundress gave £500 to stablize this Mercy mission.

17. Birr *Annals*.

18. Mother M. Catherine's religious philosophy is in accord with the recommendations of the Reverend Jean Pierre de Caussade, S. J., spiritual director for certain Visitation convents (died 1751). Though there is no evidence that she knew his *Abandonment*, she did come under Jesuit influence during her noviceship at George's Hill, and the instructions she gave her own novices the following year show the undeviating consistence and strength of a master of the spiritual life.

19. The subsequent history of Mother M. Francis Xavier Warde is one of blessings upon herself and upon the Congregation of Mercy. She lived to be the first Golden Jubilarian in the Institute and in the forty-three years remaining to her she continued the work of foundations begun in Ireland. Forty-one of those years were spent on the American missions. She not only introduced the Institute to the United States but she extended it over the entire settled and partly settled north of the country. From Pittsburgh to pioneer Chicago, from Pennsylvania again east to the New England States, she established missions from which other Convents of Mercy came into existence in such numbers that the title of American foundress has rightly been attached to her name.

20. The original "Act of Consecration" is in the community archives of the Sisters of Mercy of the Union, General Motherhouse, Bethesda, Md.

21. October 26, 1840 letter to Caroline White.

22. Father Clarke, who preached a charity sermon in Limerick.

23. Bernard William Delany carried on the family tradition of charity. Though twice married, he had no children. Both he and his unmarried brother, Edmund Scully Delany, devoted much of their income to charity.

CHAPTER XXXIV

1. Henri Ghéon, *St. Martin of Tours* (New York: Sheed and Ward, 1946), p. 179.

2. Birr *Annals*.

3. Though in Cork at the time, Sister M. Clare Augustine Moore made characteristic inquiries on her return to the motherhouse and included her findings in the manuscript she later wrote with such realism.

4. Sister M. Vincent Whitty, professed on August 19 with Sister M. Justina Fleming and the English novices, was assistant in the novitiate during Mother M. Cecilia's absence in Birmingham. In 1842 she accompanied Mother M. de Pazzi to Liverpool to help establish that foundation. In 1844 when Mother M. Cecilia became mother superior, Sister Vincent was appointed to the office of mistress of novices, and in 1849 at the death of Mother M. Cecilia, Sister Vincent became superior. During her term of office she sent sisters to the Crimea and to South

America. When she herself could not give sisters for a foundation in Arkansas, she went personally to Naas and interested the community there to undertake the mission. Later she herself went on the foundation for Brisbane, Australia.

5. See note 13 of Chapter XXXI.

6 The archives of the parent community contain a written statement by Mother M. Liguori Keenan telling of Mother M. Vincent Whitty's conversation with Father Vincent Grotti, C. P., and of his advice.

7. In her November 18, 1840 letter to Galway, Mother Catherine referred to a compliment O'Connell had paid the Sisters of Mercy in a speech at Carrick: "The foot has afforded great amusement at recreation, each claiming for her own foot the compliment paid to all. They have lately made some very nice cloth boots and got them capped and soled with leather. When finished they do not cost quite four shillings. Dear Sister M. de Sales commenced the work and it now goes on rapidly. Any kind of stocking will do. I have been long recommending these homemade boots both for neatness and economy."

8. Within five years Sister Mary Agnes O'Connor established the Institute in London proper and in New York.

9. Father Walsh's zeal in behalf of the Kingstown poor had caused him to represent their case to Archbishop Murray after the withdrawal of the sisters. He was therefore responsible for their return in 1840. In 1842, however, he was made coadjutor to the Vicar Apostolic of Nova Scotia, in 1844 Bishop of Halifax and subsequently Archbishop. Conditions again required the temporary withdrawal of the sisters. Today the Institute not only continues the work established there by Mother Catherine but staffs a modern hospital, St. Michael's.

10. November 13, 1840 letter to Mother M. Francis.

11. Letter to Sister M. Vincent Hartnett in Limerick.

12. Mother M. de Pazzi did cross the Irish Sea to help make the Liverpool foundation but she returned and lived her life out at the parent house.

13. Carroll, *Leaves from the Annals of the Sisters of Mercy,* I, 49-50.

14. Sister M. Clare Augustine Moore's detailed account (Dublin MS) of Catherine McAuley's last illness was submitted to Dr. George C. Glinsky, chief of staff of the tuberculosis division of Deshon Federal Hospital, Butler, Pa., who gave the following diagnosis: "In the opinion of the undersigned from reading an extract of her condition, this case was one of pulmonary tuberculosis which was complicated by an empyema." Dr. Glinsky added that modern early diagnosis and treatment forestalls such cases. He pointed out that the patient's general condition could produce a rapid breakdown of tissue where there was friction. The "ulcer" could have developed in a period of six weeks to two months, he said.

Bibliography

Barry, K. M. *Catherine McAuley and the Sisters of Mercy.* Dublin: Fallon and Son, 1894.
Belloc, Bessie R. *Historic Nuns.* St. Louis: B. Herder, 1911.
Bourdelot, Rev. L. F. *The Story of the Catholic Church in Bermondsey.* London: Burns, Oates and Washbourne, Ltd., 1923.
Bowen, Elizabeth. *Bowen's Court.* New York: Alfred A. Knopf, 1942.
————. *The Shelbourne.* London: George G. Harrap and Co., 1951.
Burke Savage, Rev. Roland, S. J. *A Valiant Dublin Woman, The Story of George's Hill.* Dublin: M. H. Gill and Company, 1940.
————. *Catherine McAuley, The First Sister of Mercy.* Dublin: M. H. Gill and Son, 1949.
Carroll, Mother M. Teresa Austin. *Leaves from the Annals of the Sisters of Mercy.* 4 vols. New York: The Catholic Publication Society Co., 1881, 1883, 1889, 1895.
————. *Life of Catherine McAuley.* New York: D. and J. Sadlier and Co., first edition 1866, second edition 1874.
Comerford, Rev. M. *Collections relating to the Dioceses of Kildare and Leighlin.* Dublin: James Duffy and Sons, Vol. I., n. d.
Costello, Sister Mary Loretto. *The Sisters of Mercy of Maryland.* St. Louis: B. Herder Book Co., 1931.
Cross, Arthur Lyon. *A Shorter History of England and Greater Britain.* New York: Macmillan, 1939.
Donnelly, Most Rev. Nicholas, Lord Bishop of Canea. *A Short History of Some Dublin Parishes.* Catholic Truth Society of Ireland. (in series, early twentieth century.)
Dyer, Thiselton. *British Popular Customs.* London: George Bell and Sons.
Farrell, Benjamin F. *The Rights and Duties of the Local Ordinary Regarding Congregations of Women Religious of Pontifical Approval*: a Dissertation (Canon Law). Washington: Catholic University of America Press, 1941.
Fitzpatrick, Rev. Brother J. D. *Edmund Rice, Founder and First Superior General of the Christian Brothers of Ireland.* Dublin: M. H. Gill and Son, Ltd., 1945.
Fitzpatrick, W. J. *Irish Wits and Worthies.* Dublin: James Duffy, Sons and Co., 1873.
————. *The Life, Times and Correspondence of the Right Rev. Dr. Doyle, Bishop of Kildare and Leighlin.* Dublin: James Duffy, Sons and Co., revised edition M. H. Gill and Co., 1880.

Freriks, Celestine A. *Religious Congregations in their External Relations*: a Dissertation (Canon Law). Washington: Catholic University of America Press, 1916.

Gately, Sister M. Josephine. *Supplementary Manual to the Sisters of Mercy*. New York: Macmillan, 1931.

Ghéon, Henri. *St. Martin of Tours*. New York: Sheed and Ward, 1946.

Gilbert, Sir John Thomas. *History of Dublin*. Vol. I. Dublin: McGlashan, 1854.

Green, Alice Stopford. *The Irish Nationality*. New York: Henry Holt, 1911.

Gwynn, Denis. *Cardinal Wiseman*. Dublin: Browne and Nolan, Ltd., 1950.

———. *Father Dominic Barberi*. London: Burns, Oates and Washbourne, Ltd., 1947.

———. *Father Luigi Gentili and the Second Spring*. Dublin: Clonmore and Reynolds, Ltd., 1951.

———. *Lord Shrewsbury, Pugin and the Catholic Revival*. London: Hollis and Carter, 1946; Westminster, Md.: The Newman Press, 1946.

———. *The Second Spring 1818-1852*. London: Burns, Oates and Washbourne, Ltd., 1942.

Hartley, Dorothy and Elliott, Margaret M. *Life and Work of the People of England*. Vol. II. London: B. T. Batsford, Ltd., 1931.

Hartnett, Mother (or Sister) M. Vincent. *The Life of Reverend Mother Catherine McAuley, Foundress of the Order of Mercy*. Dublin: John F. Fowler, 1864.

Harvey, John. *Dublin*. London: B. T. Batsford, Ltd., 1949.

Hayden and Moonan. *A Short History of the Irish People from the Earliest Times to the Present Time*. New York: Longmans, Green & Co., 1927; Dublin: The Educational Company of Ireland, Ltd.

Healy, Most Rev. John. *Maynooth College Its Centenary History*. Dublin: Browne and Nolan, 1895.

Howley, Very Rev. M. F. *Ecclesiastical History of Newfoundland*. Boston: Doyle and Whittle, 1888.

Jolly, Ellen Ryan. *Nuns of the Battlefield*. Providence, R. I.: Visitor Press, 1927.

Landreth, Helen. *The Pursuit of Robert Emmet*. Dublin: Browne and Nolan, 1949.

Lecky, William E. Hartpole. *History of Ireland in the Eighteenth Century*. Vol. I. London: Longmans, Green and Co., 1913.

———. *Leaders of Public Opinion in Ireland*. Vol. II. London: Longmans, Green and Co., 1912.

MacManus, Seumas, assisted by several Irish scholars. *The Story of the Irish Race*. New York: Devin-Adair, 1944.

MacSweeney, Rev. P. M. (ed.). *Letters of Mary Aikenhead*. Dublin: M. H. Gill and Son, 1914.

Malton, James. *Picturesque and Descriptive View of the City of Dublin*. London: 1794.

Maxwell, Constantia. *Country and Town in Ireland under the Georges*. Dundalk: Dundalgan Press, 1949.

———. *Dublin under the Georges*. London: Faber and Faber, Ltd.

Meagher, Rev. William. *Commemorative Oration of the Most Rev. Daniel Murray with historical and biographical notes*. Gerald Bellew, 1853.

Newton, Douglas. *Catholic London*. London: Robert Hale Ltd., 1950.

Orth, Clement Raymond. *Approbation of Religious Institutes*: a Dissertation (Canon Law). Washington: Catholic University of America Press, 1931.

Ronan, Very Rev. Myles (P. P., D. Litt.). *An Apostle of Catholic Dublin, Father Henry Young*. Dublin: Browne and Nolan, Ltd., 1944.

Schaaf, Valentine Theodore. *The Cloister:* a Dissertation (Canon Law). Cincinnati, O.: St. Anthony Messenger Press, 1921.

Sisters of Mercy. *Reverend Mother M. Xavier Warde.* Boston: Marlier and Co., Ltd., 1902.

Swayne, (Gaelic given name). *Early History of Carlow College.* Dublin: Browne and Nolan, Ltd., 1943.

Turner, Edward Raymond. *Ireland and England in the Past and at Present.* New York: Century Co., 1919.

Urlin, Ethel Lucy. *Festivals, Holy Days and Saints' Days.* London: Simpkin, Marshall, Hamilton, Kent and Co., 1915.

Walsh, James J. *These Splendid Sisters.* New York: J. H. Sears and Co., 1927.

Walsh, William Shepard. *Curiosities of Popular Customs.* London: Gibbings and Co., 1898.

Index

INDEX

A NOTE ON THE TYPE

IN WHICH THIS BOOK IS SET

This book is set in Times Roman, a Linotype face created by Stanley Morrison, world-famous typographical authority. Designed for the London *Times* which demanded a type face that should be clear and legible, it is precise but not mechanical, having a high letter but not condensed, of a "color" suitable for any paper or printing process, with character but not with annoying characteristics. Notice the clear, open characters of Times Roman. This is the secret of its clear printing on any paper, whether it be on the coarsest of newsprint or the finest coated paper. This book was composed and printed by the Wickersham Printing Company of Lancaster, Pa., and bound by Moore and Company of Baltimore. Typography and design by Howard N. King.